Also by Ganesh Sitaraman

The Counterinsurgent's Constitution:
Law in the Age of Small Wars

The Crisis
of the
Middle-Class
Constitution

THE CRISIS

OF THE

MIDDLE-CLASS
CONSTITUTION

Why Economic Inequality
Threatens Our Republic

GANESH SITARAMAN

Alfred A. Knopf · New York 2017

THIS IS A BORZOI BOOK
PUBLISHED BY ALFRED A. KNOPF

www.aaknopf.com

Portions of this work first appeared, in different form, in the following
publications: "America's Post-Crash Constitution" originally published in
Politico on October 5, 2014; "Foreword, Drift and Mastery in the 21st
Century" published in *Walter Lippmann, Drift and Mastery* (University
of Wisconsin Press, 2015); "The Puzzling Absence of Economic Power
in Constitutional Theory" published in 101 *Cornell Law Review* 1445,
in 2016; and "Economic Structure and Constitutional Structure: An
Intellectual History" published in 94 *Texas Law Review* 1301, in 2016.

Library of Congress Cataloging-in-Publication Data
Names: Sitaraman, Ganesh, author.
Title: The crisis of the middle-class constitution : why economic
inequality threatens our Republic / by Ganesh Sitaraman.
Description: New York : Alfred A. Knopf, [2017] | Includes bibliographical
references and index.
Identifiers: LCCN 2016026242 (print) | LCCN 2016026710 (ebook) |
ISBN 9780451493910 (hardcover) | ISBN 9780451493927 (ebook)
Subjects: LCSH: Constitutional law— Economic aspects.—United States. |
Equality—Economic aspects. | Income distribution—United States. |
Middle class—United States. | United States—Social conditions. |
Power (Social sciences) | Plutocracy.
Classification: LCC KF4749 .S58 2017 (print) | LCC KF4749 (ebook) |
DDC 339.2/20973—dc23
LC record available at https://lccn.loc.gov/2016026242

Jacket design by Darren Haggar
Jacket photograph by Gregor Schuster/Getty Images

Manufactured in the United States of America

First Edition

Contents

Contents

The Crisis
of the
Middle-Class
Constitution

Introduction

The number one threat to American constitutional government today is the collapse of the middle class. Not the rise of presidential power. Not the growing national security state. Not the gridlock in Washington. Not the polarization of the two political parties. These are all important developments that shape how our constitutional system works. But it is possible to have a functioning constitutional republic with slightly more presidential power, or with a bigger military, or with fewer acts of Congress, or with a more polarized electorate. It is much harder to have a functional constitutional republic without a strong middle class.

What does the middle class have to do with preserving a republican form of government? From the ancient Greeks onward, political philosophers were preoccupied with the problem of economic inequality and its relationship to the structure of government. The wealthy elites would clash with everyone else—the rich oppressing the poor, the poor seeking to confiscate and redistribute the wealth of the rich. Economic inequality led inevitably to political inequality and, as a result, instability, class warfare, and constitutional revolution.

Statesmen and philosophers therefore went to considerable lengths to design governments that would not fall prey to the tumults that accompanied economic inequality. The great republics throughout history—Rome, Florence, Venice, England—all had what we can think of as *class warfare constitutions,* governments designed on the assumption that economic inequality was inevitable and the clash between rich and poor inescapable. Class warfare constitutions experimented with many different designs to prevent economic conflict from spilling into constitutional revolution: Statesmen empowered special "tribunes," representatives of the people, not drawn from the patrician class. They created bodies that represented different classes of people. And they sought to balance class power to prevent any one economic group from dominating the political system. Class warfare constitutions took as a premise that inequality would exist in society, and because inequality was a threat to stable government, they built checks into the constitutional structure itself.

The American Constitution is different. Our Constitution isn't based on the assumption that class conflict is inevitable. Our Constitution is a *middle-class constitution*. Unlike the class warfare constitutions of earlier times, our Constitution assumes relative economic equality in society; it assumes that the middle class is and will remain dominant. The framers of the Constitution were well aware of the history of statesmen and theorists grappling with class warfare. But they did not adopt a design premised on the inevitability of class conflict. In fact, our Constitution does not have a single provision—not one—that explicitly entrenches economic class into the structure of government. There is no provision excluding poor people from the Senate, and no provision excluding the rich from the House of Representatives. Class warfare constitutions had these kinds of features.

Instead, from the time of the American Revolution through the creation of the Constitution, many Americans believed that the New World was unique because it had relative economic equality. There was neither extreme wealth nor extreme poverty, as was common in Europe. In fact, when compared with Europe, America's special providence was clear: no feudalism, no nobility, and no aristocracy-supporting land inheritance policies. Americans, as Alexis de Tocqueville would later say, were born equal rather than becoming so. Americans understood and talked about this fact throughout the founding era, including during the debates over the ratification of the Constitution. Because the new American nation had readily available land to the west, there would be economic opportunity for anyone to own property and build an economic future. Of course, all of this was within the confines of the era's views on equality between men and women and between races (more on that to come), but the big picture is that for two thousand years class warfare defined the design of government. Then America came along.

The problem today is that the basic foundation upon which our middle-class constitution was built—the prerequisite of relative economic equality—is crumbling. More than eight years after the financial crash, disparities in economic power are at the forefront of popular debate. There is widespread concern about rising inequality and the increasing share of wealth going to the top 1 percent and 0.1 percent of people. In the past generation, the average worker hasn't seen his income rise; adjusted for inflation, it's been stagnant. People are working harder and harder, with gains in productivity and rising GDP but without an increase in wealth or economic security. Economic inequality is also turning into political inequality. Political leaders increasingly express a growing popular sentiment that "the system is rigged" to work for wealthy and corporate interests, who have the means to buy influence through campaign funding and then sustain their influence with "armies of lobbyists" in Washington. This outrage also isn't partisan: it comes from both the populist right and the progressive left.

Worse yet, these populist concerns aren't imagined. In a battery of studies over the last decade, political scientists have demonstrated that economic elites dominate the American political system. The wealthy participate more at every stage of the political process—from meeting candidates, to donating, to voting. Moneyed interests get greater access to elected officials and their staffs. Elite economic interest groups (business and industry) make up the majority of interest groups and spend the most money on lobbying. Political scientists have even shown that the majority's views have effectively no impact on American public policy; the strongest predictor is the views of wealthy elites. These findings operate across all areas of policy, and they provide systematic evidence that politics is bent in favor of the wealthiest members of American society. They also raise a disturbing question: Can our constitutional system survive the collapse of the middle class?

SOCIAL STRUCTURE AND CONSTITUTIONAL STRUCTURE

When most people—including constitutional scholars—think about the structure of a constitution, they focus on the types and arrangement of offices. Is there a president or a prime minister? One house in the legislature or two? Once we know the basic structure, the question becomes how the separate branches of government check and balance each other. The way it is usually understood, constitutional structure is all about the mechanics of government offices.

Historically, this wasn't always the dominant way of thinking, and in fact, it isn't the only way of thinking about constitutions today. Imagine you are asked to advise a Middle Eastern country designing a new constitution. The country's population is divided roughly equally between Sunni and Shia Muslims, and their leaders tell you that conflict between the two groups concerns them. If you do your homework and read what political scientists have written on the topic or if you look at the constitutional design of similarly divided societies, you would probably suggest a power-sharing arrangement in which there is a requirement that a certain number of cabinet officials come from each religious sect. If the groups are geographically concentrated, you might also suggest devolution of power to different provinces, to allow each group to have greater control over its local governance. No one would blink an eye at either of those suggestions. But what is striking is that these design strategies aren't about the checks and balances between different branches of government. These design strategies take into account divisions in society.

Why exactly are *social* divisions relevant to *constitutional* structure? The most important reason is to prevent oppression. Oppression can come in a variety of forms. The one that first comes to many Americans' minds is that government might oppress the people. We are worried that elected officials and civil servants will grow out of touch with the views of the people and no longer act according to the public good. Scholars call this a principal-agent problem. The people delegate power to their agents—elected officials and civil servants—but the people's delegates might not pursue the policies that the people want. This is an important concern, and in *The Federalist Papers* James Madison developed an elaborate theory of separation of powers, checks and balances, and fragmented interests for how to address it. A second kind of oppression is even more fundamental—and is why we have government in the first place. We are worried that private actors will oppress us. Someone might rob you at gunpoint or break into your home. We create government, in part, to protect us from private oppression.

When a *society* itself is deeply divided, however, there is a third concern that mixes the first two: one social group might capture *all* the parts of government—all the branches that are supposed to check each other—and then use government to oppress the other social group or to pad their pockets. Go back to the example of designing a constitution: If the Sunni control the government completely, what's to stop them from passing laws that oppress the Shia? Or if the shoe is on the other foot, what's to stop the Shia from issuing government contracts only to themselves? Separating powers and relying on checks and balances won't work if a single social group with shared beliefs controls every part of the government.

For political and constitutional theorists throughout history, oppression and revolution were ever-present risks. If the Sunni or Shia feel oppressed, they might very well take up arms and overthrow the government. Deeply divided societies are always on the edge of instability, strife, and even outright conflict. Moments of stability are also fleeting because social conditions change over time. If a constitution divides power evenly between Shia and Sunni, what happens if, decades later, the Sunni become 90 percent of the population? Perhaps they might think the Shia minority is disproportionately or unfairly determining policy. The Sunni might revolt. What if a new minority group immigrates to the country only to find itself oppressed by the two preexisting groups? Changes in society can put pressure on a constitutional system created under different social conditions. If changes in social structure don't lead to reforms in the constitutional structure, the result is likely to be oppression—leading possibly to revolution. Social structure and constitutional structure are therefore intimately connected.

For most of the history of constitutional thinking—the twenty-three hundred years from the ancient Greeks into the modern era—the hardest, most intractable problem was at the nexus of social and constitutional structure: the economic division between rich and poor. Aristotle, Polybius, Cicero, Machiavelli, and other political thinkers all paid considerable attention to how constitutional structure would intersect with economic inequality. They worried that economic inequality would lead to political inequality and, with it, oppression and ultimately revolution. Their primary answer was to develop mixed forms of government that built economic classes directly into the structure of government. Each class would thus have a stake in government and a check on the other. But over time, some thinkers hypothesized another way out of the problem of inequality. Theorists in this second tradition recognized that if a society didn't have economic inequality—if instead there was a strong, large middle class—it would be less likely to fall prey to economic divides. Freed from economic conflict, the sensible middle would hold the balance of power between a small number of wealthy and impoverished citizens. Under both traditions, the key feature was that the political structure had to mirror the distribution of wealth.

WHY ECONOMIC INEQUALITY THREATENS THE REPUBLIC

This book makes an unconventional argument about the American constitutional tradition. It argues that the American Constitution is based on the prerequisite that the nation has relative economic equality—a strong middle class, no extreme wealth or poverty, and economic opportunity. This might seem like a counterintuitive claim. For many people, the conventional understanding of our constitutional origins is that the founding fathers were wealthy white men who wrote the Constitution in order to preserve and promote their own interests. There is some truth to this story. But it isn't the whole story, and it isn't the whole truth.

In fact, when you think about it, this often accepted story about the Federalists' Constitution—that it was a system devised to favor the elites—is really quite puzzling. Our Constitution doesn't have any explicit provisions requiring that officeholders be from a specific economic class. It doesn't even require that voters be from a specific class. With thousands of years of constitutional design explicitly incorporating economic class into the structure of government, the framers knew how to write such provisions. They had even done so in state constitutions during the 1770s and 1780s. But when it came to the federal Constitution of 1787, the framers didn't build economic classes into the structure of government. If they really wanted to benefit themselves, why didn't the framers go further?

The answer is that many of them didn't want to—and even if they did, they couldn't. During the time of the American Revolution, through the era of the Articles of Confederation, and into the ratification period and the early republic, there was a robust and strong belief that a truly republican form of government was only possible in a society with relative economic equality. Drawing on a long tradition in political philosophy, the founding generation understood that the balance of political power had to mirror the balance of economic power in society. As a result, there were only two stable ways to design a government: Where there was inequality, there had to be a class warfare constitution. When there was relative equality in society, there could be a commonwealth or republic. Unlike Europe, with its hereditary nobility, property rules that concentrated wealth, and history of feudalism, America didn't have centuries of entrenched wealth or poverty. With vast lands to the west and the possibility of education, any white man (at the time, of course, it was limited as such) had the opportunity to access the middle class. These beliefs weren't just wishful thinking: economic historians have shown that the American colonies were remarkably equal for the late eighteenth century. With this intellectual commitment to—and the reality of—relative economic equality in the background, the American Constitution departed from a structure rooted in class warfare.

But that's not the end of the story. As recent historians have shown, the politics and economics of the time also provided a brake on elite Federalists' ambitions. The relationship between economic and constitutional structures was a lively part of the political debates over the ratification of the Constitution. Participants in those debates were well aware of the class warfare constitutions of the past, and they drew upon them in making arguments both for and against the proposed constitution. Anti-Federalists were concerned that the new constitution would lead to an aristocratic form of government, in which ordinary people had little power. They even proposed returning to the class warfare designs of the past to prevent such a development from taking place. The Federalists—who are usually seen as supporting elite interests—responded by rejecting the Anti-Federalists' premise of inequality. They held that in America there were no classes and that the new constitution was rooted in the people themselves. This might have been good spin or smart campaign rhetoric, but the Federalists sold the Constitution—and won—with these arguments.

Perhaps most strikingly, the economic realities of the time supported the creation of a middle-class constitution. After the Revolutionary War, the new nation fell into a calamitous economic depression. Toward the end of the 1780s, virtually everyone was unhappy with the Articles of Confederation. Creditors, bondholders, and many of the wealthiest Americans thought that the country needed better credit and wanted a stronger federal government. Many debtors, farmers, and other ordinary Americans wanted a system of government that would be better able to alleviate the economic pressures on them. At the end of the day, surprisingly, the Constitution contained something for both sides. As we'll see, at the heart of the Constitution was a practical solution to the economic crisis of the 1780s, one that used an obscure provision on tariffs to remove financial burdens from ordinary Americans and place them instead on wealthier merchants and those who purchased luxury goods. In contrast to two millennia of constitutions premised on class inequality, our Constitution was forged, in part, on trying to rebuild the economic fortunes of ordinary people.

If this account of the founding era seems unconventional, that's because it is. But it wouldn't have been at the time. The founding era was perhaps the richest moment in the life of American ideas. In the letters and speeches of the time, statesmen and even ordinary citizens sometimes sound more like scholars or philosophers than political hacks. They studied history, law, economics, politics, philosophy, all in service of the robust debate taking place on what kind of nation they would create. As a result, their debates feature an extraordinary diversity of political ideas. Looking back from the present, commentators often interpret the founding era through ideas associated with some of the most prominent political philosophers in history: Karl

Marx, John Locke, and Niccolò Machiavelli. Devotees of Marx see society as mired in class conflict; in their version of the founding era, wealthy landowners designed a scheme of government that would preserve and promote their economic interests. Followers of John Locke emphasize instead a revolutionary tradition built on individual rights to life, liberty, and private property, the absence of feudalism, and the social contract. A third approach is inspired by Niccolò Machiavelli, one of the great theorists of republican government. The republicans argue that the founding generation valued freedom and self-government, and they believed a republic could only exist if the people and their leaders were virtuous citizens. Each of these leading traditions finds support in the historical evidence and brings a powerful perspective to understanding America's past and present.

But there is another philosophical tradition, one that has largely been forgotten today but that was well-known to the founding generation. In the seventeenth century, the Englishman James Harrington argued that a republican form of government—what he called a commonwealth—could not exist without a relatively equal distribution of wealth. In all societies, Harrington said, power followed property. If property was concentrated in the hands of a few, the wealthy would eventually turn their economic power into political power, creating an aristocracy. Only if economic power was distributed widely among the people was a commonwealth, or republic, possible. Harrington's understanding of the commonwealth stands on its own as a theme in the founding era, but it also overlaps with the more familiar interpretations of the founding. To Marxists, it acknowledges that the distribution of wealth matters. With Lockeans, it emphasizes the absence of feudalism and the relative equality of individuals. It is closest in its resemblance to republicanism, but it diverges by privileging the economic, not just the civic, preconditions for representative government.

Many in the founding generation had internalized Harrington's lessons, and they believed that the American republic was built on America's exceptional economic conditions—on the foundation of the middle class. For generations after the founding era, the tradition of the middle-class constitution remained alive. Political leaders and even ordinary Americans worried that rising inequality threatened

America's middle-class republic. The growth of a distinct rich and poor threatened republican government in two ways. When economic inequality existed, the wealthy would stop advocating for policies that promoted the common good. Instead, they would support—and use their resources to do whatever they could to promote—public policies that led to their private benefit. The wealthy would also begin to think they are inherently better than the poor and that they alone are worthy of the right to govern. The result of these dynamics is that the republic is corrupted and transformed, slowly and silently, into an oligarchy. The second threat came from the people's response to the rise of the oligarchs. Suffering from economic anxiety and without political redress from a self-satisfied opulent elite, the people might turn to a demagogue who would overthrow the government—only to become a tyrant. Oligarchy or tyranny, economic inequality meant the end of the republic.

CLASS, RACE, AND THE AMERICAN TRADITION

To claim that a middle-class ethos was a critical part of the founding might seem anachronistic. Most people think of "class" as a relatively modern term, emerging in the nineteenth and twentieth centuries. Others might think of fixed social positions, or even Karl Marx and the idea of class consciousness. But it is not the case that there was only "rich" and "poor" before the nineteenth century. Throughout history, political theorists wrote about the middle class, just using slightly different language. Aristotle, for example, talked about a "middle" between the rich and the poor and called a constitutional system dominated by this group the "middle constitution." In the founding era, Americans referred frequently to the "middling classes," the "middling peoples," and the "middling sort." In each case, they meant a group between the rich and the poor. While it is anachronistic to refer to the "middle class" per se in the time of Aristotle or even in the late eighteenth century, it would be clunky and archaic today to use the "middling sort" or any similar phrase.

What makes someone middle class? Individuals throughout history have often had slightly different conceptions. Some focus on status, others on cultural norms. Still others tie it to income levels, education, or profession. All of these definitions have something important to offer. But what is common among all the definitions, and all definitions throughout history, is that the middle class is the group of people who aren't extremely rich or extremely poor. That is the definition used here. There isn't necessarily a specific dollar figure that corresponds to middle class, and if there was, it would necessarily change based on time and context.[1] However, in today's context among developed countries, *The Economist* captures the idea well: to be middle class means that you have enough spending money to provide for yourself and your family without living hand to mouth, but not enough to guarantee their future.[2]

Throughout this book, I refer to relative economic equality and a large middle class somewhat interchangeably. The phrases are different, of course. Theoretically, a society would be economically equal if its members were all extremely poor or extremely rich. But all societies have differences in wealth, and people are able to compare themselves to each other. Relative economic equality means there aren't huge divergences between rich and poor and that the society is not bifurcated into rich and poor. A large middle class means that most members fall somewhere in the middle. The terms are not exactly the same, but they are complementary.

Perhaps the bigger challenge to thinking about economic equality in our constitutional tradition is that for most of American history many groups of people were not economically equal—and were deliberately excluded from the chance to reach the middle class. Women, African Americans, minorities, Native Americans—all were denied entry into America's promise of freedom, liberty, and justice. But we must be careful not to conflate two different traditions in American history. One tradition focuses on the distribution of wealth *within* the political community. This idea is at the heart of the middle-class constitution. A second—and separate—question is *who* should be included in the political community. Americans have struggled throughout our history to expand the political community. This is our tradition of inclusion—of abolitionists and suffragettes, of sit-ins and freedom rides, of "I will fight no more forever" and "the bullet or the ballot."

The intersection between these two stories—the economic story and the inclusive story—has never been simple. Sometimes the two traditions coincide. There were members of the founding generation who thought slavery was incompatible with republican freedom. The post–Civil War Reconstruction Republicans pushed not just for civil rights but also for forty acres and a mule. But sometimes the two traditions diverge, as when the Jacksonians advocated for poor whites while preserving and expanding slavery. Or when the Reconstruction Republicans pushed hard for racial equality but not gender equality. The story of the inclusive tradition is essential to America's past and to our values. It has been told many times before, and it deserves to be told again because the struggle for inclusion continues. But the goal of this book is not to retell that story. Rather, it is to recover and trace the middle-class constitutional tradition, the tradition of economic equality *within* the political community, and its relationship to our constitutional system.

At the same time, it is impossible to divorce economic conditions within a political community from the underlying economic and political system that excludes people from full membership. The mid-nineteenth-century economy cannot be understood without considering slavery, and the economy at virtually any time in history cannot be understood without considering the roles women played outside the workplace. For the middle-class constitution, what is perhaps most important is what happens when efforts at inclusion succeed. With every successful effort to consider a group of Americans as full members of the political community, it becomes necessary to ensure that they too share in the economic conditions that are a prerequisite for republican government. One of the central challenges for America's middle-class constitution has been that with each expansion in the political community a struggle has taken place over how to ensure that entrants into the political community can achieve the relative economic equality needed for a republic. Thus, many Reconstruction Republicans saw their task as not just civil rights but economic justice for the freed slaves of the South. After the civil rights victories of the 1960s, Martin Luther King Jr. and other leaders understood that the next stage of reform had to be improving economic conditions. While the main emphasis of this book is not on the many and complex ways in which race, class, and gender intersect, along the way we shall see some of the times when this intersection shaped the battle over the middle-class constitution.

THE CRISIS OF THE MIDDLE-CLASS CONSTITUTION

From before the revolution, through the 1780s, and into the early republic, the founding generation recognized that America was exceptional because of its relative economic equality and that this is what allowed them to embark on their experiment in republican government. The question, Alexander Hamilton said, was "whether societies of men are really capable or not of establishing good government from reflection and choice, or whether they are forever destined to depend for their political constitutions on accident and force."[3] The founders were optimistic that America's experiment would succeed. But fear travels alongside hope, and through much of our history Americans were also afraid their precarious experiment in republican government would not last. So they were vigilant, and when they debated economic issues—and they did so fiercely and frequently—their debates often took place on constitutional terms. They were usually focused not on this clause or that clause of the constitutional text but on a much broader question: Would a policy exacerbate or mitigate the threat that economic power posed to the constitutional system? If America lost its relative economic equality—a precondition for the constitutional system—it would mean the end of the Republic.

Almost immediately after the Constitution was ratified, the country's leaders worried that their equal republic was at risk of slipping away. In the 1790s, Jefferson and Hamilton dueled over the creation of the first Bank of the United States, a debate that continued into the Madison administration and reached a fever pitch with the Jacksonian-era second bank war. The Jacksonians railed against the power of economic elites, and they developed the first organized political party as a countervailing force to what they believed was the overweening power of the nation's emerging financial class. Yet despite these concerns, Americans in the early republic remained relatively equal economically, and they understood their equality as a function of their geography. With land readily available to the west, Americans believed they had a "safety valve," even as wage labor started to displace land as the source of productivity. Factory workers who faced tough hours or conditions could move west and become Jeffersonian yeomen farmers, taking up property and, as a result, joining America's society of equals.

But by the late nineteenth century, this narrative was no longer available. The closing of the frontier, massive population shifts from farms to cities, industrialization, and the rise of corporations and trusts meant greater and greater concentrations of people and power than the founding generation could ever have imagined. Concentrated economic power became the great fear of the populists and progressives, and they took up two tasks: reform the structure of the economy to redress the imbalance between workers and owners, and reform the structure of government to break the political power of the economically powerful. Populists and progressives during this time came up with some of the most innovative and creative solutions in American history: constitutional amendments democratizing the country, corporate and income taxes, antitrust laws, campaign finance reforms, the professionalization of government officials. And although reformers did not always rely on constitutional amendments, they did rely on constitutional arguments. One of the most shocking things is how many economic policy arguments throughout American history have been made in forthrightly constitutional terms. These reformers understood that economic structure and constitutional structure were interconnected.

Despite the progressives' best efforts, the crisis of the middle-class constitution persisted. During the Great Depression, New Deal reformers set the battle as one between democracy and economic royalists, and they continued to advocate for many of the same solutions that had been invented by populists and progressives a generation earlier. While the Supreme Court signaled in 1937 that it would no longer be a roadblock to reform, New Deal reformers still had not agreed on how to reshape the economy or the political system in order to preserve the equal commonwealth envisioned by the founders. But as Franklin Roosevelt remarked, the country demanded "bold, persistent experimentation." The New Dealers provided it.

When World War II broke out, the united front of the people and the business elite joined forces to defeat the Nazi and Japanese threat. After the war, America's rising prosperity buried old debates about broad structural reforms to the economy and the political system. From the 1940s to the 1970s, America saw a growing middle class, rising wages, rising productivity, rising standards of living, and progress on equality for everyone. Constitutional debate turned to issues of civil rights and eventually to the culture wars. Economic issues were less salient, and their constitutional significance was largely forgotten.

It should not be surprising that it was only after World War II that Americans' fear of aristocracy waned. The founding generation had revolted against a feudal aristocracy. Their grandchildren were but two generations removed from the Revolutionary memory, and they lived in a time when feudal aristocrats still governed much of the Western world. The immigrants of the late nineteenth and early twentieth centuries fled those very states for a new republic defined by equality and opportunity rather than class hierarchy. By the middle of the twentieth century, the alternative to republican government was no longer aristocracy but authoritarianism. Fascism and then communism, not aristocracy or oligarchy, became the central fear.[4]

The glorious years of the mid-twentieth century now seem exceptional. The last thirty years have brought stagnant wages, rising inequality, and a middle class that is on its last legs. Globalization, technology, automation, financialization, and changes in public policy have transformed how the economy works. Political power is increasingly concentrated in a smaller group, creating legitimate fears that government has been co-opted to serve corporations and wealthy individuals and to shield them from competition. And efforts are under way to reinterpret the Constitution to make it harder to rebuild economic security for the middle class. Some political scientists have even declared that America is no longer rightly called a republic; it is better described as an oligarchy. We are now in a critical moment in the life of our middle-class constitution—a moment when we must remember that republican government cannot succeed without a strong middle class and when we must acknowledge that the central threat to our republic is once again economic.

Americans of all political stripes might find this account uncomfortable. Those on the left worry about economic inequality, but too often they dismiss the inheritance of the founding generation. Those on the right value our constitutional origins, but rising economic inequality is rarely their central concern. Many in the center often ignore both the distribution of wealth and American history, preferring to focus instead on technocratic debates over economic growth and efficiency.

But the history of constitutional thought suggests that when economic and constitutional structures become misaligned, reform or revolution must ultimately get them back into sync. Political philosophers throughout history believed there could only be a stable equilibrium in one of two situations: with a class warfare constitution built on economic inequality; or with a middle-class constitution grounded in a strong, large, and accessible middle class. The question today is how Americans will respond to the crisis of our middle-class constitution: Will we accept oligarchy and the threat of demagogues and tyrants? Or will we work to restore the economic preconditions for our republic?

PART I

THE RADICALISM OF THE
AMERICAN CONSTITUTION

CHAPTER ONE

From Athens to America: The Two Traditions

By the time the Constitution was ratified, John Adams was out of touch with the mainstream of American constitutional thinking. He was perhaps the deepest thinker, the most thoughtful, and the best read among the revolutionaries, and his *Thoughts on Government* in 1776 guided them as they drafted state constitutions. Adams himself drafted the Massachusetts Constitution of 1780. But in 1787, his tome titled *A Defence of the Constitutions of Government of the United States of America* appeared to come from a bygone era. Adams himself recognized this, writing to a friend, "This Book will make me unpopular."[1]

What made Adams an outlier wasn't the structure of the government he proposed. His suggestion looked similar to the Constitution drafted at Philadelphia that summer. He, too, proposed a system of separated powers, with an executive branch and a bicameral legislature. The difference was his justification for that structure. By 1787, Americans firmly believed in popular sovereignty, and they saw both the House of Representatives and the Senate as rooted in the will of the people. Two houses in the legislature simply served as a check on the exercise of power by slowing the legislative process and cooling passions. In the *Defence* and in his other writings, Adams justified the two houses based on social class. He believed, in the words of the historian Gordon Wood, that "government bore an intimate relation to society and unless the two were reconciled no state could long remain secure."[2] While America seemed like an egalitarian society without "distinctions of ranks," Americans would

be driven to "better their condition [and] advance their fortunes[]
without limits." This natural desire to acquire more wealth would
cause social divisions between "the rich and the poor, the laborious
and the idle, the learned and the ignorant."[3] The task of constitutional government was to "regulate and not to eradicate" such divisions, which would invariably be reduced to two—the rich and the
poor.[4] No society, Adams thought, could be truly equal. There was
"no special providence for Americans," who were just "like all other
people, and shall do like other nations."[5] And so John Adams, a hero
of America's democratic Revolution, argued that there needed to be
one house for the "rich, the well-born, and the able" and another for
the common people of the country.[6] Each class would serve as a check
on the other because "[n]othing but Force and Power and Strength
can restrain" groups of people against "their Avarice or Ambition."[7]
Adams thought he was protecting against oligarchy by confining the
rich to one house of the legislature. It was an "ostracism," he said.[8]
But critics at the time found Adams's position surprising. America
did not have an aristocracy, they said. So why create one?[9] Decades
later, John Taylor ("of Caroline," as he was known) called Adams's
Defence a "caricature or travesty" of American constitutional thinking. It made a "radical errour" in envisioning "our division of power,
as the same principle with his balance of [social] orders."[10]

It might seem puzzling that the man who would become the first
vice president of the United States thought the American Constitution should align economic classes with the branches of government.
But it is only puzzling when compared with the democratic tendencies unleashed by the American Revolution and by our own modern commitment to an egalitarian democracy. To understand why
Adams was such an outlier—and how *radical* the American Constitution was—we have to go back in time, to the intellectual traditions
that Adams and the founding generation inherited.

For much of the history of constitutional thought, political theorists and statesmen believed economic inequality was inevitable
in society and was one of the central challenges, if not the central
challenge, of constitutional design. Either the rich would tyrannize
the poor, or the poor would oppress the rich. The result would be
oligarchy, mob rule, or constant strife. The way to create a stable

government was to build economic classes directly into the structure of government, thereby creating a balance between wealthy and ordinary citizens. These *class warfare constitutions* mirrored the economic inequality in society and mitigated its deleterious effects. For political theorists, the Roman republic, with its patrician senate and tribune of the plebs, served as a detailed case study in this tradition of constitutional design.

But there was a second response to this problem as well, albeit one that was much more speculative. Political theorists in this second tradition recognized that societies might not be divided only into rich and poor. There could be a third group—a middle class. In these societies, if the middle class was large enough and strong enough, it could hold the balance of power between rich and poor. The middle class would govern wisely, without any of the vices that afflict the impoverished or the affluent. *Middle-class constitutions* would not need to be defined by structures mirroring economic inequality. A different kind of governmental structure—a democracy or commonwealth—might be possible.

The intellectual history that undergirds these two traditions is obscure today, and it requires an in-depth exploration into history from ancient Greece through the eighteenth century. But it provides the baseline for understanding what made the American Constitution exceptional and for seeing the connection between political power and economic conditions. If economic power and political power became mismatched, the result would be instability, strife, and even revolution.

ATHENIAN EXCEPTIONALISM

Around 600 B.C., economic tensions in Athens were running high. Overseas colonization meant greater wealth for the already wealthy landowners, in addition to access to foreign luxuries.[11] At the same time, poorer families were at risk of being sold into slavery or forced to sell their labor to pay off their debts.[12] "The disparity between the rich and the poor had culminated, as it were, and the city was in an altogether perilous condition," the historian Plutarch wrote. "It seemed as if the only way to settle its disorders and stop its turmoils was to establish a tyranny." But the Athenians did not establish a tyranny. Instead, they called forth one of their more distinguished citizens, Solon, who "was neither associated with the rich in their injustice, nor involved in the necessities of the poor."[13]

In 594 B.C., Solon adopted two major reforms that fundamentally changed the relationship between the rich and the poor in Athens. First, he abolished debt bondage and forgave existing debts. The poor could never be truly equal citizens if they were at risk of needing to sell themselves into slavery. Ending debt bondage meant that over time poverty would not lead to political inequality.[14] The second reform was a significant revision of the political and legal system, particularly an expansion of the scope of who could hold office. Instead of relying on birth status as a qualification for holding office, Solon shifted to a wealth requirement, based on agricultural production.[15] Here, too, the reforms had longer-term significance: they expanded political mobility.[16] With the shift from birth to wealth, even the poor could potentially raise their economic standing and attain political leadership. As part of his legal reforms, Solon also created a popular law court in which anyone who was injured—rich or poor—could bring suit against those who had wronged him, and he established the Council of 400, an assembly with members from different wealth classes. Solon's reforms, Plutarch tells us, "pleased neither party." "The rich were vexed because he took away their securities for debt, and the poor still more, because he did not redistribute the land, as they had expected, nor make all men equal and alike in their way of living."[17] Solon's reforms put Athens on the path to becoming the democracy that Pericles would herald as a model for the world, where "everyone is equal before the law" and "political life is free and open."[18] Over the next few hundred years, Athenian reformers would expand political equality even further, making Athens the deliberative democracy we think of today.

What made Athenian democracy work? First was a set of political reforms that established democratic equality. The second great Athenian reformer, Cleisthenes, helped create a democratic identity with his reforms in 507 B.C. He eliminated Solon's wealth classes and instead divided Athens into ten tribes based on 139 different areas of residence, with each tribe sending members to the now-expanded

Council of 500. The result was a shift from wealth to geography, creating broader, more equal representation in the council. In addition, Cleisthenes adopted reforms to prevent notable individuals from accumulating too much power within the city. Members of the Council of 500 could serve only twice in their lifetimes and for one year each.[19] He also introduced the practice of ostracism, by which the assembly could exile a member of the city. In the fifth century, Athens used ostracism fifteen times, largely to exclude people who were feared to have grown too powerful and were suspected of wanting to become tyrants.[20] Ostracism ensured that the people writ large had a check on the wealthy and powerful.

After Cleisthenes, further reforms extended equality in Athens. The city-state shifted selection of its top officials from election to lottery.[21] Property qualifications for office were reduced and then eliminated altogether.[22] At the end of the fifth century, the march of Athenian democracy was halted by a generation of warfare during and after the Peloponnesian War. Starting in 411 B.C., Athens went through a series of constitutional revolutions in just under a decade: an oligarchy took over in 411, only to be swiftly replaced by the rule of "the 5,000," followed by the reintroduction of democracy in 410. Sparta defeated Athens in 404, and the "thirty tyrants" took over the city.[23] Finally, in 403, Athens again became a democracy.

For much of the next century, Athens flourished. This was the golden age of Athens—of Plato and Aristotle, poets and playwrights. It was also the pinnacle of Athenian democracy. The assembly was no longer restricted by wealth or property qualifications: any male citizen could participate.[24] Within the Council of 500, which set the agenda for the assembly, a tenth of the members composed the executive body, whose rotating chair was selected by lottery and only served for twenty-four hours, to prevent the chair from accumulating inordinate power.[25] The courts had juries of between two hundred and fifteen hundred people, chosen by lottery from panels of six thousand.[26] Jurors had to be citizens over the age of thirty.[27] Of the twelve hundred officials in the city, only about a hundred were elected, which included ten generals—the rest were selected by lottery.[28] Throughout this time, economic inequalities never resulted in rebellion.

Of course, by modern standards, Athens doesn't seem like the ideal democracy. Women, foreigners, and slaves were excluded from participating in politics. But although Athenian political freedom was in part built on the backs of women and slaves, the story is not so simple as that might suggest. When compared with other city-states at the time, Athens was extraordinarily open. Not only was oligarchy the most common form of government in fourth-century B.C. Greece, but, as the classicist Josiah Ober once noted, "[f]or the first time in the recorded history of a complex society, *all* native freeborn males, irrespective of their ability, family connections, or wealth, were political equals, with equal rights to determine state policy."[29]

Just as important, democratic deliberation in Athens was not limited to wealthy elites who did not need to work.[30] At the time, there were twenty thousand to thirty thousand Athenian citizens: adult men who were not foreigners or slaves. About twelve hundred to two thousand of these citizens were wealthy enough to form the "leisure class" that did not need to work, a number that jumps to forty-eight hundred to eight thousand if we include their families. In other words, only about 5 to 10 percent of citizens were in the highest echelon of economic class. When the Athenian assembly met at Pnyx, the hill that was home to the city's six-thousand-citizen democratic debates, it was not a gathering controlled or dominated by the richest Athenians. Even if all of the economically elite citizens in Athens attended, they would compose only about *one-third* of the assembly.[31]

While some at the time, like the now cheekily named "Old Oligarch," complained that the poor ran the government, Athens was remarkably wealthy and surprisingly equal in its distribution of wealth. Estimates we have of wages suggest that a great number of Athenians earned enough "to enable them to live decent lives."[32] Our evidence of housing patterns corroborates this evidence. If ancient Greece was severely stratified by wealth, we would expect to see archaeological evidence of mansions (for the rich) and small huts (for the poor). But the archaeological record instead clusters around the middle, with few extremely small or large houses.[33] "Wealth was distributed relatively equitably across Greek populations"; Josiah Ober concludes, "there was a substantial middle class of people who lived well above bare subsistence yet below the level of elite consumption."[34]

To enable the many working middle-class citizens to participate in politics, the people of Athens made a second policy choice. They did not assume that relative economic equality would prevent those who were on the wealthier side from dominating politics. To make democracy work, they paid for widespread participation. Starting in the mid–fifth century B.C., Athens paid citizens a per diem for attending the assembly and later expanded the per diem to include jury service.[35] Normally, men, women, and children all had to work simply to sustain the family. The payment for political participation offset the losses that accompanied being absent from a day of work. The result was to expand who could govern the Greek city-state to those even of modest means.

Economic equality and equal political participation were not the only features that allowed Athenian democracy to flourish. Athenian political culture worked to guard against the *informal* advantages that wealthy individuals could parlay into outsized political power. Because the wealthy could pay for education and had leisure time to develop oratory skills, they were more likely to participate in and dominate the assembly. The famed orator Demosthenes is said to have deliberately shaved off half the hair on his head. Too ashamed to leave his house, he would have to practice oratory for months at a time while his hair grew back.[36] Speakers before the assembly knew that the crowd was vigilant and skeptical of those who accumulated influence, and so orators (especially wealthy ones) were careful to flatter the people. Demosthenes himself captured the depth of this concern, attempting to clothe his oratorical preparation in a populist garb: "[H]e who rehearsed his speeches was a true man of the people: for such preparation was a mark of deference to the people, whereas heedlessness of what the multitude will think of his speech marks a man of oligarchical spirit, and one who relies on force rather than on persuasion."[37]

Athenian government also had formal rules that prevented the wealthy from taking on too much power. Those who served as magistrates were subject to a legal and financial audit upon leaving office, and speakers in the assembly could be punished for proposing unlawful ideas or speaking after taking a bribe.[38] Ostracism was an extreme fail-safe in the case of someone who was suspected of seeking too much power. But perhaps most important, Athenian democracy did not rely on elections. If leadership was determined by election, the wealthy would be more likely to get elected; they'd have the skills, time, and financial resources to dedicate themselves to public business. Athens solved the problem of the aristocratic advantages of elections through the widespread use of lotteries.

And therein lies the greatest difficulty with thinking about Athens as a model for today. In the early 1990s, the intellectual historian Bernard Manin described one of the quickest, most striking changes in the history of constitutional theory: in a matter of decades in the eighteenth century, elections became universally accepted as the sole strategy for selecting leaders.[39] In Rome, order of voting among the tribes was partly determined by lottery.[40] In Renaissance Florence, simple lotteries and multistage mixed lottery-election systems were used to choose leaders.[41] Republican Venice continued to use lottery into the late eighteenth century, when its government finally fell.[42] Philosophers in the seventeenth and eighteenth centuries—Harrington, Montesquieu, and Rousseau—all devoted attention to selecting officials by lottery.[43] And yet, in debates after the American and French Revolutions, lottery is almost completely absent.

Lost in this transformation from lottery to election was an important argument about economic class. From the Athens of Aristotle to the eighteenth century, political philosophers believed that elections were inherently aristocratic, and lotteries inherently democratic.[44] The simplest way to see the aristocratic bias in elections is to consider features of our own electoral system today. Winning an election requires being known by the population, and some candidates have a built-in advantage on name recognition. It is partly for this reason that political dynasties persist and media celebrities can rocket to front-runner status. Without that preexisting advantage, there are huge costs to becoming known as a candidate. These days, much of those costs are for television advertisements, and it is advantageous to be a candidate who can simply pay for the campaign, without needing to raise money. Deep-pocketed candidates can (usually) outspend less well-financed opponents in order to get noticed by voters. More conceptually, elections have an aristocratic bent because, compared with lotteries, they do not give everyone an equal chance to participate in government. Instead, only a few get to participate in a process by which they are *chosen*. The fact of choice means that not everyone will have an equal chance of being selected; some candidates will be more likely to win than others.

Today, we see these features as a great strength of elections—and there are many strengths to elections. But when compared with a lottery system, elections will be more likely to lead to rule by wealthy or privileged elites.[45] Lottery, in contrast, has no aristocratic bias; it is inherently democratic because it treats and selects people on equal terms. Everyone has an equal chance of being chosen. To put it in statistical terms, lotteries lead to a standard distribution in the population serving in government. Elections lead to a distribution skewed toward the wealthy.

The disappearance of lottery from constitutional theory was fundamentally rooted in the idea that government legitimacy comes not from equal participation in public affairs, as the Athenians believed, but from "the consent of the governed."[46] With the emergence of the modern philosophy of representation, the Athenian model for preventing class warfare became obsolete.

THE THEORY OF THE CLASS WARFARE CONSTITUTION

In the second century B.C., the Greek historian Polybius asked how it was that the Romans conquered the entirety of the known world in merely fifty-three years.[47] The rise of the Roman republic had been the defining fact of Polybius's life. Born around 200 B.C. in the city of Megalopolis, Polybius was the son of a leading family in the capital city of the Achaean League, a federation of southern Greek city-states. Because his father had served as a general for the league, he was destined for a career in diplomacy and politics.

Rome blocked that future. In the decades before Polybius's birth, Rome had consolidated its power in Italy and waged war against Carthage, in North Africa. It defeated Macedon, the empire once led by Alexander the Great, and it expanded east into modern-day Turkey. Rome required uncompromising loyalty from its allies and supplicants. When it defeated Macedon for a third time in just over thirty years, the Romans punished not only those who had rebelled against their power but also those who had not been supportive enough. You were either with Rome or against her.

According to historians, Polybius's political rivals put him on a list of people who were halfhearted in their support for Rome during the third Macedonian war. In 168 B.C., Polybius was taken to Italy as a prisoner along with a thousand others. Detained for the next seventeen years, he had the good fortune to be selected to serve as tutor to one of the leading families in Rome. His student Scipio Aemilianus went on to become the greatest military commander of his generation, and the two men remained close even after Polybius was free to return home. When Scipio undertook the siege—and ultimately the defeat and destruction—of Carthage in 146 B.C., his old tutor joined him in North Africa for the battle. In that same year, for inexplicable reasons, the southern Greeks again declared war on Rome. Upon their defeat, the Achaean League was disbanded, and the great city of Corinth, like Carthage, was destroyed. Polybius returned to Greece and used his connections, worldly travel, and understanding of Roman practices to help with the reconstruction of his homeland.

Although Polybius gained fame in his own time for rebuilding Greece, his fame today stems from another of his endeavors: documenting the rise of Roman power over the previous century. Polybius argued in *The Histories* that Rome was able to conquer the known world in such a short period of time because of its political system. Most political systems, he observed, fall into one of six categories: kingship, aristocracy, and democracy, and their perversions, tyranny, oligarchy, and mob rule. Each of these systems suffers from natural decay, a cyclical process that leads to frequent constitutional revolutions and instability. As a result, no city-state with one of these types of governments could ever maintain an empire. The Roman republic solved this problem by mixing the forms of government. Rome created a stronger and more stable political system by combining features of each. World domination followed.[48]

Polybius wasn't the first to describe government in this way. Greek political theorists had classified governments along the lines of monarchy, aristocracy, and democracy since at least Pindar, three hundred years earlier. Herodotus, Thucydides, and Plato also all gave accounts of constitutional forms along these lines, with varying degrees of specificity.[49] The best-developed account, however, was that of the fourth-century B.C. philosopher Aristotle.

In the *Politics,* Aristotle set as his task determining what the best constitution is for a state. Not just the best constitution in theory (which he called the "constitution of our prayers"), but more important, the best constitution that can actually be achieved in the real world.[50] Like other political philosophers throughout history, Aristotle identified the main forms of government as kingship, aristocracy, and what he called "constitutional government." Each of these perfect systems had a corresponding imperfect form of government: tyranny, oligarchy, and democracy.[51]

Today we think of these "forms" of government as based on the number of rulers. Kingship and tyranny involve a single ruler. Aristocracy and oligarchy, the rule of the few. Constitutional government and democracy, government by the many. But that is not what Aristotle believed. While he recognized the link between the number of rulers and the type of government, he did not think it was the defining feature of these forms of government.[52]

What could be more relevant than the number of rulers? The answer is one of Aristotle's most important insights and the key to understanding a critical feature of constitutional design from the ancients until the eighteenth century. For Aristotle, social conditions could not be divorced from politics. The fact that a community has some rich people and some poor people, or was unified or divided in its beliefs, mattered.[53] Political outcomes were dependent on the power of different social groups, so social factors were central when thinking about the structure of government.[54] To gain any real insight into the best constitution for a society in the real world, therefore, Aristotle held that it was not sufficient to think only about the number of leaders. Rather, we also have to consider the relationships and actions of powerful groups in society. "[T]he constitution," Aristotle commented, "is a community," and the "community is the constitution."[55]

Because Aristotle believed social conditions and government were intertwined, when he looked at the different types of government, the number of rulers wasn't the critical feature. The critical feature was *which class* ruled.[56] Oligarchy was rule in the interest of the wealthy. Democracy was rule in the interest of the poor.[57] "The real difference between democracy and oligarchy is poverty and wealth," Aristotle wrote. "Wherever men rule by reason of their wealth, whether they be few or many, that is an oligarchy, and where the poor rule, that is a democracy."[58] It was simply an "accident" that in most cases a few are wealthy and many are poor.[59]

For Aristotle, one of the central problems of constitutional design was the possibility of class warfare between the wealthy and the poor. Aristotle believed that in a democracy the poor would govern because democracies are based on free and equal citizenship. The problem, however, was that because the poor are equal in one respect (freedom), they will believe they should be equal in all respects.[60] So if the poor control government, they are likely to confiscate and redistribute the wealth of the rich.[61] The rich, in turn, will be threatened by these efforts and revolt, bringing strife and instability to the state.

But Aristotle also believed that giving control to the wealthy through an oligarchy was no better. The wealthy are susceptible to thinking that because they are "unequal in one respect" (their wealth), they should be unequal in all respects.[62] If the wealthy control government, they are likely to hoard money and property for themselves and oppress the poor, because they will believe the poor are less worthy of respect and less worthy of governing.[63] The poor then have cause for rebellion. Aristotle outlined some suggestions on how to prevent class warfare, including honoring those who rule without personal gain and giving power and respect to the class not in power. However, he was not optimistic these solutions would stabilize the community. The division between the rich and the poor meant constitutional revolution was an ever-present risk.[64]

For two millennia after Aristotle, statesmen and philosophers seeking to address class warfare adopted one of Aristotle's two solutions to this problem. Aristotle's first solution—the one best known in history—was what he and Polybius called mixed government.[65] Most people today think of mixed government as blending the three different "pure" types of government: rule by one (monarchy), by the few (aristocracy), and by the many (democracy). But Aristotle thought of constitutional government as blending economic classes, not just the number of rulers. As a result, we can consider mixed government as creating a *class warfare constitution*. Such a constitution assumes that economic inequality in society is inevitable and that class conflict presents a serious risk of internal discord. In response, class warfare constitutions incorporate each economic class into government itself, bringing together different structures to create a hybrid political system that should, in theory, be more stable than any of the pure forms of government alone. For Aristotle, a class warfare constitution worked because it gave each economic class a share and a stake in governing. As a result, neither class would have reason to destabilize the regime.

Aristotle identified three strategies for how to create these constitutional governments.[66] The first was to combine elements of both democracy and oligarchy. For example, in an oligarchy, Aristotle says, the rich are fined if they do not serve on juries. The fine serves as an incentive for their participation. In contrast, in a democracy, the poor are paid to serve on juries, because this enables their participation. Aristotle recommended adopting both policies so that both groups would participate. Aristotle's second strategy was to take the middle point between the policies that a democracy and an oligarchy would adopt. In an oligarchy, there would be high property qualifications to participate in government; in a democracy, no property qualifications. The middle way was a moderate property requirement.

Aristotle's final strategy for mixed government has been the most influential: take something from each political system. For example, the democratic approach is to have no property qualifications and to pick officials by lottery instead of election. That ensures that anyone and everyone can partake in governance. The oligarchic approach is the opposite: elections only by those who met property qualifications. Aristotle suggested adopting a system of elections as a nod to oligarchies but requiring no property qualifications for voting or service. The result was that only those chosen few could serve in government but that everyone could participate in their selection. In this way, democracy and oligarchy are blended together. A simpler example of this kind of mixing is limiting one part of the government to each class—for example, a house of lords for the wealthy and a house of commons for everyone else. Rich and poor both participate, reducing the risk of either side dominating the other.

Two hundred years later, when Polybius saw Rome's mixed government as the reason for its successful conquest of the known world, he added another element to Aristotle's understanding of class warfare constitutions. The Greek historian remarked that the Roman republic had consuls who controlled warfare and administration and were akin to kings or monarchs. The Roman senate looked like an aristocracy because it was composed of elite patricians with power over revenues and expenditures, among other things. The Roman people—the democratic element—were essential to approving legislation, going to war, and choosing leaders. Each of these groups was locked together in the government. But Polybius also pointed out that each of these three parts of the Roman government was dependent on the others to accomplish its goals and that each could block the aims of the others.[67]

Polybius concluded that stability and peace were not only due to the fact that each class had a share and stake in government, as Aristotle had argued. Rather, stability also came from the fact that each part of society "can be effectively counteracted and hampered by the others."[68] Today, we know this idea as "checks and balances," and for Polybius it explained Rome's success. Checks and balances made Rome powerful precisely because they prevented one class from exploiting or oppressing the other.

THE LIBERTY OF THE PLEBS

According to the historian Livy, in 493 B.C. a haggard, skinny old man made his way into the Roman forum. Unshaven and dressed in tattered clothes, he looked as if he had been lost in the wilderness and somehow survived. He told the people in the forum that he had served in the army as a company commander, showing them the scars on his chest that proved his valor. But while he was on his tour of duty, his farmhouse was razed to the ground, his crops destroyed, and all of his possessions taken. At that very moment—when he had lost everything back home—came a war tax. The man took on debt but fell behind in his payments. First he lost his ancestral property, then his remaining possessions, and finally he was forced to sell himself into bondage. His creditor imprisoned and tortured him. To the growing crowd, he now revealed his back, still raw with scars from recent whippings.[69]

The crowd was apoplectic. "They complained that while fighting in the field for liberty and empire they were taken prisoner and maltreated at home by their fellow citizens," Livy tells us. "[T]he liberty of the plebs was better served in war than in peace and among the enemy than among citizens."[70] The crowd clamored for the senators and consuls to show themselves and bring relief to the indebted veteran and to all debtors. But the senators who were in the forum, already fearful of their lives, didn't have a quorum. Then, at that very moment, a horseman arrived with an urgent warning: an army was marching on the city.

At the time, Rome was merely a small city-state, frequently at war with the neighboring Volsci and Aurunci (to the south), Aequi (to the east), and Sabines (to the north), among others. The impoverished plebeians of Rome responded to the horseman's signal, taking up arms and defeating the Volsci, and then the Sabines, and then the Aurunci. With victories in hand, they returned to Rome, only to be sent back to their creditors and watch as the senate failed to address their complaints.[71] When the Volsci, Aequi, and Sabines attacked the following year, the plebs again took up arms and defeated them.[72] Now worried that disbanding the army would lead to citywide strife, the senators invented a new threat from the Aequi. But the plebs had finally had enough. In what is called the First Secession of the Plebs, they refused to fight and decamped to the Sacred Mount, three miles outside the city, just beyond the Anio River.[73] Worried about the possibility of more wars on the horizon and the threat of civil strife, the patricians gave way in negotiations.

What emerged from the Secession of the Plebs was not an end to their debt-fueled grievances but a change in the structure of government. Instead of a pure aristocracy, run by patrician senators, Rome would now have new features in its government: the office of tribune of the plebs and a plebeian assembly. Tribunes—there were at least two when the tribunate was founded—would provide assistance to ordinary Romans, especially against the actions of consuls. Patricians and senators were prohibited from serving as a tribune. And perhaps most important, the plebs vowed to avenge any violence against a tribune, in effect rendering his person sacrosanct. Anyone who harmed a tribune would be killed. Over time, the tribunate expanded to ten, and tribunes became some of the most powerful men in Rome. They had the authority to grant clemency (including from the death penalty), veto legislation at any stage in the process, block the actions of other magistrates, initiate legislation through plebiscites, call public assemblies, initiate prosecutions against magistrates who had abused their office, and keep a written record of the laws of Rome.[74] The creation of the tribunate is what first made Rome a class warfare constitution. It instituted economic class directly into the structure of government, with the tribunate and the assembly giving plebeians a share and stake in government and a check on the power of the patrician senate.

The details in the tribunate's origin story, like all stories from early Roman history, may be apocryphal, shaped by the politics and mythmaking of later Roman historians.[75] Still, throughout history, many of the great political philosophers used the experience of the Roman tribunate to explore whether class warfare constitutions could be stable forms of government and to explain their own views on the relationship between economic and constitutional structures. Studying the history of the tribunate—and the history of thinkers who reflected upon the tribunate—allows us to see the possibilities and pitfalls of class warfare constitutions.[76]

Rome's class warfare constitution—the one Polybius celebrated as enabling the republic to conquer the known world—did not emerge fully formed after the Secession of the Plebs. For the next two hundred years after the secession, Rome was defined by what later historians called the "struggle of the orders"—a persistent state of tension between patricians and plebeians—that culminated in the government of checks and balances that Polybius observed.[77]

The central issues in the struggle of the orders were economic, and the most significant issue was the distribution and use of agricultural lands, because agricultural property was both critical to subsistence and the most important source of wealth for most people.[78]

Rome's mythical founding king, Romulus, had supposedly given two *iugera* (about two-thirds of an acre of land) to each family. The rest of the land was public land, available for families to use for grazing and cultivation. Given the agricultural techniques of the time, a family needed more than fourteen *iugera* merely to sustain themselves.[79] The combination of private and public land use could accommodate these needs. But over time, the wealthiest Romans increasingly took control over public land and treated it as part of their estates.[80] The plebs responded with calls for reform. Between 486 and 367 B.C., there were twenty-five attempts to address the issue of public lands.[81] The most important reform, in 367, placed a limit of five hundred *iugera* on the possession of public land.[82] While it did not go as far as plebeian desires for public lands to be redistributed more equitably, it did impose a fine for possession beyond the limits.[83]

The second issue in the struggle of the orders was political power. Starting in 462 B.C., the plebeians began to demand that Rome's laws be codified and made publicly available.[84] "When the laws are written down, weak and rich men get equal justice," Euripides had written. "[T]he weaker, when abused, can respond to the prosperous in kind, and the small man with justice on his side defeats the strong."[85] In 451, the Romans suspended their constitution and appointed ten men to draft a code of substantive laws. They came up with ten laws, but the people thought there needed to be two more. The following year another ten men were appointed to finish the job.[86] Having written the Twelve Tables, Rome's first codified set of laws, this second group of ten took power for themselves and refused to restore the constitution. Then the leader of the junta, Appius Claudius, attempted to seize and rape a young woman, Verginia. In a dramatic telling by the historian Livy, Verginia's own father killed her in order to save her from the tyrant's grasp. Offended by this literally rapacious exercise of power, the plebs again seceded, this time to the Aventine Hill. Appius Claudius committed suicide, and the constitution was reinstated—with further reforms.[87] Tribunes became sacrosanct as a matter of statutory right, not just convention. The reforms prohibited the creation of any magistracy that did not give citizens a right to appeal. Plebeian officers were given the right to keep public records of senatorial decrees. And perhaps most important, the reforms established that plebiscites could bind the entire population, though with procedural caveats.[88]

Over the next two centuries, plebeians won many other concessions. By 300 B.C., plebeians gained the ability to serve in the most powerful political offices and in religious offices.[89] A law required that at least one of Rome's two consuls be plebeian.[90] Laws reformed interest rates and debt repayment and abolished some forms of debt bondage.[91] And in 287 B.C., after another debt-motivated secession of the plebs, popularly passed legislation became immediately binding on the general population without any caveats or procedural hurdles.[92] With that law in place, the struggle of the orders—and the first phase of the Roman republic—came to an end.[93]

DESTINED FOR SEDITION?

The view from 146 B.C., when Polybius watched Rome destroy Carthage, was one that showed how powerful the Roman republic had become. But had Polybius lived a hundred years later, he wouldn't have asked how Rome conquered the world in just fifty-three years. He would have asked how, in just fifty-three years, Rome descended from stable republic to civil war.

Living in that era of turmoil and conflict, Cicero didn't quite pose the question that way. But he did outline a theory of government that held that mixed government was the best possible design for a constitution. In his dialogue *On the Republic,* Cicero echoed Aristotle, Polybius, and other ancient theorists, noting that the three forms of government were kingship, aristocracy, and popular government and that each of these had a "depraved form."[94] Like Aristotle and Polybius, he noted that there is a "fourth form" of government, a "mixture" of the three pure forms.[95]

"The best constitution for a State," Cicero wrote, was one that is a "balanced combination of the three forms."[96] Such a constitution, particularly if it evolves over time organically, rather than being the product of a single founder, would be less susceptible to revolution than any of the pure forms of government.[97] "[U]nless there is in the State an even balance of rights, duties, and functions, so that the magistrates have enough power, the counsels of the eminent citizens enough influence, and the people enough liberty, this kind of government cannot be safe from revolution."[98] Cicero's mixed constitution, like that of Aristotle and Polybius, was designed to prevent revolution, and it linked social class to political power. The "eminent citizens" are separate from the "people," and both must affirm and accept the power and limits of government.

In a dialogue called *On the Laws,* a companion to his *Republic,* Cicero fleshed out what he saw as the best constitution in practice. The design of his ideal constitution was identical to the actual structure of Roman government. But through a clever narrative device, Cicero hinted that he didn't actually believe the Roman republic as it had been constituted was the best. He had strong misgivings about the tribunate.

The *Laws* is a dialogue conducted primarily between Cicero and his brother Quintus. After Cicero outlines the structure of Roman government, Quintus attacks his brother's position on the tribunate. He charges tribunes throughout history with inciting violence, making conflict and bloodshed a normal part of Roman politics, and stirring the mob to a frenzy.[99] Cicero defends the tribunate against these criticisms, noting that while the tribunate was flawed, it had also done much good. When it was created, "conflict ceased, rebellion was at an end," and it was clear to all Romans that "compromise was the only salvation of the state."[100] Moreover, without the tribunate, mob rule might have been even more radical. Cicero then tells Quintus that the convention in a dialogue of this sort is for the interlocutor to agree wholeheartedly with the teacher's comments so the lesson can go on. But surprisingly, Quintus refuses. He tells Cicero that he does not agree with his views on the tribunate. The third participant in the dialogue, Atticus, then chimes in, declaring that he, too, is unconvinced by Cicero's defense of the tribunate. Outnumbered, Cicero makes no reply. He simply moves to the next topic.[101] As a result, the reader is left with the distinct impression that Quintus has won the argument. The tribunate, in his memorable phrase, "was born in sedition and destined to create sedition."[102]

Was the tribunate really the cause of the civil wars and the Roman republic's collapse? For an answer, we have to go back a century, to the expansion of Rome in the second century B.C.—the years that Polybius describes as leading to Rome's domination of the known world. Between 264 B.C., when the First Punic War began, and 146 B.C., when Corinth and Carthage were destroyed, Rome gained control over the land surrounding most of the Mediterranean.[103] During this period, Rome is better understood less by the traditional divide of patrician and plebeian and more by a new division between the *nobiles*—the set of patricians and elite plebeians whose families had held the consulship—and the ordinary, non-elite plebeians.[104] The empire brought enormous wealth to Rome in the form of war spoils and profits from territorial administration, taxation, and trade.[105] The riches of empire went mostly to wealthy elites, as did contracts from the senate for services (like tax collection and building projects).[106] The historian Sallust described the consequences of imperial wealth: "The generals divided the spoils of war with a few friends. Meanwhile the parents or little children of the soldiers, if they had a powerful neighbour, were driven from their homes. Thus, by the side of power, greed arose, unlimited and unrestrained, violated and devastated everything, respected nothing, and held nothing sacred, until it finally brought about its own downfall."[107]

Sallust's description of the curse that came with Rome's rising power highlighted the greater and greater stress placed on the poor. Long wars meant that the poor had to neglect their farms at home and many did not return alive; only the wealthiest could pay to have someone manage the land while they were abroad fighting in a seasonal campaign. In addition, as the rich got richer, they purchased more and more land, and land speculation became a common practice, particularly in regard to public lands.[108] The existing rule limiting any person's use of public lands to five hundred *iugera* went unenforced.[109] The number of dispossessed former smallholders grew, as did the degree of economic inequality.[110] Importantly, it was these small landholders that had been the backbone of the army.[111]

With riches flowing into Rome, wealth soon became a prerequisite for holding office, which only pushed officials to use their offices to make still more money.[112] Sallust described the effect that this new "lust for money" had on the republic: "[A]varice destroyed honour, integrity, and all other noble qualities; taught in their place insolence, cruelty, to neglect the gods, to set a price on everything. . . . When the disease had spread like a deadly plague, the state was changed and a government second to none in equity and excellence became cruel and intolerable."[113] When Rome entered the age of civil war, Crassus would say "that no one could be counted rich unless he could maintain an army from his income."[114]

The prologue to the republic's decline and fall started in 133 B.C., when the thirty-year-old Tiberius Gracchus became tribune of the plebs. As tribune, Tiberius set himself immediately to addressing the issue of public land use. He seems to have been concerned with both economic inequality and the sustainability of the army, which was recruited largely from poorer Romans.[115] Tiberius proposed an agricultural law that would make public lands available for distribution in allotments to poorer citizens. Any person who had more than 500 *iugera* of land (the existing, though unenforced, legal limit) would have to give up excess land, save for an additional 250 *iugera* for each of two sons. Land reclaimed from the rich would be redistributed in small allotments of 30 *iugera,* thus expanding economic opportunity for a wider population of Romans.[116]

Unsurprisingly, Tiberius's agrarian law met with immediate opposition. When he "began to assert the freedom of the commons and expose the crimes of the oligarchs," Sallust writes, "the nobility, who were guilty, were therefore panic stricken."[117] While the reasons behind Tiberius's political strategy have not survived, we know that instead of taking his bill to the senate, which was common practice, Tiberius dusted off an archaic precedent that allowed land bills to go directly to the popular assembly.[118] Perhaps because of this unconventional move (or because he was under the influence of the senate and the patricians), another tribune, Octavius, vetoed the measure and continued to block its consideration. Blocking a tribune's bill was unprecedented in the history of the assembly, so Tiberius countered with another unprecedented step: he called for Octavius to be disqualified from the tribunate for opposing the will of the plebs.[119] Winning that motion, Tiberius again raised the agrarian law, and the people carried the bill.[120] Funding the bill was a different story.

Finance was a power allocated to the senate, and the senators had little interest in cooperating with Tiberius. So Tiberius threatened to circumvent the senate.[121]

Had Tiberius stopped there, everything might have been fine. But he decided to run for reelection as tribune. While it wasn't illegal to serve two consecutive terms, no tribune had run for reelection in 200 years.[122] Worse yet, Tiberius was slowly gaining a following among the plebs, who were building a political organization around him—something that hadn't happened since the last secession of the plebs 150 years earlier.[123] To his opponents, Tiberius was increasingly taking on the mantle of a tyrant and demagogue. He had to be stopped. Before the election could take place, Publius Nasica, Tiberius's cousin and rival, took the opportunity. Nasica's men chased the tribune down and clubbed him to death in the forum, along with three hundred of his supporters. As a final insult, their bodies were unceremoniously dumped into the Tiber River.[124] In the aftermath, the senate punished the remaining supporters of Tiberius, and Nasica left the city (he had, after all, killed a sitting—and therefore sacrosanct—tribune).[125] But the senate didn't revise Tiberius's agricultural law.[126] While it had initially been unwilling to compromise, Tiberius had given the plebs power and a voice, and the senate was not going to risk further strife with the plebs by rolling back the law.

A decade later, Tiberius Gracchus's brother Gaius became tribune (like his brother, at the age of thirty).[127] As much a reformer, he was more politically savvy given the demise of his brother. Instead of redistribution, Gaius proposed creating new colonies in Italy and on the site of Carthage so the poor could benefit from available land. He offered a new grain law: Rome would buy and store corn in bulk and then sell it over time at below-market rates, thereby reducing price variation, preventing profiteering, and lowering prices.[128] He also proposed giving all Latins citizenship and expanding the rights of all people in Italy.[129] Despite these more measured reforms, Gaius's fate was no better than his brother's. The senate opposed Gaius's proposals, and when the tensions again turned violent, Gaius and his supporters were cut down on the Aventine Hill.[130]

Historians have concluded that the Gracchi episodes were critical moments in the path to civil war. For the first time in generations, the people saw the intransigence of the senate and at the same time learned that they could exercise considerable power.[131] From that moment on, the division between rich and poor would only grow more acute, particularly as the agrarian problem took on a new phase in the form of demands from military veterans for land.[132] As one historian has concluded, "The Senate triumphed over the Gracchi with the sword, but the sword was to fall into other hands."[133]

In the decades after the Gracchi, Roman politics became increasingly intertwined with military power. The expanding empire gave military commanders a following among rank-and-file soldiers, who increasingly looked to their commanders for the benefits and bounty that came from victory. As with the alignment of military power and economic poverty during the First Secession of the Plebs, the frustrations of soldiers raised the possibility of revolution. In 88 B.C., the general Sulla marched on Rome; his erstwhile rival Marius did the same in 86 and used his power to become consul and exile Sulla.[134] In 83, with Marius now dead, Sulla returned to Italy with an army of forty thousand, fresh from a victory in Asia Minor.[135] Taking power in 81, he became dictator and consul, with the aspiration of returning the republic to some form of order.[136]

Sulla's central goal was to strengthen the power of the senate, particularly against the tribunate. He increased the number of senators, especially those he considered allies, because that body had been decimated during the conflicts of the previous decade; senators' heads were left to rot in the forum.[137] But more important, Sulla stripped the tribunes' powers: abolishing their authority to propose legislation, limiting their veto rights, and barring tribunes from holding higher office (making the tribunate a dead end for ambitious leaders).[138] Sallust called the new tribunate an "empty shell of a magistracy," and another commentator said the post was now a "shadow without substance."[139] Reforms in place, Sulla retired in 79 B.C. and died the following year.[140]

With his death, clamor for the return of the tribunate revived.[141] In 70 B.C., the consuls Pompey and Crassus restored the tribunate's powers fully, to great acclaim from the people.[142] But the damage to the Roman constitution was done. Sallust captured well the dynamics of the years after the restoration of the tribunate: "[Y]oung men, who gained the height of power, and whom youth and high spirits made impetuous, began, by accusing the Senate, to rouse the plebs, and then by largess and promises to inflame them further, and thus to make themselves famous and powerful. Against them, the majority of the *nobilitas* strove with all their might, apparently on behalf of the Senate, in reality to preserve their own importance."[143] The politics of class warfare was no longer a stabilizing force. It was the problem.

The political system Polybius thought was the most stable in the world—the one he thought conquered the world precisely because of its unique checks and balances on power—ended up failing to manage class conflict. As Rome conquered more and more territory, it grew wealthier, reshaping the economic and social structure of the republic. The wealthy forgot the lessons of compromise that had been learned on the Sacred Mount in 494 B.C. And once the people's grievances captured the attention of military commanders, the republic swiftly descended into a chaotic civil war that culminated in Julius Caesar's seizing power.

THE VIEW FROM FLORENCE

For later political philosophers, the Roman republic was the main case study of a class warfare constitution. It offered the chance to reflect on how best to organize a republican form of government. Looking back on their ancient ancestors, two gentlemen from Florence—one (in)famous and one virtually unknown today—had very different assessments of the class warfare structure of a republic.

For most people, the name Machiavelli is synonymous with advocating for a ruthless leader who will stop at nothing to gain and maintain power. *The Prince* gave Machiavelli his reputation. But *The Prince* wasn't the only book Machiavelli wrote, and for many scholars it isn't actually his most important or compelling work. As a Renaissance thinker, Machiavelli was part of that era's revival of ancient philosophy and culture. In the dauntingly titled *Discourses on the First Ten Books of Titus Livy*, Machiavelli turned his attention from princes to republics. While scholars often focus on the Florentine's emphasis on the virtues needed for republican government, Machiavelli also had a surprisingly populist streak.[144]

Machiavelli's birthplace of Florence was not the paradigm of stability during the Renaissance. The city had multiple governments and constitutions from the thirteenth through the fifteenth century, including an oligarchy from 1381 to 1434 and a sham republic that was in reality government by the Medici family from 1434 to 1494.[145] The city was also rife with class conflict. The wealthy aristocracy in Florence preferred a regime in which only a few prominent families (from the patrician class or from wealthy guilds) governed, rotating among themselves through leadership positions. The people and the members of the lower-tiered guilds wanted a government in which more people participated, with shorter terms of office and reduced property requirements.[146]

In 1494, Charles VIII, the king of France, invaded Italy to claim the throne of Naples. Without asking the *Signoria* (Florence's lead governing body), Piero di Lorenzo de' Medici collaborated with Charles. Florence erupted in anger, exiling the Medici family and reorganizing the government in a more popular fashion. Machiavelli served in this government until 1512, including as secretary for the "Ten of War," the council responsible for warfare.[147] His time in politics was hardly positive. Although he came from a family with a long tradition of service, Machiavelli wasn't wealthy, his father was mired in debt, and he was rumored to be illegitimate.[148] The Florentine aristocracy blocked him from the city's top offices, and they frequently interfered with his initiatives.[149] In 1512, the Florentines allowed the Medici to return, because they now believed strong Medici rule would help Florence drive the French out of Italy. This put Machiavelli on the wrong side of the leading political powers, and he was briefly imprisoned, before he exiled himself to his farm ten miles outside the city. It was then that Machiavelli wrote *The Prince* and, during 1517 to 1519, the *Discourses*. He died in 1527, and his writings were published posthumously in 1531.[150]

In the *Discourses,* Machiavelli took on the question of the best constitution for a state. He adopted the Aristotelian and Polybian convention of six forms of government: princedoms, aristocracies, and democracies, and their corrupted versions.[151] Because of the cycles of constitutional revolution, which Polybius had described, he concluded that a "more solid and more stable" form is one that "partakes all three," in other words, mixed government.[152] Looking for models, Machiavelli considered contemporary Venice, ancient Sparta, and the Roman republic and settled on Rome as the best.

What made Rome a better model? First was the now well-worn cliché that Rome wasn't built in a day. In Machiavelli's simplified view, Sparta's government was the product of a single founder, Lycurgus, who established a mixed government that remained stable for generations.[153] While Machiavelli thought single-founder republics are "fortunate," Rome was extraordinary because it built a successful government organically over a long period of time.[154] The second reason Rome was a better model is that it didn't just want to preserve its power; it wanted to expand into an empire.[155] Sparta never admitted foreigners, which translated into a stable and homogeneous population. Venice never called upon its citizens to fight in wars. Both factors—population increase from immigration and imperial expansion—are essential for the growth and power of a city, but they are also the causes of riots, corruption, and strife.[156] A powerful republic, Machiavelli thought, must address these problems by giving the people a real stake in government. Thus, for any government that wanted power, "it is essential to follow the Roman organization, not that of other republics."[157]

Machiavelli makes a number of surprising claims about Rome, his "perfect republic."[158] The first is that Rome "attained this perfection on account of the dissension between the Plebs and the Senate."[159] While most people would think that conflict and clashing interests contribute to disorder and instability—and are to be avoided— Machiavelli saw the tension between these countervailing forces as the strength of the republic. "I say that those who condemn the conflicts between the Nobles and the Plebs appear to me to be blaming the very things that were the primary reason for Rome's remaining free," he wrote.[160] The central error in most people's thinking is that they ignore the fact that "in every republic there are two opposing humors—the people and the upper classes."[161] Citing the three hundred years without significant strife between the creation of the tribune of the plebs and the Gracchi, Machiavelli argues that conflict between these classes led directly to laws that ultimately promoted freedom.[162]

Machiavelli was not naive, and he wasn't blind to the view that the tribunate, starting with the Gracchi's assertive populism, is what eventually led to the downfall of the republic. But he tells the story differently from Cicero. Machiavelli notes that debates over the agrarian laws came up repeatedly in Roman history.[163] By the time of the Gracchi, the problem had become acute because the Romans had failed to deal with it adequately. "[E]ither [the law] was not made in such a way at the outset as not to need constant revision, they put off rewriting it so long that looking back caused turmoil, or, if it was drawn up well at the outset, it became corrupted later by usage."[164] The tribunate was part of the issue but not the central cause. Indeed, "if the conflict over agrarian law struggled three hundred years before enslaving Rome, it would perhaps have been enslaved much sooner had the Plebs not always checked the Patricians' ambition both by this law and by their other desires."[165]

Given his reputation from *The Prince,* it is perhaps surprising that Machiavelli doesn't follow Cicero and blame the tribunes and the plebs for causing Rome's downfall. In fact, he does just the opposite. He blames the nobles, and he consistently argues that the nobles (whom he defines by wealth) are the biggest threat to the state.[166] Nobles have "a great desire to dominate," unlike the common people, who "merely . . . desire not to be dominated."[167] But the problem isn't just their desire for power; it's also their wealth. Gentlemen, Machiavelli writes, are those who "live richly in idleness and on the income from their estates without having any care for either agriculture or other work essential for living." They are "destructive to any republic and any land; but still more destructive are those who, in addition to the wealth mentioned above, have strongholds under their command and subjects who obey them."[168]

Machiavelli read Roman history to support his view. With the expulsion of the kings, "the Roman Nobility became arrogant," and they "began spitting out all the poison against the Plebs that they had kept pent up . . . [and] they insulted them every way they could."[169] The tribunate, Machiavelli argues, was a positive development. It made the republic "more stable," gave "the people a role in administration," and helped "safeguard Roman freedom."[170] Tribunes even "acted as intermediaries between the Plebs and the Senate, preventing the Nobles' insolence."[171] Machiavelli, it turns out, was a populist: "[I]f we examine all the disorders of the people and all the disorders of the princes, all the glories of the people and all those of princes, the people will be seen to be far superior in goodness and glory."[172]

This wasn't just theory and history for Machiavelli. In another work, called the *Florentine Discourses*, Machiavelli actually proposed a new constitution for Florence—one that revived a tribune-like office called the provost.[173] Machiavelli's plan is complicated, but it is important because it shows that when he turned to designing a constitution for the real world, it wasn't a constitution dominated by a powerful prince; it was a constitution modeled on Rome's class warfare constitution, with a powerful tribunate. Indeed, Machiavelli cleverly designed his proposed constitution to give more and more power to the people over time.

Machiavelli's structure of government had five main parts. First was the *Signoria,* a body of sixty-five life-tenured citizens, which was led by a rotating executive committee composed of eight people and the head of the republic, the *gonfalonier* of justice. The second body was the Council of the Select, another life-tenured body, but with two hundred people, which Machiavelli said should initially be picked by the pope. Machiavelli's proposal was dedicated to the pope, so this provision was meant to curry his support. The third body was the *Consiglio Grande,* a body of six hundred to a thousand, which would, in the future, fill all positions in the council and the *Signoria* and select other officeholders. The fourth body was the Companies of the People, sixteen groupings from the broader population that *excluded* those eligible for the *Signoria*. Finally came the provosts. The provosts would be picked by lottery from the Companies of the People, meaning that no member of the elite *Signoria* could serve as provost. In addition, provosts would attend the *Signoria* and the Council of the Select, and neither body could conduct business without them. In essence, they had a tribunate-like veto if they failed to attend. Each provost would serve for only a week or a month—to prevent elite Florentines from bribing or threatening them. Provosts were also empowered to delay any enactment and to appeal decisions to the *Consiglio*.[174] The consequence of this design was not rule by a powerful prince or even by the aristocracy. Real power was with the

Consiglio and the provosts, and that power would only grow stronger over time as the *Consiglio* exercised its ability to fill offices.

Many people these days think of Machiavelli as an amoral political operator, and his name is synonymous with political intrigue and backstabbing. Scholars often concentrate on Machiavelli's emphasis on virtue and its role in sustaining republican government. But in an important sense, he was also part of a long political tradition on how to create political stability in a divided society. He was deeply concerned with the problem of economic inequality, and he supported constitutional structures to prevent inequality from spilling over into conflict.

A generation younger than Machiavelli, Donato Giannotti had a somewhat different take on Florentine politics. Giannotti taught at the University of Pisa from 1520 to 1525 and then spent the next few years in Padua and Venice writing a book on the structure of the Venetian government. When the Medici fell from power in Florence in 1527, Giannotti took up Machiavelli's old position as secretary to the Ten of War. He was exiled in 1530, after which he decided to write a book on how to reform the Florentine system of government.[175] Giannotti isn't well-known today, but he had two insights that challenged the conventional thinking about the checks and balances theory of class warfare constitutions.

Like most constitutional theorists, Giannotti starts with the three pure forms of government. But he departs from Polybius, Machiavelli, and other theorists of mixed government in important ways. Giannotti did not believe it was possible to establish the pure, uncorrupted forms of government in the real world, because he presumed that men are corrupt.[176] He also rejected Polybius's hypothesis that Rome effectively fused the three forms of government. When foreigners interacted with the republic, they did not think they were interacting with a mixed form of government; they interpreted consuls as kings, the senate as an aristocracy, and the people as a democracy. For a truly mixed form to work, foreigners should have recognized the interdependence between the parts. Giannotti argued that there was no evidence that foreigners recognized this kind of interdependence. The failure to reach a true fusion of powers led to the instability and conflict that ultimately caused Rome's fall.[177] In reaching that conclusion, Giannotti also disagreed with Machiavelli. He thought tensions in Rome were a weakness, not a strength.

Giannotti's first brilliant insight came from reflecting on the clash of powers in Rome. Giannotti concluded that it would *always* be impossible to reach the stable equilibrium that Polybius and other theorists desired. In a mixed government that is at equilibrium, the "pressures and counterpressures" between the forces "will be equal." But that means that there will never be a "resolution of the contest" when groups disagree.[178] In other words, the fact that someone must ultimately decide a contested question means that there could never be a truly equal balance between separated forces within government. There would always have to be a winner and a loser.[179] Needing to choose a winner in contested cases, Giannotti, like Machiavelli, threw his hat in with the people, rather than the aristocrats.[180] He advocated for Florence to revive the *Consiglio Grande* and make it open to the people, not just the elites.[181]

The reason why he sided with the people was specific to Florentine social conditions, and this was Giannotti's second insight. Giannotti rejected the paradigm that Florence was made up of rich and poor—the staples of mixed-government thinking since ancient Greece. Yes, the city was made up of the "rich and great" who desired command and the many poor who wished not to be commanded. But it also had a third group—the *mediocri*, the middle, who wanted liberty but also had enough money to desire a share in command.[182] Looking back at Florentine history, Giannotti observed that the Medici had allowed poor people to advance to office and that they had restricted opportunities for aristocrats to show their greatness. The result was the creation of a "new and growing class" that was not so great as the highest nor as low as the poor. These *mediocri* "hold the balance of power and make a stable [mixed government] possible in Florence."[183]

The *mediocri* were the type who could rule and also be ruled in turn, and Giannotti theorized that it was possible for the *mediocri* to become so large in a city that they would "absorb the category of the 'many poor' altogether."[184] Because this middle class would be less likely to have irrational desires to command others, Giannotti thought it might even be possible to have something approaching a pure democracy in a society where the middle class was big enough.[185] Giannotti didn't believe there was a society with a big enough middle class for that—Florence certainly didn't have a middle class of that scope—but he recognized that if the middle class were stronger than the rich and the poor together, or at least equal to them in power, they could hold the balance of power in the city.[186]

While Giannotti didn't develop the relationship between his two insights, the ideas can be easily combined. In a class warfare constitution, the fact that a decision must be made means that one side or another—rich or poor—will inevitably be more powerful. Equilibrium between economic classes will never be possible and such a regime will always be unstable. But if the deciding assembly for any contested issue is composed of members of the middle class, then neither the rich nor the poor will be the ultimate ruler. The ultimate rulers will be the middle class. And the middle class, Giannotti's *mediocri*, will be less likely to take extreme positions. By designing Florentine government to lean toward popular power, via the *Consiglio Grande*, Giannotti made it possible for the middle class to hold the balance of power in Florence.

Giannotti wasn't the first person to recognize the existence of the middle class and its importance to constitutional structure.[187] "I have taken all the fundamentals of my brief discourse," Giannotti wrote, from "a superabundant spring that has spread through all the world."[188] The source was Aristotle.

THE THEORY OF THE MIDDLE-CLASS CONSTITUTION

When philosophers throughout history looked back at Polybius and Aristotle, they focused primarily on class warfare constitutions. But while Aristotle believed that class warfare structures could help stabilize a society brimming with economic tensions, he did not think a class warfare constitution was the best constitution for a state, or even the best achievable constitution in the real world. The best achievable constitution is what Aristotle called a middle constitution.

"In the multitude of citizens there must be some rich and some poor," Aristotle wrote in the *Politics*, "and some in a middle condition."[189] This middle class held great promise as the core of a political community. The psychological and material condition of the middle class made it a stable foundation for government. By disposition, the middle class was less likely to be overconfident, and therefore it would have greater aptitude for both ruling and being ruled.[190] Unlike the poor, the middle class was financially secure enough that they would not covet the wealth and property of the rich.[191] Unlike the rich, the middle class would not constantly be involved in plots against each other to gain ever-greater power.[192] "[W]here some possess much, and others nothing, there may arise an extreme democracy, or a pure oligarchy; or a tyranny may grow out of either," Aristotle said. "[B]ut it is not so likely to arise out of the middle constitutions."[193] This is why Aristotle, who was no evangelist for democracy, still favored democracies over oligarchies. "They have a middle class which is more numerous and has a greater share in the government," he wrote. "For when there is no middle class, and the poor are excessive in number, troubles arise, and the state soon comes to an end."[194]

For Aristotle, a constitution built on a strong, large middle class held the greatest promise for stability and, as a result, for human flourishing. A society divided into rich and poor would become "a city, not of freemen, but of masters and slaves, the one despising, the other envying; and nothing can be more fatal to friendship and good fellowship in states than this."[195] A large middle class made it less likely that there would be "factions and dissensions"[196] that could destabilize the community, because the middle class would have a shared economic status and, as a result, a shared ethical and cultural worldview.[197] A unified political community would be stronger than a divided one.[198]

Stability was also a by-product of political dynamics. When it came to middle-class stability, Aristotle engaged in what we'd think of today as game theory.[199] The premise is that the rich and the poor will never agree to be subservient to the other. As a result, if the rich or the poor ever wanted to establish a different kind of government, one more favorable to their interests, they'd have to unite with the middle class. But the middle class's interests are not fully aligned with either the rich or the poor, so there is a limit on how far the middle class would be willing to go before it shifted its allegiance to the other class. As a result, an equilibrium emerges in which the middle class is an "arbiter" between the rich and the poor.[200] "[T]he best political community is formed by citizens of the middle class," Aristotle said. "[T]hose states are likely to be well-administered in which the middle class is large, and stronger if possible than both the other classes."[201]

With so many benefits to the middle-class constitution, why didn't Aristotle focus more on it? And why did democracies and oligarchies predominate in the ancient world if the middle-class constitution was the best constitution? "[T]he middle class is seldom numerous," Aristotle explained, and "whichever party, whether the rich or the common people . . . predominates, draws the constitution its own way."[202] Most societies suffered from economic inequality. The middle-class constitution was elusive simply because a strong middle class was elusive.

THE RISE OF THE MIDDLE-CLASS CONSTITUTION

Born in 1611 to an old country family, James Harrington attended Trinity College, Oxford, though he did not earn a degree.[203] From the available sources, he seems to have stayed out of the political crises in England during the 1630s that led to the English Civil War in the 1640s.[204] In 1647, however, he was appointed to serve the captive king Charles I, and he remained in that position until Charles was beheaded in 1649.[205] A seventeenth-century commentator, who included Harrington in a collection of short biographies, reported that the king and Harrington would discuss forms of government frequently but that the king "would not endure to heare of a Commonwealth."[206] The two men apparently got along well, and Harrington was distraught when the king was executed.[207]

Despite his rapport with the king, Harrington was no monarchist. Quite the contrary: scholars consider his *Commonwealth of Oceana* (1656) "a moment of paradigmatic breakthrough" precisely because Harrington wasn't a monarchist.[208] Harrington's great contribution was a constitutional theory that helped justify the English commonwealth. And more than a century later, he would be cited by Americans as one of their guides for designing their republic.

Like previous constitutional theorists, Harrington recognized "the doctrine of the ancients"—that there were three pure types of government, a corrupted version of each, and a mixture of the three.[209] But Harrington was the first theorist to make explicit—even more so than Aristotle—that the forms of government were based on property ownership.[210] "If one man be sole landlord of a territory," he wrote, "his empire is absolute monarchy."[211] "If the few or a nobility, or a nobility with the clergy, be landlords . . . the empire is mixed monarchy. . . . And if the whole people be landlords, or hold the lands so divided among them, that no man, or number of men . . . overbalance them, the empire . . . is a commonwealth."[212] This was Harrington's first great contribution: property was the basis of political power, and the design of government must be attentive to the distribution of property in society. Harrington's focus on property as land (rather than on wealth) is certainly a limitation of his theory. A general theory would have linked political power to economic power more broadly. But his narrower approach is understandable given the context of the seventeenth century and the alignment of property with wealth and class.[213]

Looking back at Rome, Harrington agreed with Machiavelli's view that a powerful nobility would destroy popular government. But he rejected Machiavelli's optimistic view that a class warfare constitution could create stability.[214] Like Giannotti (whose name is invoked as the first word of *Oceana*), Harrington thought class warfare constitutions were a problem. The structure of Rome's government "divide[d] it into parties" and led to "perpetual strife."[215] In a surprisingly modern turn of phrase, Harrington argued that Rome was really "two commonwealths"—one rich, one poor—each with "contrary interests" that led to "perpetual feud and enmity."[216]

Then came his key insight: If inequality between rich and poor created strife, relative economic equality should eliminate internal conflicts, create a stable government, and guarantee freedom.[217] "[E]quality of estates causeth equality of power," Harrington said, "and equality of power is the liberty not only of the commonwealth, but of every man."[218] In an "equal commonwealth," there would "be no more strife than there can be overbalance in equal weights."[219] Because class warfare would simply not exist, the equal commonwealth would, in the words of one scholar, "prove theoretically immortal."[220]

But how could a society achieve equality in the distribution of property?[221] The answer was agrarian laws—laws governing the acquisition and transmission of property. In fact, Harrington felt so strongly about agrarian laws that he frequently turned the adjective into a noun, referring simply to a society's "Agrarian." "The Agrarian" was necessary to organize the commonwealth. Without one, government "hath no long lease."[222] The Romans had failed because they did not enforce their agrarian law.[223] The nobility had "by stealth possess[ed]" lands that the people should have had access to, and they grew "vastly rich" in the process.[224] By the time of the Gracchi, it was simply "too late."[225] Romans failed to maintain their republic because of "negligence committed in their agrarian laws."[226]

Having developed the doctrine that political power follows the distribution of property, Harrington was uniquely positioned to make a second breakthrough: if the balance of property changed, the political system would change as well. Harrington argued that the political transition from feudalism to the English Civil Wars to the establishment of parliamentary sovereignty under the commonwealth was based on changes in the underlying social and economic structure of England. Under the feudal-era "Gothic Balance," there had been a monarch, wealthy landowning nobles, and the rest of the people. This created a "mixed monarchy," which operated somewhere between aristocracy and monarchy. Over time, kings worried about the power of the nobility, and successive Tudor monarchs pursued legal changes that expanded landownership among the common people at the expense of the nobles.[227] The most important change, during the time of Henry VII, prohibited lords from evicting tenants holding twenty or more acres. This guaranteed widespread property ownership to "the yeomanry, or middle people, who . . . were much unlinked from dependence upon their lords."[228] Together with other reforms by subsequent monarchs, the nobility became weaker and weaker. As the power of the "middle people" grew in politics, the commons finally wrested power from the monarchy.[229] As one scholar put it, "When the land was in the possession of a few barons and dignitaries of the Church dependent on the Crown, the natural form of government was a regulated monarchy; but with the enormous increase in the number of landowners, monarchical institutions had finally become impossible."[230] In other words, Harrington had rooted constitutional design in economic conditions, and he then theorized that constitutional change was partly the result of underlying economic changes.

Harrington's property-based theory of the commonwealth explained not only the English revolution and Civil War, which overthrew King Charles and the monarchy in the 1640s, but also provided a foundation for a more equal form of government—one without a king altogether. A political system had to follow the distribution of property in society. The rise of the "middle people" in England meant that the ancient constitution was no longer viable and a new constitution—one built on the foundation of the middle class—would be necessary.[231] "[W]here there is equality of estates, there must be equality of power;" Harrington concluded, "and where there is equality of power, there can be no monarchy."[232]

In the century between *The Commonwealth of Oceana* and the American founding, Harrington's ideas spread to some of the leading constitutional theorists of the age. In the 1720s, Thomas Gordon and John Trenchard, writing under the pseudonym Cato, took up Harrington's themes in a series of pamphlets known as *Cato's Letters,* which were well known in America during the founding era. Writing in the wake of the corruption and failure of the South Sea Company, Cato argued that "the first principle of all power is property; and every man will have his share of it in proportion as he enjoys property."[233] Cato accepted that England's current circumstances meant that it could not have "a republican form of government" because property was not distributed in "average" among the people; as a result, "it is impossible to settle a commonwealth here."[234] The only way for England to become a commonwealth was with the adoption of "an agrarian law, or something equivalent to it."[235]

The leading philosopher of the Scottish Enlightenment, David Hume, commented on the widespread acceptance of Harrington's views. He recognized that "most of our political writers" accepted that property is "the foundation of all government," though Hume himself thought that other factors mattered more.[236] Hume also embraced a Harringtonian understanding of the dynamic relationship between power and property. He argued that if there is an imbalance between power and property, the "order of men who possess a large share of property" will find a way to "stretch their authority, and bring the balance of power to coincide with that of property."[237] Affirming Aristotle and Harrington, Hume even wrote an essay in lavish praise of the "middle station." The middle station was best suited to "the calm voice of reason," because "[t]he great are too much immersed in pleasure, and the poor too much occupied in providing for the necessities of life."[238] Only those in the middle station could exercise the virtues of "patience, resignation, industry, and integrity" in addition to those of "generosity, humanity, affability, and charity."[239] They had more wisdom and ability than the rich or the poor, and they would also be better suited to friendship because they had no jealousy of others (like the poor) or suspicion of others (like the rich).[240]

Perhaps most strikingly, Montesquieu, the celebrated French philosopher who is best known for his theory of the separation of powers, also incorporated elements of Harrington's approach into his *Spirit of the Laws*. Montesquieu noted that some constitutions divided lands equally, but he warned that if the founders of governments do "not give laws to maintain" the balance of property, the constitution will be "transitory." "[I]nequality will enter at the point not protected by the laws, and the republic will be lost."[241] This is what Montesquieu believed happened in ancient Rome:

> The indefinite permission to make testaments [that is, to pass down wealth through inheritance and gifts], granted among the Romans, gradually ruined the political provision on the sharing of lands; more than anything else it introduced the ominous difference between wealth and poverty . . . some citizens had too much, an infinity of others had nothing. Thus, the people, continually deprived of their share, constantly asked for a new distribution of lands.[242]

The answer, Montesquieu suggested, was to "regulate to this end dowries, gifts, inheritances, testaments, in sum, all the kinds of contracts." Passing on wealth to others in an unregulated fashion would "disturb the disposition of the fundamental laws."[243] After a long discussion of innovative methods for regulating the transfers and concentration of wealth, Montesquieu recognized a practical reality: "Although in a democracy real equality is the soul of the state, still this equality is so difficult to establish that an extreme precision in this regard would not always be suitable." He therefore suggested establishing outer bounds of wealth and then passing laws that will "equalize inequalities" through "burdens they impose on the rich and the relief they afford to the poor."[244] We remember Montesquieu today for the separation of powers between different government branches—for example, dividing the executive and the legislative—but even he recognized that economic equality was critical for a well-functioning government.

While there have been important attempts to restore Harrington to the canon of political philosophers and constitutional theorists in the Western tradition, Harrington is rarely at the center of the American constitutional story.[245] And yet, more than any theorist since Aristotle, Harrington took seriously the relationship between the distribution of wealth in society and the structure of the constitution. He argued that the two were intertwined, and he went beyond Aristotle in exploring how economic change could force constitutional change. For American colonists an ocean away, his insights would prove invaluable.

CHAPTER TWO

America's Middle-Class Constitution

The New York Times called it a "startling theory."[1] *The Sun* concluded in its review, "[T]he facts set forth in this volume cannot be brushed aside; they must be reckoned with."[2] The year was 1913; the book, *An Economic Interpretation of the Constitution of the United States.* In it, a young Columbia University historian named Charles Beard described in detail the occupations, property holdings, and economic interests of the framers of the Constitution. His conclusion: America's founding document was designed by wealthy elites who were bent on promoting their own economic interests.

Every generation tells and retells the story of the Revolution and the creation of the Constitution, putting its own spin on America's origins. Since the beginning of the twentieth century, three interpretations have dominated. Beard's is the first. His specific claim—that the personal economic interests of the founders shaped their support for the Constitution—was debunked decades ago.[3] But his book remains significant because it advanced a school of history that saw economic interests as critical to the new nation's beginnings. The more general "Beardian" claim is familiar to us all.[4] The Articles of Confederation was a system of government that placed altogether too much power in the hands of the people. When an economic depression hit in the 1780s, the state legislatures relented to populist pressure from farmers, passing legislation to support irresponsible debtors and imprudently printing paper money. The Constitution was the elites' response. At the heart of the American project was an aristocratic counterrevolution.[5] Even today, a new generation of neo-

Beardians emphasizes material, and especially economic, interests in their version of the founding.[6]

Other historians rejected the Beardian emphasis on interests and instead focused on philosophical ideas.[7] Starting in the 1960s and 1970s, historians began to argue that the republican tradition shaped the founders' actions.[8] If Beard had echoes of Karl Marx in his work, these scholars wrote under the tutelage of Niccolò Machiavelli. The Florentine author's *Discourses on Livy* was seen as a central text in the revival of republicanism in Western philosophy, and these historians emphasized the founding generation's commitment to civic virtue, disinterested statesmanship, and deliberation over the public good. In contrast to the "republicans," the "liberal" historians stressed the inheritance of John Locke. Whether in Jefferson's Declaration of Independence or the era's culture of limited government and personal rights, what mattered was individualism, the social contract, private property, and the absence of feudalism.[9]

Despite their prominence, there is something unsatisfying at the heart of each of these philosophical accounts of the founding era.[10] Are we really supposed to believe that the founders were philosophers who fought only for high-minded ideals? If so, what of the economic pressures of the 1780s? What of their political disagreements and personal rivalries? But a puzzle emerges if we take seriously the more cynical, self-interested story about the founders. If the founders were so intent on creating a counterrevolutionary government that would support the interests of wealthy elites, why didn't they advance their interests even further?

Beardians, republicans, and liberals have all contributed a great deal to understanding the founding. But there is another tradition, one that speaks directly to some of these lingering questions.[11] The founding generation learned from James Harrington that political power followed economic power. An economically unequal society could not be politically equal. Only a society that was relatively equal economically could therefore achieve a republican form of government. When they looked at their own economic conditions and compared them to the countries of Europe, the founding generation saw that America was exceptional because it had a relatively equal distribution of wealth. It was perhaps the only place on earth suited to republican government.

The tradition of the middle-class constitution does more than just link America's economic conditions to philosophical ideas. When the founding generation moved to replace the Articles of Confederation in the 1780s, they were responding in part to an economic crisis and the need to alleviate the economic pressure on ordinary Americans. During the battle over the ratification of the Constitution, both Federalists and Anti-Federalists harked back to Harrington's lessons in debating representation and political power. And even James Madison—father of the Constitution and hardly a populist—understood that the economic conditions in society were critical to the proper functioning of American government.

The Constitution is far from being a counterrevolutionary document. We should interpret it as a radical culmination to the Revolutionary era. It was radical because it rejected two thousand years of thinking on class warfare constitutions. Instead, the Constitution was built on the bedrock of America's middle class.

ECONOMIC EQUALITY IN EARLY AMERICA

"We are on an equality as to property [compared] to what they are in the old countries," the laborer William Manning observed in 1799.[12] Manning was not naive. He did not believe there was perfect economic equality in America. There are differences in wealth during every era, and the founding era was no exception. But the reality— the reality that Manning saw—is that early America was astonishingly equal for its time.

Compared with England and other western European countries in the late eighteenth century, America didn't have either a super-rich tier of elites or a bottom rung of desperate poor. American estates were minor compared to their English counterparts. George Washington's estate, for example, earned £300 per year in the 1770s. This would have made him a "better sort of yeoman" in England.[13] And while Washington's Mount Vernon is a beautiful home, it was hardly comparable with the Duke of Marlborough's massive baroque-style palace at Blenheim. The lack of a wealthy elite extended to the merchant class too: the wealthiest urban American merchants were worth £25,000 to £50,000; their counterparts in London were worth £200,000 to £800,000.[14] Charles Chauncy of Massachusetts was right to note in 1766, "There is scarce a man in any of the colonies, certainly there is not in the New England ones, that would be deemed worthy of the name of a rich man in Great Britain."[15] The contrast was equally true at the lower end of the economic spectrum. Conditions approaching the slums of London were unknown in America. During an economic downturn, 10 percent of the American population might be poor, but this was a far cry from the 50 percent of people in England who occasionally or regularly relied on charity for survival.[16]

In recent years, economic historians have created new data sets to measure historical levels of inequality. The challenge when measuring inequality in the founding period is that data is difficult to come by. Recently, however, economists Peter Lindert and Jeffrey Williamson have resurrected a practice started in the seventeenth century called "social tables." Social tables are data sets that identify and count people by occupation and social class and then connect the data to evidence about average incomes for those occupations (drawn from exhaustive and exhausting archival research). The result is a social profile of colonial America.

What Lindert and Williamson have found is that the America of 1774 was surprisingly egalitarian. Considering all households, including slaves, the top 1 percent in America had 8.5 percent of total income. When only free households are taken into account, the number drops to 7.6 percent.[17] In 2012, for comparison, the top 1 percent of Americans took 19.3 percent of total income.[18] In fact, you have to go back to 1973 to find a recent number—7.7 percent—even in the range of free 1774 America.[19]

When economists measure inequality, the most common number they use is called the Gini coefficient, which captures the dispersion of income for households from zero (completely equal) to one (completely unequal). Based on their social tables, Lindert and Williamson were able to construct a Gini coefficient for early America. In 1774, the Gini coefficient for American households, including slaves, was .441. It was .409 without slaves.[20] To put that into perspective, the Gini coefficient for America in 2012 was .463.[21] What that means is that the America of 2012 was actually more unequal than the America of 1774—*even including slavery*. In fact, the data is even more surprising because the Gini coefficient for America in 2012 is based on household incomes *after* taking into account taxes and transfer payments (like welfare and the earned income tax credit), which reduce inequality—and obviously 1774 America did not have a welfare state.[22] To even get close to America's 1774 Gini coefficient, we would have to go back to 1996 (.44), and to approximate the Gini coefficient of free 1774 America, we would have to go back to 1982 (.408).[23]

Most of the inequality in colonial America was between regions, so when Lindert and Williamson broke down the data by region, they found even greater egalitarianism. New England's Gini coefficient was .367, the Mid-Atlantic .376, and the free South .341.[24] Those numbers are similar to America in the late 1960s period (the Gini in 1968 was .371). As a comparison, the South, including slaves, had a Gini coefficient of .464, almost identical to 2012 America (.463) after tax and transfer payments.[25] In other words, America today is almost exactly as unequal as the slave-owning South in 1774.

Of course, relative economic equality didn't mean that there were no distinctions at all within the new nation. From before the Revolution through the early republic, there were still differences between people, but they were less about "economic class" as we think of it today and more about manners, education, culture, and merit.[26] Early Americans were passionately opposed to hereditary classes and hierarchies. George Mason's draft of the Virginia Declaration of Rights in 1776 rejected all hereditary offices, noting that "the Ideal of Man born a Magistrate, a Legislator, or a Judge is unnatural and absurd."[27] Article I, section 9 of the Constitution declared, "No title of nobility shall be granted by the United States." As David Ramsay said in his Fourth of July oration in 1778, "[A]ll offices lie open to men of merit of whatever rank or condition . . . even the reins of state may be held by the son of the poorest man, if possessed of abilities equal to the important station."[28]

Americans' egalitarian spirit was closely tied to geography. At the time, people believed that manufacturing was linked to poverty. In an agricultural society, men could work the land and gain a measure of independence and self-sufficiency. Manufacturing was only necessary when there ceased to be enough land for the population, pushing people into wage work that would necessarily mean poverty. But America was different. As long as America had the potential to expand westward, there would be equal economic opportunity.[29] Benjamin Franklin commented, "Land being thus plenty in America, and so cheap as that a labouring Man, that understands Husbandry, can in a short Time save Money enough to purchase a Piece of new Land sufficient for a Plantation, whereon he may subsist a Family." Laborers were also not locked into poverty in America. Until land was fully settled, Franklin continued, "Labour will never be cheap here . . . no man continues long a Journeyman to a Trade, but goes among those new Settlers and sets up for himself."[30]

As historian Gordon Wood has argued, the founding generation "believed that equality of opportunity would necessarily result in a rough equality of station, that as long as the social channels of ascent and descent were kept open it would be impossible for any artificial aristocrats or overgrown rich men to maintain themselves for long."[31] And so it was. Americans experienced great economic mobility—both upward and downward.[32] Many of the most famous members of the founding generation were "first-generation gentlemen": the "first in their families to attend college, to acquire a liberal arts education, and to display the marks of an enlightened . . . gentleman." Wood's list is long: Samuel Adams, John Adams, Thomas Jefferson, James Otis, John Jay, James Madison, David Ramsay, Benjamin Rush, James Wilson, John Marshall, William Paterson, Elbridge Gerry, Thomas McKean, Hugh Henry Brackenridge, Nathaniel Chipman. Still others, like Benjamin Franklin, George Washington, and Nathanael Greene, never went to college at all but made up for it through rigorous individual study.[33] *The Pennsylvania Packet* noted in 1776 that half the property in the colony was owned by men in leather aprons and the other half by men whose fathers or grandfathers wore leather aprons.[34]

Mobility wasn't just equality of opportunity in the upward direction. It also meant a risk of failure. Without the risk of downward mobility, there was nothing to stop a permanent class of elites from emerging. Indeed, for many of the leading men of the age, downward mobility was a harsh reality. James Iredell of North Carolina refused an appointment to the Continental Congress in 1776 because of his "cursed poverty."[35] Many of the most important Federalist leaders in the 1790s lost everything they had, including Robert Morris, previously the richest man in America and the financier of the Revolution. James Wilson, one of the most erudite and eloquent members of the Constitutional Convention of 1787 and one of the first justices of the Supreme Court, was actually held in a debtors' prison while still serving on the Supreme Court. He died penniless.[36]

Of course, economic equality and equal opportunity did not extend to everyone. Women, slaves, free African Americans, Native Americans, and indentured white men—none experienced fully the American Revolution's promise of democratic equality. In recent years, historical research has uncovered, in rich detail, what life was like for these groups during the late eighteenth century. Some of the most innovative histories also show how these groups had a profound effect on the colonists' decision to revolt against Britain and on the events that led to the creation of the Constitution.[37]

How can we square the claim of economic equality with the reality that so many were excluded from the American economy? With our modern values in mind, we have to acknowledge and condemn the significant failures of the era: the brutal conditions of slavery; violence and theft against Native Americans; secondary status for women. But we cannot only judge with modern values in mind. To do so condemns virtually all of history, throwing out courageous revolutions and inspirational achievements. It also condemns us, living here in the present, because the people of the future will look back and judge our time as a failure in accordance with *their* values. We must criticize the faults of the past, but we must also establish a baseline that allows us to recognize the astonishing achievements of the Revolutionary era. In addition to comparing Revolutionary America to our situation today, we have to compare it to the historical traditions it inherited and to other countries at the time. Only with these comparisons in mind can we understand how striking the extent of Revolutionary Americans' idea—and their reality—of equality truly was.

Foremost, the Revolutionary era unleashed ideas of political equality that were recognized at the time as flatly incompatible with the lack of equality for women and African Americans. James Otis, writing in his 1764 *Rights of the British Colonies Asserted and Proved,* questioned slavery, declaring that "[t]he colonists are by the law of nature free born, as indeed all men are, white or black.... Does it follow that tis right to enslave a man because he is called black?"[38] Richard Henry Lee of Virginia, a signer of the Declaration of Independence, supported women's suffrage, arguing that women had "as legal a right to vote as any other person."[39] The 1776 New Jersey Constitution actually gave women the right to vote and hold office—a provision that stayed in effect until 1807.[40] In Pennsylvania, the 1780 constitution not only abolished slavery but also gave African Americans the right to vote—a provision that remained in force until 1837.[41] Indeed, some historians have concluded that the Revolution's radical premise of equality set in motion an intellectual tradition that ultimately foreordained the end of slavery and other forms of inequality.[42] Equality was by no means a reality, and we should not celebrate the inequality of the time. But we must acknowledge that the spirit of the Revolution put pressure on continued forms of inequality and that the conditions in America differed from other places around the world.

If we look to Europe, for example, the American colonies were far more economically equal than the imperial homelands. While international data isn't available for 1774, we can still make helpful comparisons to foreign countries in the mid- to late eighteenth century: In 1759, England and Wales had a Gini coefficient of .522. By 1802, it had risen to .593. Holland in 1732 was even more unequal at .610, though by 1808 the Dutch were slightly better off at .563.[43] To put that in perspective, European countries were about as unequal as Brazil, Haiti, or South Africa in the early twenty-first century.[44] America was substantially more equal, with a Gini coefficient of .441. Where the top 1 percent in 1774 America picked up 8.5 percent of income, the top 1 percent in England and Wales in 1759 took more than twice as much—17.5 percent of income.[45] America's middle and upper-middle classes were also doing far better than their English counterparts. The 40th–80th percentile took 39.6 percent of the income in colonial America, compared with only 30 percent in England in 1759.[46] As Lindert and Williamson conclude, "there was no documented place on the planet that had a more egalitarian distribution in the late eighteenth century."[47]

Historical estimates on landownership also align with these findings. In England, only 20 percent of the population owned land and more than 60 percent owned no property at all. In America, two-thirds of the white population owned land, and those who didn't were usually young men and recent immigrants who were readying themselves to go west.[48] Samuel Peters, writing his *General History of Connecticut,* summed up the condition of his fellow Americans well: "In no part of the world are *les petits* and *les grands* so much upon a par as here, where none of the people are destitute of the conveniences of life and the spirit of independence."[49]

THE INTELLECTUAL ORIGINS OF AMERICA'S MIDDLE-CLASS CONSTITUTION

A country with such extraordinary equality stood in contrast to two thousand years of thinking on class warfare constitutions. But Revolutionary Americans were not without an intellectual muse. Inspiration came instead from the middle-class constitutional tradition and in particular from James Harrington. Harrington's analysis of power and property found a receptive audience among the founding generation, many of whom took the English philosopher's lessons to heart in thinking about the relationship between power, the relatively equal division of property in society, and the commonwealth.[50] "Harrington has shown that power always follows property," John Adams wrote in 1776.

> This I believe to be as infallible a maxim in politics, as that action and reaction are equal, is in mechanics. Nay, I believe we may advance one step farther, and affirm that the balance of power in a society, accompanies the balance of property in

land. The only possible way, then, of preserving the balance of power on the side of equal liberty and public virtue, is to make the acquisition of land easy to every member of society; to make a division of land into small quantities, so that the multitude may be possessed of landed estates. If the multitude is possessed of the balance of real estate, the multitude will have the balance of power, and in that case the multitude will take care of the liberty, virtue, and interest of the multitude, in all acts of government.[51]

Others followed Adams in embracing Harrington's lessons.[52] Phillips Payson, in a 1778 sermon, argued that "free government and public liberty" were possible only "if there is a general distribution of property, and the landed interest not engrossed by a few, but possessed by the inhabitants in general through the state."[53] During the ratification debates in Pennsylvania, Anti-Federalist Samuel Bryan, writing under the pseudonym Centinel, echoed the sentiment in forceful terms: "A republican, or free government, can only exist where the body of the people are virtuous, and where property is pretty equally divided[;] ... for when this ceases to be the case, the nature of the government is changed, and an aristocracy, monarchy or despotism will rise on its ruin."[54]

The most thorough exposition of Harringtonian principles, however, came from Noah Webster, who is best known today as the author of the first American dictionary. Responding to Anti-Federalist arguments during the ratification debates, Webster asked where the source of power lay in society. "The answer is short and plain—in *property*."[55] Once this truth was understood, it became clear how to preserve freedom. "*A general and tolerably equal distribution of landed property*" was the "*whole basis of national freedom*."[56] If property was equally distributed, so too would power be distributed. If property was unequal, then power would also be unequal and freedom at risk.

In an economy primarily driven by land, the critical safeguard was to prevent an aristocracy from emerging through land inheritance. "Make laws, irrevocable laws in every state, destroying and barring entailments," Webster wrote. "[L]eave real estates to revolve from hand to hand, as time and accident may direct; and no family influence can be acquired and established for a series of generations—no man can obtain dominion over a large territory." The result would be that "the laborious and saving, who are generally the best citizens, will possess each his share of property and power, and thus the balance of wealth and power will continue where it is, in the *body of the people.*"[57]

Webster's explanation that property needed to remain with the people rested in part on ancient Rome's experience with agrarian policy. "Rome," he wrote, "exhibited a demonstrative proof of the inseparable connexion between property and dominion." Applying Harrington's lessons to the ancient republic's government, Webster had a different reading of Roman history. He argued that Rome's monarchy and aristocracy—the governments before the establishment of the tribunate—could not possibly have succeeded because "they were not supported by property."[58] Too many people, he thought, had property, and so over generations power was wrested from the kings and patricians and increasingly granted to the people. It was not until "they established a commonwealth" that property and power were aligned in the city.[59]

Webster's conclusion could hardly have been more clear: "An equality of property, with a necessity of alienation, constantly operating to destroy combinations of powerful families, is the very *soul of a republic*—While this continues, the people will inevitably possess both *power* and *freedom;* when this is lost, power departs, liberty expires, and a commonwealth will inevitably assume some other form."[60] "Let the people have property," he said, "and they *will* have power."[61]

Luckily, America had the economic conditions that were a prerequisite for establishing a commonwealth. In 1787, Webster wrote that America had "small inequalities of property . . . every man has an opportunity of becoming rich."[62] This fact distinguished "the governments of Europe and of all the world, from those of America." In the rest of the world, rights had to be protected from other classes of men. Americans often forgot, Webster said, that "the objects of the contest *do not exist in this country.*"[63]

Webster wasn't unique in his belief that what made America

exceptional was its economic equality. Throughout the founding period, Americans recognized that they were uniquely suited to republican government precisely because the people were relatively equal and the middle class was strong.[64] Perhaps most striking was the Pennsylvania Constitution of 1776. The most radical of the Revolutionary constitutions, the Pennsylvania charter completely rejected the class warfare model, and instead adopted a unicameral legislature, "for we have not, and hope never shall have, a hereditary nobility, different from the general body of the people."[65] An early draft of the new state's declaration of rights went even further in seeking to preserve the equality of property. It announced that "an enormous Proportion of Property vested in a few individuals is dangerous to the Rights, and destructive of the Common Happiness of Mankind." The draft even gave the legislature the power to prevent such concentrations of wealth.[66] As one historian has summarized, Pennsylvanians believed that "[b]ecause the people of other societies had not been equal, they had been compelled to incorporate great social distinctions into their constitutions." In contrast, Pennsylvanians "had an opportunity unknown to previous societies."[67]

While Pennsylvania was the most radical of the American states, America's economic equality was widely recognized in every region, and even overseas. Federalist Jonathan Jackson of Massachusetts noted in 1788 the "small inequality of fortune throughout the country, compared with others which we know."[68] There was even a proposal in 1780, inspired by Harrington, to change the Commonwealth of Massachusetts's name to Oceana.[69] A response to John Adams's *Defence of the Constitutions* commented that "[w]e have no such thing as orders, ranks, or nobility; and . . . it is almost impossible they should ever gain any footing here."[70] Even in South Carolina, the least equal of America's jurisdictions, inhabitants saw that America was uniquely equal in the world.[71] In 1777, one South Carolinian noted that Americans were "a people of property; almost every man is a freeholder."[72] Charles Pinckney believed America had "fewer distinctions of fortune & less of rank, than among the inhabitants of any other nation . . . a very moderate share of property entitles them to the possession of all the honors and privileges the public can bestow."[73] David Ramsay said that tyranny was unlikely in the new republic because America was composed of "free men all of one rank, where property is equally diffused."[74] In Britain, the English radical Thomas Pownall noted that America had "a general equality, not only in the Persons, but in the power of the landed Property of the Inhabitants." Europe, in contrast, was striving for "that natural equal level Basis on which Ye, American Citizens, stand."[75]

Nor did this sense of equality end in the Revolutionary period. In the decades after the ratification of the Constitution, Americans continued to believe that they were exceptional precisely because of their equality. Speaking in Middlebury, Vermont, in 1801, Jeremiah Atwater said that "property, in this country, is pretty equally divided among the people." Unlike in most European countries, "[t]he feudal distinctions of tenant and lord are here unknown."[76] By the early years of the nineteenth century, Americans were even referring to themselves as "dominated by the 'middling' sort."[77] Charles Ingersoll concluded in 1810, "Patrician and plebeian orders are unknown. . . . What in other countries is called the populace, a compost heap, whence germinate mobs, beggars, and tyrants, is not to be found in the towns; and there is no peasantry in the country."[78]

How would the new republic maintain the level of equality that Harrington suggested was necessary for republican government? Many of the founders categorized the strategies for preserving America's equal and mobile commonwealth similarly. Jefferson focused on land policies (entail and primogeniture) and education.[79] Noah Webster similarly focused on land policies and education, calling them "fundamental articles: the *sine qua non* of the existence of the American republics."[80]

In a 1792 essay, James Madison provided a slightly different, but in some ways more helpful, framework for thinking about the range of options. The brief essay was on parties, and much of it focused on what to do when "the existence of parties cannot be prevented." Madison suggested that one party must check the other, akin to Polybius's idea of the class warfare constitution, and he also suggested ensuring that one group was not favored "at the expence of another."

But the more interesting advice was on how to prevent such parties from emerging at all. Republicanism would be preserved first "by establishing political equality among all."[81] Over time, this notion would lead to the expansion of the right to vote. Indeed, John Adams even endorsed the ancient Greek practice of paying for political participation to ensure that political power isn't skewed by economic power. He commented in the 1780s that unless there is pay for those holding political office, "all offices would be monopolized by the rich; the poor and the middling ranks would be excluded and an aristocratic despotism would immediately follow."[82] With equal political influence, economic elites would not wield unequal political power.

Second on Madison's list was "withholding *unnecessary* opportunities from a few, to increase the inequality of property, by an immoderate, and especially an unmerited, accumulation of wealth."[83] With property as the dominant form of wealth at the time, many in the founding generation focused on restricting the transfer of property, as a way to prevent the creation of an aristocracy.[84] Thomas Jefferson famously said that one of his proudest moments was the abolition of the entail (a legal device to pass on property to one's descendants) and the abolition of primogeniture (a legal rule by which property is passed on to the oldest son) in Virginia.[85] In a letter to John Adams in 1813, he remembered "[t]hese laws, drawn by myself, [which] laid the axe to the root of Pseudoaristocracy."[86] Jefferson believed that while "an equal division of property was impracticable," legislators "cannot invent too many devices for subdividing property."[87] The linkage between property inheritance laws and preventing aristocracy was well understood throughout early America. James Kent held that the entail was "recommended in monarchical governments, as a protection to the power and influence of the landed aristocracy; but such a policy has no application to republican establishments."[88] In 1784, when North Carolina adopted a bill restricting primogeniture and entails, the bill gave as its justification that "it will tend to promote that equality of property which is of the spirit and principle of a genuine republic."[89] St. George Tucker wrote "that entails would be the means of accumulating and preserving great estates in certain families, which would . . . be utterly incompatible with the genius and spirit of our constitution and government."[90]

Madison's third strategy was to rely on "the silent operation of laws, which, without violating the rights of property, reduce extreme wealth to a state of mediocrity, and raise extreme indigence toward a state of comfort."[91] This category included a wider range of policy options than the others and in some ways it is the most surprising from a modern perspective, because it shows that some of the founders thought redistributing wealth was critical to sustaining the Republic. Before the Revolution, Jefferson wrote of the importance of laws that might "equalise" people "by laying burthens on the richer classes, & encouraging the poorer ones."[92] After the Revolution, Jefferson and others declared their support for a progressive system of taxation. Another means of "silently lessen[ing] the inequality of property," the sage of Monticello wrote, "is to exempt from all taxation below a certain point, and to tax the higher portions of property in geometrical progression as they rise."[93] An anonymous writer in Charleston in 1783 took a similar approach, arguing that if laws on transferring property were insufficient to maintain "portions not greatly dissimilar," then "further increase of property must be positively restricted."[94] Placing a ceiling on the wealthy was one strategy; the other was expanding access for ordinary people. Jefferson also believed the unemployed should be free to take up uncultivated land,[95] and he proposed that every man who didn't have fifty acres of property be given property so he met that minimum threshold.[96] The best example of a federal policy to ensure the availability of property was the Northwest Ordinance of 1787, which pushed expansion westward, opening lands for settlers and providing for all the necessities for republican government.[97]

Together, these policies would enable Harrington's equal commonwealth to remain a reality in America. This story—the story of the Harringtonian tradition in America—in some ways confounds the usual divisions in thinking about America's philosophical heritage. It is clearly "republican," because Harrington and the founders were both preoccupied with what it would take to create and preserve a representative democracy. But while most republicans tend to emphasize ideals of virtue and the public good, this tradition also appeals to the "liberal" emphasis on economic equality and highlights the relatively egalitarian structure of the New World.[98] As Alexis de Tocqueville in the nineteenth century and Louis Hartz in the twentieth both recognized, Americans had the benefit of never experiencing feudal inequality. But most liberals tend to focus on individualism and natural rights, not on the distribution of wealth and its connection to the form of government.[99] The Harringtonian tradition merges republican and liberal themes, and it taught the founders that America's egalitarian economic structure permitted a republican form of government. It is this tradition—the tradition of the middle-class constitution—that allows us not only to reinterpret the origins of our Constitution but also to see the threat that the collapse of the middle class poses to our constitutional system.

THE CRISIS OF THE CONFEDERATION: THE ECONOMIC ORIGINS OF THE MIDDLE-CLASS CONSTITUTION

In July 1786, the town leaders of Pelham, Massachusetts, called for county-wide conventions to discuss their frustrations with the state government and its policies. Angry townspeople gathered in Bristol County, Worcester County, Middlesex County, and Berkshire County, but the biggest convention was in Hampshire County, with fifty towns present. The Hampshire Convention agreed on a list of grievances and an affirmative agenda: They wanted to abolish the upper house of the state legislature, make the election of lower house members more democratic, get rid of the courts of common pleas and general sessions, and move the legislature out of Boston. They objected to taxes imposed on them, to the high costs of the legal system, and to the state's approach to what satisfied as legal tender.[100]

Over the next few months, hundreds of men, led by Revolutionary War veterans and officers, turned their grievances into insurrection. In August, they marched on the Northampton courthouse, in western Massachusetts, forcing the judges to adjourn court without doing any business.[101] In September, a hundred men with bayonets blocked the court in Worcester. When the governor called up the militia the next day, the militiamen refused to take arms, and many even joined the insurgents, now numbering three to four hundred.[102] In Great Barrington, in the far west of the state, armed men seized the court. When a thousand-man militia came to open the court, someone suggested they vote first, and eight hundred of the militiamen joined the rebels. The rebels then demanded that the judges agree not to hold court "until the Constitution of the Government shall be revised or a new one made." Three of four judges complied immediately.[103] Courts were even shut closer to Boston, in Concord and Taunton.[104]

The men called themselves Regulators. We know them as part of Shays's Rebellion. The Regulators were not all poor debtors.[105] Some were debtors but not necessarily impoverished; one of the leaders, Luke Day (who had once been jailed for his debts), was among the wealthiest men in his town. Most felt the state government was unfairly benefiting wealthy speculators who had bought up bonds at very low prices. Chief Justice William Whiting of the Berkshire County Court, writing under the name Gracchus, argued that the leaders of the state had become "overgrown Plunderers" and that it was time for "the People at large" to "watch and guard their Liberties, and to crush the very first appearances of incroachments upon it."[106]

The Massachusetts leadership responded with carrots and sticks. The carrots seemed sensible: they would extend the dates for paying taxes, accept payments in kind, sell land in Maine to reduce future tax burdens, and pardon those who took an oath of allegiance to the state. The sticks were far harsher. Rioters would forfeit their property, be whipped publicly, and be imprisoned without habeas corpus. Sheriffs would be held guiltless for killing rioters. And any officer or soldier who abandoned his post to support the rebels would be put to death.[107] The state government raised an army under former Revolutionary War general Benjamin Lincoln, whose forces defeated the Regulators in a battle at the federal arsenal at Springfield.[108] Attempting to regroup, the rebels even sought help from Ethan Allen, the leader of the Green Mountain Boys in Vermont, who was himself a former insurgent against wealthy land speculators.[109]

Shays's Rebellion is famous, but it wasn't the only uprising in America. Throughout the 1780s, unrest was bubbling up across the country. In New Jersey, agitators boarded up local courthouses to prevent legal actions against debtors from going forward.[110] The court in Camden, South Carolina, was shut down. Goods and property that had been taken to pay taxes were "rescued" by armed force in York, Pennsylvania.[111] In three Virginia counties, there were at least 155 cases of debtors who used armed force to prevent sheriffs from seizing their property.[112] Arsonists burned the King William

County courthouse in May 1787, and three hundred men stormed the Greenbrier County court in August 1787, even as the Constitutional Convention was ongoing in Philadelphia.[113]

How should we interpret these insurrections and the creation of the Constitution that followed them? One of the important debates over the founding era is whether there was a social or political revolution in America and when it took place. Social revolutions involve addressing a major problem in society, and at least since the French and Russian Revolutions they have been understood as focused primarily on poverty. Political revolutions, in contrast, involve changing the form of government. Some historians, like Louis Hartz, believed revolutions had to be social, and because America did not have widespread poverty or feudalism, there was no "genuine revolutionary tradition" in America at all.[114]

Others, like Charles Beard and his followers, hold that the creation of the Constitution was a social revolution or, more precisely, a social *counter*revolution.[115] The wealthy elites rejected the democratic ethos of the American Revolution and overthrew that system, replacing it with an aristocratic constitution that was designed to advance their own economic interests. During the period of the Articles of Confederation, their argument goes, the states' pro-debtor policies—shutting down courts, printing paper money, impairing contracts—threatened the wealth of creditors and bondholders. A new regime would enable these economic elites, a group that included the framers of the Constitution, to ensure that they got paid and that states couldn't pursue such "levelling" policies in the future.[116]

A third story, best captured by philosopher Hannah Arendt and constitutional scholar Bruce Ackerman, argues that the American Revolution was a political revolution and that any political revolution requires both overthrowing the old regime and establishing a new one. The creation of the Constitution was therefore the *culmination* of the American Revolution. For Arendt, the goal was to establish a framework for public freedom—a republican government, defined by virtuous leaders deliberating toward the public good. For Ackerman, the Constitution's political revolution involved the active role of "We the People" in shaping their destiny. There are different interpretations of the 1780s under this political revolution theory, but what is most important is that these thinkers do *not* focus on economic conditions or economic conflict.[117]

None of these stories is totally satisfying. It is hard to believe, as the political story holds, that economic issues and conditions were not crucial. It is equally hard to believe, as the Beardians suggest, that the only important factors are economic and that they exclusively favor the elites. This is where the Harringtonian tradition comes in. It is attentive to *both* economic conditions *and* public freedom. It requires us to think about the economic realities of the time, in addition to the worldview and background assumptions that people held. According to Harrington, it was simply not possible to have a republic without relative economic equality. The significant economic challenges of the 1780s put so much pressure on ordinary Americans that they threatened the future of republican government itself. The American founding was not a social revolution focused primarily on alleviating poverty or supporting the wealthy. It was a political revolution, but one that was necessary not just to build the political structure for a free republic but also to reestablish the economic conditions necessary for a free republic.[118]

To understand why the Articles of Confederation had to be replaced, we have to go back to the time of the Revolution. The Revolutionary War devastated the economy of the fledgling American republic. Production dropped because men were fighting in the war. Trade ground to a halt. Farms and property were utterly destroyed throughout the states. In the South, where slavery was a central part of the economy, many slaves fled or joined the British.[119] To pay for the war, the Continental Congress printed money, which led to rapid inflation. The Continental dollar, valued in specie (gold and silver), fell from one hundred cents in September 1777 to fifty-six cents in March 1778 to twenty-four cents by September 1778 to ten cents by 1779.[120] Individuals throughout the rebelling states felt this shift strongly at home. In early 1776, for example, a gallon of molasses cost two shillings. By early 1778, it cost twenty shillings and, by the end of 1779, two hundred shillings.[121]

For ordinary American families, the economic crisis led to increasing concern, even conflict, particularly because some people seemed untouched by these economic ills. The situation in Philadelphia provides evocative examples. Speaking at the Philadelphia statehouse, Daniel Roberdeau, a general in the Pennsylvania militia, argued for price controls and condemned financiers who were "getting rich by sucking the blood" of ordinary people.[122] The writer "Mobility" threatened Philadelphia's elites directly: "We cannot live without bread—hunger will break through stone walls and the resentment excited by it may end in your destruction."[123] In October 1779, rhetoric spilled into violence as militiamen grabbed the merchants John Drinker, Thomas Story, Buckridge Sims, and Matthew Johns and marched them around the city toward the home of James Wilson (later one of the most active members of the Constitutional Convention). Wilson and his friends armed themselves. The militia arrived and attempted to break down the doors of "Fort Wilson." Shots were fired, and the two groups fell into hand-to-hand combat that left five dead and fourteen wounded.[124]

Despite the end of the Revolutionary War in 1783, the economic crisis persisted. Economic historians estimate that real per capita incomes fell by as much as 30 percent between 1774 and 1790.[125] The data on foreclosure orders in Pennsylvania shows the extent of the calamity. In Berks County, Pennsylvania, which had a taxable population averaging five thousand between 1782 and 1792, there were thirty-four hundred writs of foreclosure issued. Lancaster County, Pennsylvania, with a fifty-nine-hundred-person taxable population, saw thirty-nine hundred writs of foreclosure between 1784 and 1789. In Northumberland County, the number of foreclosure orders actually exceeded the taxable population between 1785 and 1790.[126] Looking at all available evidence across the newly independent states, some historians have concluded that the economic depression of the 1780s was actually *worse* than the Great Depression of the 1930s.[127]

The central problem was that the Confederation Congress needed money, particularly in the form of gold or silver.[128] Congress needed money to pay the debts incurred to foreign countries that had helped the revolutionaries expel the British. It needed money to pay the army to defend the West against Indians. It needed money to pay pensions and bonuses to officers in the army.[129] Congress had been printing fiat paper money, taking loans, and impressing specific supplies into service during the Revolution. But now that the conflict was over, federal credit was laughable, and the value of paper currency had completely collapsed.[130]

At the time, there were only three options, and as historian Woody Holton argues, Americans tried all three. First, to stop hemorrhaging gold and silver, Americans instituted campaigns to promote "industry and frugality" in hopes of reducing the trade deficit with Britain. These efforts failed because the British blocked American ships from trading in Caribbean ports and the Americans' attempt to retaliate by barring the British from American ports failed.[131] Second, the Confederation Congress tried to gain revenue through the sale of western lands, ultimately passing the Northwest Ordinance in 1787. Earlier ordinances required land to be surveyed prior to sale, but these surveys turned out to be difficult to complete because surveyors encountered hostile Indians. When Congress repealed the survey requirement, most of the remaining buyers were land speculators, and even they only bought 108,000 acres.[132] Finally, Congress tried to raise revenues through tariffs by first proposing a 5 percent tariff on imports. The Articles of Confederation required unanimity for any such policy, and Rhode Island blocked the measure.[133] When Congress tried again a few years later, New York was the holdout.[134]

Left with no other choices, the Confederation Congress issued "requisitions."[135] At the time, Congress did not have the power to collect taxes. It could only ask, or requisition, the states for funding.[136] The states attempted to fulfill their obligations by putting into place new taxes.[137] They imposed head taxes, excise taxes, and property taxes.[138] One historian estimates that taxes increased three to eight times in the early 1780s.[139] In some cases, the desire to fulfill these obligations led to some strange bedfellows. At one point, backcountry South Carolinians actually petitioned the South Carolina assembly to suspend the transatlantic slave trade to keep wealth in the state: when slaves came into the country, gold and silver went out.[140] Between October 1781 and August 1786, states complied with federal requisitions at a 37 percent rate.[141] But for ordinary middle- and lower-class Americans, the burden was too great. Depressed commodity prices meant low incomes and a limited ability to pay.[142] For those in rural areas, the problem was particularly acute, because gold and silver were scarce.[143] Then, in one of the most important but least remembered actions of the era, in September 1785, Congress presented the states with a new $3 million requisition.[144]

The requisitions of the 1780s—and the 1785 requisition in particular—sparked a popular backlash, which manifested itself in political change, protest, unrest, and outright revolt. "For a long time the people of America will not have money to pay direct taxes," Gouverneur Morris later said. "Seize and sell their effects and you push them into Revolts."[145] Farmers, debtors, and others feeling economically squeezed wanted to use produce and property to pay their debts and taxes and to shift the tax burden to traded luxury goods. They wanted creditors and bondholders to accept less than they were owed on their speculative investments. They tried to reduce attorney's fees in legal actions and in some places closed the courts to prevent actions against debtors. And they wanted to print more paper money so the currency would be inflated and they could more easily pay their debts.[146]

In some states, the people ousted their state legislators and replaced them with new members who pursued tax and debt relief policies.[147] In Massachusetts, where two-thirds of the taxes needed to pay their share of the requisition would have gone to state and federal government creditors, angry voters ousted 74 percent of the state house of representatives in a single election. Massachusetts had already relaxed its policies based on popular pressure: the state decreased penalties imposed on delinquent tax collectors and agreed to let citizens postpone deadlines and even pay their debts with fruits and vegetables.[148] Seeking to avoid the fate of their predecessors, the newly constituted assembly imposed no taxes that year.[149] Other states followed a similar path: angry voters burdened by taxes voted out their state legislatures, and the new, more populist assemblies took action to alleviate their burdened constituents.[150]

For rebellious ordinary Americans, the issue was not that they were irresponsible, that they thought debts unimportant, or that they did not want to pay.[151] The problem was that they genuinely could not pay given the economic distress of the time, that the government's harsh economic policies were making things worse, and that they didn't think their payments were being put to good use. The tax and debt policies put pressure on the driving force of the economy: the people's work. Debtors were forced to sell their tools and livestock to pay their debts, leaving them unable to "save their estates" and continue as "useful members of the community," as one New Jersey writer put it in 1785.[152] Debtors were further burdened in time and money by having to go to court to defend themselves against creditor actions. For those who didn't lose their livelihoods, productive working hours were wasted: Artisans had to determine if someone could pay in commodities instead of money. If so, artisans then had to spend time after the workday bartering tea, salt, or other commodities for items they needed. Farmers became increasingly discouraged; any attempt to extricate themselves from their debt seemed impossible. Worse yet, in the event that they could pay their taxes in gold and silver, it would go to bondholders and creditors, who had made speculative investments at rock-bottom prices. Ordinary people thought it unfair that speculators be rewarded, and they recognized that any payment was unlikely to help the economy because the bondholders and creditors were continually sending gold and silver to Britain in return for manufactured goods.[153]

By the late 1780s, virtually everyone agreed the Articles of Confederation system wasn't working, but for different reasons. Ordinary citizens believed they had been squeezed too hard in tough times. Elites felt aggrieved as well. Bondholders like Abigail Adams thought they were victims who had been "cheated."[154] They thought the government had to pay its debts, or else the declining creditworthiness of the new nation would dry up foreign credit permanently.[155] The states' pro-debtor stance was contributing to the country's economic problems.[156] In a sense, the impetus for a new federal constitution from the elite was itself a backlash to the popular backlash created by the requisitions.

While conventional history books tell of the worries of insurrection from below, a nascent class hierarchy was also seen as a threat to the fledgling republic.[157] "Rapidly are you dividing into two Classes—extreme Rich and extreme Poor," warned Brutus in *The Boston Gazette* in April 1787.[158] A Connecticut assemblyman, writing in May 1787, declared, "We may as well think to repeal the great laws of attraction and gravitation" as to "continuing a popular government without a good degree of equality among the people as to their property." He even called upon a form of biblical economic justice, when "lands were to revert to their former owners at the end of every fifty years."[159]

Others thought that the Confederation's inability to manage the economic crisis was justification enough to return to a monarchical form of government. Peregrine Foster of Providence wrote in July 1786, "[I]f this is the way in which we are going on, I pray the Lord soon to raise up some good Monarch or even an Oliver Cromwell to establish a government." Benjamin Tupper of Massachusetts concurred: "I cannot give up the idea that Monarchy in our present situation is to become absolutely necessary to save the States from sinking into the lowest abbiss of Misery." In December 1786, an anonymous writer in Connecticut admitted that he "was once as strong a republican as any man in America" but now thought that a republic was "almost the last kind of government I should choose. I should infinitely prefer a limited monarchy." Leading figures noticed the rise in monarchical sentiments. Madison worried in February 1787 that "the late turbulent scenes in Massts. & infamous ones in Rhode Island, have done inexpressible injury to the republican character in that part of the U. States; and a propensity toward Monarchy is said to have been produced by it in some leading minds."[160] Hector St. John de Crèvecoeur said that New Englanders "[s]igh for Monarchy & that a very large number of persons in several Counties would like to return to English domination."[161] When Madison and Hamilton remarked that the Constitutional Convention would "decide for ever the fate of Republican Government," it was in part because of the threat posed by the economic vices of the Confederation.[162]

THE CONSTITUTION'S ECONOMIC COMPROMISE

The economic crisis of the Confederation reminds us that the founders were practical political leaders who had to solve a challenging economic policy problem: The central government needed revenue to be able to operate. The revenue had to come from somewhere, and it couldn't overly burden the middle class, unless they wanted the new government to suffer from the same persistent revolts and insurgencies that afflicted the Articles of Confederation. The Constitution is often described as originating from a series of compromises: the Great Compromise, a Senate with two members from each state; the three-fifths compromise, on representation; the slave trade compromise.[163] But from the perspective of the economic crisis of the Confederation, we should imagine one more compromise at the heart of the Constitution. The Constitution's economic compromise is hidden from view if we think the original charter was constructed to serve the interests of the wealthy elites. It is hidden from view if we think of the founders as high-minded philosophers. And it is also hidden from view if we look for evidence of the compromise only in the secret debates in Philadelphia. The compromise that addresses the economic problems of both farmers *and* merchants, debtors *and* creditors, ordinary people *and* elites, is buried deep in Article I of the Constitution.

Article I, section 10 of the Constitution prohibits the states from engaging in a number of activities, including two that were of critical economic importance during the 1780s: "impairing the obligation of contracts" (which states did to protect debtors) and "lay[ing] any imposts or duties on imports or exports" (which states did to raise revenues). Article I, section 8 of the Constitution is the other side of prohibiting state imposts: it empowers Congress to create "duties, imposts and excises." Usually these clauses are not read together. Constitutional lawyers analyze the first clause—the contracts clause—along with the Constitution's provisions on protecting property.[164] They normally group the impost, or tariff, clauses with the commerce clause.[165] This conventional grouping betrays modern concerns. Libertarians and classical liberals are concerned primarily with the protection of contract and property rights, and so they like to group those provisions together. Debates on the national government's power to regulate commerce were especially fierce throughout the twentieth century, so provisions on that topic are usually linked.

But thinking about these provisions from the perspective of the economic debates of the 1780s suggests another way to interpret these clauses. The contracts clause prevents states from passing laws that undermine contracts, such as pro-debtor laws that require creditors to take less for their investments.[166] This provision clearly supports creditors vis-à-vis debtors and is one piece of evidence for the

Beardian analysis of the Constitution. For the elites at the time, the provision would have forced debtors to pay their debts and, critically, strengthened the ability of the government and individuals to obtain credit in the future.

The impost or tariff clauses are a way for the federal government to generate revenue—something it could not do sufficiently well during the Confederation. Indeed, the failure of the states to unanimously agree to lay an import tariff is what forced the Confederation Congress to continue to requisition additional funds from the states. The effect: states imposed taxes, the people rose up against the state legislatures, and the newly elected legislatures enacted pro-debtor legislation. If the new Congress had the tariff power, the revenue model for the country would shift significantly. Coastal merchants engaged in international trade and wealthier people who bought imported goods would bear the lion's share of the national government's revenue burden, which was necessary to pay debts, cover the cost of the army, and fund the national government's activities. States could then alleviate the tax burden they had imposed on ordinary people, who were still being crushed by the post–Revolutionary War economic depression. Ordinary people would now have the ability to engage in economic activity without the fear that any money they earned would go to taxes or creditors.[167]

Taken together, the two provisions were an effort to solve the problems of *both* the creditor and bondholder elites *and* the ordinary people who were most heavily hit by the economic crisis. In fact, this is just what happened. Almost immediately after Congress first reached a quorum, in April 1789, James Madison introduced the tariff bill into the House of Representatives. "A national revenue must be obtained," Madison said. "[B]ut the system must be such a one, that . . . shall not be oppressive to our constituents."[168] The bill became the second piece of legislation passed by the First Congress. President Washington signed it into law, appropriately, if not poetically, on July 4, 1789.[169] The new government, one historian has noted, "obtained almost all of its revenue from tariffs levied in the port towns, so farmers almost never had to try to come up with scarce gold and silver to pay federal taxes."[170] The states followed suit in alleviating the tax burden on their citizens. In Massachusetts and

North Carolina, the poll tax was reduced by 90 percent, and in North Carolina land taxes were cut by just under 80 percent.[171] A study of eleven states between 1785 and 1795 shows that on a per capita basis taxes dropped by 75–90 percent, just as the federal import tariff increased.[172]

While there is little historical evidence discussing the contracts clause, and virtually nothing discussing the contracts clause and tariff clause in conjunction with each other, it wasn't because these provisions were unimportant. Alexander Hamilton wrote in his notes for a speech at the New York ratification convention, "Impost begat Convention."[173] John Adams noted in 1790 that Rhode Island's refusal to adopt the impost was "the instrument which Providence thought fit to use for the great purpose of establishing the . . . Constitution."[174] Historians have argued that the paucity of discussion during the ratification debates was a strategic choice. The critics of the Constitution thought that as a political matter, they would be better off if they could not be pegged as desperate debtors.[175] More important, according to one historian, they also "viewed the widely circulated claim that the Constitution would relieve the tax burden as the deadliest weapon in their opponents' arsenal."[176] We often forget that ratification was a fiercely contested political battle. Silence was strategic.

Still, there is evidence that people at the time understood the economic compromise at the heart of the Constitution and were particularly clear-eyed in seeing the tariff clause as designed to help alleviate ordinary people's economic woes by shifting the financial burden to merchants and those buying imported goods. Writing in *The Massachusetts Centinel*, "One of the Middle-Interest" discussed how trade and taxes were linked: "[I]t is well known how the trade of Massachusetts is gone to Connecticut, and that for want of a revenue, our own *State taxes* are increased. The insurrections that disgraced this Commonwealth the last winter, may be all traced up to this source."[177] He continued, "[T]axes may not have been necessary if we had enjoyed national regulations; and that the same constitution which is to give this authority [taxing power] to Congress, is also to give those commercial powers before mentioned, which will make proper impositions on foreign trade, and derive such revenues by

way of impost and excise, as will greatly diminish direct taxation."[178]
"A Farmer" in Connecticut explained how the provision would have
the effect of redistributing the tax burden toward purchasers of luxury imports:

> So long as taxes continue to be laid on us directly, according to
> the list, we farmers must inevitably sweat under the pressure
> of them. It is grievous to be borne, but I fear we must bear
> it until we can agree to throw some part of it upon the mer-
> chants, by way of an impost. . . . Had the general impost been
> granted at first, with the proposed regulations and restrictions,
> how happy would it have been for us! We should not lie, as we
> now do, smarting at every pore and bleeding fast from every
> vein. . . . A great part of our foreign debt would probably have
> been paid before this time. The weight of our taxes cannot
> be shifted from our polls and our farms to foreign luxuries
> and the unnecessary goods of the merchants without vesting
> in Congress the power of laying imposts, duties, and excises.[179]

As a result, the farmer concluded that the Constitution was
"peculiarly favorable to the agricultural part of the United States."[180]
Recognizing the power of the claim, skeptics of the Constitution
responded. They argued that an import tariff could not possibly raise
enough revenue to fund all of the government's debts and ongoing
expenses.[181] Supporters disagreed, holding that outside wartime the
import tariff would be sufficient to cover the government's needs.[182]

Interpreting the tariff clause as supporting the economically distressed also helps explain some puzzling features of the ratification
debates. Why was it that some of the most pro-debtor, pro-paper-
money areas of the country sent pro-ratification delegates to the ratification conventions? For example, in New Hampshire, almost half
of the towns that were pro-paper-money during the Confederation
era elected pro-Constitution delegates to the ratification convention.[183] The answer is that the economic compromise solved one of
their primary fears. Why was it that three of the first five states to
ratify the Constitution—Delaware, New Jersey, and Connecticut—
had almost no debate and scarcely token opposition to the Constitu-

tion?[184] The answer is the tariff provisions. None of these states had a major port, and so none could issue state import tariffs on foreign goods to raise meaningful revenues. As a result, they had been forced into imposing more burdensome direct taxes on their populations. The Constitution let them shift their share of the national government's revenue from direct taxes on their citizens to tariffs paid by those in New York or Philadelphia.[185] By placing greater burdens on urban merchants than on rural farmers, the Constitution's economic compromise established, in effect, a progressive revenue base that could save the equal commonwealth.

THE DOCUMENT AND ITS DEFENSE: THE POLITICAL ORIGINS OF THE MIDDLE-CLASS CONSTITUTION

On June 21, 1788, the delegates to the New York ratifying convention assembled in Poughkeepsie, about halfway between New York City and Albany, just east of the Hudson River. While located in Anti-Federalist Dutchess County, the twenty-five-hundred-person town was a fair-minded venue for such a momentous—and often contentious—debate. Four days earlier, the delegates had arrived at the town's Dutch-style courthouse.[186] By the twenty-first, they were fully engaged in debating the Constitution, when the hometown representative, Melancton Smith, rose with a reasoned, thoughtful argument on the nature of political representation. At forty-four, Smith was an able and active speaker at the ratification convention, presenting disciplined, clear, and cogent arguments. But without a fancy education or background, he had none of the oratorical abilities of his Federalist interlocutors. As James Kent said of Smith, he was "a man of remarkable simplicity, and of the most gentle, liberal, and amiable disposition."[187]

The debate that Saturday concerned the number of constituents per member of Congress, which the Constitution set at thirty thousand. Smith thought that number was too large and that the House of Representatives would, as a result, be far too small to truly represent the people. Smith rejected the idea that legislators could faithfully represent people from different walks of life. Representatives needed to "resemble those they represent," he said. "[T]hey should be a true picture of the people; possess the knowledge of their circumstances and their wants; sympathize in all their distresses, and be disposed to seek their true interests."[188] It wasn't enough for them to understand politics or commerce, the kinds of subjects that come from having a "refined education"; they needed to know about the "common concerns and occupations of the people," something "men of the middling class of life" knew better than elites.[189]

The problem with the new Constitution, Smith argued, was that "representatives will generally be composed of the first class in the community."[190] "Every society naturally divides itself into classes" because people are born with different abilities. It wasn't the trappings of formal aristocracy—"titles, stars and garters"—that created social classes but rather "birth, education, talents and wealth."[191] The problem with the "natural aristocracy" that emerged from any society is that its members will come to control the government.[192] Unlike the poor or middling class, the elites "easily form associations," which makes it easier for them to take power.[193] In addition, they "command a superior degree of respect" and are well-known, making them more likely to be elected.[194] But the elite could not govern in the interest of the entire population, because they "consider themselves above the common people," they "do not associate with them," and they think they "have a right of pre-eminence in every thing."[195]

Whether or not he knew it, Smith was repeating arguments from ancient Greece. He held first that social divisions had political ramifications and that elections would have aristocratic consequences by favoring elites. Most commentators focus on Smith's argument that representatives must mirror the people and that the makeup of Congress was unlikely to match the different groups within American society. But as Smith continued his address, he made a second argument: he contended that the middle class would be *better* at governing than even the natural aristocracy or a body with class representatives. "Those in middling circumstances," he said, "have less temptation." "[T]hey are inclined by habit and the company with whom they associate, to set bounds to their passions and appetites." The middle class "are more temperate, of better morals and less ambition than the great"; they had "frugal habits" and "would be careful" in allocating public burdens on the people.[196] Just as Aristotle had argued that the middle class could maintain the balance of power between the rich and the poor, because it could align itself with both groups—but not completely—so, too, did Smith. Because "the interest of both the rich and the poor are involved in that of the middling class," a government of the middle would be less likely to fracture. "A representative body, composed principally of respectable yeomanry," he concluded, "is the best possible security to liberty."[197]

Rising in response to Smith was Alexander Hamilton. At only thirty-three, the self-made man from the Caribbean was already an important figure, having served as an aide to General George Washington during the Revolutionary War and then as a member of the Constitutional Convention. The idea of an American aristocracy of government officials was "ridiculous," Hamilton countered. "The image is a phantom."[198] Smith had missed perhaps *the* central feature of the Constitution's system of representation, indeed, of all electoral systems. Representatives are "dependent on the will of the people." Because an elected representative must "return to the community," it "cannot be his interest to oppose [the people's] wishes." "[T]he general sense of the people will regulate the conduct of their representatives," Hamilton said. Outside some exceptional situations, "popular views and even prejudices will direct the actions of the rulers."[199]

In addition to the "most intimate conformity between the views of the representative and his constituent," the new government had two other protections against aristocracy.[200] First, the Constitution had no provision that would "render a rich man more eligible than a poor one" to serve in office.[201] There were no economic requirements for office holding. Second, Hamilton argued that the new republic's economic equality was a safeguard of political liberty: "While property continues to be pretty equally divided, and a considerable share of information pervades the community; the tendency of the people's suffrages, will be to elevate merit even from obscurity."[202] In a nation without vast economic disparities, there would be no need to elect only the wealthy. The middle class would recognize men of talent—including plainspoken men like Melancton Smith. Sounding a warning to the chamber, Hamilton conceded Harrington's old lesson about property and power: "As riches increase and accumulate in few hands ... the tendency of things will be to depart from the republican standard."[203] But this problem, he noted, could in theory afflict any society.

The Smith-Hamilton debate on June 21 showed just how powerful the idea of the equal commonwealth was in American politics. Smith had taken up a variation on the old class warfare argument. His theory of representation was built on the fact that society was made up of different orders of people, each of which needed representation in government. Hamilton outmaneuvered Smith by rejecting the premise. Hamilton—the same Hamilton known to us today as an advocate for elite-run government—said aristocracy in America was "ridiculous" and, in valorizing public opinion, effectively agreed with Smith that the new government should be controlled by the broad middle class. Denying the existence of different orders altogether, and relying on the "pretty equally divided" allocation of property in America, Hamilton held that the Constitution rooted political power entirely in the people themselves. Smith's class-based populism ran up against Hamilton's invocation of the equal commonwealth. Indeed, at the time, some observers noticed how Hamilton turned the tables. In a letter recounting the day's events, Charles Tillinghast skeptically wrote to John Lamb, "You would be surprised, did you not know the Man, what an *amazing Republican* Hamilton wishes to make himself be considered—*But he is known.*"[204] As a leading historian concludes of the rhetorical battlefield, "The Antifederalists could never offer any effective intellectual opposition to the Constitution because the weapons they chose to use were mostly in their opponents' hands."[205]

Of course, Hamilton and the Federalists engaged in a little sleight of hand of their own. Hamilton claimed, rightly, that the Constitution had no formal rules entrenching economic power in office. Madison had made the same claim in *Federalist* No. 57, responding to charges that the House of Representatives would be made up of elites rather than the "mass of the people."[206] Madison had responded by noting that voters would be drawn from "the great body of the people," "[n]ot the rich, more than the poor; not the learned, more than the ignorant; not the haughty heirs of distinguished names, more than the humble sons of obscure and unpropitious fortune."[207] Similarly, candidates would emerge from the whole population, because "[n]o qualification of wealth, of birth, of religious faith, or of civil profession is permitted to fetter the judgment or disappoint the inclination of the people."[208] Once in office, members of Congress would be faithful to the people because of "[d]uty, gratitude, interest, ambition itself," and frequent elections.[209]

But such *formal* rules were not what concerned the skeptics of the Constitution. One Anti-Federalist, Samuel Chase, concluded that "there is no probability of a farmer or planter being chosen . . . only the gentry, the rich, the well born will be elected."[210] The Federal Farmer, one of the most insightful commentators on the Constitution, made the stakes clearest. He said there were three types of aristocracy discussed in America. The first was "constitutional" aristocracy, "which does not exist in the United States," because we did not have any formal trappings of or provisions for aristocracy. The second was an aristocratic faction or "junto of unprincipled men, often distinguished for their wealth or abilities, who combine together and make their object their private interests and aggrandizement." The third was the natural aristocracy, which comprised "a respectable order of men."[211] His concern, like that of many of the Constitution's skeptics, was with the latter two forms of aristocracy.

In focusing on the *informal* ways in which elites could dominate government, the Anti-Federalists contributed one of the most significant theoretical insights into the middle-class constitution, and perhaps into republicanism itself. Whatever a republic is, it is not an oligarchy or an aristocracy. But without a formal place for classes built into the design of the government, a middle-class constitution is particularly susceptible to elites' capturing all the levers of power. To be sure, elites could gain total control in a class warfare constitution as well. It is not hard to imagine an aspiring oligarch bribing, cajoling, or threatening a Roman tribune of the plebs and the tribune succumbing. But elite capture in a class warfare constitution requires such machinations. In a middle-class constitution, in contrast, a small group simply needs to win elections. Middle-class constitutions are at risk not necessarily of class uprising and armed revolution but of a quiet, gradual descent into oligarchy. "Eternal vigilance is the price of liberty," republicans like to say, in no small part because the threat to the republic is silent, rooted in activities that look otherwise banal: participation, organization, fame, election. But beyond arguing that the people had the power to choose their representatives, neither Madison nor Hamilton directly addressed the skeptics' fear of elite capture through informal means.[212]

What is truly shocking, though, is that the locus of constitutional debate took place on these terms at all—formal versus informal aristocracy. This itself is confirmation of the radical change from the class warfare constitutions of the past to America's middle-class constitution. During the Revolutionary era, the possibility of creating a class warfare constitution to protect elites was still very much alive in constitutional thought. Nowhere was this more evident than in Massachusetts in the late 1770s. In 1778, Massachusetts considered the adoption of a new constitution, arguably the most conservative of the Revolutionary period. The proposed 1778 constitution allowed all free white men to vote in elections for the lower house, but that was the end of its democratic tendencies. Candidates for the lower house needed to have an estate of £200. Voting for the upper house meant meeting a £60 wealth requirement, and holding office required a £400 estate. Candidates for governor had to have a £1,000 estate to stand for office.[213] The people of Massachusetts resoundingly rejected that constitution; nearly four-fifths of the towns objected, many unanimously. But remnants of the class warfare constitutional thinking persisted, and some people in Massachusetts actually thought the 1778 constitution didn't go far enough. In Essex County, north of Boston, Theophilus Parsons penned an essay known as the *Essex Result,* in which he opposed the 1778 constitution because it provided too *little* protection for property owners. Parsons opposed popular election for members of the upper house and wanted to require that legislation affecting property be approved not just by a majority of the legislature but by a majority of the propertied class.[214]

During the Constitutional Convention itself, delegates debated a wide variety of antidemocratic ways to entrench elite power. Most strikingly, many discussed the Senate in openly aristocratic terms. John Dickinson hoped the Senate would "consist of the most distinguished characters, distinguished for their rank in life and their weight of property, and bearing as strong a likeness to the British

House of Lords as possible." He wanted it to "establish a balance that will check the Democracy."[215] To advance that goal, some, like Charles Cotesworth Pinckney of South Carolina, wanted to ban senators from taking a salary. Without a salary, only the wealthy could afford to serve in the Senate, and Pinckney believed that body "ought to be composed of persons of wealth."[216] Some convention delegates also considered restricting suffrage to property owners, and some thought about granting the Senate power to initiate legislation on fiscal issues.[217]

But the document that emerged from Philadelphia included none of these counterrevolutionary policies. These ideas are nowhere to be found in the Constitution. Instead, Hamilton emerges from Philadelphia to stand in a two-story building a mile from the Hudson River and argue Harrington's republican philosophy. The question is, why? If the rich, property-owning delegates to the Constitutional Convention really wanted to skew the new government in their favor, why didn't they go further?

Part of the answer was practical. The participants in the debates in Philadelphia often did not agree. For example, when it came to setting property requirements for officeholders, they could not agree on what level to set them at, or whether they should be set in the Constitution itself, or by Congress, or by linking requirements to those in the state legislatures.[218]

Part of the answer was political: the framers knew the people would not accept a class warfare constitution.[219] When Hamilton claimed in Poughkeepsie that public opinion mattered in a free republic, at some level he must have genuinely believed it. Public opinion, with its preference for economic equality and a free republic, acted as a constraint on even him, perhaps the most counterrevolutionary of the founders. Indeed, during the convention, the delegates recognized openly how the views of the people restricted their ability to entrench elite power in the Constitution.[220] In debates over the Senate, James Wilson said, "The British government cannot be our model. . . . Our manners, our laws, the abolition of entails and of primogeniture, the whole genius of the people, are opposed to it."[221] Elbridge Gerry was even more pointed: "[I]t was necessary to consider what the people would approve."[222] In debates on the restriction of suffrage, Oliver Ellsworth remarked, "The people will not readily subscribe to the Natl. Constitution, if it should subject them to be disfranchised."[223]

But it is also important to remember that the proceedings in Philadelphia were secret, and that Hamilton, Madison, and the Federalists who made the case for ratifying the Constitution did not emphasize political expediency or social hierarchy. Americans believed they were relatively equal and their new nation could be a middle-class republic. Hamilton therefore argued that ordinary people would be elected to office because property was "pretty equally divided." Madison's *Federalist* No. 51 did not explain "checks and balances" based on the different classes in society but based on the rival theory of the separation of powers. The Constitution created different branches of government, each of which exercised a different function—legislative, executive, and judicial. The checks and balances in the American system were between these functions of government, not between social classes.[224] After all, what sense would it make to rely on class conflict in a society whose defining characteristic was relative equality? The shift away from class warfare constitutional designs was widely understood, even by skeptics. Patrick Henry thought there was "no check" in the structure of government because "The President, senators, and representatives all, immediately or mediately are the choice of the people." [225] John Adams continued to embrace the class warfare design in his *Defence of the Constitutions*. But for many Americans, the old class warfare theory was manifestly inapplicable to the new republic: Adams's critics thus attacked him for making a "travesty" of the American system.

The repudiation of the class warfare constitutional structure was one of the most important and most radical shifts in the history of constitutional design. The American Constitution certainly looks less democratic when compared with the Pennsylvania Constitution of 1776. Restrictions on suffrage were left to the states. Election of senators was made indirect, placed with the state legislatures. But these provisions are a far cry from the proposed 1778 Massachusetts Constitution, the views of the *Essex Result*, and even some of the proposals debated at Independence Hall. If the story is that the Constitution is a counterrevolutionary document, what is striking is how timid the counterrevolution was.

Still, some lingering doubts remain. What about the Senate? What about property requirements for voting? Were these not just *indirect* ways to establish an aristocratic constitutional system? There is certainly truth to these arguments; some of the framers did have aristocratic tendencies. But while it might seem hard to believe in light of the democratic and egalitarian ethos of our time, both institutions can and should be interpreted in ways that were distinctly not about surreptitiously adopting a class warfare constitutional regime.

Today, it is hard to see the Senate as anything but an elite body. Its name echoes the patrician class deliberating in Rome, and for those with more contemporary ears, as Hannah Arendt once commented, it is "automatically equated with the House of Lords."[226] But the Senate is not best interpreted as an institution designed to replicate class warfare constitutions. Perhaps most important, the Senate does not have any economic class requirement for admission. The Roman senate and the House of Lords both required that members come from an elite class. The American Senate has no such requirement. In fact, that requirement was explicitly rejected during the Constitutional Convention. Gouverneur Morris, one of the more influential delegates to the convention, believed that the rich would act in ways to oppress everyone else and that the only answer was to isolate them in a separate political body. "By thus combining and setting apart the aristocratic interest," he said, "the popular interest will be combined against it. There will be a mutual check and a mutual security."[227] Morris's approach—the class warfare approach—was rejected.

It is also hard to argue that placing selection of senators in the hands of the state legislatures was a serious strategy for guaranteeing elite domination. To accept this argument, one would have to believe that the same framers who distrusted the pro-debtor, pro-paper-money, populist state legislatures during the Articles of Confederation period trusted those same state legislatures to choose elite senators. But why would a state legislature that passes pro-debtor measures select an anti-debtor senator? Indeed, James Wilson recognized this logical flaw during the Constitutional Convention. "If the

Legislatures, as was now complained, sacrificed the commercial to the landed interest," Wilson asked, "what reason was there to expect such a choice from them as would defeat their own views"?[228] In the very first Senate, at least in some states, the state legislatures sent non-elites to the upper chamber. In Pennsylvania, for example, the state legislature chose elite banker Robert Morris from Philadelphia, and non-elite western farmer William Maclay.[229]

So how can we understand the purpose of the Senate in a way that doesn't collapse into an informal class warfare constitution? The Senate existed as a second veto point—an independent institution—to evaluate and assess policy. The purpose of bicameralism, according to this interpretation, is not to entrench the power of the wealthy but to prevent ill-considered policies based on the swift changes in public opinion that can happen in the more responsive House of Representatives.[230] Indeed, James Madison described the purpose of the Senate in precisely these terms during the Constitutional Convention: its goals were "first to protect the people against their rulers: secondly, to protect the people against the transient impressions into which they themselves might be led."[231] James Wilson worried that if legislation was vested in a single body, that body might make mistakes based on "violent fits" of opinion. Two bodies, with different qualifications and terms (two years for the House, six for the Senate), would allow for both representation and wisdom.[232] Importantly, Wilson argued, the American structure of government was still "purely democratical." Although "that principle is applied in different forms, in order to obtain the advantages, and exclude the inconveniences of the simple modes of government," all the "streams of power . . . flow from one abundant fountain . . . THE PEOPLE."[233] Members of the House of Representatives, with its frequent elections, were to be responsive to swift changes in public opinion. Senators, chosen by state legislatures and with longer terms of office, were meant to deliberate in line with the long-term public interest. As Wilson explained, this did not betray democratic principles.[234]

Property requirements for voting are equally hard to understand. How could they be anything but a way to disenfranchise the poor and guarantee rule by economic elites? Surely they must undermine the argument that America's Constitution is a middle-class constitu-

tion. Perhaps not. First, we have to remember that property requirements were not constitutionally mandated. In fact, they do not
appear anywhere in the federal Constitution. Not for holding office.
Not for voting. And it is not as if the framers of the Constitution did
not know how to write such requirements. They put in minimum
age requirements for members of both the House and the Senate,
and they debated whether to include property requirements in their
state constitutions. But when it came to the federal Constitution, the
framers decided not to include any such requirements.

As a result, requirements for suffrage were specifically left up to the
states and differed from state to state. What is perhaps most surprising is how expansive suffrage actually was in the founding era. There
were obviously significant limitations on suffrage—African Americans, Native Americans, and women. But the Revolution unleashed a
democratic spirit that severely reduced the barriers to voting among
adult white men. Before the Revolution, somewhere between 50 percent and 80 percent of adult white men had suffrage.[235] During the
Revolution, many of the states reformed their suffrage requirements
to reduce—and in some cases eliminate—property requirements.[236]
Pennsylvania removed property ownership as a criterion for suffrage
in 1776, giving the vote to all male taxpayers. North Carolina allowed
all taxpaying freemen to vote for the assembly. Georgia went from
a fifty-acre property requirement to either a £10 property qualification or service in the "mechanic trade," which meant that most
adult white men qualified. New Hampshire shifted from a property
requirement to a poll tax. New Jersey allowed all inhabitants—even
women—to vote, as long as they had £50.[237] These changes meant a
significant increase in the voting population. In Pennsylvania, New
Hampshire, Georgia, North Carolina, and New Jersey, about 90 percent of adult white men could vote. In Massachusetts, 60–70 percent
of adult white men in the seacoast towns could vote, and that number was 80–90 percent in rural areas.[238] To be sure, in some states
the rates were far lower—in New York, for example, only about 58
percent of adult white men could vote in 1790—but the overall trend
in the Revolutionary era was, in the words of a famous study, "from
property to democracy."[239]

Most important, however, property and taxpaying requirements were not thought of as a way to entrench rule by the wealthy. Under the prevailing republican theory of the time, property ownership was essential to good citizenship. Citizens were supposed to participate and govern with only the public good in mind, not with an eye to their own personal, private interest. This ideal of unbiased action, perhaps the most important of the republican virtues, was captured by the word "disinterested," which meant being "free of interested ties and paid by no masters."[240] If a person was "interested," he would serve his interests, not the public good. Owning property meant that a citizen was autonomous, not dependent on anyone else for his livelihood, and as a result the citizen could act in accordance with the public good.[241] The historian Drew McCoy summarizes this view well:

> The personal independence that resulted from the ownership of land permitted a citizen to participate responsibly in the political process, for it allowed him to pursue spontaneously the common or public good, rather than the narrow interest of the men—or the government—on whom he depended for his support. Thus the Revolutionaries did not intend to provide men with property so that they might flee from public responsibility into a selfish privatism; property was rather the necessary basis for a committed republican citizenry.[242]

Indeed, some in the founding generation explained that property requirements were actually meant to *restrain* the wealthy from unjustly gaining power. Jefferson believed that without property ownership men would be dependent on others. "[D]ependence," he said, "begets subservience and venality, suffocates the germ of virtue, and prepares fit tools for the designs of ambition."[243] In defending property qualifications for voting, Gouverneur Morris outlined this fear with remarkable clarity: "Give the votes to the people who have no property, and they will sell them to the rich who will be able to buy them."[244] What Morris feared is that the mass of the people would be dependent on their wealthier employers, and the people would sell freedom to the highest bidder. Property requirements would ensure the people were independent of the wealthy: neither

bribery nor poverty would tempt the people to relinquish their freedom. Morris was primarily concerned with America's future. "The
time is not distant when this Country will abound with mechanics
& manufacturers who will receive their bread from their employers.
Will such men be the secure & faithful guardians of liberty? Will they
be the impregnable barrier against aristocracy?"[245] While it may be
hard to understand today, many in the founding generation paradoxically saw property requirements not as a way to guarantee the
rule of the wealthy but as a way to *prevent* the wealthy from seizing
power.[246]

THE RELEVANCE AND IRRELEVANCE OF JAMES MADISON

When James Madison arrived in Philadelphia in 1787, he wasn't the
Father of the Constitution, and the delegates to the convention did
not realize they were there to write a constitution that would endure
for more than two centuries. Their task, as Madison put it, was to
"revise" the "federal Constitution" that already existed.[247] Madison's
notes on the convention are now one of the most important sources
for historians and constitutional scholars, but even they have had a
complex history. Madison revised and added to them in the years
after the convention, and the assembled notes were not published
until 1840, after his death.[248] Even *The Federalist Papers,* the most
important contribution of the American founders to political philosophy, was designed not as an exercise in grand philosophy but as part
of a political campaign to get the Constitution ratified. But twists
and reinventions of history aside, Madison undoubtedly remains
one of the great thinkers and architects of our constitutional system.
And no part of Madison's thought is more celebrated than his essay
Federalist No. 10. *Federalist* No. 10 is one of the most scrutinized documents in American history, but its treatment of factions is worth
revisiting—and reinterpreting—in light of the economic structure
of American society at the time and the Harringtonian theory that
formed the foundation for America's middle-class constitution.

The traditional view in political philosophy was that a republic
by necessity had to be small. A small republic allowed for a homogeneous population, a population that knew each other and could

act with the virtue needed to sustain a republican form of government.[249] Attempting to create a republic in a large society was an ill-fated experiment, because factions would emerge that would lead the republic to collapse into oligarchy or mob rule. In *Federalist* No. 10, Madison challenged this view. Drawing on the Scottish philosopher David Hume, Madison argued that in a large republic—what he called the "extended republic"—the problem of faction would be minimized. The tyranny of a minority was easily dispensed with: "[R]elief is supplied by the republican principle, which enables the majority to defeat [the minority's] sinister views by regular vote."[250]

The tyranny of a majority was also unlikely, but for a different reason. Madison suggested that in an enlarged republic there would be a multiplicity of interests. Speaking directly to questions of property and economic power, he identified debtors' and creditors' interests but also noted that "[a] landed interest, a manufacturing interest, a mercantile interest, a moneyed interest, with many lesser interests, grow up of necessity in civilized nations, and divide them into different classes, actuated by different sentiments and views."[251] With so many interests, it would be difficult for any particular interest to coalesce into a majority. Even if a few factions did coalesce into a majority, it would be harder for that majority to dominate politics on a repeat basis. As a result, self-interested factions would cancel each other out, enabling the rise of leaders who were committed to the public good.[252] Madison offered the same theory in *Federalist* No. 51: "In the extended republic of the United States, and among the great variety of interests, parties, and sects which it embraces, a coalition of a majority of the whole society could seldom take place on any other principles than those of justice and the general good."[253]

Much of the attention to Madison's theory has centered on the problem of the tyranny of the majority. But it is worth noting that despite Madison's familiarity with the long history of class warfare in republics, his *Federalist* No. 10 says virtually nothing about the possibility of the tyranny of a wealthy *minority*. There is no further analysis than the "republican principle" by which the minority's "sinister views" are defeated through elections. Yet we know Madison was aware of this possibility. In a letter to John Brown of Kentucky—who had asked him for advice on the new constitution of that state—

Madison warned against two different threats: "Give all power to property, and the indigent will be oppressed. Give it to the latter and the effect may be transposed."[254]

Alexander Hamilton had a different misgiving about Madison's theory. When Madison presented a version of the theory during the Constitutional Convention, Hamilton thought Madison misjudged how a system with many interests would work in the real world. Most interests were not sufficiently important to rise to the level of creating "factions," and the people would inevitably coalesce around one or two interests that would define the terms of political debate. The most likely source of faction was the "inequality of property"; it was "the great & fundamental distinction in Society."[255] In addition, Madison's theory neglected the possibility of demagogues, including wealthy demagogues inciting popular passions. "Demagogues are not always *inconsiderable* persons," Hamilton wrote in his notes. "Patricians were frequently demagogues."[256]

Madison himself conceded in *Federalist* No. 10 that the "unequal distribution of property" was the most common source of faction. But at the same time, he did not focus on this central problem in constitutional theory. Instead, he asserts that property interests were "various"; they were not polarized along the lines of rich and poor. Why not?

The unstated assumption that made Madison's "variety of interests" theory work was the relative economic equality that characterized the American republic. As the historians Douglass Adair and Drew McCoy have both argued, America's agricultural economy provided the necessary background conditions for the extended republic.[257] Because the country was predominantly agricultural and the people writ large had access to uncultivated lands, they would be virtuous farmers, small landowners who each held property. With relative equality, factions would not emerge along the lines of rich and poor. The point, so fundamental as to go unmentioned in *Federalist* No. 10, was one Alexis de Tocqueville would make explicitly forty years later. "In democracies," he wrote, "where individuals never differ much from one another . . . a multitude of artificial and arbitrary classifications are created." These associations, Tocqueville thought, allow the individual to "set himself apart, out of fear of being carried away into the crowd."[258] "Various" factions, along lines not as salient or polarizing as rich and poor, were possible in America *precisely because* people were so economically equal.[259] Relative equality meant that people would organize for other, less divisive reasons. It is perhaps no surprise that *Federalist* No. 10 gained its iconic status during the 1950s, when political scientists living in a time of economic equality and a growing middle class redefined American politics as rooted in pluralist interest groups.[260] As Louis Hartz once noted, "The Founding Fathers devised a scheme to deal with conflict that could only survive in a land of solidarity."[261]

Of course, there was no solidarity over the issue of slavery. There were already those who opposed the vicious institution. Benjamin Rush declared in 1773 that slavery was a "national crime[]" that would lead to "national punishment."[262] Some expected the coming end of slavery, with enlightened state legislators in the South following the path of their northern brethren.[263] Jefferson proposed gradual emancipation in Virginia in 1779, only to meet with defeat in the assembly. St. George Tucker's attempt failed in 1796.[264] Jefferson now thought the great task would have to fall to the next generation. But neither he nor the other founders could foresee the ascension of King Cotton and the stranglehold it would have over the economy. Nor could they foresee that the next generation of Southern leaders would resurrect class warfare constitutional theories and even feudalism in hopes of justifying their emerging empire of slavery.

When it came to the specter of rising economic inequality destroying the solidarity among citizens in the new republic, there were differences of opinion. During the Constitutional Convention, one of the delegates, Charles Pinckney, argued that it would be "centuries" before America needed a government that incorporated an aristocratic class, as the English government did. America was "not only very different from the inhabitants of any State we are acquainted with in the modern world; but [also] . . . distinct from either the people of Greece or Rome, or of any State we are acquainted with among the antients." The aristocratic features of the British constitution "can not possibly be introduced into our System," because "we neither have nor can have the members to compose it." Pinckney believed that America had "a greater equality, than is to be found among the people of any other country" and that equality would continue because the new nation "possess[ed] immense tracts of uncultivated lands," which would ensure "there will be few poor, and few dependent."[265]

Madison disagreed with Pinckney's projection. "In all civilized Countries the people fall into different classes having a real or supposed difference of interest. There will be creditors & debtors," he said, among other groups. "There will be particularly the distinction of rich & poor." Pinckney said America would not face the problem of rich and poor for "centuries." John Adams, author of *A Defence of the Constitutions,* thought America had to address the threat of divisions into rich and poor immediately. Madison's position was in the middle. "An increase in population will of necessity increase the proportion of those who will labor under all the hardships of life, & secretly sigh for a more equal distribution of its blessings," Madison said. "These may in time outnumber those who are placed above the feelings of indigence. . . . No agrarian attempts have yet been made in this Country, but symptoms, of a leveling spirit . . . have sufficiently appeared in a certain quarter to give notice of the future danger."[266] Madison's primary fear was with populist agitation, of the sort that Daniel Shays's rebellion represented, and he realized this "danger" was linked to whether the "equal distribution of blessings" continued and to the future conditions under which America's growing population would labor.

But what would guarantee the equal distribution of blessings? Jefferson advocated for ending primogeniture and the entail. There was the Northwest Ordinance of 1787 and the possibility of settlers continuing to expand westward. Madison would later fight Hamilton in the 1790s to arrest the acceleration of commerce and manufacturing in the new republic, in vain hope that America would never progress to the next stage of development after agriculture.[267] None of these policies, nor any similar policy, however, made it into Madison's Constitution or into the theory of *Federalist* No. 10. Harrington had noted that agrarian laws were essential to the preservation of an equal commonwealth. John Adams supported a class warfare constitution because he feared that economic inequality would inevitably emerge. Madison's constitutional theory—with its checks and balances, varieties of interests, and extended republic—simply trusted to the persistence of America's egalitarian economic conditions.[268]

By the time of the Virginia ratifying convention in 1788, Madison estimated America had twenty-five years before the population density throughout the country would match that of the eastern states.[269] Only then would the risk of inequality become real for the Republic. With the growth of the nation westward over the next few decades, Madison revised his estimates. By 1821, he thought there was "precious advantage . . . in the actual distribution of property" in America. Americans remained "among the happiest contrasts in their situation to that of the old world. . . . There may be at present, a Majority of the Nation, who are even freeholders, or the heirs, or aspirants to Freeholds." The time was not "very near" when the "Majority shall be without landed or other equivalent property."[270]

Less than a decade later, in 1829, Madison compared the availability of land with his estimates for the rate of population growth. He now predicted that by 1930 the population would be so concentrated that the people would be "necessarily reduced by a competition for employment to wages which afford them the bare necessities of life." Over time, the "proportion being without property" would increase. When it did, Madison concluded, "the institutions and laws of the Country must be adapted, and it will require for the task all the wisdom of the wisest patriots."[271]

PART II

A BRIEF HISTORY OF THE
MIDDLE-CLASS CONSTITUTION

On September 22, 1932, 100,000 people lined the streets of San Francisco, hoping to catch a glimpse of Franklin Delano Roosevelt.[1] The New York governor was in the midst of his campaign for president, and on the next day he was set to give two major speeches. At the Civic Auditorium on the evening of the twenty-third, Roosevelt outlined the stark differences between the Republican and the Democratic tickets to a crowd of 16,000 and rallied the crowd with his pledge to repeal Prohibition.[2] But the speech that was more revealing, more significant, actually took place earlier that Friday.

Speaking to a crowd of two thousand businessmen at the Commonwealth Club, Roosevelt outlined what was probably the best expression of the philosophy behind the New Deal. "The issue of government," he said, "has always been whether individual men and women will have to serve some system of government and economics, or whether a system of government and economics exists to serve individual men and women." He reminded the audience how easy it is to forget that people fought to "win the privilege of government" and that a strong government was in fact a "haven of refuge to the individual" from the "exploitation and cruelty" of local power brokers. Without government, petty barons would bring war and oppression to ordinary people.

Telling a brief history of the United States, Roosevelt noted that fears of petty tyrants were far less salient at the birth of the American nation. Thomas Jefferson, Roosevelt said, recognized that ours was a society with "no paupers." The rich were "few and of moderate wealth." And the "laboring class" owned property and were paid appropriately enough that they could "labor moderately and raise their families." The early republic was one characterized by relative economic equality and by economic opportunity. Jefferson's vision dominated throughout much of the nineteenth century, Roosevelt argued, in large part because of the vast western frontier, with land available to anyone willing to take a covered wagon to the "untilled prairies." So great was the promise of America that individual economic opportunity was possible not just for our own people but also for "the distressed of the world" who came in droves from Europe.

The industrial era changed that. Coupled with the closing of the frontier, the rise of the corporation threatened the "economic freedom of individuals to earn a living." Small-business men saw opportunities narrowing, "preempted altogether by the great corporations." America could now only provide "a drab living for our own people," let alone welcome immigrants from abroad. With economic life dominated by only around six hundred corporations, Roosevelt warned the audience, "we are steering a steady course toward economic oligarchy."

The answer, Roosevelt announced, was the "development of an economic declaration of rights." As a country, we did not deny the role of government in the eighteenth century, because we knew it could oppress individuals, nor should we now eliminate corporations because they too threaten freedom. Rather, "the common task of statesman and businessman" was the creation of "an economic constitutional order."[3]

An economic constitutional order.

When Roosevelt spoke in 1932 he believed that the economic challenges of his time—the Great Depression, financial panics, the political power of the wealthy—were tied up in the "constitutional order." Today, that idea seems shocking. Can we really imagine President Barack Obama—or any political leader—talking about the 2008 financial collapse, underwater homeowners, and Dodd-Frank financial reforms as a *constitutional* issue? Can we imagine political leaders arguing that the passage of the Affordable Care Act was necessary to fulfill a constitutional principle, in the way that Roosevelt thought making a "drab living" had constitutional implications?

As surprising as it might seem, for most of our history there was a robust tradition of thinking along precisely these lines. Americans saw economic challenges, and especially rising economic inequality and pressure on the middle class, as a threat to the Republic—as a problem of constitutional significance. From the very start, they were vigilant about the economic threat to their constitutional experiment. They vigorously debated economic policy issues, the most famous of which was the creation of a national bank, a topic that was central to policy debates from the 1790s to the 1830s. But during the mid-nineteenth century, it was the vastness of North America that provided peace of mind; Americans could move west, preserving the equality necessary for a republic. At the same time, however, a different tradition emerged in the South. The planter aristocracy rejected virtually every aspect of the American political tradition, and it resurrected class warfare constitutional theory and even feudalism in order to preserve slavery. With the defeat of the Confederacy, Reconstruction Republicans tried—but ultimately failed—to bring Harrington's equal commonwealth to the freedmen of the South. By the end of the nineteenth century, a transportation revolution, industrialization, the rise of corporations and trusts, and urbanization had transformed the political economy of the Republic. Economic power grew increasingly concentrated in the hands of the few, and political power followed. Activists, thinkers, workers, and farmers tried to adapt the agrarian republic of the founding to the industrial age, only to fall victim to Gilded Age plutocrats.

In the early decades of the twentieth century, the people struck back. Progressive reformers passed new legislation and constitutional amendments to rebalance both the economic and the political systems. They came up with some of the most creative, innovative arrangements to address the concentration of economic and political power. During the Great Depression, Franklin Roosevelt's New Deal experimented with many of these models, but with World War II and the looming threat of fascism the battle between the plutocrats and the people turned into a war between democracy and dictatorship. After the war, America entered a thirty-year period of economic growth and relative economic equality. Constitutional debates over economic inequality subsided as a consensus emerged on economic policy and constitutional law related to economic regulation. But the consensus was short-lived. With the economic shocks of the 1970s, the postwar system began to fall apart, once again risking the viability of America's middle-class constitution.

CHAPTER THREE

The Emergence of the Plutocracy

Daniel Webster was already one of the great orators of the age when, in 1820, he spoke at the two hundredth anniversary of the Pilgrims' landing at Plymouth Rock. Among the many topics covered in Webster's seventy-five-page speech was an assessment of America's unique constitutional system.[4] "[T]he nature of government," Webster said, "must essentially depend on the manner in which property is holden and distributed."[5] "The freest government . . . would not be long acceptable, if the tendency of the laws were to create a rapid accumulation of property in few hands, and to render the great mass of the population dependent and pennyless." In that situation, either the people would revolt and "break in upon the rights of property," or "[t]he holders of estates would be obliged . . . to restrain the right of suffrage."[6] In essence, the "natural influence" of inequality in property would lead either to "despotism" or to "unrestrained popular violence."[7] The lesson, Webster told his audience that December, was "to found government on property; and to establish such distribution of property . . . as to the interest of the great majority of society."[8]

Looking two centuries back to the first inhabitants of Massachusetts, Webster saw the roots of the American republic. "Our ancestors began their system of government here under a condition of comparative equality in regard to wealth, and their early laws were of a nature to favor and continue this equality."[9] The Pilgrims came to a new country with "no lands yielding rents, and no tenants rendering service. . . . They were themselves . . . nearly on a general level, in respect to property." This fact and the subsequent division of lands among themselves *"fixed the future frame and form of their government.* The character of their political institutions was determined by the fundamental laws respecting property."[10] The result of this "great subdivision of the soil" was "a great equality of condition." Citing Harrington, Webster said this was the "true basis most certainly of a popular government."[11] So important was this link that Webster claimed a government "like ours" could not exist if property was distributed "according to the principles of the feudal system; nor, on the other hand, could the feudal Constitution possibly exist with us."[12] "With property divided, as we have it, no other government than that of a republic could be maintained, even were we foolish enough to desire it."[13]

Webster told his audience that the new republic had little to fear from the future. "[A] great revolution, in regard to property, must take place before our governments can be moved from their republican basis." In America, the "people possess the property, more emphatically than could ever be said of the people of any other country," and the American people would never allow a government that undermined this equality.[14]

In the early nineteenth century, many perceptive commentators, like Webster, held fast to the idea that America was still the most equal commonwealth the world had ever known and that its equality was the key to its constitutional system. A decade after Webster's oration at Plymouth, in the midst of the second bank war and tumultuous Jacksonian populism, commentators continued to embrace equality as a precondition for American government. Supreme Court justice Joseph Story, for example, wrote in his 1833 *Commentaries on the Constitution* that there was an "intimate connexion" between the "general equality of the apportionment of property among the mass of a nation, and the popular form of government." The general equality in property meant that a government would have "the substance of a republic," and "[o]ur revolutionary statesmen were not insensible to this silent but potent influence."[15]

The most prescient and insightful observer, however, was the French aristocrat Alexis de Tocqueville, who journeyed through Jacksonian America and explained the fledgling nation—its politics, culture, social norms—to the European world. Tocqueville's *Democracy in America* has been called "the best book ever written on democracy, and the best book ever written on America."[16] In the very first paragraph, Tocqueville declares that the most important fact about America is its remarkable "equality of conditions."[17] Not equality of opportunity, which commentators and political figures celebrate today, but "equality of conditions," an "almost perfect equality in fortunes."[18] In America, Tocqueville said, you will not find "either commoners or nobles."[19] The people in America were "more equal in their fortunes . . . than [people] are in any country in the world and than they have been in any century of which history keeps a memory."[20]

The political significance of America's economic equality was not lost on Tocqueville. "When the rich govern alone, the interest of the poor is always in peril; and when the poor make the law, that of the rich run great risks," Tocqueville noted. "What therefore is the advantage of democracy? The real advantage of democracy is not, as has been said, to favor the prosperity of all, but only to serve the well-being of the greatest number."[21] In a democracy, majorities would rule, and in an equal commonwealth, like America, the culture and morality of democracy would be moderate—and therefore superior to a system with rich and poor facing off against each other. Equality of conditions meant a "government of the middle classes," which would be the "most economical" in its taxation and spending.[22] The middle class would seek material well-being but also understand that they "constantly change place," such that no person is fixed into a single class for perpetuity.[23] With a dominant middle class, there would be fewer revolutions because the members of the middle class "are naturally enemies of violent movements."[24] Indeed, what made America so extraordinary is that it did not have to go through the process of change that took place in France or England—a shift from feudalism to commerce, and thus from aristocracy to more democratic government.[25] "The great advantage of the Americans is to have arrived at democracy without having to suffer democratic revolutions, and to be born equal instead of becoming so."[26]

Like Webster, Tocqueville thought that American equality of conditions was preserved most fundamentally by property laws, and he also emphasized the importance of available land to the west and the egalitarian habits and culture of the American people.[27] But unlike Webster, Tocqueville saw a looming threat to the American republic. In a chapter titled "How Aristocracy Could Issue from Industry," Tocqueville described how industrial change might undermine the Republic.[28] "As the principle of the division of labor is more completely applied" and workers take on narrower, routinized roles in factories, "the worker becomes weaker, more limited, and more dependent." Over time, as employers and employees become less and less similar, the division between them would grow. The consequences were self-evident. "What is this if not aristocracy?" Tocqueville asked.[29]

Paradoxically, it was democracy itself that created the potential for the emergence of an aristocracy in America. In an equal republic, the middle class believes it can strive for something better; members of the middle class are not locked into the fixed economic status of patrician and plebeian, noble and peasant. This possibility—this hope for improvement—creates a vibrant spirit of commerce and industry. But the resulting flourishing of industry, with the inevitable division of employer and employee, owner and worker, threatens to undermine the very democracy that brought it into existence.[30] Tocqueville was optimistic that America would not fall prey to an aristocracy, but he advised "the friends of democracy" to be wary of the consequences of manufacturing. "[F]or if ever permanent inequality of conditions and aristocracy are introduced anew into the world, one can predict that they will enter by this door."[31]

The course of the nineteenth century saw Tocqueville's predictions come true. The first generations of Americans feared the rise of an aristocracy, but they lived in an era before industrialization. The concentration of wealth and power was less significant, except in the South, where the planter aristocracy began to revive class warfare constitutions to justify slavery. By the mid-nineteenth century, inequality was rising. With the failure of Reconstruction Republicans to establish a middle-class constitution that worked for freedmen in the South, the country's attention turned to industrialization and the rise of corporations. Farmers, workers, and thinkers all focused on how to adapt the Republic to the challenges of modernity, but with little success. What emerged from the Gilded Age was a plutocracy—a government in which the levers of power were pulled by the wealthy.

THE BANK WARS

Even as the ink on the Constitution was drying, the world that the founders had inherited was changing rapidly. Commerce had already been expanding prior to the Revolutionary War, creating a growing middle class.[32] In the decades after the Constitution was ratified, the flow of commerce gained in volume. Exports, including goods passing through the new republic, grew from $20.2 million to $108.3 million between 1790 and 1807. Exports of American-made goods more than doubled from $19.9 million to $48.7 million. Related industries boomed: American shipbuilders now captured 92 percent of American trade, up from 59 percent.[33] The commercial centers of the republic saw growing populations. Philadelphia was up by 114 percent; Boston, 84 percent; Baltimore, 156 percent; New York, 191 percent.[34]

With the growing importance of commerce, the founders almost immediately descended into clashes over economic issues, with the Constitution acting as the battlefield. In 1791, Alexander Hamilton, the secretary of the Treasury, proposed a plan for the creation of a national bank, to create greater monetary stability and improve economic growth. Madison, Jefferson, and their allies opposed the bank, arguing that Congress did not have the requisite constitutional authority. Article I of the Constitution granted Congress a set of express powers, and chartering a national bank was not one of them. As a matter of policy, they argued that the national bank would disproportionately benefit commercial and wealthy interests. John Taylor of Caroline captured the sentiments of the bank's opponents. The bank proposal was evidence that there were still "design[s] for erecting aristocracy and monarchy" in America. The bank would "make the rich, richer, and the poor, poorer" by giving "public property to private persons." Echoing Harrington, Taylor declared that "[m]oney in a state of civilization is power" and "[a] democratic republic is endangered by an immense disproportion in wealth."[35]

Hamilton believed the Constitution gave Congress the power to take any action "necessary and proper" to implement the powers granted by Article I. As a policy matter, he was less concerned with the Jeffersonians' fear of aristocracy. He embraced America's commercial future, arguing that the new government had to be able to facilitate economic growth and prevent monetary instability. Hamilton won the immediate debate, and President Washington signed the bank into law, with a twenty-year charter.

When the national bank's charter expired in 1811, Madison— now president—opposed reauthorizing the bank. It was a mistake he would soon regret. During the War of 1812, monetary instability crippled the infant republic's economy and the war effort. Madison, who had once so fiercely argued against the national bank, reversed course, and he approved chartering a second national bank in 1816, the final year of his presidency. Support for the bank even came from some more surprising corners. John C. Calhoun, who would become most famous in the decades to follow as an opponent of national government power, argued for the bank. "No man," he said, "could possibly have foreseen the course of these institutions." There had been a "revolution in the currency of the country," and without a national bank the power to regulate currency, undoubtedly one granted to Congress, would be in the hands of banking institutions.[36] Three years later, the Supreme Court's landmark decision *McCulloch v. Maryland* established the constitutionality of the national bank and in the process interpreted the "necessary and proper" clause as giving Congress broad authority to act to regulate the economy, pursuant to its Article I powers.[37] Hamilton's vision of a government that had the power to shape, channel, and guide the economy had won an important victory.

Over the next decades, America would experience what historian Charles Sellers called "the market revolution."[38] Commerce, trade, and interdependence increased. In 1819, Americans experienced a major economic crisis, caused not by war but by commercial speculation and global economic ties. Americans were also becoming proto-industrialists. A sleepy town in Massachusetts with a population of two hundred in 1822 became the mighty factory city of Lowell, with a population of seven thousand in 1830.[39] The cotton industry had only 10,000 wage workers in 1810; by 1860, that number was up to 122,000.[40] This growth, as we shall see, was built on slavery and a set of political theories designed to justify the vicious institution.

With these changes also came the first strains on the economic theory undergirding the Constitution. In 1829, the top 1 percent held 29 percent of the wealth in New York City.[41] Workingmen's associations sprang up, and inequality became a question of public debate. Advocates penned tracts like Langton Byllesby's *Sources and Effects of Unequal Wealth* and Thomas Skidmore's emphatic *The Rights of Man to Property!*[42] In the fall of 1830, Samuel Clesson Allen shocked western Massachusetts by declaring, "All wealth is the product of labor and belongs of right to him who produces it." To "renovate society," he said, "you must begin with its economical relations." There were now a class of producers and a class of non-producers who gained wealth through currency, money, and commerce, even though they "produced none of the objects of wealth."[43] The artisanal middle class was being squeezed by declining incomes.[44] Meanwhile, the non-producers were "a new sort of aristocracy, of a more uncompromising character than the feudal, or any landed aristocracy, ever can be." Allen feared that government was becoming little more than "the combinations of the rich and powerful to increase their riches and extend their power."[45]

With the second national bank's charter set to expire in 1836, the first bank war replayed itself in the early 1830s. Jacksonian Democrats decried the bank as stealing gold and silver from the hardworking people in the South and West. Senator Thomas Hart Benton thus condemned the eastern capitalists who used the bank to "gorge to repletion, then vomit their load into the vast receptacles of the Northeast, and gorge again."[46] Commentator David Henshaw praised Jackson's opposition to the bank as preserving the republican character of America. The country had a "vindictive hatred of a MONIED OLIGARCHY," and Jackson would gain fame when he "exterminate[ed] this aristocratic monster—this bank hydra—and rear[ed] upon its ruins a people's bank, an institution of which the people can reap the profits."[47] Others agreed that the bank was a form of monopoly that would result in "the establishment of a *monied Aristocracy*" because "a few individuals reap the greater part of the profit and direct its operation."[48] Congressman John Bell of Tennessee captured the Harringtonian stakes of the bank war, arguing that "the accumulation of great wealth in the hands of individual citizens" undermines the "equality of rank and influence" that is "the fundamental principle upon which [our Government] is erected."[49] Defenders of the bank, like Daniel Webster, held that the bank was a necessary part of maintaining economic stability. Webster even argued that the end of the national bank would harm the lower classes far more than the wealthy. "A disorderly currency . . . ," he said, "wars against industry, frugality, and economy; and it fosters the evil spirits of extravagance and speculation."[50] The only answer was to grant the government power—through the bank—to preserve monetary stability.

When Congress ultimately reauthorized the bank, President Andrew Jackson vetoed the bill. Rejecting Chief Justice John Marshall's decision in *McCulloch,* he argued that the Court's views did not bind the president and that he believed the bank was unconstitutional. His opposition to the bank extended to both its economic consequences and its political effects. The bank's stock was held by some foreigners and "a few hundred of our own citizens, chiefly of the richest class," and because the bank was a monopoly, its financial benefits would accrue only to these rich few. The political consequences were just as stark. The bank meant "a concentration of power in the hands of a few men irresponsible to the people." These men would "put forth their strength to influence elections or control the affairs of the nation." The problem was that "the rich and powerful too often bend the acts of government to their selfish purposes." Jackson conceded there would always be some "[d]istinctions in society," but the laws should never "undertake to add to these natural and just advantages artificial distinctions," particularly if they "make the rich richer and the potent more powerful." "Every man is equally entitled to protection by law," Jackson said. "[W]e can at least take a stand against all new grants of monopolies and exclusive privileges, against any prostitution of our Government to the advancement of the few at the expense of the many."[51] Congress censured Jackson after his veto of the bank, but the bank's charter expired anyway.

The market revolution and the second bank war also reshaped the American political system by leading to the creation of America's first major political party. The founders had rejected political parties, seeing them as "factions" rather than as groups advocating for the common good. The critical figure in the creation of Andrew Jackson's Democratic Party was future president Martin Van Buren. In imagining a party of the people, Van Buren looked back to English precedent. With the rise of finance in London in the early eighteenth century, Robert Walpole used patronage to reshape the balance of power in English politics, breaking the checks and balances in the system.[52] Opponents of Walpole, like Viscount Bolingbroke, argued that a "country" party needed to play the role of mobilized opposition against the corrupt, self-interested "court" of professional politicians.[53] Bolingbroke's party was paradoxically an *antiparty*, a party that identified with the nation and the common good, against the corruptions of the Walpole government. Van Buren analogized his emerging Democratic Party explicitly to Bolingbroke's experience fighting "the money power" in England a century earlier.[54] For Van Buren, the Democratic Party would be an extra-governmental vehicle that could operate across geography, time, branches of government, and candidates, to ensure the rule of the people rather than the elites. As Frederick Grimke, writing in 1848, explained, "[P]arties take the place of the old system of balances and checks. The latter balance the government only, the former balance society itself."[55]

The rise of the party system was tied in large part to the fear of an emerging commercial aristocracy and to opposition to the Bank of the United States.[56] In balancing society, the new Democratic Party would counteract the power of elites. It would, in Van Buren's words, fight "the selfish and contracted rule of a judicial oligarchy, which, sympathizing in feeling and acting in concert with the money power, would assuredly subvert the best features of a political system that needs only to be honestly administered."[57] Jacksonian partisans even described themselves as "the Democracy," to show their commitment to replacing elite rule with the rule of the people at large.[58]

The Democracy's economic principles were rooted in three separate intellectual traditions.[59] The first was the Jeffersonian tradition, which saw America as a land of smallholding yeomen farmers and thought government action would likely support the interests of the aristocracy and wealthy. The second was the antimonopoly tradition that had emerged with the rise of the corporation. In the early nineteenth century, government granted charters for the establishment of corporations. Members of the Democracy believed these charters were special privileges that amounted to monopolies. Monopolies were incompatible with republican government because they both concentrated power in private hands and favored an aristocratic distribution of wealth.[60] The Democratic commentator William Leggett gained prominence for adapting Adam Smith's theory of competition to the corporation: "If we analyze the nature and essence of free governments, we shall find that they are more or less free in proportion to the absence of *monopolies*."[61] Democrats thus supported breaking special privileges and ending corporate monopolies. "Every corporate grant is directly in the teeth of the doctrine of equal rights," said Theodore Sedgwick. Equal rights eventually meant that *anyone* should be able to start a corporation.[62]

The final element of the Democracy's political economy, especially among the most committed members, was support for labor. Drawing on the thinking of the workingmen's associations that emerged in the 1820s, Democrats (and in particular a group of New York Democrats called the Locofocos) emphasized the importance of strengthening and supporting workers.[63] In a particularly notable instance, Congressman Ely Moore defended labor in a rousing speech, before collapsing on the House floor in the midst of his remarks. In the speech, which was reprinted four times within two months, he declared that "there is much greater danger that capital will unjustly appropriate to itself the avails of labor, than that labor will unlawfully seize on capital." Unions, he said, were simply "counterpoises against capital, whenever it shall attempt to exert an unlawful, or undue influence."[64] Orestes Brownson described the Locofocos as Jeffersonian Democrats, "who having realized political equality, passed through one phase of the revolution, now passes on to another, and attempts the realization of social equality, so that the actual condition of men in society shall be in harmony with their acknowledged rights as citizens."[65] The way to ensure social equality, to guarantee that labor is fairly compensated, said Martin Van Buren, was to prevent all the evils that operate against working people: "partial legislation, monopolies, congregated wealth, and interested combinations."[66]

Of course, the great irony of the Jacksonians' economic agenda is that it backfired. The Jacksonians hoped to preserve the political economy of an agrarian society, even as that society was increasingly disappearing. A commercial society requires a banking and monetary system, but the Jacksonians opposed an organized monetary system. After the second bank war, state banks started issuing notes without any federal oversight, leading to speculative bubbles all across the country. The resulting panic of 1837 led to one of the worst depressions in American history. "In abolishing one efficient central banking system," the historian Robert Remini concludes in his study on the bank war, "Jackson can be faulted for not substituting another: one better controlled but one able to provide the country with adequate currency and credit."[67] The Jacksonian position on corporations suffered a similar fate. In setting the stage for laws allowing anyone to create a corporation, Jacksonians unleashed *more* corporations into the economy, eventually leading to an even greater concentration of wealth and power than was wrought by the market revolution. As Arthur Schlesinger Jr. once observed, the Jacksonian economic policy unwittingly "promoted the very ends it was intended to defeat."[68]

THE SLAVOCRACY'S CONSTITUTION

The market revolution did not take place only in northern factory towns. Industrial growth was inextricably tied to the production of cotton and therefore to slavery in the South. After the invention of the cotton gin, production of the white gold of the South skyrocketed. In 1796, cotton amounted to 2.2 percent of U.S. exports; by 1820, the commodity accounted for 32 percent of exports.[69] By 1831, nearly 50 percent of global cotton was produced in the United States, and more than 70 percent of British cotton imports came from America.[70] Cotton production in the United States increased tenfold between 1820 and 1860.[71] For the South's cotton empire to continue expanding, the planter aristocracy needed more and more slave labor: the factories in Lowell, Massachusetts, alone required 100,000 days' worth of slave laborers' cotton production each year.[72] Slavery was critical to the economic success of the South, the North, and indeed much of the industrializing world.

With the growth of slavery and the emergence of a more aggressive abolitionist movement in the North, southern intellectuals increasingly worked to develop political theories that could justify and defend slavery. Among the pro-slavery spokesmen and theorists, none was better known or respected than John C. Calhoun. For forty years, the South Carolinian was one of the leading figures in American public life, serving as a member of the House of Representatives during James Madison's administration; secretary of war for James Monroe; vice president under both John Quincy Adams and Andrew Jackson; secretary of state under John Tyler and James K. Polk; and senator from South Carolina for sixteen years. As a political thinker, Calhoun is best known for his theory of the concurrent majority, which justified a state's right to nullify federal law. But what is perhaps most surprising is that Calhoun's political theory—designed to protect slavery—was built on the foundation of class warfare constitutional theory.[73]

The basics of the South Carolina Doctrine were not complicated. In all societies, the "most difficult work of man" was addressing "the conflict of opposing interests."[74] Unlike Madison, who theorized that interests would be so fragmented that they would not coalesce around two parties, Calhoun saw the emergence not just of the party system but also of increasing sectional differences between North and South. Madisonian pluralism was unlikely because "a combination will be formed between those whose interests are most alike," and the "community will be divided into two great parties."[75] Locked in a contest for permanent control, each party—in the American case, the northern and southern states—will seek to dominate the other, leading ultimately to conflict.[76] The answer was to "mak[e] it impossible for any one interest or combination of interests or class, or order, or portion of the community, to obtain exclusive control."[77] Veto, interposition, nullification, check, or balance of power—the point was the same. Each faction had to have a "negative power—the power of preventing or arresting the action of the government."[78] Only when both factions agreed would there be a "concurrent majority" and therefore a just administration of government. This, Calhoun thought, was the fundamental principle not only of the American Constitution but of all constitutional governments.[79]

Calhoun could make such a bold claim of constitutional universality because he acknowledged that the theory was nothing more than a revival of the class warfare constitutional tradition. "Where the diversity of interests exists in separate and distinct classes of the community, as is the case in England, and was formerly the case in Sparta, Rome, and most of the free States of antiquity," Calhoun reasoned, "the rational constitutional provision is, that each should be represented in the government, as a separate estate, with a distinct voice, and a negative on the acts of its co-estates, in order to check their encroachments."[80] Calhoun himself thought the Roman tribunate was the best model for a constitutional veto, and he interpreted Roman history in line with Polybius's optimistic account two millennia earlier. Rome was divided into patricians and plebeians, and the plebeians, fed up after years of oppression, "in a word, seceded." The creation of the tribunate, with its power to veto policy, was an inducement to reunification. This was "the very power," Calhoun said, "which I contend is necessary to protect the rights of the States, but which is now represented as necessarily leading to disunion."[81] Far from leading to disunion, the tribunate, Calhoun argued, "proved to be the bond of concord and harmony" in Rome, reducing conflict, harmonizing interests, and leading to "devotion to country in the place of devotion to particular orders."[82] Of course, Calhoun's American tribunate would not be organized along economic class lines. "Happily for us, we have no artificial and separate classes of society." Rather, the distinctions between Americans "are almost exclusively geographical, resulting mainly from difference of climate, soil, situation, industry, and production."[83]

At first, Calhoun's preoccupation seemed to be the tariff and other economic policies. By the early 1830s, the southern states opposed high tariffs, and South Carolina, by state convention, exercised the very power Calhoun would theorize, refusing to accept the tariff. The "nullification crisis" led to some of Calhoun's most eloquent statements in the Senate, including a response to the Jackson administration's "Force Bill," which would have allowed the federal government to enforce the tariff against South Carolina's will.[84] The southern agricultural system, Calhoun said, relied on an "immense amount of capital and labor" to produce "cotton, rice, and tobacco" for export to the "general market of the world."[85] But in his *Discourse on Government,* Calhoun tips his hand to show that his real concern is preserving slavery. Two hundred pages into his essay on American constitutional structure and history, he admits that the problem is *not* protective tariffs or other economic policies like the Bank of the United States or extensive spending on internal improvements. In all of these cases, policies can be reversed simply through ordinary elections. The Democratic Party was fighting to do just that, and its victory would settle these policy disagreements.[86]

The real problem was that ordinary politics could not resolve the emerging conflict over slavery. The coming crisis, Calhoun thought, had its first hints as early as the Northwest Ordinance of 1787, which banned slavery in the territories between the Ohio and Mississippi Rivers.[87] Once Missouri was admitted to the Union in 1821 and slavery prohibited in the northern territories, it became clear that the northern, non-slave states would gain political power over time. Combine that with the growing belief in the North that "slavery was a sin," and the southern system was under significant threat.[88] If slavery was excluded from the southern and western territories, the non-slave states would gain "an overwhelming preponderance in the government." They would then attempt to "destroy[] the existing relations between the races in the southern section."[89] These changes were irreversible. North and South were becoming two different nations, "with a hatred more deadly than one hostile nation ever entertained towards another." The South would not give up slavery, which meant, starkly: "Abolition and Union cannot co-exist."[90]

But maybe there was another option, something to prevent "drenching the country in blood."[91] Maybe there could be "a change which shall so modify the constitution, as to give to the weaker section, in some form or another, a negative on the action of the government."[92] So it was that John C. Calhoun, the defender of liberty and union, who twice served as vice president of the United States, proposed not just nullification but constitutional revolution. The presidency had to be split into two, Calhoun argued. One president from the North, one from the South. Each would have to agree before any law could take effect. "Nothing short of this" would protect the South, and nothing less than this could "restore harmony and tranquility to the Union."[93]

In attempting to preserve slavery, Calhoun had now mired himself in contradictions and heresies. Somehow, according to Calhoun's theory, faction led to unity; strife led to tranquillity; struggle led to harmony. Calhoun himself conceded that the tribunate was unable to address the "increase of wealth" in Rome.[94] And yet he could not see that his archetype of a class warfare constitution failed to accomplish the one thing it was designed to do. How would giving a veto to two sides with "conflicting and hostile interests"—sides with a deadly "hatred" for the other—how could that possibly lead to a level of concord that would "bind the whole in mutual affection" and "brotherhood"?[95] Why would "faction, strife, and struggle for party ascendency" yield to "patriotism, nationality, harmony, and a struggle only for supremacy in promoting the common good"?[96] Calhoun would nullify the tariff clause, one of the critical compromises of 1787. He would revise the structure of American government to feature two presidencies. He would argue that America had to return to the tradition of class warfare constitutions. All to defend slavery. And what of the slaves? Calhoun posited that strife between two groups was the most difficult challenge for constitutional theory, and the answer was for each group to have a stake in government and a veto over policy. So why didn't the theory of nullification, class warfare, concurrent majorities, and the veto apply to *blacks and whites* in the South?

Pro-slavery thinkers like Calhoun all started with a variety of arguments. Slavery was in the Bible. It was a fact in the ancient world. It was common in Africa. American slave conditions were better than conditions in Africa. Slaves were humanely treated. Slaves lived better than English industrial workers. Northern prosperity depended on slavery. Emancipation would lead to a race war.[97] But every time they attempted to develop a coherent political theory that justified slavery, they ended up either wallowing in contradictions, like Calhoun, or repudiating virtually every aspect of the American constitutional tradition.

There was Abel Upshur, who served as secretary of state under John Tyler. "There are no original principles in Government at all," Upshur said.[98] As a result, nothing was mandatory. People could choose whatever principles they wanted. Upshur chose property and argued to the Virginia Constitutional Convention of 1829–30 that the state constitution should give greater power to the owners of land and slaves. William Harper of South Carolina—state representative, judge, U.S. senator—chose to repudiate egalitarianism. Man was born as a baby, and in that state no man is free or equal. Rather, all men are totally dependent on others and controlled by others. Slavery was therefore not abnormal; it was simply another kind of patriarchy. Harper was willing to admit that slavery was an evil, but "[t]o say that there is evil in any institution is only to say that it is human." There was simply no reason to think that a regime with slavery was any worse than a different regime, which would have a different bundle of evils.[99] William Smith, who served twenty years as president of Randolph-Macon College, took a similar position. He defined slavery as any subjection to the control of another. With this definition, *any* government involved slavery. The question was only what balance between freedom and slavery existed in any particular society.[100] It was just a matter of degree.

Henry Hughes was one of the most eccentric pro-slavery thinkers. Hughes thought individuals had no rights except those granted to them by the state. Society was divided into a variety of fields—politics, economics, hygiene, ethics, religion, philosophy, aesthetics—and each field needed an administrative structure. Hughes's resulting totalitarian welfare state would regulate insurance markets, inspect products, adjudicate wages, interest rates, rents, and prices, set food and drug standards, and even govern the structure and design of homes. But the key was that Hughes's state would enforce hygiene. "[H]ygienic progress forbids ethnical regress." "Hybridism is heinous. Impurity of races is against the law of nature. Mulattoes are monsters."[101] Forward thinking in the worst possible way, Hughes destroyed individualism to enforce segregation.

But the most idiosyncratic, and perhaps the most serious, pro-slavery thinker was George Fitzhugh. "We do not agree with the authors of the Declaration of Independence," Fitzhugh wrote, "that governments 'derive their just powers from the consent of the governed.'" The American revolutionaries did not ask for the consent of "[t]he women, the children, the negroes," or the "non-property holders." For these groups, "the new governments were self-elected despotisms, and the governing class self-elected despots. Those governments originated in force, and have been continued by force."[102] The revolutionaries might have *claimed* they acted for freedom, but "[a]ll governments must originate in force, and be continued by force." Freedom, consent, and individualism were little more than rhetoric. Jefferson's muse, John Locke, was nothing more than "a presumptuous charlatan."[103]

Having rejected the Declaration of Independence, the American Revolution, Locke, the social contract, consent, and individualism, Fitzhugh built a vision of government on the foundations of feudal force rather than free society. Free society's capitalistic economic regime was devoid of morality or mutual care, turning wage laborers into "slaves without masters." Free societies were defined by the ethic of every man for himself; it was only in slave societies that "it is natural for men to love one another."[104] Christian morality characterized slave societies; competition, antagonism, and selfishness defined free societies. Indeed, Fitzhugh claimed, there was "no pauperism in Europe till feudal slavery was abolished."[105] Free society and capitalism brought with it "famine."[106] Slavery was not an aberration, a blight on the American system, but instead a central feature of government anywhere—a natural part of organizing society along the feudal principles of force. The only way to get beyond the ills of competition and selfishness was for "free society sternly to recognize slavery as right in principle, and necessary in practice . . . to the very existence of government, of property, of religion, and of social existence."[107]

Fitzhugh's critique of capitalism was thoroughgoing but hardly unique. As early as 1837, Calhoun had framed slavery as an alternative to the ills of capitalism. In any wealthy and civilized society, the South Carolinian said, there would be "a conflict between capital and labor." "The condition of society in the South"—that is, slavery—is what would keep the South free of the "disorders and dangers result-ing from this conflict."[108] But it was Fitzhugh who took this argument to its logical conclusion. So strongly did Fitzhugh believe slavery had to be defensible in principle that he—alone among the southern pro-slavery thinkers—also endorsed *white* slavery.[109] The social system had to "formally recognize[] inequality, the necessity of authoritar-ian order and human interdependence."[110] The answer—the only path for government—was slavery.

Seeking to justify the vicious institution, these southern thinkers repudiated virtually every aspect of the American tradition: individu-alism, personal rights, the social contract, egalitarianism.[111] Fitzhugh resurrected feudalism. Hughes created a totalitarian Jim Crow state. Calhoun revived class warfare constitutions. Every American princi-ple collapsed in the search for a political philosophy that could justify slavery.

By the 1850s, northerners and southerners had developed diver-gent visions for the expanding capitalistic economy. James Henry Hammond best explained the southern approach. The son of a schoolmaster, Hammond built a plantation empire before becoming governor of South Carolina in the 1840s. At one point, his wife left him after she discovered his affair with a mother-daughter pair of his slaves (he admitted that he might be the father of children with each of them).[112] Entering the Senate in 1857, Hammond rocketed to national prominence with a speech he delivered in 1858. "In all social systems," Hammond declared, "there must be a class to do the menial duties, to perform the drudgery of life." This class was like the bottommost foundation of a building; it was "the very mud-sill of society and of political government." Without this lower class, there could be no "progress, civilization, or refinement." The South, Ham-mond said, was lucky to have found "[a] race inferior to her own. . . . We use them for our purpose, and call them slaves."[113] The way to continue the booming economic growth associated with cotton while also preserving "political government" for whites was to sup-port slavery. Pushing to expand slavery, some prominent southern officials worked to build up the U.S. military, contemplating expan-sion into Latin America and the creation of an American empire of slavery.[114] Others suggested reopening the African slave trade. More slaves would not only support economic growth in the booming Mississippi valley but also enable non-slave-owning white men to become slaveholders.[115]

With the rise of the Republican Party, the northern vision came to be associated with "free soil" and "free labor."[116] The mudsill theory, Horace Greeley wrote, expressed "the sentiment of all aristocracies."[117] Responding to Hammond's ideas in a speech to the Wisconsin State Agricultural Society in 1859, Abraham Lincoln said it was wrong to believe work had to be forced upon a lower class of hired laborers or slaves. Not only were capital owners dependent on labor, but a "large majority belong to neither class—neither work for others nor have others working for them." This majority was made up of both farmers and artisans, and they "work[ed] for themselves, on their farms, in their houses and in their shops." Free men would not be "fatally fixed for life" as hired laborers. Even the "penniless beginner" could "labor[] for wages awhile," save enough to "buy tools or land, for himself," and eventually even "hire another new beginner to help him." With its farmers and artisans, this system of free labor "opens the way for all—gives hope to all, and energy, and progress, and improvement of condition to all."[118]

THE FREEDMEN'S REPUBLIC

After four years of warfare and 620,000 dead, the age of the slavocracy formally came to an end. The question now was how to treat the freedmen across the South. Some believed that the abolition of formal slavery was sufficient; as long as the freedmen now had an equal opportunity to participate in the economy, no further action was needed.[119] But against these groups, one strand of Reconstruction Republicans tried to bring the former slaves of the South into America's middle-class constitution.[120] Their views were diametrically opposed to the feudal and class warfare theories of the slavocracy. They wanted to transform southern society from a planter aristocracy into a republic of small landowners—one that now included blacks as well as whites.

After the Emancipation Proclamation was issued in 1863, freeing slaves in the Confederate states, the War Department created the

American Freedmen's Inquiry Commission to assess the needs of the freedmen. Their report and recommendations ultimately led to the creation of the Freedmen's Bureau, which had the authority to split confiscated and abandoned lands into forty-acre plots for freedmen and loyal white refugees.[121] Many Reconstruction Republicans supported such land confiscation and redistribution policies in order to break the feudal power of the planter aristocracy and replace it with a more egalitarian distribution of property. George Julian, chairman of the House Committee on Public Lands, pushed for permanent seizure of Confederates' land. Both houses of Congress passed versions of his legislation, but they could never agree on a single bill.[122] Other leading Republicans, like Wendell Phillips and, at times, Benjamin Butler and Charles Sumner, also supported land distribution policies.[123]

The most eloquent advocate for confiscation and redistribution was Thaddeus Stevens. The clubfooted Pennsylvania congressman proposed confiscating the estates of the top 10 percent of wealthy rebel planters, which at the time amounted to those with more than $10,000 or more than two hundred acres in land. With that land, which he pointed out would leave 90 percent of southerners untouched, every freedman could be given forty acres. The remainder would be sold at auction and used to fund veteran pensions, compensate the injured, and retire the war debt.[124] Stevens's reasoning acknowledged that this action would be revolutionary, but he also deemed it necessary for preserving republican government. "The whole fabric of Southern society must be changed," he declared in a speech to constituents in 1865.

> Without this, this government can never be, as it has never been, a true republic. Heretofore, it had more the features of aristocracy than of democracy. The Southern States have been despotisms, not governments of the people. It is impossible that any practical equality of rights can exist where a few thousand men monopolize the whole landed property. The larger the number of small proprietors the more safe and stable the government. As the landed interest must govern, the more it is subdivided and held by independent owners, the better. . . .

If the South is ever to be made a safe republic, let her lands be cultivated by the toil of the owners, or the free labor of intelligent citizens. This must be done even though it drive her nobility into exile. It they go, all the better.[125]

Stevens's goal was to bring the freedmen into America's political community, and that required more than just civil rights; it required economic independence. After his death in 1868, one of his colleagues summed up his views well: "He knew that a landed aristocracy and a landless class are alike dangerous in a republic, and by a single act of justice he would abolish both."[126]

Stevens's position was held even more strongly by the freedmen themselves, though they framed the need for land reform less on republican philosophy than on practical experience. Some argued for confiscation and distribution, fearing that without land they would be at the mercy of their former white owners to provide them with opportunities for wage labor. "Gib us our own land and we take care ourselves," one Charleston man told then newspaper correspondent Whitelaw Reid. "[W]idout land, de ole masses can hire us or starve us, as dey please."[127] Others thought that it was their past labor that "entitled them to at least a portion of their owners' estates," and they emphasized that their labor had enriched northerners as well as southerners.[128] Bayley Wyat at Yorktown, Virginia, stated, "We has a right to the land where we are located. For why? I tell you. Our wives, our children, our husbands, has been sold over and over again to purchase the lands we now locates upon; for that reason we have a divine right to the land. . . . And den didn't we clear the land, and raise the crops. . . . And den didn't dem large cities in de North grow up on de cotton and de sugars and de rice dat we made? . . . I saw dey has grown rich, and my people is poor."[129] For many of the freedmen, land was a matter of both freedom and justice—freedom from their past owners, and justice for their past sacrifices.[130]

While military commanders and other leading officials rarely went so far as Stevens in supporting confiscation and redistribution, they too emphasized the beneficial possibilities of landownership and advanced policies that would help freedmen become homesteaders. The first confiscations were a wartime policy to damage the Confederate cause. Union commanders across the South settled freedmen on the plantations they had once worked. At the same time, Congress passed two Confiscation Acts in 1861 and 1862 to advance the Union cause in the war.[131] President Lincoln and cabinet officials were also involved. Lincoln issued a December 1863 order allowing black families to occupy forty acres of land (and single adult men twenty acres), which could be purchased at $1.25 an acre. Secretary of the Treasury Salmon P. Chase attempted to use the Captured and Abandoned Property Act of 1863 to lease land to former slaves in small parcels.[132]

The most famous military action was General William Tecumseh Sherman's Special Field Order No. 15. After his March to the Sea in 1864, Sherman ordered that thirty miles deep of land, from the ocean inward and from South Carolina to Florida, be reserved for freedmen. Each family would, famously, get forty acres of land and be lent animals, like mules, to help them work the land. Some forty thousand families benefited from Sherman's policy.[133] Others had complementary proposals: Quartermaster General Montgomery Meigs suggested that as a condition to receive a pardon, rebels with a net worth of more than $20,000 should have to give five to ten acres of land to each family of their former slaves.[134] This would redistribute land and prevent freedmen from migrating and leaving the South without a sufficient labor force. Carl Schurz and John Sprague suggested giving freedmen land along the Union Pacific Railroad. Their plan not only settled the land but also meant a population that could defend the railways from Indian attacks.[135]

In Congress, Republicans in the middle-class constitutional tradition put their efforts behind the Freedmen's Bureau and Southern Homestead Acts. The Second Freedmen's Bureau bill provided that loyal refugees and freedmen would be eligible to receive up to forty acres of abandoned and confiscated land, as long as they used it for three years.[136] The bill also opened up three million acres of public land and protected the Sherman freedmen for three years. The bill passed Congress with huge majorities, only to be vetoed by President Andrew Johnson. The congressional attempt to override Johnson's veto failed by merely two votes.[137] Two days after the Second Freedmen's Bureau bill passed in Congress, George Julian's Southern Homestead Act passed as well. The bill was an extension of the wartime Homestead Act, which opened up land in the West. The southern version gave freedmen and loyal whites a preference for homesteading in new public lands until 1867.[138] Johnson signed that bill in 1866.

Importantly, Stevens, Sumner, and the egalitarian faction of the Republican Party justified their policies—and particularly the economic policies underlying the Freedmen's Bureau bill—on constitutional grounds. While they referred to a variety of constitutional provisions, two were particularly important: the republican guarantee clause and the Thirteenth Amendment. Article IV of the Constitution states, "The United States shall guarantee to every State in this Union a Republican Form of Government." The clause had lain dormant in the courts for most of American history.[139] But the congressional Republicans—and most people in the nineteenth century—didn't see the Supreme Court as the only or even necessarily the primary authority on constitutional questions. Richard Yates of Illinois called the guarantee clause "the jewel of the Constitution." Sumner said it was "a sleeping giant . . . never until this recent war awakened, but now it comes forward with a giant's power. There is no clause in the Constitution like it. There is no other clause which gives to Congress such supreme power over the states."[140] Sumner explained that the Freedmen's Bureau bill and the Civil Rights Act of 1866 could easily be justified as "carry[ing] out the guarantee of a republican form of government."[141] Economic policies—land distribution and redistribution—were constitutionally permissible, in part, to ensure that states reentering the Union were truly "republican."

Republicans in Congress also justified economic measures under the newly passed Thirteenth Amendment. The "immortal" amendment banned slavery and involuntary servitude, giving Congress the power to pass "appropriate legislation" to enforce those bans.[142] Senator Henry Wilson of Massachusetts, the manager of the Freedmen's Bureau bill, explicitly said the constitutional authority for his economic agenda was based on the amendment.[143] But the amendment did not just *empower* Congress. One participant in the debates claimed that it "creates *the duty* for just such legislation as this bill contains, to give them shelter, and food, to lift them from slavery into the manhood of freedom, to clothe the nakedness of the slave, and to educate him into that manhood that shall be of value to the State."[144] As one scholar has summarized, "[T]he Enforcement Clause provided constitutional foundations for federal laws forbidding racial discrimination, providing goods and services to freedmen, and providing the same goods and services to destitute white refugees."[145] It was powerful enough to "revolutionize Southern society."[146]

Two things made the Thirteenth Amendment argument powerful and revolutionary. The first is that it did not have a "state action" requirement. Many constitutional provisions prevent the state or federal government from acting. The First Amendment, for example, says that "*Congress* shall make no law" abridging the freedom of speech (among other things). The Fourteenth Amendment says that "[n]o *State* shall make or enforce any law" denying the equal protection of the laws. The Thirteenth Amendment, in contrast, is not limited to government conduct.[147] It simply says, "Neither slavery nor involuntary servitude . . . *shall exist* within the United States." Indeed, in the decades after the Civil War, every justice on the Supreme Court recognized that the amendment applied to private actors directly, whether or not government was involved.[148]

The second is that the word "slavery" had a more capacious (albeit contested) meaning in the nineteenth century. Today, most people think of slavery as exclusively "chattel slavery"—when people are defined as the property of others. In earlier times, however, there was debate over how far exactly "slavery" extended. Some used "slavery" to mean the lack of independence and freedom, which was of particular concern to republican forms of government. Thus, some of the American revolutionaries in the 1770s considered themselves "slaves" to Parliament, rhetoric they inherited from English revolutionaries a century before.[149] Theorists of the slavocracy often said that banning "slavery" would apply to the "wage slavery" of the northern industrialists. Southerners hoped such a broad reading would scare northerners into not criticizing chattel slavery. Instead, many northern abolitionists argued that chattel slavery was different from wage slavery and that the latter should not be considered slavery at all.[150] The leading proponents of the Thirteenth Amendment took the more capacious view that the amendment had implications beyond race and beyond chattel slavery. Thus, Senator Henry Wilson explained, "[W]e have advocated the rights of the black man because the black man was the most oppressed type of the toiling men of this country.... The same influences that go to keep down and crush down the rights of the poor black man bear down and oppress the poor white laboring man."[151] After the amendment was passed, Congress received reports of southern economic practices designed to return to the functional equivalent of antebellum slavery. For example, planters would conspire to hire freedmen only with their former employer's permission, thereby preventing a fluid labor market and preventing freedmen from leaving the planter.[152] Members of Congress decried these practices as violating the intentions of the amendment.

After the Civil War, what made the Thirteenth Amendment so "dangerous" to the wealthy is that slavery and involuntary servitude could be interpreted to include these economic imbalances of power.[153] Conflict between poor whites and wealthier whites had already emerged, escalating in parts of the South to what the historian Eric Foner has called a "civil war within the Civil War."[154] Alexander Jones, a North Carolina newspaper editor, thus declared, "The great national strife originated with men and measures that were . . . opposed to a democratic form of government. . . . The fact is, these *bombastic, highfalutin* aristocratic fools have been in the habit of driving negroes and poor helpless white people until they think . . . that they themselves are superior; [and] hate, deride and suspicion the poor."[155] Indeed, the first case on the Thirteenth Amendment to come before the Supreme Court engaged the question of economic power. In *The Slaughterhouse Cases,* butchers in Louisiana were required to use the slaughterhouses of seventeen specific individuals, who had been granted a state-sanctioned monopoly. They argued that this was a form of feudalism, in which they were akin to serfs required to labor only on specified tracts of land for their lords. The purpose of the Thirteenth Amendment, they said, was to eradicate precisely such elements of feudalism.[156] With the issue of chattel slavery settled in the Civil War, the central conflict of the coming era,

Republican senator Benjamin Wade said, would be economic: "Property is not equally divided, and a more equal distribution of capital must be wrought out."[157]

But in spite of the breadth of the Thirteenth Amendment and the efforts of the Reconstruction Republicans in the 1860s and 1870s, the freedmen would not gain full admission to America's political or economic communities.[158] President Johnson opposed land confiscation efforts, including for the Sherman land, and quickly granted amnesty to most southern rebels.[159] Congress's efforts floundered over practical considerations. The Freedmen's Bureau was overly optimistic about the possibility of labor and capital having aligned interests, particularly in the context of racial and class antagonism.[160] The lands under the Southern Homestead Act were ill-suited to cultivation, and many freedmen were locked into labor contracts that prevented them from getting a homestead before their preference expired.[161] Many freedmen also had little money with which to purchase land.[162] Perhaps most important, southern whites rejected the Reconstruction Republicans' vision of an egalitarian republic and passed laws to restrict black workers' economic options and political rights. One prescient commentator predicted in 1865 that southerners' "whole thought and time will be given to plans for getting things back as near to slavery as possible."[163] Violence, night raids, the Ku Klux Klan, guerrilla warfare against civilians and reformers— all emerged as part of the bloody reign of terror that "redeemed" the South for its white inhabitants.[164] While northern Republicans were outraged at the cruel insurgency, they soon lost their resolve.[165] The panic and depression of 1873 shifted attention to monetary and labor debates in the North and enabled the South to backslide into white supremacy.[166] With the failure of Reconstruction, the planter and merchant classes continued to dominate poor whites in the South.[167] For the freedmen, the situation was even worse. Through force and fraud, white supremacist southern Democrats rigged elections to gain power. "A *revolution* has taken place and a race are disfranchised," former Union general Adelbert Ames observed. "[T]hey are to be returned to a condition of serfdom—an era of second slavery."[168]

THE RACE BETWEEN LAND AND INDUSTRY

In their 2008 book, *The Race Between Education and Technology*, economists Claudia Goldin and Lawrence Katz argue that America's education system was largely responsible for the reduction in inequality throughout much of the twentieth century.[169] Because some people have lower skills than others, technological progress invariably increases economic inequality between these groups. But widening inequality is not inevitable. When access to education and the quality of education have kept up with the pace of technological change, inequality narrowed. Only in the late twentieth century, when education failed to keep up with the pace of technological change, did economic inequality widen. Goldin and Katz's argument is distinct to the twentieth century, when technological change proceeded with great speed. But it does have a nineteenth-century analogue, which we can think of as the race between land and industry.

In an 1857 letter to Jefferson biographer Henry Randall, the English historian Thomas Babington Macaulay explained the coming challenge. The conservative Macaulay was opposed to American government because "[e]ither the poor would plunder the rich, and civilization would perish; or order and property would be saved by a strong military government, and Liberty would perish." Americans might think they had "an exemption from these evils," he noted, but this was mistaken because America's fate was simply "deferred." "As long as you have a boundless extent of fertile and unoccupied land," he wrote to Randall, "your laboring population will be far more at ease than the laboring population of the old world." The equal commonwealth would continue according to Jeffersonian political economy. "But the time will come when New-England will be as thickly peopled as Old England. Wages will be as low. . . . You will have your Manchesters and Birminghams . . . [and] hundreds of thousands of artisans will assuredly be sometimes out of work." This was America's inevitable future, Macaulay warned, and when it came to pass, "your institutions will be fairly brought to the test." He wished Americans the best in surviving the coming trial, but he feared the worst. "Your Constitution is all sail and no anchor."[170]

Throughout the nineteenth century, leading Americans developed theories and policies to delay the inevitable fate that Macaulay predicted. The most important was to expand availability and access to land in the West. The Confederation Congress's passage of the Northwest Ordinance (1787), Jefferson's purchase of the Louisiana Territory (1803), and laws like the Homestead Act (1862) were justified in part as solving the problem of population growth and equal opportunity: as long as these lands became available to people from the East, the constitutional system was safe. Horace Greeley, whom we associate with the phrase "Go west, young man," held fast to this theory in the age of the factory. "The public lands," he said, "are the great regulator of the relations of Labor and Capital, the safety valve of our industrial and social engine."[171] Under the "safety valve" theory, any wage worker in America's version of Manchester or Birmingham could take advantage of the Homestead Act, move west to the frontier, and become an independent farmer.[172] As long as the availability of land kept ahead of industrial development, the constitutional prerequisite of economic equality would hold for those within the political community.

The "safety valve" theory, however, suffered from two problems. First was the closing of the frontier. In 1893, Frederick Jackson Turner argued in *The Significance of the Frontier in American History* that America was defined by its frontier culture, which is partly what made the country so egalitarian and devoid of social and political hierarchies. The closing of the frontier three years earlier meant, according to one late nineteenth-century Kansas commentator, "the absence of the safety valve heretofore existing in the public domain."[173] Without expansive lands to the west, America could not ensure the equal economic opportunity that the founders' vision of republican government required. The second problem with the safety-valve theory was that it was a fiction. Greeley's advice and the Homestead Act might have encouraged some wage workers to move west, but the real trends in the late nineteenth century were away from agriculture and toward urbanization and industrialization.[174] In 1870, American agricultural production was $500 million greater than industrial production. By 1900, industrial production dwarfed agricultural production—$13 billion to $4.7 billion.[175] The population was also increasingly living in cities. In 1870, 23.2 percent of Americans lived in urban areas; by 1910, the percentage of Americans living in urban areas had doubled to 46.3 percent.[176] The country was no longer one defined by small landowners.

With the founders' economic assumptions collapsing under the weight of industrial transformation, the critical question was whether the republican constitutional system could survive the shift from productive property ownership to wages. Wage labor posed challenges to republicanism. Wage laborers were dependent on other people for their economic survival, and that dependence conflicted with republicanism's requirement that citizens be free and independent. As historian Eric Foner has said, for many late nineteenth-century Republicans, "A man who remained all his life dependent on wages for his livelihood appeared almost as unfree as a southern slave."[177] For citizens to be free, they needed a measure of economic independence, which had generally been linked to ownership. The second problem was that in an industrial system, economic gains would accrue disproportionately to a small few—the owners. Relative economic equality was at risk in a system in which wage laborers earned little while big profits went to their bosses. Years later, the Supreme Court justice John Marshall Harlan remembered how widespread this understanding was in the 1880s: "The conviction was universal that the country was in real danger from another kind of slavery . . . that would result from the aggregation of capital in the hands of a few individuals controlling, for their own profit and advantage exclusively, the entire business of the country."[178]

In addition to expanding the availability of land, policy makers reimagined the tariff as a way to forestall the coming "labor question." Before the 1840s, the tariff was largely justified as protecting and promoting infant industries, enabling America to be economically independent of Britain.[179] The panic of 1837 and the resultant economic crisis brought forward a new justification. With the panic came widespread unemployment and early hints of labor organizing as well as anticapitalist sentiments.[180] In response, policy makers began to embrace the tariff as a strategy to protect wage earners from competition with "pauper labor" in Europe.[181]

For these supporters of the tariff, political economy could not simply be reduced to an aggregation of self-interest. The problem with the political economists of the age—Smith, Ricardo, Malthus—was that they had crafted their economic theories for European aristocracies, not for republics. Aristocracies and feudal societies were based on "pauper labor," which conflicted with the equality required for a republic (as did slavery, which members of this tradition also opposed). To compete on a free-trade basis with an aristocracy's system of pauper labor would mean lower wages in America—something that threatened the Republic itself.[182] Daniel Raymond, the leading American political economist of the early nineteenth century, wrote that republics were organized around the good of the nation. As a result, "every citizen" had a duty to "forego his own private advantages for the public good."[183] If a poor working class emerged in America, Francis Bowen feared, this "class of laborers, who must always form the majority in any community, and who, with us, also have the control in politics, will not be satisfied without organic changes in the laws, which will endanger at once our political and social system."[184] The tariff republicans also rejected the idea that the goal of the economy was to increase efficiency. As historian James Huston writes of the nineteenth-century republican protectionists, "[A] society did not strive to attain a maximum efficiency but rather chose the amount of efficiency that it believed the social structure could withstand. The protectionists treated efficiency more like a commodity than a standard by which economic activity was to be judged."[185] In a sense, the republican justification for protectionism was a return to the tariff's constitutional origins. As part of the economic compromise at the heart of the Constitution, the tariff would fund the federal government, enabling states to reduce the economic burden on ordinary Americans that had caused so much strife in the 1780s. In an industrializing age, the tariff would again serve as a policy that promoted the economic security of ordinary Americans.

The high tariff persisted throughout the nineteenth century, though it too came under increased pressure by the end of the century. During the Civil War, Congress passed the Morrill Tariff, named after Justin Morrill, who also sponsored the Morrill Land Grant College Act. (Indeed, high tariffs, homesteading in the West, and higher education can be seen as a Republican economic package to ensure a broad middle class.[186]) When Grover Cleveland proposed to *lower* tariffs in 1887, he nonetheless committed not to adopt tariff rates that would result in "either the loss of employment by the working man or the lessening of his wages."[187] But by the end of the nineteenth century and the start of the twentieth century, the tariff's republican justification seemed less and less persuasive. The tariff protected workers only so long as there was a competitive domestic market. If a corporation raised prices to benefit from high tariffs, it would lose out to the competition. But domestic competition now seemed weaker than ever. A new kind of monopoly was transforming the economy. It was a combination of corporations under one umbrella—and it was known as the trust.[188]

THE CRISIS OF CONCENTRATION

The "star attraction" at the 1899 Chicago Trust Conference was Hazen Pingree. The Republican governor of Michigan had a storied past. During the Civil War, he had fought at Bull Run, was taken prisoner and sent to Andersonville, and escaped from Confederate captivity only to return to the front. Moving to Detroit after the war, Pingree rose to become one of the leading shoe manufacturers in America before running for mayor in 1889. As mayor, Pingree was best known for fighting corruption. By the end of his tenure, he had won lower prices for streetcars, established a working system of public street lighting, fixed the sewer system, and become a national leader in debates over the municipal ownership of utilities. In 1896, he was elected governor of Michigan. As a Republican reformer, Pingree was celebrated (and sometimes criticized) for his efforts to help ordinary people. When the depression of 1893 hit, for example, Pingree pushed owners of empty lots to allow the people to plant food and vegetables on them, earning him the simultaneously heroic and derisive nickname "Potato Patch Pingree."[189]

When he arrived at Central Music Hall in Chicago on September 14, 1899, Governor Pingree was greeted with a thunder of applause. Reporters at the time noted that the "applause [was] so fervent that it was several minutes before he could proceed."[190] That night, in a speech titled "The Effect of Trusts on Our National Life and Citizenship," Pingree linked the industrial changes of the age to the economic preconditions for American government. "In this republic of ours we are fond of saying that there are no classes. In fact, we boast of it. We say that classes belong to monarchies, not to republics." Pingree continued, "The strength of our republic has always been in what is called our middle class. . . . It would be little short of calamity to encourage any industrial development that would affect unfavorably this important class of our citizens."

The central question for Pingree was not whether industrial change, corporations, or combinations like the trusts would be more economically efficient. Pingree was concerned with their "effect upon our middle class." The problem, as even advocates for trusts acknowledged, was that the new industrial behemoths made "it impossible for the individual or firm to do business on a small scale." Larger corporations and trusts "concentrate the ownership and management of all lines of business activity into the hands of a very few." The consequences for America's middle class were disastrous. The trust is "the forerunner, or, rather, the creator of industrial slavery," Pingree said. In this dystopian world, the new masters are the managers who "serve the soulless and nameless being called the shareholder," while the new slaves are "the former merchant and business man and the artisan and mechanic, who once cherished the hope that they might sometime reach the happy position of independent ownership of business." If the trusts continue to dominate the economy, the future would be one of "[c]ommercial feudalism." "We cannot be true to our republic by ignoring these things," Pingree concluded. "The degrading process of the trust means much to the future of a republic founded upon democratic principles. A democratic republic cannot survive the disappearance of a democratic population."[191]

After the Civil War, many Americans still held firm to the idea that America was a classless society.[192] But in the decades after the Civil War, the economic changes wrought by industrialization and the rise of corporations threatened this inherited assumption from the founding era. It is hard to imagine the extraordinary scale of the revolution that took place in the late nineteenth and early twentieth centuries, but virtually every aspect of American life was transformed. Elevators meant cities could grow vertically rather than horizontally. Electricity changed the experience of nighttime. The country became ever more connected by the railroad and telegraph. Mass production changed the nature of work.[193]

Industrialization meant growth and concentration in every sector. In the wake of the Civil War, railroads exemplified the changes of the era. The final leg of the transcontinental railroad united the country in 1869, shortening the trip from east to west from months to less than a week. Already by 1870, 50 percent of American capital industry and 10 percent of nonfarm labor were involved in railroad construction.[194] Massive growth followed in the subsequent decades. Between 1865 and 1900, the American rail network expanded from 35,000 miles to 193,000 miles.[195] The economic challenge for the railroad industry was the high initial capital expense—that is, the cost of laying track. Entry into the market was expensive and doomed competition because a price war meant that participants would fail to recover the high costs of construction. Most countries, over time, solved this problem by nationalizing their railways. But the United States didn't take that path. Instead, railroads frequently went bankrupt throughout the late nineteenth century, leading to consolidation in a small number of firms.[196] By 1896, the railroad industry amounted to 15 percent of gross national product, was highly concentrated, and was controlled by the most famous industrialists of the era—Vanderbilt, Stanford, Harriman.[197]

As in railroads, a small number of titans dominated other industries. By 1890, Andrew Carnegie's steel empire was alone responsible for one-fourth of all American steel.[198] From his place in the banking industry, J. P. Morgan's tentacles extended throughout virtually every sector. In 1900, the house of Morgan had seats on the boards of companies that collectively made up one-fourth of all the wealth in America.[199] John D. Rockefeller expanded his oil-refining business into production, tanker manufacturing, and real estate. By 1904, the vertically integrated Standard Oil Company was responsible for 90 percent of crude oil production in the United States and 85 percent of sales.[200]

The problem with monopoly was that it concentrated wealth and power. "Nature is rich; but everywhere man, the heir of nature, is poor," declared Henry Demarest Lloyd in the opening lines of *Wealth*

Against Commonwealth. Lloyd observed that America was rich in natural resources like oil and coal but that "syndicates, trusts, combinations" were doing all they could to "control production" and prevent competition so that they could make more money.[201] In sensational muckraking detail, Lloyd's book regaled the country with descriptions of corruption and greed in the oil industry. Declaring that "[l]iberty and monopoly cannot live together," he feared that the continuation of monopoly would inevitably mean "[t]he concentration of wealth, the wiping out of the middle classes."[202]

In 1895, the question of monopoly reached the Supreme Court. The issue in *United States v. E. C. Knight Co.* was whether the Sherman Antitrust Act of 1890 applied to the manufacturing trust that controlled 98 percent of the sugar market.[203] Deciding in favor of Knight, the Court held that the Sherman Act did not extend to regulating monopolies in manufacturing. While Congress had the power to regulate commerce, the Court thought manufacturing was different from commerce and that it only *indirectly* impeded commerce.[204] In dissent, Justice John Marshall Harlan feared the consequences of the decision: "We have before us the case of a combination which absolutely controls, or may, at its discretion, control the price of all refined sugar in this country." A similar "combination, organized for private gain and to control prices," might emerge in every sector of the economy, Harlan said. If that happened, "[w]hat power is competent to protect the people of the United States against such dangers except a national power,—one that is capable of exerting its sovereign authority throughout every part of the territory and over all the people of the nation?"[205] The case was immediately criticized. An author in the *American Law Review* called *E. C. Knight* the "most deplorable" case in decades because the Court had decided "in favor of incorporated power and greed against popular rights."[206]

In the next decade, from 1895 to 1904, a tidal wave of corporate mergers and consolidations took place. More than 1,800 firms disappeared in the "great merger movement," leaving the remaining behemoths with dominance of their sectors.[207] General Electric emerged from a combination of 8 firms, with 90 percent control of its market. DuPont was the result of 64 firms merging, taking 65–75 percent of the market. American Tobacco was built from 162 firms and controlled 90 percent of the market.[208] Nearly half of mergers ended with the resulting firm having at least 70 percent market share.[209] By 1904, 300 corporations controlled more than 40 percent of American manufacturing and influenced 80 percent of American industry.[210]

With industrialization proceeding apace and economic power becoming concentrated in fewer and fewer firms, unrest spread throughout the country. In 1877, the major railroads held secret meetings to stop the competition that had forced them to cut rates drastically after the panic of 1873. The railroad cartel could now raise prices and cut pay for workers. Still reeling from the depression that followed the panic, railroad workers went on strike. First on the Reading Railroad. Then on the Pennsylvania. Then, in Martinsburg, West Virginia, strikers seized a cattle train and detached the locomotive, blocking the rail line. The local government sent in the militia, and President Hayes ordered in federal troops to quell the insurgents. The Great Strike of 1877 soon spread. Ten were killed and dozens wounded in Baltimore. More than twelve were killed in Pittsburgh, where the wounded included women and children. In Chicago, a reporter recounted the condition of a rioter who was clubbed: "The blood and brains were oozing down his neck." Tens of thousands now went on strike across the country, with protests reaching to Omaha, uniting blacks and whites in Galveston, and migrating even to San Francisco, where strikers celebrated as a wharf owned by a railroad subsidiary went up in flames.[211]

Labor unrest continued throughout the country in the ensuing decades. In 1886, a Chicago rally in support of an eight-hour workday turned into the site of the Haymarket riot when a bomb exploded, leading to gunfire and many dead and wounded.[212] In 1890, the United States witnessed more strikes than ever before.[213] With the economic depression after the panic of 1893, output dropped by 64 percent, and farm income fell 18 percent.[214] When the Pullman Company, maker of railcars, cut wages in the midst of the economic crisis, workers decided to strike. The 1894 Pullman Strike shut down the railways in much of the country, including most of the traffic in and out of Chicago.[215] Henry Demarest Lloyd thought, "This crisis is greater than that of 1776 or 1861."[216] The organizer of the strike,

Eugene Debs, was jailed, with the federal circuit court justifying his conviction under the Sherman Antitrust Act. The Supreme Court upheld his conviction on other grounds; earlier that year, it had held the Sherman Act inapplicable to the sugar trust.[217] When Debs emerged from prison to a crowd of 100,000 supporters, Lloyd said he was "the most popular man among the real people today."[218]

With violence around the country, Governor Pingree was by no means alone in his fear that industrialization was leading to economic inequality and that the division of the country into rich and poor was a threat to the Republic. David Kinley, a professor of economics at the University of Illinois, worried that the "elimination of producers and middlemen" will result in the "destruction of the independent middle class," leading to "only two classes in industrial society, the employers and employed." "This danger," Kinley wrote, "is one of very great importance in a republic. The stability of our institutions depends upon the existence of a numerous middle class of economically independent people. Any movement, industrial, political or social, which tends to prevent this, is a menace to a republican government."[219] The Reverend T. DeWitt Talmage echoed Aristotle in explaining how the virtues of the middle class sustained American government: "The middle classes, who have hitherto held the balance of power and acted as mediator between two extremes, are diminishing, and at the present ratio we will soon have no middle classes, for all will be very rich or very poor, and we will be divided between princes and paupers, between palaces and hovels."[220]

One of the more radical critiques came from Milford Howard, a member of Congress from Alabama, who feared that the middle class was "rapidly disappearing and being absorbed by the very poor."[221] In *The American Plutocracy*, Howard wrote that "[t]he middle class in this country was formerly larger than both the capitalistic and wage-slave classes combined; now the wage-slave class is larger by almost five millions than both the other classes combined. Soon the middle class will entirely disappear."[222] For Howard, like many others, this was a constitutional problem because political power would inevitably follow the distribution of wealth. "How long will it be," he asked, "if the present ratio of gain be maintained, ere a few hundred men will own all the wealth of this magnificent country? Then what will be the fate of our boasted Constitution, our blood-bought liberty?"[223] Howard's solution—a constitutional amendment—channeled the most radical of the Pennsylvania revolutionaries of 1776. Under Howard's proposed amendment, no citizen would be allowed to have more than $1 million in property of any kind. The excess would be "condemned as a public nuisance and a public peril and be accordingly forfeited into the United States Treasury."[224]

THE COOPERATIVE COMMONWEALTH

Industrialization posed a threat to the middle-class constitution, and a flurry of thinkers and activists in the 1880s and 1890s tried to address it. Some looked backward with a Jeffersonian eye to land distribution. In *Progress and Poverty* (1879), one of the best-selling books of the time, Henry George argued that the problem of the age wasn't the divide between labor and capital. The problem was land monopolists, who did no work but took in unearned income from rents. As progress increased—machines, development, productivity—poverty increased too because the monopolists increased the rent they charged. The solution was a single tax, an extremely high land tax that would restrict the emergence of a rentier class of land monopolists. With such a tax, he argued, progress would reduce poverty rather than accompany it.[225]

Other innovative thinkers were more forward-looking. George McNeill was a giant in the labor movement—father of the eight-hour workday movement, president of the International Workingmen's Union, co-author of the Knights of Labor's constitution, and co-founder of the American Federation of Labor (AFL). He explained the problem in 1887: "[O]ur rulers, statesmen and orators have not attempted to engraft republican principles into our industrial system."[226] Industrialization had increased economic inequality, and "[t]hese extremes of wealth and poverty are threatening the existence of the government." McNeill was stark about the constitutional consequences: "[T]here is an inevitable and irresistible conflict between the wage-system of labor and the republican system of government."[227] Corporate power was a "greater power than that of the State"—a "State within a State"—that is "quietly yet quickly sapping the foundations of the majority-rule."[228] This was an affront to the Constitution's demand that each state have a republican form of government, and it was a challenge to the Republic itself. "Republican institutions are sustained by the ability of the people to rule," McNeill argued. "The foundation of the Republic is equality."[229]

McNeill was a member of the Knights of Labor, perhaps the most innovative reform organization when it came to reinventing republicanism for the industrial age.[230] Formed in Philadelphia in the 1860s, the Knights of Labor saw their membership spread like wildfire beginning in 1883 alongside the eight-hour workday campaign and railroad strikes.[231] At their peak, in 1886, the Knights had an official membership of 700,000 and an unofficial membership of likely more than 1 million, or about one in sixty Americans.[232] The Knights, like many others at the time, saw themselves as part of the "middle social stratum, balanced between the very rich and very poor."[233] As John W. Breidenthal, chairman of the aligned Union Labor Party, said in 1887, they represented "the middle class of society . . . not the extremely rich or extremely poor. We stand on middle ground. We have come here to organize and save this Government from the extremes of the one and the robbery of the other."[234]

The Knights' solution was what they called "the co-operative commonwealth." The Knights believed the American republic relied on equal freedom and economic independence and that wage labor could not replace landownership as a way to maintain the founding era's principles. Translating the principle of equal economic power to the industrial age, they argued for "joint ownership and control over industrial enterprises."[235] While some reformers of the era, like Laurence Gronlund, advocated socialism, the central thrust of the Knights' vision was neither socialist nor communist.[236] A cooperative simply involved shared employee ownership over the enterprise. It transformed each industrial organization into a mini-republic of its own, in which workers would have a say over how the enterprise was run—an idea that later reformers would call "industrial democracy." As Henry Demarest Lloyd said, "[T]here is to be *a people* in industry, as in government."[237] The Knights' platform, as declared in their 1878 constitution, provided a succinct but comprehensive set of goals. In addition to cooperative institutions, they advocated for laws that treated capital and labor on a level playing field; health and safety regulations; laws requiring corporations to pay employees on a weekly basis; a ban on child labor; the eight-hour workday; and a national monetary system.[238]

These "labor republicans," as one scholar has called them, also embraced the Aristotelian idea that it was the large mass of working people—those who "had not yet realized their freedom"—who would be best equipped to hold the balance of power in American government.[239] "[T]he ruling few had an interest in domination[;] the class of dependent workers had a common interest in economic independence."[240] The labor republicans recognized that republican institutions "require[d] the economic independence of all, not just some." As a result, the long-term interests of workers were aligned with "the general interests of a republic," and that made "workers potentially agents of republican transformation."[241]

In the cooperative commonwealth, workers would need a modernized form of civic virtue, focused now on the "habits of cooperation and collective action."[242] Labor republicans established reading rooms, educational centers, and newspapers and advocated for maximum-hours laws, in part so that workers would have the education they needed to be good republican citizens.[243] But the Knights also recognized the bourgeois culture of the middle class and hoped the cooperative commonwealth would help bring workers into it. New York City's tailors' union sent a circular to its members asking about their labor conditions: "Are you compelled to work on Sunday to support your family?" "Have you got time and means to visit Central Park or any other places of pleasure? Does your family or you go to hear public lectures?" A Saginaw, Michigan, Knight, referring to lumbermen working fourteen to fifteen hours a day, said they were "not free men—[they] had no time for thought, no time for home."[244] George McNeill made clear that the result of the shorter workday and the cooperative organization of industry would be that workers would become part of the middle class, "using the morning hours in the duties and pleasures of the sunlit-home; taking his morning bath before his morning work, reading his morning paper in the well-equipped reading-room of the manufactory."[245] The Knights' economic agenda was one that would enable workers to enter and remain in the middle class, economically through cooperative ownership and culturally through leisure time well spent.

From a modern perspective, what is most surprising is how progressive the Knights' vision was. The Knights organized black and white workers, without regard to race.[246] Indeed, Terence Powderly, the head of the Knights, made a special—and provocative for the time—point of having a black worker introduce him at a major gathering in the South.[247] The Knights also admitted women to their membership, and plank thirteen of their 1878 constitution established as one of their goals "to secure for both sexes equal pay for equal work."[248] Taken together with their advocacy against child labor and for health and safety regulations, they presaged many of the twentieth century's public policy goals.

The labor republicans overlapped in their membership with the populists of the 1880s and 1890s. United as the People's Party in the 1892 presidential election, the populists comprised a hodgepodge of largely nonpartisan, antiparty reform groups, from the Farmers' Alliance and Knights of Labor to women's groups and followers of Henry George's single-tax plan.[249] Historians over the last century have viewed the populists in very different lights. They were first seen as "primitive" or "traditional," harking back to bygone days before industrialization. Then they were reinvented as part of a clash between East and West, in which their democratic tendencies were the foundation for the Progressive Era. By the 1970s and 1980s, they were critics of progress, antimodernists who resisted the new economic order. Most recently, scholars have looked at what the Populists supported—not just what they opposed—and found them to be surprisingly creative. They were innovators who confronted the concentration of economic power with their own, and prescient, solutions.[250]

The populists recognized that the central economic transformation of the time was the concentration of power, and they sought economic and political reforms that would adapt to the new world of large organizations. As Charles Macune, the head of the Farmers' Alliance, explained, "All the different classes and occupations of society are engaging in organization for mutual advancement and protection to a greater extent than ever before in the history of the world. In fact, we may say that every calling is organized. This thorough organization has created a new order of things."[251]

Farmers couldn't just stand by. They needed to organize too. In Johnson County, Illinois, they created the Farmers' Mutual Benefit Association, which used farmers' exchanges, instead of local grain buyers, to centralize their power so they could get a better price in the Chicago grain markets.[252] In Jefferson County, Kansas, Walter Allen took the deliberately provocative action of creating the "Farmers' Trust" in 1888. Trusts were abhorrent to many of the populists, but the Farmers' Trust sought to fight fire with fire, leveling the playing field between agrarians and industrialists. The goal of the trust was to "centralize control of warehouses, grain elevators, stockyards, and other strategic points of agricultural trade" so that the trust would have, in the words of Allen, "a monopoly in the commission business and power to control shipments and regulation of the price of farm products." The trust would "wipe out ninety per cent of the retail men" and create "direct communication with local shippers by telegraph and telephone."[253] Organization would confront organization.

The Farmers' Alliance and its populist allies went so far as to offer what one historian has called an "agrarian statist agenda."[254] Far from embracing a proto-libertarian, hands-off government, the agrarian populists pushed for "scientific government" that would operate like a "business organization."[255] They praised Napoleon's state-building efforts in France, even though he was hardly a democratic leader.[256] They exalted the post office, an efficient national organization that they hoped would inspire similar government agencies for addressing weather information, labor and farm statistics, warehousing, and even banking.[257] Their most extensive proposal was Macune's "subtreasury" system. First proposed in 1889, the subtreasury system was to be a government-run cooperative, which would make loans to farmers, secured by their crops. The subtreasury would have offices and warehouses in farming districts around the country to store crops, and it would release them into the market in a controlled manner, in order to keep prices stable. It would, in effect, take agricultural financing away from Wall Street.[258] The Populists also proposed a slew of constitutional and policy reforms that they saw as combating the growing inequality of economic and political power in the country. In their 1892 platform, the Populists endorsed the progressive income tax, secret ballot, direct election of senators, and eight-hour workday.

The Populists were also clear that their forward-looking economic agenda had constitutional implications. In the 1892 Populist platform's preamble, authored by Minnesota farmer and activist Ignatius Donnelly, the reformers declared that their aim was "to restore the government of the Republic to the hands of 'the plain people,' with which class it originated." Their goals, they said, were "identical with the purposes of the National Constitution."[259] In *A Political Revelation* (1894), James "Cyclone" Davis made this argument most directly. Davis was a star advocate for the Populists in the 1890s and gained his nickname from overpowering his debate opponents.[260] Surveying the different types of governments, Davis concluded that "Republics, or Democracies as they are sometimes called . . . deny the rights of special classes."[261] Had Jefferson been around, he would have seen that "there is another *hereditary high-handed aristocracy* in our land, with far more stupendous accumulation of property, held in single lines of 'corporate names' or titles, whose castles, palaces, mansions and estates, the kings and princes of Britain's realm cannot rival."[262] Action was essential. Davis argued that the Constitution allowed all of the reforms that the Populists desired and in fact that these reforms were necessary for the Constitution to be "carried out in its full and complete sense."[263]

In some parts of the South, populism followed a different arc. Despite some early Reconstruction attempts to unite poor whites and freedmen against the planter aristocracy, the "redemption" of the South and the end of Reconstruction in 1877 meant that populism was largely a white movement. But in the early 1890s, there was a moment when biracial populism briefly emerged as a possibility. In Georgia, the agrarian radical Tom Watson campaigned on the platform of uniting poor blacks and whites. "You are kept apart that you may be separately fleeced of your earnings," Watson declared. "You are made to hate each other because upon that hatred is rested the keystone of the arch of financial despotism which enslaves you both. You are deceived and blinded that you may not see how this race antagonism perpetuates a monetary system which beggars both."[264]

Watson nominated a black man to the Populist Party's state executive committee. He spoke to mixed-race audiences. He had black speakers join him on the platform at events. He pushed the Populists to "make lynch law odious to the people."[265] But as Watson grew more and more successful, the establishment took action to stop his rise to power and to prevent his disruptive views from spreading. Violence, force, fraud, bribery: They did everything they could to intimidate black voters and block Watson from taking power in 1892. "They have incited lawless men to a pitch of frenzy which threatens anarchy," Watson said. "Threats against my life were frequent and there were scores of men who would have done the deed and thousands who would have sanctioned it." Watson was right. No less a figure than Georgia governor William Northen was reported to have said that "Watson ought to be killed and that it ought to have been done long ago."[266]

Watson lost in 1892, but in 1896 he was the Populist Party's nominee for vice president, alongside William Jennings Bryan, who served as both the Democratic and the Populist candidate for president. In one of the most fiercely contested presidential races in history, Bryan lost to the full force of the Republican machine and its innovative fund-raising tactics. Populists were divided over whether to create "fusion" tickets with Democrats or Republicans, and the election marked the beginning of the end for the insurgent third party. By 1904, Watson wanted to rehabilitate his political career. And so, in the words of his biographer, the legendary historian C. Vann Woodward, Watson "abandoned his old dream of uniting both races against the enemy, and took his first step toward the opposite extreme in racial views."[267] Watson reinvented himself. He now supported limiting primary elections to whites because a white populist revolt was only possible if whites were not afraid of blacks' taking power. He eventually even became a proponent of lynching.[268] So ended the brief Populist dream of a biracial union in the South against the economically powerful.

Despite their creative solutions, the labor republicans and populists consistently ran aground in the courts, where a laissez-faire approach dominated. Legally, debates over the democratic control of industrial power have come to be symbolized by a single case, *Loch-*

ner v. New York.[269] In the 1905 case, the Supreme Court struck down a New York law limiting the number of hours a baker could work to ten a day and sixty a week. The Court held that "liberty of contract" was a substantive right implicitly included in the Fourteenth Amendment's declaration that "no state shall . . . deprive any person of life, liberty, or property, without due process of law." On the laissez-faire theory, labor was equivalent to property, and the New York law infringed on the baker's freedom to sell his labor for more than the maximum hours allowed. As a result, the New York legislature could not infringe on this economic right in order to help workers. In a famous dissent, Justice Oliver Wendell Holmes wrote that the Constitution "is not intended to embody a particular economic theory," and he condemned the majority for making economic philosophy into a constitutional doctrine.[270]

Constitutional scholars have clashed over the right interpretation of *Lochner* and the "*Lochner* era." The first generation of progressive scholars followed Holmes and saw *Lochner* as embracing a laissez-faire ideology. Revisionists over the last half century have taken a different view. Some scholars have argued that the Supreme Court's decision was based on the Court's preference for judge-made common law, rather than democratically enacted statutes, as an economic regulatory regime.[271] Others have argued that the Court's decisions during this era are best explained by the Court's aversion to "class legislation."[272] According to one reading of republican constitutional theory, legislation is supposed to be in the public good. "Class legislation" was policy that helped one interest group over another. The New York law pitted bakers against employers, and was therefore class legislation in support of bakers that had to be struck down. Most recently, libertarian scholars have argued that the *Lochner* era was defined by justices' finding unspecified, fundamental rights— like liberty of contract—in the Constitution.[273]

In an important sense, the laissez-faire courts saw themselves as heirs to the free labor philosophy of the Republican Party. Coming out of the Civil War, laissez-faire supporters held that wage labor was free labor.[274] Some proponents of this position came from a strand of antebellum abolitionism in which the legal freedom to work wherever and for whomever fulfilled the independence that republican

political economy required. "Where are the slave auction-blocks. . . .
They are all gone!" William Lloyd Garrison declared in 1869. "From
chattels to human beings. . . . Freedmen at work as independent
laborers by voluntary contract!"[275] As long as a worker was not forced
to work for a particular master, he was considered free. Yale's William
Graham Sumner perhaps put it best: "A society based on contract is
a society of free and independent men."[276]

In a series of decisions, Gilded Age courts relied on this general
approach, refracted through different constitutional provisions—
with the effect of blocking the efforts of the reformers. In 1884, the
New York legislature passed a law prohibiting cigars from being manufactured in tenements. Landlord-employers had transformed their
tenement housing into sweatshops, exploiting tenants to make cigars
in their rooms. The New York City cigar makers' union pushed for
the prohibition, only to see the New York Court of Appeals (which
is the supreme court of New York) strike it down in the 1885 case of
In re Jacobs. With willful blindness to the new economic realities, the
court considered the sweatshop workers akin to "artisans" who were
engaged in "innocuous trades . . . in their own homes," only to be
deprived of their property and liberty by not being allowed to work
from home.[277] The court's vision was rooted in the bygone economic
assumptions of the prior age: small artisans, like small landholders,
had economic mobility.[278] The Pennsylvania Supreme Court's decision in *Godcharles v. Wigeman* was similar.[279] Factory, mill, or mine
owners would often build entire towns, including housing, churches,
and schools. In these company towns, the factory owner would pay
workers not with currency but with goods or scrip that was usable
only in the company-owned stores. Workers and their families were,
in effect, completely dependent and attached to the company: their
labor was for the company, their income was in company scrip, and
their debts were owed to the company. Pennsylvania's law mandated
that laborers in and around these towns be paid in cash and paid at
regular intervals. The Pennsylvania Supreme Court thought the law
was an "insulting attempt to put the laborer under a legislative tute-
lege" because the law prevented the worker from "sell[ing] his labor
for what he thinks best, whether money or goods."[280] Courts around
the country engaged in similar reasoning.[281]

The reformers, as can be expected, strenuously objected to the intersection between laissez-faire economics and the constitutional system. In the words of McNeill, it was a "false and pernicious system of political economy" that was "subvert[ing] . . . the high positions attempted by the Fathers."[282] But with frequent losses in the courts, organized labor increasingly took a different approach. Starting in the 1890s, it abandoned the vision of the cooperative commonwealth and instead advocated for a system of what legal historian Willy Forbath has called "collective laissez-faire."[283] Labor now argued that the Constitution required that combinations of persons should have the same rights as "combinations of capital."[284] According to this theory, the right to strike was rooted in the Thirteenth Amendment's prohibition on involuntary servitude, and the right to picket and boycott attached to the First Amendment's freedom of speech and association.[285] This new labor program—crafted in response to the laissez-faire courts—became one of the central sites of contestation in the early twentieth century. The labor republicans' vision, which turned Harrington's property-based equal commonwealth into an industrial-era cooperative commonwealth, became one of the paths not taken.

PLUTOCRACY IN AMERICA

Marcus Daly was determined to stop William Andrews Clark. Clark, like Daly, was an industrial magnate who owned copper mines, mills, smelters, lumber, banks, retail stores, newspapers, and utilities. But what Clark really wanted was to win elected office in Montana.[286] Partly he wanted the status and power that came with public leadership. Partly he wanted to support policies that would improve his business holdings and harm those of Daly. When Clark stood for Congress in 1888, Daly men pasted their handpicked candidate's name over Clark's on ballots, leading to Clark's loss in an instance of spectacular fraud.[287] So began Montana's War of the Copper Kings.

Over the next two decades, copper magnates in Montana would engage in some of the most blatant, surprising, and shocking efforts at corruption to gain political power in American history. Daly canceled business contracts with those who would not support his political aims. He started his own newspaper to compete with Clark's. The two fought over whether the state capital would be located at Anaconda (Daly's company town) or Helena (which Clark supported to block Daly), and they "gave away cigars, bought rounds of drinks, and sometimes just handed out money in an effort to garner support for one city or the other."[288]

Clark decided that 1899 was his last best chance to get into the Senate, and he was willing to pay legislators whatever it cost. The opening bid for a bribe was $10,000 a vote, with many reportedly coming in at $20,000 and one rumor of $50,000 for a single vote.[289] Clark's son remarked that they would "send the old man to the Senate or to the poor house."[290] For his part, Clark said that he "never bought a man who wasn't for sale."[291] By some estimates, Clark spent $431,000 to buy forty-seven votes in the state legislature and offered more than $200,000 more that was rebuffed.[292] Commenting on the brazen corruption in the election, Mark Twain said of Clark, "He is said to have bought legislatures and judges as other men buy food and raiment. By his example he has so excused and so sweetened corruption that in Montana it no longer has an offensive smell."[293] Senator William Clark took office in Washington, only to have investigations open immediately. After hearing testimony from state legislators and even Montana Supreme Court justices whom Clark's agents attempted to bribe, the Senate investigations committee declared Clark's election void.[294] In an amazing maneuver, Clark resigned and his allies in Montana contrived to get the governor out of the state, making the lieutenant governor (a Clark ally) the acting governor—at which point the lieutenant governor appointed Clark to fill the now-vacant Senate seat Clark had just been denied.[295]

By the early years of the twentieth century, a new copper king, F. Augustus "Fritz" Heinze, emerged on the scene. Heinze was opposed to Amalgamated Copper, the Standard Oil–linked owner of the now-deceased Marcus Daly's Anaconda Copper Company. Heinze controlled two local judges who consistently ruled against Amalgamated. Fed up after a significant adverse ruling, Amalgamated Copper closed down all of its industrial and mining operations in 1903, putting 80 percent of Montana's workers out of a job.[296] It refused to restart operations unless the governor called a special session of the legislature and passed legislation that would protect the company from these adverse rulings. After three weeks, the governor and the legislature complied.[297]

Amalgamated Copper returned to politics in 1908, proposing a bill that would have, in effect, made monopolies legal by allowing one corporation to have a controlling stake in others. The law would have allowed Amalgamated to control every corporation in the state.[298] The Republican W. F. Meyer worried that it was "simply a means by which one corporation can control the whole state, body and soul."[299] Thomas Everett argued that the "most baleful power of the trusts is not that of fixing prices. The most baleful power of the trusts is that they can go into the halls of legislation and control the passage of laws."[300] In the wake of the "great shutdown," Amalgamated had gotten out of politics briefly, during which time populists gained influence in the state legislature and passed a state constitutional amendment allowing for popular initiatives and referenda.[301] With this new tool in hand, populists in 1912 pushed four reform initiatives, including the Corrupt Practices Act—a campaign finance reform law that blocked corporate spending in elections.[302] Montana's Corrupt Practices Act passed with 76 percent of the vote—a landslide victory against the copper kings' political influence. A century later, in the aftermath of the *Citizens United* decision, the Supreme Court of the United States would strike down Montana's Corrupt Practices Act by a 5–4 vote, without even hearing an argument in the case.[303]

The events in Montana were some of the most extreme and shameless in the country, but they were a powerful indicator that the wealthiest Americans would not confine themselves to gaining power in the economic realm. Daly, Clark, and Heinze attempted to gain control of every part of the government—the legislature, courts, and executive. They even tried to control the newspapers to shape public opinion in their favor. Some commentators had trouble describing this new state of affairs. Charles Francis Adams pondered the problem: "We know what aristocracy, autocracy, democracy are, but we have no word to express 'government by moneyed corporations.'"[304] Other commentators knew exactly what word to use: "plutocracy."

The emergence of the plutocracy initiated a vicious cycle that threatened the Republic. Plutocrats used their money to control every aspect of the government. Then they used the government to give themselves special privileges. Those privileges meant widening inequality, more wealth to the plutocrats, and, as a result, more political power. In *The New Plutocracy,* John Reed in 1903 lamented the decline of the American system from a revolution and constitution that "made all our citizens equal in political and civil rights and privileges" to a system where "rulers buy their places."[305] "We are governed by an elective aristocracy, which in its turn, is largely controlled by an aristocracy of wealth," Frank Parsons wrote. "Behind the legislatures and congresses are the corporations and the trusts; behind the machines, the rings and the bosses, are the business monopolies, the industrial combinations and the plutocrats; behind the political monopolists are the industrial monopolists."[306] Former South Dakota senator Richard Pettigrew reflected back on his time in Congress in the 1890s: "I could form only one possible conclusion— that the power over American public life, whether economic, social or political, rested in the hands of the rich." America was no longer a republic. "Plutocracy is a word that means rule by and for the rich. The United States is a country run by and for the rich. Therefore, it is a plutocracy."[307]

Henry George Jr., son of the agrarian reformer, told the story of how America had changed. "Except for the slaves and Indians," he wrote in *The Menace of Privilege,* "there was at the beginning of the Republic full political and approximate social equality. . . . [R]eal poverty was casual and nowhere deep or chronic. The reason of this was plain. The easy access to land made it a comparatively simple matter for all men to get subsistence."[308] Now, however, "privileges granted or sanctioned by government" had created inequality that is "ominous in the Republic."[309] Privileges were everywhere: private ownership of natural resources, the tariff and other taxation on production, special government grants, grants under general laws, and immunities in the courts.[310] And the privileged used their wealth to further their privilege, by controlling not just the federal government and state and local governments but by trying to influence the press, universities, and the church.[311] Even the courts were captured. "[C]orporate lawyers now lead the bar everywhere," John Reed said, "nobody but a corporation lawyer can get an important judgeship."[312] Richard Pettigrew wanted to abolish the federal courts altogether.[313] In an almost complete reversal from Tocqueville's comments on equality in America, Supreme Court justice Henry Brown remarked at Yale Law School in 1895, "Probably in no country in the world is the influence of wealth more potent than in this, and in no period of our history has it been more powerful than now."[314]

In his two-volume *American Commonwealth*, first published in 1888, the British aristocrat Lord James Bryce argued that the American system suffered most not from mob rule but from wealth-related dangers: "the existence of a class of persons using government as a means of private gain"; "the menacing power of wealth"; capitalists who "have not unfrequently abused the powers which the privilege of incorporation conferred upon them"; and those who "employed their wealth to procure legislation opposed to the public interests."[315] In the conventional understanding of the forms of government, plutocracy was a kind of oligarchy, opposed to democracy. But "there is a strong plutocratic element infused into American democracy; and the fact that it is entirely unrecognized in constitutions makes it not less potent, and possibly more mischievous."[316] While "[s]ixty years ago there were no great fortunes in America, few large fortunes, no poverty," America in 1888 had some poverty, "many large fortunes, and a greater number of gigantic fortunes than in any other country of the world."[317] Bryce remained optimistic that Americans' "faith in equality and love of equality are too deeply implanted" to be "rooted out by any economic changes," but he cautioned Americans that "[t]he influence of money is one of the dangers which the people have always to guard against, for . . . its methods are as numerous as they are insidious."[318]

Writing in his diary, former president Rutherford B. Hayes worried about how the "influence of money" had resulted in "excessive wealth in the hands of the few" and that there was now a "maldistribution of property," which meant "extreme poverty, ignorance, vice, and wretchedness of the many."[319] The consequences for the Republic were clear. "This is a government of the people, by the people, and for the people no longer," Hayes wrote. "It is a government by the corporations, of the corporations, and for the corporations."[320]

CHAPTER FOUR

The Search for Solutions

Theodore Roosevelt once remarked that Walter Lippmann was "the most brilliant young man of his age in all the United States."[1] This sentiment was widely shared. An elderly William James sought out Lippmann in his college dorm room to praise an essay the undergraduate had published. The British Fabian Graham Wallas found Lippmann so appealing that he dedicated his book *The Great Society* to his former student. And after graduating from Harvard in three years, Lippmann served as a course assistant to the philosopher George Santayana and a research assistant to the famed journalist and muckraker Lincoln Steffens.[2]

So began one of the most spectacular careers in American public life. Lippmann was a founding editor of *The New Republic* (along with Herbert Croly and Walter Weyl); an adviser to Woodrow Wilson's closest aide, Colonel House; the author of most of the Fourteen Points; and the nation's leading newspaper columnist—first at the New York *World* and then at the *Herald Tribune*. Within a year of starting his *Tribune* column in 1931, Lippmann had a national audience of ten million people. For half a century, he would shape public opinion through his column (syndicated in more than two hundred newspapers) and through twenty-three widely read books. Lippmann even coined the term "Cold War" with the title of his 1947 book.

In 1914, only a few years out of college, Lippmann published a book diagnosing the tumult of the Progressive Era. *Drift and Mastery* described the lack of control, a lack of "mastery," over the forces unleashed by industrialization. Attempts to reclaim the past or achieve a utopian future were misguided and furthered "drift." The only option was to face modern challenges head-on. What was necessary was not just "freedom for the little profiteer" but freedom from "the chaos, the welter, the strategy of industrial war."[3]

Drift and Mastery was one of the most important books of the Progressive Era, and it provides the key to understanding the ethos behind what is probably the most underappreciated period in American history. When it is used today, "progressive" is not usually thought of as describing someone with a coherent worldview or philosophy. Instead, it is generally thought of as a term to describe those who prefer not to be called "liberal," those who are on the far left side of the political spectrum, or those who are part of a conglomeration of center-left groups in American politics.

Even historians have trouble with the "progressives." The earliest historians spoke not of a "movement" but instead of two groups within the Progressive Era, such as new-stock urban liberals and old-stock patrician reformers, or western democratic Bryanites and eastern elite Rooseveltians.[4] In the early 1970s, the idea of a progressive movement was criticized as ideologically incoherent, a mere grab bag of policies and traditions. According to this reading, the Progressive Era was simply a time of "shifting, ideologically fluid, issue-focused coalitions" that anticipated and created the system of interest groups that came to define American politics in the post–World War II period.[5] One historian characterizes the Progressive Era as a time of transformation, from America's many diffuse and eroding "island communities" to a bureaucratic national order.[6] Another sees progressives as drawing on three distinct themes: antimonopoly, the social bonds between human beings, and efficiency.[7] A third characterizes the progressives' work as improving people through social and moral policy, controlling big business, and ending class conflict, all while endorsing segregation.[8] With so many interpretations and variations, it is hard not to agree with the historian Richard Hofstadter when he wrote that progressivism was "a rather widespread and remarkably good-natured effort of the greater part of society to achieve some not very clearly specified self-reformation."[9]

But *Drift and Mastery* suggests there was something at the heart of progressivism. Lippmann argued that the nation had entered a period of "drift"—a lack of control over dynamic forces in the world—and that drift was the source of the "current unrest" in the country. Business had been radically transformed by "the huge corporation, the integrated industry, production for a world market, the network of combinations, pools and agreements," and the rise of consumerism.[10] Social life had been transformed as well. Urbanization shifted people from country to city, breaking the "loyalties of place."[11] And the traditional order—"the sanctity of property, the patriarchal family, hereditary caste, the dogma of sin, obedience to authority"—now "survive[d] only as habits or by default."[12] The deepest anxieties were brought on by what Lippmann called the "fear economy": "The fear of losing one's job, the necessity of being somebody in a crowded and clamorous world, the terror that old age will not be secured, that your children will lack opportunity—there are a thousand terrors which arise out of the unorganized and unstable economic system under which we live."[13]

Lippmann's answer to drift was *mastery*. Mastery involved "the substitution of conscious intention for unconscious striving," and Lippmann used "mastery" as a catchall to describe people taking control of their circumstances and making active choices about the path forward.[14] "We can no longer treat life as something that has trickled down to us," he wrote. "We have to deal with it deliberately, devise its social organization, alter its tools, formulate its method, educate and control it."[15] Politically, mastery was the spirit of democracy. "Democracy is more than the absence of czars, more than freedom, more than equal opportunity," Lippmann argued. "It is a way of life, a use of freedom, an embrace of opportunity."[16] Democracy allowed people to break free from tradition and theory. It was only through a robust democracy that the people could shape their destiny.

Lippmann's concept of mastery provides perhaps the best explanation of what united thinkers and activists during the Progressive Era. Scholars and commentators have long struggled to connect the movements of the time—expansion of suffrage and the direct election of senators; active government regulating private actors; social settlements and voluntary efforts; Prohibition and social legislation; scientific management principles; eugenics and racial supremacy;

labor organizing. Positive or negative, all were different pathways for gaining mastery over changing forces in society. They were attempts to address the deep human needs that massive social and economic transformations laid bare in the early twentieth century. In his review of *Drift and Mastery*, Theodore Roosevelt captured the heart of Lippmann's project. "There can be no real political democracy unless there is something approaching an economic democracy," he wrote. "There can be neither political nor industrial democracy unless people are reasonably well-to-do, and also reasonably able to achieve the difficult task of self-mastery."[17]

The progressives wanted mastery over the forces around them. They passed constitutional amendments and legislation bringing power back to the people. They devised new, innovative ways to reform and control the economic and political influence of big corporations. And they did all of these things because they knew it was necessary to preserve America's middle-class constitution—to save the Republic. A generation later, in the midst of the Great Depression, the New Dealers would follow many of these same strategies. The stakes were the existence of democracy itself. If democracy couldn't solve the economic problems of the Depression, they feared the rise of a dictatorship in America and the end of the Republic. When World War II required full mobilization, the emphasis shifted—from the people against the plutocracy to democracy against dictatorship. Victory in 1945 initiated a postwar boom that lasted thirty years. The glorious decades saw rising prosperity, rising growth, and relative economic equality. While these changes didn't apply equally to everyone, the boom years allowed debates on civil rights and improved living standards even for those still excluded from the full promise of American equality. But by the 1970s, the age of equality was ending. Economic shocks combined with racial and cultural fragmentation. The result was an America that was once again at risk of losing its middle-class constitution.

THE PEOPLE STRIKE BACK

When the Sixteenth Amendment, which established Congress's power to create an income tax, was ratified in 1913, it was only the third time the American people reversed a Supreme Court decision through constitutional amendment. The first was the Eleventh Amendment, dealing with sovereign immunity, in 1795, and the second was the Civil War amendments, reversing the infamous *Dred Scott* decision.[18]

The origins of the income tax are rooted in the declining fortunes of the tariff and the rising fortunes of the wealthy. From the founding through the nineteenth century, the government derived its revenues primarily through the tariff. While the tariff started as a way to raise revenue while alleviating the economic burdens on ordinary Americans in the 1780s, its justifications changed frequently during the nineteenth century from countering British power to developing infant industries and protecting wage labor. By the turn of the twentieth century, economists had started revising their theories of trade, and Americans increasingly believed the tariff had become a tool of the special interests to prevent competition, in the process contributing to the rise of trusts and increasing costs for ordinary people.[19]

At the same time, new data emerged in the early 1890s documenting the rise in inequality during the Gilded Age. In studies surprisingly similar to those conducted today by economists Thomas Piketty, Emmanuel Saez, and others, Thomas Sherman and George K. Holmes gathered data on the share of income held by the wealthiest Americans. Sherman concluded that the top 6 percent of Americans owned two-thirds of all wealth in the country. Holmes found the top 9 percent holding 70 percent of America's wealth. Sherman's and Holmes's work reached a wide audience, and it contributed to the idea that taxation should be based on one's ability to pay.[20] The rich should "not be permitted to shirk" their civic duties, Cordell Hull said. It would be better to "tax wealth not poverty."[21]

Between these sentiments, the rising power of the populist movement, and the panic of 1893 and the depression that followed, the country reached a crisis point.[22] In 1894, Congress passed a corporate income tax, which was intended to be a convenient, workable way to tax shareholders (who were usually wealthy individuals).[23] Almost immediately, shareholders of a corporation, who didn't want the corporation to pay the tax, challenged it as unconstitutional. The Constitution required that "direct taxes" be apportioned proportionally according to the number of people in each state and that "duties" be "uniform" throughout the United States.[24] Few worried that the corporate tax was at risk under either provision, given Supreme Court opinions from 1796 and 1881.[25] Overturning those cases in 1895, the Supreme Court struck down the tax by a 5–4 vote in *Pollock v. Farmers' Loan and Trust Co.* In his concurrence, Justice Stephen J. Field, well-known for his laissez-faire views, announced, "The present assault upon capital is but the beginning. It will be but the stepping-stone to others, larger and more sweeping, till our political contests will become a war of the poor against the rich,—a war constantly growing in intensity and bitterness."[26] Dissenting, Justice Edward Douglass White chastened the Court for taking part in the "animosities of factions" and called the decision "fraught with danger to the court, to each and every citizen, and to the republic."[27] The Court's decision in *Pollock* only emboldened proponents of the tax. The following year, the graduated income tax made it into the Democratic Party platform for the first time, and reformers increasingly pushed for taxation along progressive lines.[28]

In 1907, another financial panic and recession called attention to issues of wealth and economic power, setting the stage for Congress to pass a corporate tax and send the income-tax constitutional amendment to the states for ratification. There were many justifications for these initiatives, but both proposals rode a wave of popular support for controlling corporations and combating the political power of economic elites. In his message to Congress initiating debate on the corporate tax, President William Howard Taft recognized the benefits of corporations but at the same time noted, "[S]ubstantially all of the abuses and all of the evils which have aroused the public to the necessity of reform were made possible by the use of this very faculty." His bill would take a "long step toward that supervisory control of corporations which may prevent a further abuse of power."[29] During the debate in Congress, Senator Robert Owen declared that "[t]he most important need of the people of the United States of this generation requires the abatement of the gigantic fortunes being piled up by successful monopoly, ... which have brought about a grossly inequitable distribution of the proceeds of human labor."[30] The corporate tax passed in 1909, in part because businesspeople and elites wanted to prevent more radical proposals to have the federal government, rather than the states, incorporate, license, and regulate corporations.[31]

The debate over the income-tax amendment was justified along similar lines. Senator William Borah of Idaho linked the tax directly to America's form of government. The framers of the Constitution did not want the tax burden to fall "upon the backs of those who toil" while "the great accumulated wealth of the Nation" paid nothing. "It was never so intended," he explained. "[I]t was a republic they were building, where all men were to be equal and bear equally the burdens of government, and not an oligarchy, for that must a government be, in the end, which exempts property and wealth from all taxes."[32] Representative Champ Clark recognized that at the time of "the Constitution, population was about equally distributed, and wealth was also; but times change and men change with them, and things change too."[33]

In February 1913, the income-tax amendment was ratified, and that same year Congress passed the first, modest, graduated income tax. It placed a 1 percent "normal" tax on incomes of $3,000 ($4,000 for married couples), and a "rich man's tax" of between 1 percent and 6 percent on incomes between $20,000 and $500,000.[34] Over time, corporate and personal income taxes revolutionized the fiscal structure of the government. In 1880, customs and excise taxes made up 90 percent of federal revenues. By 1930, they were only 25 percent. The income tax contributed nothing in 1880 to the Treasury. By 1930, it accounted for 59 percent of funds.[35]

As extraordinary as the Sixteenth Amendment was the Seventeenth Amendment. Under the original Constitution, the state legislatures selected U.S. senators. The Seventeenth Amendment instead provided for the direct election of senators by the people. What is astonishing is what was required for this constitutional amendment to pass: two-thirds of the sitting senators, all of whom had been selected under the old method, had to agree to change the system that put them in power. And three-fourths of the state legislatures had to give up their power to pick senators. How did this happen?

The answer partly has to do with the political consequences of economic wealth. By the late nineteenth century, many Americans believed the Senate had been captured, filled with men "who never would have gone there but [f]or the corrupt use of money to secure their election."[36] From 1857 to 1899, the Senate dealt with ten cases of bribery allegations leading to the selection of its members.[37] Commentators thought it was "beyond dispute that bribery is the rule rather than the exception," because senators were hesitant to expose their colleagues' (and in some cases, it was believed, their corporate sponsors') corruption in all but the most obvious cases.[38] Edgar Lee Masters expressed the characteristic concern of the era: "No system is free where there is an upper legislative branch whose members owe their selection to plutocratic intrigue, whose stock-in-trade is preserving for the rich and paltering with the poor."[39]

Outright bribery was not the only problem. The selection of senators by the state legislatures also resulted in the composition of the Senate being skewed toward the rich and toward those whose lives and careers were intertwined with corporations. Lord Bryce noted that "[t]he Senate now contains many men of great wealth. Some, an increasing number, are senators because they are rich; a few are rich because they are senators."[40] People increasingly worried that elites took on "a senatorship as some decoration granted them by a state legislature at the behest of the boss in recognition of their having piled up millions in mining copper or selling oil or watering gas stock."[41] In many cases, senators even retained their connections to the corporate world. New York senator Chauncey Depew held a shocking seventy-four corporate directorships while serving in the Senate.[42] Critics commonly and cleverly modified the old biblical proverb: "It is harder for a poor man to enter the United States Senate than for a rich man to enter Heaven."[43]

Once rooted in the Senate, the economically powerful spread their influence throughout the government through the Constitution's system of checks and balances. Senators were necessary to confirm executive branch officials and federal judges. Commentators argued that the courts' laissez-faire mentality was directly tied to the corporate capture of the Senate. "Plutocracy appoints the Federal judges," Edgar Lee Masters said.[44] The corporations "can prevent the appointment of any man to the Federal bench, or to any other Federal position, who is not the choice of the corporations," wrote another reformer.[45] The chief justice of the North Carolina Supreme Court, Walter Clark, thought the problem so significant that he went so far as to advocate for the election of federal judges. The Senate was filled "by the influence of corporate power and very often by the selection of the attorneys of those corporations."[46] Corporate wealth "exert[ed] influence" over the president and the Senate, so no judge could get confirmed "without the approval of allied plutocracy."[47] Clark was smart enough to recognize that in most cases the judges were not taking bribes. The influence of wealth was more subtle. Judicial nominees were frequently lawyers for corporations; over time, they ended up "believing sincerely in the correctness" of the views of "aggregated wealth."[48] The bench, he said, was filled with people who had a "natural and perhaps unconscious bias from having spent their lives at the bar in advocacy of corporate claims."[49]

One commentator looked back to the class warfare constitutions of the ancient world and suggested the Constitution be reformed so that there would be one house elected by the people and "a second legislative chamber in which the representatives of property interests shall sit."[50] But he was an outlier. For most reformers, the answer wasn't the revival of a class warfare constitution; it was popular election. It was "dangerous to democracy" for senators to gain power "solely because of their wealth."[51] If America wanted to retain its "republican form of government," then bribery and corruption had to end.[52] Because "[a] small body of men (as a legislature) is easier stacked up and handled and bought than the whole body of people at the polls," the election of senators by the people would "render the efforts of the briber futile."[53] Under popular election, corporations and the wealthy would not be able to exert as much influence as they could under legislative selection.[54]

Between 1893 and 1911, the House of Representatives voted for a constitutional amendment to change the method of selecting senators six times, only to meet defeat in the Senate.[55] But over time, populists and progressives gained ground. The most innovative tactic started in Oregon. Under the "Oregon System," voters forced state legislators to sign pledges declaring they would obey the popular will on selection for the Senate.[56] Coupled with a nonbinding referendum on the people's preference for senator, voters in Oregon were able to wrestle control of the election of a senator from the state legislature. Senators elected under the Oregon System knew they owed their positions to the people, and state legislatures were already pledged to support popular preferences. A constitutional amendment—even one that stripped entrenched power—became harder to oppose. Grassroots action led to greater democracy.

The direct election of senators was but one part of a package of progressive reforms designed to reduce the political power of the plutocracy. Popular initiatives, referenda, and direct primaries—in which voters would choose party candidates during primary elections, rather than having conventions of party elites pick the candidates— were among the other leading reforms that spread throughout the states. Both were based on the same theory as the direct election of senators: popular power could counteract the political power of the wealthy elites. But progressives also recognized that the economically powerful would try anything to influence elections. As a result, they came up with campaign finance restrictions as a complementary tool to restore republican government in America.

The flood of money into politics started in the latter part of the nineteenth century. In 1888, Matthew Quay, the Pennsylvania Republican leader, raised millions for Benjamin Harrison from steelmakers and oil companies.[57] The undisputed champion of organizing donations from the wealthy was Mark Hanna, William McKinley's campaign manager. Hanna once famously remarked, "There are two things that are important in politics. The first is money, and I can't remember what the second is." In 1896, Hanna argued to the finance industry that the election of populist William Jennings Bryan would threaten their interests. But he didn't simply ask for voluntary contributions. He made "assessments" of corporations based on their size and wealth, and he demanded a percentage of their overall capitalization. As one commentator wrote, "Hanna shook down the business world for $2.5 million."[58]

Across the country, reformers feared corporate power over elections. Kentucky banned corporate contributions in elections in 1891.[59] Tennessee, Florida, and Nebraska passed similar bans in 1897.[60] In New York, Elihu Root proposed banning corporate money in elections in the 1894 state constitutional convention. The ban would "prevent . . . the great railroad companies, the great insurance companies, the great telephone companies, the great aggregations of wealth, from using their corporate funds, directly or indirectly, to send members of the Legislature to these halls in order to vote for their protection and the advancement of their interests as against those of the public."[61] Senator William Chandler, a Republican from New Hampshire, lost his seat because he was insufficiently supportive of the Boston and Maine Railroad's interests and influence.[62] In response, he introduced the first federal restriction on corporate contributions in 1901, and he became a leading advocate for campaign finance reform.[63] "A republic is supposed to be individual government," he said in 1904. "But when corporations can furnish money to carry elections from corporation treasuries, individualism in government is gone. . . . When the custom grows broad enough the whole character of government is changed, and corporations rule, not men."[64]

A year later, a scandal broke out that energized public support for reform. Life insurance companies were supposed to be "better" than other companies, because their work was related to the welfare of individuals. Investigatory reporting and hearings exposed that the Equitable Life Insurance Company had used its corporate treasury funds to support the McKinley and Roosevelt campaigns.[65] The scandal dominated the press, leading to damning information. Senator Chauncey Depew of New York had received a $20,000 retainer from Equitable since 1888, while Senator David Hill (also of New York) got $5,000.[66] Senator John Dryden of New Jersey—who was also the founder and president of Prudential Insurance—was called to testify, and he admitted to using corporate funds to support Republican candidates in 1896, 1900, and 1904. In the accounting books, Dryden had recorded the contributions simply as "expenses."[67] Contrary to the approach of the Supreme Court in 2010's *Citizens United,* the *New-York Tribune* raised the stakes of the Equitable Life scandal to one of constitutional dimensions: "In the United States the government is intended to be a government of men. A corporation is not a citizen with a right to vote or take a hand otherwise in politics."[68] In the wake of the scandal, Chandler and Congressman Perry Belmont started the first campaign finance reform group, the National Publicity Bill Organization.[69]

In 1907, the New York *World* published a letter from railroad magnate E. H. Harriman claiming that he had raised $250,000 at President Theodore Roosevelt's request in 1904 and that he expected, in return, that Senator Depew would be named as an ambassador. With Depew overseas, his New York Senate seat would be available for someone favorable to Harriman's faction in state politics.[70] At the time, the idea of a president's asking for money to support a campaign was anathema to political culture, a violation of decorum. Roosevelt denied the charges, but the news provided the momentum necessary for Congress to ban corporate contributions to campaigns. The Tillman Act of 1907, named after the populist reformer and vicious racist "Pitchfork" Ben Tillman of South Carolina, became the first major federal campaign finance reform law.

Scholars have debated precisely why the Tillman Act passed. Some argue the central motivation was to protect shareholders.[71] The Equitable Life scandal, after all, was about a corporation's misallocating its funds—spending that should have gone to the shareholders of the company but instead advanced the political preferences of corporate managers. Others argue that corporations were in favor of the reforms because they were tired of getting shaken down for contributions by the Mark Hannas of the political world.[72] These corporate-law explanations are certainly important parts of the story. But these explanations miss the bigger picture. The Tillman Act was but one plank of the reformers' platform to restrict corporate influence in politics—a platform that included direct election of senators, direct primaries, initiatives and referenda, and public disclosure.

Indeed, after the Tillman Act, campaign finance reform efforts continued. During the 1908 election, both presidential candidates—William Howard Taft and William Jennings Bryan—announced they would voluntarily disclose all of their campaign contributions.[73] The consequences were immediately noticeable. The wealthy gave surprisingly less during the 1908 race than the 1904 campaign. More than 50 percent of Theodore Roosevelt's campaign funds in 1904 came from only nine donors, who each put in six-figure sums of money.

In 1908, there was only one donor who contributed six figures, and that was Taft's brother, who gave $110,000.[74] With Taft's victory, the reformers passed the Publicity Act in 1910, requiring post–Election Day reporting of the national parties' receipts and expenditures.[75] The following year, now with Democratic majorities, Congress expanded the Publicity Act. The 1911 amendments required pre–Election Day reporting, expanded the scope from parties to Senate and House campaigns, and limited expenditures in House races to $5,000 and in Senate races to $10,000 (or lower if state law provided for a lower cap on spending).[76] James Reed, the freshman member from Missouri who added the Senate and House restrictions, said they were necessary because the importance of money in campaigns "bars the aspiration to the House of Representatives or to the Senate of any man who does not possess the means."[77]

These changes—the income-tax amendment, the direct election of senators, campaign finance reform—marked a sea change in the American political system. And yet, surprisingly, the Progressive Era is rarely considered one of the central moments in America's constitutional story.[78] When constitutional scholars describe the American constitutional tradition, they usually focus on three moments: the founding, the Civil War, and the New Deal. The founding sets the framework for government. The post–Civil War era, often called the "second founding," provides the Thirteenth, Fourteenth, and Fifteenth Amendments, ending slavery, giving African Americans the right to vote, and creating the right to "equal protection of the laws" that has been central to ensuring racial and gender equality. Although no constitutional amendments were adopted, the New Deal is seen as the critical moment in the creation of the regulatory state—the moment when the Supreme Court abandoned the laissez-faire philosophy of the Gilded Age and allowed democratic majorities to regulate the economy. In recent years, scholars have even argued there is a fourth "constitutional moment"—the civil rights revolution of the 1960s.[79]

But it was during the Progressive Era that some of the most consequential reforms to the new industrial economy took place. The progressives understood that economic transformations were a threat to the Republic, and they fought to simultaneously reform the

Constitution and restructure the economy. The progressives passed four constitutional amendments in seven years—establishing an income tax, shifting the structure of the Constitution to require the direct election of senators, prohibiting the sale of alcohol, and giving women the right to vote. At the same time, in response to the changes wrought by the Industrial Revolution, the progressives engaged in some of the most creative and important legislative reforms in American history. Through food and drug regulation, conservation, income taxes, and antitrust, they sought to constrain the economic powers of corporations and wealthy elites that had been unleashed during the Gilded Age.

THE VARIETIES OF PROGRESSIVE REFORM

The progressives recognized the importance of the rise of corporate capitalism in America. As Richard Hofstadter put it half a century later, "[N]othing less was at stake than the entire organization of American business and American politics, the very question of who was to control the country."[80] The idea of mastery united the progressives, but it took on many manifestations—each seeking to address the challenges that accompanied the Industrial Revolution. Constitutional lawyers and theorists pay too little attention to these movements and to the political thinkers who shaped and explained them. Yet it was Progressive Era thinkers who crafted the most creative and best-theorized approaches to wrangling, constraining, shaping, and reimagining the relationship between economic power and political power.[81]

"Big business," Theodore Roosevelt declared in 1910, "has become nationalized and the only effective way of controlling and directing it and preventing the abuses in connection with it is by having the people nationalize the governmental control in order to meet the nationalization of the big business itself." It was folly to try to break up big businesses, Roosevelt believed. They were "the result of an imperative economic law" that couldn't be willed away by political action. The only viable answer was government control, or else corporations would become "the ruler of the people."[82]

For Roosevelt, a vigorous, engaged national government was the fulfillment of American constitutional principles. "The chief reason ... that led to the formation of the National Government," he wrote in his annual message to Congress in 1908, "was the absolute need that the Union, and not the several States, should deal with interstate and foreign commerce, and the power to deal with interstate commerce was granted absolutely and plenarily to the Central government." In the early republic, the only forms of interstate commerce were "the waterways, the highroads, as well as the partnerships of individuals." But that had all changed with the Industrial Revolution. In the new economy of the early twentieth century, "[i]nterstate commerce is now chiefly conducted by railroads; and the great corporation has supplanted the mass of small partnerships or individuals." Roosevelt's desire for national governmental power over the economy was "merely a proposal to carry out to the letter one of the prime purposes, if not the prime purpose, for which the Constitution was founded."[83]

When it came to corporate power, Roosevelt advocated for an approach that might seem surprising today. In 1903, Congress created the Bureau of Corporations within the newly created Department of Commerce and Labor. Roosevelt ran the bureau as an adjunct to his own office, working closely with bureau leaders in the ensuing years. The bureau did not have the power to license corporations, but it did have investigatory and subpoena powers. As a result, it was in a position to help Roosevelt shape public opinion and recommend regulatory reforms.[84] Roosevelt and the bureau's leadership were clear to distinguish between the size of corporations and unfair competition, and they set their crosshairs on unfair competition.[85] The bureau initiated voluntary investigations with major corporate conglomerates like U.S. Steel and International Harvester, searching their books and advising them on which practices to stop. In return, Roosevelt promised not to initiate prosecutions under the Sherman Antitrust Act.[86]

But the bureau's investigatory powers weren't enough for its leaders or for Roosevelt. The bureau advocated for a licensing power: corporations would have to get a federal license to operate, and preserving their license would be contingent on disclosing basic features of the corporations' structure and finances.[87] Roosevelt wanted to go even further. In his annual message in 1908, he called for a federal agency that had "full power of control and supervision" over combinations.[88] In an age of national interconnectedness, Roosevelt thought the federal government, not the states, needed to have the power of incorporation. His federal incorporation law would give the agency the power to incorporate businesses, require disclosure, and even prevent the issuance of stock without the authorization of the secretary of commerce (the latter reflected Roosevelt's fierce opposition to stock speculators).[89]

In the context of corporate governance, which today remains with the states, Roosevelt's preference for federal regulation might seem unconventional. But his basic approach came to pass across virtually all areas of public policy. As Frederick Winslow Taylor's principles of scientific management gained traction, progressives began to see expertise and a professional civil service as a way to insulate policy making from corruption. During Roosevelt's time, the Pure Food and Drug Act and the Meat Inspection Act (both passed in 1906) created federal regulation of food and pharmaceuticals. Throughout the twentieth century, federal regulation would become the dominant model in a variety of areas. Aviation, occupational safety, consumer products, clean water, clean air, hazardous materials—all are areas in which the national government regulates markets to protect the public from the misuse of corporate power and to advance the public interest. Roosevelt's incorporation law simply applied this approach to corporate governance.

In *The Promise of American Life* (1909), Herbert Croly gave Roosevelt's presidential actions historical and philosophical foundation. America's national promise was one of "improving popular economic condition, guaranteed by democratic political institutions, and resulting in moral and social amelioration."[90] From the founding onward, there had been a tension between two traditions that sought to fulfill this promise. The Jeffersonians, who feared national government action, tended to side with ordinary Americans. The Hamiltonians embraced a strong national government but often used it to protect elites. Roosevelt's great innovation was to fuse the best of both traditions, to achieve Jeffersonian ends of supporting the people by the Hamiltonian means of a strong national government. The New Nationalism, as Croly called it, would help address the "prevailing abuses and sins" that were associated with "the prodigious concentration of wealth, and of the power exercised by wealth."[91] Labor unions, graduated inheritance taxes, public service commissions, and regulation were all part of the program.

Five years later, Croly fused his nationalism with the rising democratic impulses of the progressive movement across the country. In *Progressive Democracy,* he focused on economic change and political reform. Like many others at the time, he started with the Beardian thesis that the Constitution was an undemocratic document, largely put together by the wealthy classes (though he took the argument from J. Allen Smith rather than Beard).[92] In this second book, Croly sought to explain a deep puzzle: When the Jeffersonian opponents to the Federalists and their elite Constitution took power in 1801, why didn't they reform the Constitution and make it more democratic? The answer, Croly argued, is that the "American democracy rallied to an undemocratic Constitution" because it was in Americans' economic interests.[93] In England, the protection of property rights and the limited restrictions on acquiring property "resulted in the concentration of wealth in comparatively few hands." But not in America. In America, the government's economic policies—like encouraging settlement in the West—benefited the majority of American citizens.[94] The problem was that by the end of the nineteenth century the "pioneer conditions" had given way to industrial production. Government policies to promote growth were based on "the supposition that every economic class was benefitting equally from the stimulation."[95] But this was no longer the case. "Harmony between industrial and social interest could no longer be automatically created."[96] Instead, policies that stimulated growth were now "creating real and irreconcilable antagonisms between class and class."[97] The system was not producing "economic results traditionally associated with American popular government—a socially desirable distribution both of wealth and of economic responsibility, and a steady improvement in the general standard of living."[98]

What was needed now, Croly thought, was Progressive Democracy, a set of structural reforms—constitutional and nonconstitutional—that would reshape democracy and realign government policy and the distribution of economic gains. Croly focused largely on "direct government," including the need to make the process of amending the Constitution simpler and more responsive to majority preferences. More democracy meant the structures of American government could better adapt to the racing changes of the industrial age. Politically, Croly embraced the package of reforms first dreamed up by the Populists and implemented by progressives throughout the states: the direct primaries, direct election of senators, initiatives and referenda, recall elections. Economically, he expressed support for industrial democracy, an updated and rebranded version of the Knights of Labor's cooperative commonwealth.

Where Croly and Roosevelt supported a centralizing approach to controlling economic power, Louis Brandeis best exemplified the decentralizing vision. Lawyer, Zionist, adviser to Woodrow Wilson, and future Supreme Court justice, Brandeis was a giant in the legal profession. Known as the "People's Lawyer" for his frequent advocacy on behalf of ordinary people and their interests, Brandeis was the first to call for a "right to privacy," and he revolutionized legal practice with his frequent use of statistics and data in legal argument.[99]

During the Progressive Era, Brandeis recognized industrial change as a crisis of the highest magnitude. "The struggles of the eighteenth and nineteenth centuries both in peace and in war were devoted largely to overcoming the aristocratic position," Brandeis wrote.[100] But "[s]ince the adoption of the Federal Constitution, and notably within the last fifty years," the country had been through "an economic and social revolution" that had greater significance "than any political revolution known to history." Machinery, communications, transportation—all have "wrought changes in the conditions of life which are in many respects greater than those which had occurred in civilized countries during thousands of years preceding." With these changes came opportunity to free people from the "thraldom of drudgery," but at the same time emerged "new dangers to liberty." While some politicians had recognized and attempted to adapt to these changes, the law "was largely deaf and blind to them." The courts, in particular, blocked political action to the point that the judiciary's laissez-faire position "became dangerous; because constitutional limitations were invoked to stop the natural vent of legislation."[101]

The struggle for "social and industrial justice" was the third great trial in American history—comparable only to the Revolution and the Civil War.[102] And the stakes couldn't have been higher. "Either political liberty will be extinguished or industrial liberty must be restored," Brandeis thought.[103] The problem was that while most Americans had political liberty, they experienced industrial absolutism. "We are as free politically, perhaps, as free as it is possible for us to be. Every male has his voice and vote. . . . On the other hand, in dealing with industrial problems the position of the ordinary worker is exactly the reverse. The individual employee has no effective voice or vote."[104] The Republic could not persist without a free and independent citizenry, and people were "not free if dependent industrially upon the arbitrary will of another."[105] But Brandeis did not think constitutional amendment was necessary. "Instead of amending the Constitution," he said, "I would amend men's economic and social ideals."[106]

If America was to retain its tradition of "rule by the people," political democracy would not be enough.[107] Citizens needed to have the qualities necessary for self-government, and that was impossible unless economic conditions allowed them to be independent. Higher wages, reduced hours, safe conditions, collective bargaining—all were important, but they were not enough to form citizens of the Republic.[108] Political democracy required "industrial democracy."[109] In an industrial democracy, there would be shared responsibility, collaboration between labor and management.[110] "The employees must have the opportunity of participating in the decisions as to what shall be their condition and how the business shall be run," Brandeis said in his testimony before the Commission on Industrial Relations in 1915. "They must learn also in sharing that responsibility that they, too, must bear the suffering arising from grave mistakes, just as the employer must."[111] Profit sharing was a start, labor representatives on the board of directors a second step, but there had to be still more.[112] The future, Brandeis hoped, would bring something more like cooperatives than the hierarchical corporation. Importantly, Brandeis recognized that economic structure paralleled political structure. "We already have had industrial despotism. With the recognition of the unions, this is changing into a constitutional monarchy, with well-defined limitations placed about the employers' formerly autocratic power. Next comes profit-sharing. This, however, is to be only a transitional, half-way stage. The eventual outcome promises to be a full-grown industrial democracy."[113]

Industrial democracy was best fulfilled in smaller settings, in economic institutions in which workers could have a meaningful stake and share in governance. An economy composed of small players also allowed for greater competition and, importantly, allowed for democratic control.[114] As a result, Brandeis was skeptical that national government regulation was the path forward.[115] Instead, he became a champion—and turned Woodrow Wilson into a champion—of antitrust as a way to maintain an economy of small producers. Norman Thomas, who had been a student of Wilson's at Princeton at the turn of the century, remembered years later, "[I]f [Wilson] had ever heard Harrington's dictum that the distribution of power follows the distribution of property, he never discussed it with his students in the classroom."[116] But Wilson was not ignorant of the economic changes of the era. In the 1880s, he became a friend of Frederick Jackson Turner's, and while Wilson the professor is remembered most for his book on congressional government, he was also an adherent to and evangelist for Jackson's frontier thesis. Wilson argued frequently that the economic changes of the industrial era required new thinking, and under Brandeis's tutelage he became a leading advocate for antitrust as a way to realign economic and political power.[117] His presidency saw the passage of the Clayton Antitrust Act, the creation of the Federal Trade Commission, and significant legislation on the Interstate Commerce Commission.[118]

These days, most scholars think the purpose of antitrust law is to promote consumer welfare through efficient markets.[119] Restrictions on trade are evaluated almost exclusively on economic grounds, with a focus on "their overall effect on the efficiency underlying markets."[120] As leading scholar Herbert Hovenkamp has said, antitrust has no "moral content"; its "sole purpose is to make the economy bigger."[121] Brandeis, Wilson, and other decentralizing progressives would have disagreed. In the Progressive Era, antitrust was focused on the fact that "the vast accumulation of wealth in the hands of corporations and individuals . . . [could] oppress individuals and injure the public generally."[122] The problem with big corporate entities is that they "threatened self-government in two ways—directly, by overwhelming democratic institutions and defying their control, and indirectly, by eroding the moral and civic capacities that equip workers to think and act as citizens."[123] Antitrust was a way to break up these big institutions, enabling democratic control of society and the economy. In *Liggett v. Lee,* a 1933 case involving a Florida anti-chain-store law, Brandeis recognized that the "concentration of economic power" was so great "that so-called private corporations are sometimes able to dominate the state."[124] He worried that the corporate system was becoming akin to the "feudal system" and that "this 'master institution of civilised life' is committing [society] to the rule of a plutocracy."[125] "Americans seeking escape from corporate domination," Brandeis wrote, "have open to them under the Constitution another form of social and economic control—one more in keeping with our traditions and aspirations. They may prefer the way of co-operation, which leads directly to the freedom and the equality of opportunity which the Fourteenth Amendment aims to secure." There was a "fundamental difference between capitalistic enterprise and the co-operative—between economic absolutism and industrial democracy."[126]

Fifteen years later, Justice William O. Douglas took the same approach, arguing that "[p]ower that controls the economy should be in the hands of elected representatives of the people, not in the hands of an industrial oligarchy."[127] The Sherman Antitrust Act was "founded on a theory of hostility to the concentration in private hands of power so great that only a government of the people should have it."[128] But by the time of Douglas, the old progressive antitrust philosophy was no longer dominant. Antitrust had shifted from a fear of concentrated power to competition and consumerism.[129] A generation later, Judge Robert Bork's *Antitrust Paradox* declared that "the only legitimate goal of American antitrust law is the maximization of consumer welfare," not the "survival or comfort of small business," and certainly not the restriction of the political power of gigantic corporations.[130]

In some ways, the least-known founder of *The New Republic* might have been the most revolutionary—and prophetic—thinker about political economy. Unlike Lippmann and Croly, Walter Weyl had been trained in economics. After studying at the University of Pennsylvania's Wharton School and in Germany, Weyl spent years as an investigative journalist.[131] In *The New Democracy* (1912), Weyl agreed that the constitutional system of the founders was ill-suited to the industrial age.[132] "Since Washington's inauguration," he wrote, "our population has increased twenty-three fold and our national wealth probably over one hundred fold, while the whole structure of society has been metamorphosed by steam, electricity, railroad, and telegraph."[133] The democracy of the founders, simply defined as an "*absence* of kings, of nobles, of political oppression," was not adapted to a "complex, closely knit industrial system."[134] This new regime brought with it a "swaggering plutocracy," a group of "very wealthy men," who "exert an enormous, if not preponderating, influence over industry, politics, and public opinion."[135] In the plutocratic economy, private corporations with natural or legal monopolies were capturing society's wealth and then entering politics to ensure that democracy would not change the status quo.[136] The complexity of the Constitution—with its multiple veto points, nominating systems, gerrymandering, and judiciary—favored plutocracy, giving it ample opportunity to exert influence and block democratic action.[137] "In no country is public opinion so powerful as in the United States," Lord Bryce once wrote. Weyl responded that the plutocrats also seek to control public opinion through their ownership of newspapers and magazines and their attempts to influence churches, universities, and the "tribunes of the people."[138]

Change was necessary, and Weyl believed it would not come through communism. Communists believed in class warfare, that industrialization would produce such misery that it would lead to mass uprising and the establishment of a socialist state. Weyl thought Marx had gotten it wrong.[139] People who were "too poor, too ignorant, and, by their very economic dependences, too inconstant and fearsome" could never lead the "tenacious, long-continued campaigns which must precede any revolutionary change."[140] Those who are oppressed lose morale, lose hope, and are unable to break free from their oppressive bonds. "A man or class, crushed to earth—is crushed to earth."[141] With insight connecting back to Harrington, Weyl believed instead in the theory of "progress through prosperity."[142] Society's increasing wealth, which he called the "social sur-plus," is what would enable some people to have the education, wealth, and political influence to bring about democratic change.[143] Once people had a stake in society, democracy would become "ulti-mately inevitable."[144]

In industrializing America, reform would come from the new democracy—the democracy of consumers. America had been, "until recently at least, what one might style a middle-class nation," and while Americans were never attached to "a rigid equality of wealth," the emerging inequality was so significant that it was uniting "in opposition factory workers, farmers, shopkeepers, professional men" against the plutocracy.[145] In the old way of thinking about political economy, this level of unity would have been impossible, because workers were differentiated by what they produced. But industrial-ization was transforming Americans into undifferentiated consum-ers. Bankers, lawyers, farmers, and mechanics were all consumers of the same goods, and they had shared economic needs and desires.[146] Seeing the wealth of the growing nation, and recognizing their role in creating it, the new democracy of consumers would question why the distribution of wealth was not more equitable and why political power was concentrated with the plutocracy. They would clamor for reform to satisfy their interests as consumers.

Weyl's new democracy shared many of the political and economic goals that the progressive movement embraced. He supported the secret ballot, the creation of a professional civil service, propor-tional representation in the states, changes to the Constitution to make amendment more democratic, direct election of senators, and direct legislation by the people.[147] Economically, Weyl believed in producing "equality of opportunity" and "more widely distributed" wealth.[148] In the new democracy, taxes would be not just a matter of revenue but a way to change the distribution of wealth in society.[149] Taxes would go to "improve education, health, recreation, commu-nication, 'to provide for the common defense, and promote the gen-eral welfare.'"[150] Weyl largely predicted the modern state's approach to social policy, but in doing so, he also marked a break from the traditions of the past. The other progressives—Lippmann, Brandeis, Croly, Wilson, Roosevelt—saw a link between the distribution of wealth and constitutional structure. Their rationale for reform was as much moral and constitutional as it was economic. Weyl had less to say about the project of ensuring a republican citizenry.[151] Instead, his consumerist democracy focused on satisfying the *economic* wants of the people. Still, more than most of the other progressives, Weyl saw the dynamic relationship between economics and politics. He knew the rising middle class would bring about political change. But the irony was that in the new democracy Americans would demand changes to satisfy their consumer desires, not to preserve their republican form of government.

Roosevelt, Croly, Brandeis, Wilson, and Weyl all recognized that economic reform was constitutionally significant. But there were other equally important attempts to reform political economy that were not framed in constitutional terms. "Perhaps the most significant policy tendency at the turn of the century," Felix Frankfurter wrote, was the idea of public utilities and public service corporations.[152] The phrase "public utilities" is likely today to elicit groans, if not snores. But at the turn of the twentieth century, it was a cutting-edge subject for reformers, and some of the most important theorists of administrative law and the regulatory state over the next generation—Bruce Wyman, Felix Frankfurter, James Landis, Rexford Tugwell—started their careers with an emphasis on public utilities regulation.[153] Public utilities regulation had its origins in common law. Traditionally, some professions—innkeepers, common carriers (that is, transportation services), surgeons, bakers, and others—were considered "public callings," and therefore subject to a duty to serve all comers.[154] States enforced this obligation on members of these professions. In addition, states had a broader "police power," which they could use to regulate even the use of private property for the general welfare.[155] The police power is what empowered states—and still does today—to issue health and safety regulations of all kinds. Public utilities advocates drew upon and expanded these traditional notions. Reformers argued that modern necessities were "as truly public services as the traditional governmental functions of police and justice" and therefore subject to regulation as industries "affected with a public interest."[156] "Who would say milk, bread, meat, working clothes, and adequate shelter for each are not necessities?" asked Rexford Tugwell, who was later one of Franklin Roosevelt's brain trust.[157] If these commodities were necessities, why didn't the government have a role in regulating their provision? Public utilities regulation famously came to define railroad pricing and electric power, but its scope was far broader, extending to tobacco warehouses, tugboats, and stock exchanges.[158]

Another group, the institutional economists, stressed the possibility of public-private cooperation and self-government by trade associations.[159] In *The New Competition* (1912), Arthur Jerome Eddy declared, "[C]ompetition is war, and war is hell." Eddy argued that cooperation, not competition, was the foundation of all society, and cooperation, not competition, should be at the center of economic policy.[160] Though this approach was hardly a serious check on corporate power and influence, the "associational" model became the dominant form of economic policy during World War I.[161] The War Industries Board, established in 1917, regulated the production and prices of war materials through five hundred War Service Committees, divided by industry and made up of industry representatives.[162] Herbert Hoover's Food Administration, for example, relied on trade associations to manage priorities, prices, production, and services, with government and business leaders working together to jointly manage these efforts.[163] So promising was wartime cooperation that Harry Garfield, the son of the slain president James A. Garfield and head of the Fuel Administration, declared that the time for individualism in America was over: "[W]e must boldly embark upon the new principle of cooperation and combination."[164] Cooperation, combination, public-private partnerships, were directly at odds with antitrust enforcement because government and industry worked together to set and regulate production, wages, and prices. As associationalism gained steam during World War I, Wilson's antitrust efforts fell by the wayside, and after the war, the impetus for structural reforms to the economy waned.

DEMOCRACY AGAINST ECONOMIC ROYALISM

"Under a cloud-veiled moon, in skies suddenly cleared of rain, a mass of more than 100,000 people gathered in the stadium of the

University of Pennsylvania," reporter Arthur Krock wrote in *The New York Times*. It was a Saturday night, June 27, 1936, and the crowd had assembled to hear Franklin Roosevelt accept the renomination of the Democratic Party for the presidency. With his eldest son, James, and Vice President John Nance Garner helping at each side, the polio-stricken president took the platform at Franklin Field as "The Star-Spangled Banner" and thunderous applause filled the arena.[165]

Philadelphia, the president said to the Democratic faithful, was a fitting place to dedicate themselves to the campaign ahead. In 1776, Americans had started a revolution to achieve "freedom from the tyranny of a political autocracy." The "eighteenth-century royalists who held special privileges from the crown" had governed the New World without the consent of the governed. Their only aim was the preservation of their own privilege. But the Americans of that generation would not accept the "mercenaries of dynastic power," and each fought battle after battle to win "the right with his neighbors to make and order his own destiny through his own Government." On July 4, 1776, "political tyranny was wiped out at Philadelphia."

In the decades since, new forces—machinery, railroads, steam, electricity, telegraph, radio, and mass production and distribution—"combined to bring forward a new civilization and with it a new problem for those who sought to remain free." From industrialization came "economic royalists" who "carved new dynasties" and built "[n]ew kingdoms" out of corporations, securities, banks, industry—none of which the founders could have imagined. Soon enough, the "privileged princes" stretched their hands out to grab control of the government itself. "They created a new despotism and wrapped it in the robes of legal sanction." Now, in the "new industrial dictatorship," the basic fundamentals of economic life—the hours worked, the wages paid, the conditions of work—were "beyond the control of the people." Competition and personal initiative withered under the shadow of monopoly control. "[T]he political equality we once had won," Roosevelt said, "was meaningless in the face of economic inequality. A small group had concentrated into their own hands an almost complete control over other people's property, other people's money, other people's labor—other people's lives."

The great crash of 1929 had exposed the economic tyranny of

the new royalists, and for four years Roosevelt waged battle after battle to end it. While "[t]he royalists of the economic order have conceded that political freedom was the business of the Government,"
Roosevelt said, "they have maintained that economic slavery was
nobody's business. They granted that the Government could protect
the citizen in his right to vote, but they denied that the Government
could do anything to protect the citizen in his right to work and his
right to live." This generation, Roosevelt declared, would not accept
such a fate. This generation had a "rendezvous with destiny." It was up
to them to ensure that the "average citizen" had "equal opportunity
in the marketplace." The royalists would accuse them of attempting
a constitutional revolution that would overthrow America's institutions, but Roosevelt reminded the audience what the Constitution
and the flag stood for: "Now, as always, they stand for democracy, not
tyranny; for freedom, not subjection; and against a dictatorship by
mob rule and the over-privileged alike."

Reaching the end of his remarks, Roosevelt made reference to the
gathering storms of dictatorship around the world. In other lands,
people had "grown too weary to carry on the fight. They have sold
their heritage of freedom for the illusion of a living." America had
to succeed in its "war against want and destitution and economic
demoralization," because this war was not just a war over living standards, but a "war for the survival of democracy." In this conflict, Roosevelt concluded, "[w]e are fighting to save a great and precious form
of government for ourselves and for the world."

Roosevelt's speech put the economic challenge of the time in distinctly constitutional terms. At stake was the survival of the American system of government, the preservation of democracy. Four
years earlier, on the cusp of election, Roosevelt had spoken in similar
terms, calling for the creation of an "economic constitutional order"
so America could adapt to the changes of industrialization. During
his first term, Roosevelt took quick action in economic, financial,
and social policy, trying programs of all sorts as part of his New
Deal for the American people.[166] Looking back from 1936, he said he
hoped people would say that his first term was when "the forces of
selfishness and of lust met their match" and the second would be the
one where they "met their master." He welcomed the hatred of the

businessmen and monopolists, speculators and bankers, because he knew that "Government by organized wealth is just as dangerous as Government by organized mob."[167] As historian Alan Brinkley put it, the New Dealers believed "the nation's greatest problems were rooted in the structure of modern industrial capitalism and that it was the mission of government to deal somehow with the flaws in that structure."[168]

But from the vantage point of 1936, it still wasn't clear *which* structure would replace the existing form of industrial capitalism. At times, the New Dealers appeared heirs to the New Nationalism of Theodore Roosevelt and Herbert Croly. The Securities Act of 1933 and the Securities Exchange Act of 1934 governed the regulation and disclosure of primary and secondary markets for securities and established a new federal agency: the Securities and Exchange Commission (SEC). At other times, the early New Dealers looked more like the heirs of Brandeis and Wilson. The Banking Act of 1933 broke up commercial and investment banks through the famous Glass-Steagall provisions and established the Federal Deposit Insurance Corporation (FDIC), making banking with small institutions safe. Some legislation was designed as relief and protection from economic insecurity. The Agricultural Adjustment Act subsidized farmers to raise the value of crops; the Civilian Conservation Corps, the Federal Emergency Relief Administration, and the Civil Works Administration aimed at getting people back to work; and the Social Security Act sought to protect people in old age, poverty, and unemployment. In still other cases, they were associationalists, who combined eclectic approaches to restructuring the relationship between the state and the economy. The National Industrial Recovery Act, passed in 1933, created the National Recovery Administration (NRA), the heir to the War Industries Board of World War I. The NRA suspended antitrust law and established industry-wide associations that set up codes of fair competition to regulate wages, hours, and prices. Section 7(a) of the bill provided a foothold for labor unions, by protecting collective bargaining.[169] The third part of the bill created the Public Works Administration, which put $3.3 billion toward infrastructure projects that would get people back to work.[170] When Roosevelt said in

1932 that "the country demands bold, persistent experimentation," he meant it.[171] The New Dealers tried everything—and then some.

Despite majorities in Congress, Roosevelt worried that the Supreme Court would overturn what the New Dealers saw as necessary and democratically authorized actions. In the first few years of his presidency, they were pleasantly surprised. In 5–4 votes, the Court upheld price controls on milk, Minnesota's mortgage moratorium, and the federal government's ability to regulate currency.[172] The administration thought the latter power was so important that Roosevelt was ready to start a constitutional crisis if the Court ruled against him on the currency question.[173]

But then, in 1935, the Supreme Court turned against the New Deal. It struck down provisions of the National Industrial Recovery Act and the Railroad Retirement Act.[174] Justice Owen Roberts, the fifth vote in the latter case, called the rail workers' pension system a "naked appropriation of private property" and held that Congress did not have power to create such a system under the commerce clause. On "Black Monday," May 27, 1935, the Court struck down the totality of the National Industrial Recovery Act and the Frazier-Lemke mortgage moratorium.[175] Days later, Roosevelt said that the country had been "relegated to the horse-and-buggy definition of interstate commerce."[176]

The following year, the Court continued its assault on Roosevelt's economic constitutional order. Striking down the key feature of the Agricultural Adjustment Act, Justice Roberts said the processing tax was "an expropriation of money from one group for the benefit of another."[177] The Court overturned the Guffey Coal Act and the Municipal Bankruptcy Act, and it even struck down New York State's minimum-wage law.[178] For Justice Harlan Fiske Stone and the dissenters, the issue was one of democratic politics versus economic preferences. "The Fourteenth Amendment," Stone said, "has no more embedded in the Constitution our preference for some particular set of economic beliefs than it has adopted, in the name of liberty, the system of theology which we may happen to approve."[179]

The national outcry after the New York minimum-wage case was significant. Roosevelt received letters from across the country about the need to combat the justices' myopic and restrained view of the Constitution. Members of Congress grew impatient: in the 1936 session alone, they introduced more than one hundred proposals to curb the powers of the Supreme Court.[180] And after his landslide victory in the 1936 election—the largest victory since James Monroe in 1820—Roosevelt introduced the famous "court-packing" plan, to increase the size of the Supreme Court.

The plan, however, would never be implemented. In 1937, in *West Coast Hotel v. Parrish,* the Supreme Court reversed course—upholding Washington State's minimum-wage law 5–4, with Justice Roberts switching sides. Chief Justice Charles Evans Hughes, now in the majority, struck directly against embedding economic preferences into the Constitution. "The Constitution does not speak of freedom of contract," he wrote. "[T]he liberty safeguarded is liberty in a social organization which requires the protection of law against the evils which menace the health, safety, morals and welfare of the people." Washington's legislature was therefore allowed to act to stop "the exploiting of workers at wages so low as to be insufficient to meet the bare cost of living."[181] That same day, dubbed "White Monday," the Court upheld a rewritten farm mortgage law.[182] Two weeks later, it upheld the National Labor Relations Act.[183] The following month, it upheld the Social Security system.[184] So complete and so swift was this reversal that commentators declared court packing dead and called Justice Roberts's change of heart the "switch in time that saved nine."[185]

Leading constitutional scholars have dubbed the 1936 election and the "switch in time" a "constitutional moment," a revolution that was on a par with the Civil War amendments and the founding. As a matter of constitutional authority, it surely was. For the next six decades, whether through depression or recession, war or civil protest, the Supreme Court would not again restrict Congress's power to regulate the economy. The debate was effectively over. If powerful economic interests lost battles in Congress, they could no longer rely on the Supreme Court to bail them out, at least when it came to the commerce clause. The Constitution did not incorporate any particular set of economic preferences. Rather, democratically elected officials had the power to craft economic rights and regulations as they saw fit. But while the Court would no longer stand as a roadblock to economic reform, the question still remained: Could the New Dealers restructure industrial capitalism to preserve the middle-class constitution?

DEMOCRACY AGAINST DICTATORSHIP

Having experienced a slight recovery during FDR's first term, the country was sinking back into depression by 1937. In a speech that year, Roosevelt's aide Harold Ickes pulled no punches in presenting an account of how concentrated economic power threatened the Republic.[186] America was in the midst of a struggle between "the power of money and the power of the democratic instinct." The conflict would need to be "fought to a finish—until plutocracy or democracy" triumphed. Ickes incorporated the Harringtonian lesson into his diagnosis of the nation's travails: "Economic power in this country does not rest in the mass of the people as it must if democracy is to endure." Citing a recent book by Ferdinand Lundberg, he called out "America's 60 families," the sixty families who controlled the two hundred most powerful corporations in America and more than a quarter of America's wealth. They had "lulled the American people into the conviction that if the people would grant conditions in which these 60 families would have confidence that they would do as they pleased, the 60 families would put capital to work; enterprise would boom, wages would rise, stocks would soar and there would be two cars in every garage." Americans tried this theory, and the result was "the worst peacetime catastrophe ever known." In strikingly contemporary terms echoing critics of the 2008 bank bailout, he described how FDR's administration "bailed the 60 families out" of their own "mesmeric miscalculations" and even "preserved the corporate structures," the "capital structure," and the "management structure." The government then abandoned the theory of letting the "gravy" of the sixty families "trickle down upon the exploited millions" and replaced it with policies that got "120 million people at the bottom standing on their own feet."

With progress moving steadily, the administration increasingly changed course and listened to the calls of private industry to cut public expenditures, balance the budget, and give managers greater responsibility. What happened? The sixty families "did little or nothing to increase the purchasing power of labor," they "ran prices to the sky," and, worst of all, they threatened to "refuse to do business at all unless the President and Congress and the people will repeal all that we have gained in the last five years and regrant them the suicidal license they had enjoyed in 1929." America's sixty families, Ickes charged, were involved in a general sit-down strike—a strike not by labor but "of the capital created by the whole American people of which the 60 families have obtained control." If the people yielded, the country would become a "big-business Fascist America."

Referencing Daniel Webster's speech at the anniversary of the Pilgrims' landing, Ickes explained that America's democratic institutions depended on "the fact that wealth was equitably distributed, that everyone had a real and not an illusory chance to acquire an economic stake in the welfare of the country and that, in consequence, a democracy involved no irreconcilable conflicts because both economic power and political power existed in the great mass of the people." Since the start of the Republic—since Jefferson imagined relatively equal distribution and access to property—Americans had feared "the concentration of private economic power" and "not without reason." "It has been a hard fight to preserve a free democracy and a system of free individual enterprise against the inroads of concentrated economic power," he said. The "money aristocrats, or corporate earls," were "an even greater menace to our institutions" than feudal barons and titled classes. The fight against the power of big business had to be won "if our democracy is to survive."

What is striking about Ickes's speech is not that he embraced the seventeenth-century Harringtonian idea that power follows property or the fear of oligarchy and plutocracy that had been part of the American tradition since the founding. What is striking is that he did not mix these concerns with the kinds of broader structural reforms that earlier American reformers who spoke in these terms proposed. Nowhere present is the idea of the cooperative commonwealth or industrial democracy familiar in labor circles. There is no hint that the country needs political reforms like direct democracy or campaign finance laws, the things populists and progressives demanded.

In fact, for all their clamor about economic royalists and corporate earls, unlike the populists and progressives, the New Dealers did little to push for reforms that would seek to safeguard political decisions from the influence of wealth. Instead, Ickes's framework is one that is surprisingly modern: the debate, as he frames it, is whether the country's economic success is best preserved with policies allowing wealth to "trickle down" from the top or whether the economy succeeds through a large and growing middle class.

The unique mix of eighteenth-century republican rhetoric and twentieth-century liberal economics in Ickes's speech was part of a series of shifts that were under way at the time and consolidated by the end of World War II. The first was the rise of economic theories centered on consumption, rather than production, and the importance of public spending. Back in 1912 Walter Weyl had prophesied that the consumer would be the foundation of the "new democracy"; by the late 1920s, political economists were increasingly emphasizing consumption. William Foster and Waddill Catchings's *Road to Plenty* argued in 1928 that underconsumption was the central problem in economies and that public spending was the solution. Stuart Chase, in his presciently titled 1932 book *A New Deal*, held that underconsumption was the driving problem and that it was necessary to increase the purchasing power of consumers. And most famously, John Maynard Keynes's *General Theory of Employment, Interest, and Money* appeared in 1936. While the early New Deal's NRA focused primarily on regulating producers rather than increasing consumers' purchasing power, as Keynes's ideas gained favor through the 1930s, so too did a shift from changing the structure of capitalism to managing levels of demand.[187] In 1940, Roosevelt's National Resources Planning Board (NRPB) issued a report titled *The Structure of the American Economy Part II*. The NRPB argued that structural changes were *less* important than the operating characteristics of the economy. Structural changes "would always be inadequate to the task of achieving full employment, which had more to do with changing the way consumers and producers alike behaved in their daily lives than changing the structure of institutions." The right path forward was not "reforming or regulating production" but "policies designed to encourage consumers to spend more and producers to produce and invest more, as well as policies to discourage everyone from excessive, unproductive saving."[188] With this shift, one historian concludes, the New Dealers "detached liberalism from its earlier emphasis on reform—its preoccupation with issues of class, its tendency to equate freedom and democracy with economic autonomy, its hostility to concentrated economic power. They had redefined citizenship to de-emphasize the role of men and women as producers and to elevate their roles as consumers."[189]

The second shift was political, with Roosevelt and the New Deal-ers losing their power in Congress. To protect white supremacy, southerners in Congress worked to prevent New Deal reforms from transforming the South. As one historian has said, the New Deal was trapped in a "southern cage," unable to make progress without com-promising with white supremacists determined to retain their hold on power in the South.[190] Conservative Democrats and Republicans strategized together to defeat Roosevelt's court-packing plan, fear-ing that if Roosevelt's plan succeeded, he would be unstoppable.[191] In April 1938, tired of the constant defections from his own party and confident of his popularity, Roosevelt announced his intention to purge the Democratic Party of its more conservative, anti–New Deal elements—especially southern senators who had opposed him on economic and racial issues like sit-down strikes, labor standards, antilynching laws, and housing.[192] When the purge failed, the liberal-conservative split within the Democratic Party grew worse than ever, weakening Roosevelt's hand over domestic policy. With World War II at the center of events, Roosevelt grew increasingly careful in picking his domestic battles. He appointed Republicans to his cabinet and protested little when Congress rolled back some of his signature New Deal programs: the Civilian Conservation Corps, the Works Progress Administration, the National Youth Administration, the National Resources Planning Board, and the Farm Security Administration.[193]

The rising fear of (and fearmongering over) communism also pushed liberal reformers away from bold action. Beginning as early as the 1930s and continuing through the 1940s, conservatives depicted reformers as communists and Soviet sympathizers. From the start, they targeted labor activists, but they also turned their attention to members of the growing consumers' movement, employees of the

Social Security Administration, and others.[194] Red Scare conservatives even attacked the Marshall Plan and those who worked on European reconstruction as Soviet sympathizers who were trying to advance socialism.[195] Afraid of being condemned as communists, liberals rebranded themselves. They were no longer leftists but rather cold warriors who occupied what Arthur Schlesinger Jr. called "the vital center."[196] Between 1947 and 1956, more than five million federal employees were screened by an anticommunist loyalty program; twenty-five thousand were subjected to an FBI full field investigation; and twenty-seven hundred were dismissed.[197] While the threat of espionage was real, so too was the use of communist accusations as a way for conservatives to block policy changes they disagreed with. The Red Scare and the McCarthy witch hunts of the post–World War II era reined in bold initiatives for economic reform by putting pressure on reformers in a variety of fields: health care, public housing, women's employment.[198] Many of those subjected to searching, bruising investigations were neither socialists nor communists. They were just talented reformers (and, disproportionally, talented women) who believed that raising living standards would be good for the economy and for democracy.

The relationship between labor, business, and government also changed. For decades, labor had seen its goal as industrial democracy, as a restructuring of labor relations into constitutional terms. Labor scholar and mediator William Leiserson had once said that trade unionism was "a form of constitutional government."[199] Harvard economist Sumner Slichter analogized collective bargaining to "civil rights [in] industry."[200] The Wagner Act of 1935, which created the National Labor Relations Board and the system of collective bargaining, had fulfilled part of this ambition.[201] In the lead-up to World War II, labor leader Walter Reuther pushed still further toward industrial democracy. He introduced a plan for the big car companies to build airplanes, by pooling their efforts and introducing industrial councils with worker participation. The auto companies opposed the Reuther plan, as did the emerging war bureaucracy, led by former General Motors (GM) president William Knudsen at the Office of Production Management. Once Pearl Harbor was attacked, there was no longer any question that the auto companies would convert to airplane production, and the Reuther plan lost its force.[202] Instead, labor took a no-strike pledge and accepted a freeze on wages with a small cost-of-living increase based on inflation. In return, labor was granted "maintenance of membership," which expanded unions by a third over the course of the war.[203]

At the same time, "dollar a year" men flooded into government from the business world (while continuing to collect their private sector salaries).[204] Roosevelt often complained that the same anti–New Deal businessmen whose hatred he once welcomed were now staffing his administration.[205] I. F. Stone went further, noting that the "arsenal of democracy" was being run "with one eye on the war and the other on the convenience of big business."[206] But many corporate leaders gained high praise from liberals as industrial statesmen, and the New Dealers and businessmen who worked closely together often shed their previous suspicions of each other. "As I leave Washington," one businessman wrote of his colleague, "I leave behind me in you a man whom I have learned to work with, to like and to respect."[207] For many, this mutual respect came to replace earlier antipathy toward economic royalists.

After the war ended, General Motors workers, steelworkers, electrical equipment workers, and meatpackers went on strike for wage increases. It was the largest strike wave in American history, and stoppages that year contributed to a conservative political climate that brought forth Republican majorities in Congress in 1946 and the Taft-Hartley Act in 1947.[208] Passed over President Truman's veto, Taft-Hartley stripped power from labor unions by allowing states to ban union shops, by prohibiting unions from engaging in secondary boycotts (when members of a union boycott another company in support of that company's workers), and by preventing foremen and low-level supervisors from unionization.[209] In the new postwar era, Taft-Hartley's restrictive regime of collective bargaining would define labor relations. As one labor historian notes, by the 1940s and 1950s "[t]he phrase 'industrial democracy' [had] practically vanished from the vocabulary of political life and union discourse."[210]

The emergence of the modern administrative state followed a similar path. Prior to "the switch in time," conservatives battled the New Deal through the courts. But with the Supreme Court out of the picture, the battle shifted to legislative constraints on the emerging regulatory state.[211] The fierce debate is best exemplified through two deans of Harvard Law School. In 1938, the American Bar Association (ABA) asked Roscoe Pound, the legendary dean of Harvard Law School, to chair its committee on administrative law. Pound's committee attacked the New Deal agencies for establishing "administrative absolutism." The committee's report declared that America was becoming a dictatorship and compared Roosevelt's administration to the Soviet Union.[212] Pound, the ABA, and their allies would offer administrative law legislation over the next few years designed specifically to hamstring FDR's New Deal agencies—particularly the National Labor Relations Board and the Securities and Exchange Commission, which they saw as overly pro-labor and antibusiness.[213] Indeed, one version of the legislation included exemptions for *pre–New Deal* agencies.[214]

That same year, James Landis wrote *The Administrative Process*. Landis was Pound's replacement at Harvard and had previously served as chairman of the Securities and Exchange Commission. The New Dealer rooted the administrative state in the "rise of industrialism" and the "rise of democracy."[215] Landis argued that there were "concentrations of power on a scale that beggars the ambitions of the Stuarts" and that government action was necessary because "certain enterprises possess such great public significance that their pursuit and control cannot be intrusted to private industry."[216] The common law was inadequate because it was not enough to "presume[] the existence of an equality" between individuals, such that common-law litigation led to evenhanded treatment with a judge as umpire deciding between the two parties in court. In fact, "the absence of equal economic power generally is so prevalent that the umpire theory of administering law is almost certain to fail."[217] The common-law regulatory system had to be superseded because of the number and types of economic problems in society. The "accumulation of . . . unredressed claims is of itself a serious social threat." It demanded "positive solutions" and a government that exercised ongoing "control over the economic forces which affect the life of the community."[218] With this preference for regulatory agencies instead of common-law courts, Landis saw the administrative state's reliance on expertise as more than just a restraint on bureaucratic discretion for fear of unchecked government power.[219] It was a strategy to prevent capture by economically powerful actors in society. A professional, expert-driven civil service would insulate policy making from political and economic influence. Because civil servants are chosen for their technical knowledge, rather than by election, political preferences, or connections, they will be less likely to cower to influence.[220]

The war transformed the Pound-Landis debate too. In the early years, Roosevelt fought and ultimately vetoed conservative attempts to tie the government's hands when it came to administrative procedures. But the challenges of wartime administration, in particular the problems faced by the Office of Price Administration and the War Production Board, created a new consensus around reform.[221] By 1946, when the Administrative Procedure Act was passed, there was little opposition or even debate. The war had proven both the need for a robust state and the need for procedural checks on the state's power.[222]

The shift took place in antitrust as well, with the replacement of future Supreme Court justice Robert Jackson with Yale Law School professor Thurman Arnold as the head of antitrust efforts at the Department of Justice. Jackson's vision of antitrust aligned with the progressive antimonopolists. He opposed chain stores despite lower prices for consumers. His opposition was "not economic so much as it is a social objection." The core problem is that "[w]e do not like to have any one man or corporation own the town." In his unpublished autobiography, Jackson revealed the source of these views. He grew up in an area that was "socially classless." It was "truly and deeply democratic, democratic in an economic and social as well as in a political sense . . . the nearest Paradise that most of us ever know." That way of life had now "largely disappeared" because of giant economic organizations, and Jackson wondered "[w]hether democracy can survive in this atmosphere."[223] Arnold, his successor, didn't think bigness was a problem in itself; he was only concerned with the specific bad behaviors of big institutions. "There can be no greater nonsense than the idea that a mechanized age can get along without big business," he said in 1942. "Not only our production during the war, but our way of life after the war, depends on big business."[224]

For Arnold, antitrust was not the "expression of a religion" but an economic issue, fundamentally about cartels and monopolies raising prices on consumers. Arnold undertook aggressive industry-wide prosecutions on these terms, bringing more cases than at any time in the history of the country.[225] The shift from Jackson to Arnold was a shift in the underlying theory of antitrust. But antitrust itself quickly fell out of favor, as a casualty of the war-production effort. Arnold, disillusioned and outgunned by the dollar-a-year men, soon departed the administration.

The most important shift, however, was in the terms of debate—the vision of Roosevelt's administration. In 1936, Roosevelt framed America's choice as between democracy and economic royalism, his version of the old debate between republics and oligarchy. If America continued as an oligarchy, popular unrest and an enterprising demagogue would lead to dictatorship. "The great adventure of the Recovery Act," Don Richberg had said in the early days of the New Deal, "lies in the effort to find a democratic and truly American solution of the problem that has produced dictatorships in at least three great nations since the World War."[226] Joseph P. Kennedy, the chairman of the SEC and father to a future president and two senators, agreed, noting in 1936 that "democracy will not be safe for this country unless we constructively deal with the causes of dictatorships. . . . We must solve the problem of [economic] security."[227] Economic reform was necessary to protect the Republic.

But by the 1940s, the threat of oligarchy and demagogues preying on the poor had largely dropped out of the conversation, replaced by fear of dictatorship. "Dictatorship" had not always been a uniformly bad word in American culture. The Studebaker car company even introduced a model called the Dictator in 1927. But with the rise of Hitler and the Nazis in Germany, the choice facing Americans shifted from republic-or-oligarchy to democracy-or-dictatorship. (Studebaker seems to have noticed this shift in real time; it stopped selling the Dictator in 1937.[228]) After the experience of the National Recovery Administration, big business turned against the public-private associational model and started to lump Roosevelt's New Deal in with fascism and communism.[229] The president's court-packing plan didn't help. In response to the plan, the conservative newspaper magnate Frank Gannett created the National Committee to Uphold Constitutional Government, claiming that Roosevelt's success would put America "on the road to dictatorship such as they have in Italy and Germany."[230] Gannett's committee would send 15 million letters, at one point averaging 100,000 per day, to mobilize Americans against the Supreme Court bill.[231] With the Court battle won, Gannett turned to another Roosevelt initiative. The president had created a committee to assess how to reform and modernize the executive branch. The Brownlow Committee's recommendations included creating six executive assistants to the president, expanding the civil service merit system, encouraging budget planning, placing each of the increasing number of New Deal agencies under one of twelve cabinet departments, and giving the president managerial direction over all executive branch agencies.[232] The plan was hardly dictatorial, but it was announced just weeks before court packing and came to a vote in the spring of 1938, just after Hitler annexed Austria. Conservatives latched onto the plan as setting up an American dictatorship: Gannett's group sent 850,000 mailers out to build support against Roosevelt. Father Charles Coughlin incited listeners to go to Washington to prevent Roosevelt from becoming another Julius Caesar. Roosevelt even had to issue a statement saying that he did not want or intend to become a dictator.[233] Dictatorship, not oligarchy, was increasingly the enemy. By the 1940s, with big business now enlisted in Roosevelt's war effort, economic reform gave way to military necessity. The decades-old battle between populist reformers and plutocrats had been reshaped, with populists and plutocrats joining forces to defeat Hitler and the specter of dictatorship.[234]

While structural reforms fell out of favor, Roosevelt did not completely abandon the constitutional terms of economic debate. In 1944, he declared that the end of World War II would not be followed by the chaos that followed World War I. "[W]e shall not repeat the tragic errors of ostrich isolationism," he said in his annual message to Congress.[235] Nor would we "repeat the excesses of the wild twenties when this Nation went for a joy ride on a roller coaster which ended in a tragic crash." The objective for the future would not be structural reform, but security—"not only physical security which provides safety from attacks by aggressors. It means also economic security, social security, moral security." After discussing what was needed to win the war and establish international security, he turned to America. "This Republic had its beginning, and grew to its present strength, under the protection of certain inalienable political rights—among them the right of free speech, free press, free worship, trial by jury, freedom from unreasonable searches and seizures," Roosevelt said. But as the country grew and "our industrial economy expanded— these political rights proved inadequate to assure us equality in the pursuit of happiness." Americans now understand that "true individual freedom cannot exist without economic security and independence. 'Necessitous men are not free men.' People who are hungry and out of a job are the stuff of which dictatorships are made." The last few decades had made these economic truths self-evident.

Roosevelt declared that it was time for a "second Bill of Rights" that would provide "a new basis of security and prosperity . . . for all regardless of station, race, or creed." It would guarantee the right to a useful job; to earn enough to provide food, clothing, recreation, and a decent living for a family; to enterprise free from unfair competition and monopolies; to a decent home; to medical care; to protection from the economic fears of old age, sickness, accident, and unemployment; to education. World War II shifted Roosevelt from a debate over the structure of economic institutions to the creation of an economic bill of rights. Roosevelt didn't call for a constitutional amendment or for revolution, but he saw his economic bill of rights as just as necessary for the protection of the Republic as was the political bill of rights that had been adopted 150 years earlier. The war had tested whether democracy could survive the threat of dictatorship. The united democracy of business and the people had won. The second bill of rights would become a way to preserve democracy without having to reform the structure of corporate capitalism. And for decades to come, it would be the hope of American economic reformers.

THE GLORIOUS YEARS

The New Deal and World War II ushered in an era of middle-class growth and economic equality, which economists Claudia Goldin and Robert Margo have called "the great compression."[236] Over the next generation, America experienced an economic boom whose benefits were broadly shared. Between 1948 and 1978, American productivity (measured by GDP) rose by 107.8 percent.[237] During that same period, the median male worker's income continually rose, tracking GDP closely; by 1978, hourly compensation was up 96 percent.[238] Shared growth and prosperity meant a stronger middle class on metrics other than wages. In 1940, 43.6 percent of Americans were homeowners. With the postwar boom, that number had hit 64.4 percent by 1980.[239]

To be sure, the wealthiest Americans did better than those in the middle class. But their share of America's wealth was nowhere near as large as it had been in the decades before the Depression. In 1928, at the height of the Roaring Twenties, the top 10 percent of Americans took home 46 percent of the country's income excluding capital gains and 49 percent including capital gains. Between 1951 and 1982, the top 10 percent share never hit 33 percent excluding capital gains and never reached 35 percent including capital gains.[240] The top 0.1 percent of Americans in the late 1920s had 25 percent of the nation's wealth. By 1950, their share was down to about 10 percent, and it hovered there or below until the 1980s.[241] At the other end of the spectrum, shared prosperity and government policy meant that the poverty rate dropped precipitously in the postwar years, reaching a low point of 11.1 percent in 1973.[242] In other words, whether we look at the median worker, the wealthiest Americans, or the number of Americans in poverty, economic inequality was becoming less of a problem in the rising tide era after World War II.

Government policies were critical to building the middle class and growing a middle-class economy. The GI Bill, for example, sent 2.2 million veterans to college, and it provided many veterans with loans to start small businesses and buy new homes. Between World War II and 1966, one-fifth of all homes built in the United States were financed through the GI Bill.[243] The bill cost $7 billion, but for every dollar invested, between $5 and $12 were returned over thirty-five years in higher productivity and tax revenues.[244] President Dwight D. Eisenhower's massive interstate highway system—which at the time was projected to cost $25 billion—was partly intended to serve as a public works project, which Eisenhower hoped would put millions of people to work and smooth out the peaks and valleys in unemployment.[245] Estimates are that highway spending was responsible for 31 percent of yearly productivity growth in the late 1950s and 25 percent of yearly productivity growth in the 1960s.[246]

Federal policies also reined in the financial sector and the economic gains and power of the wealthy. From the founding of the country until the Great Depression, the United States saw financial panics and crises roughly every twenty years—1819, 1837, 1857, 1873, 1893, 1907, 1929.[247] But the New Deal financial regulatory system—safe depository banking through the FDIC, enforcement through the Securities and Exchange Commission, and separation of functions through the Glass-Steagall Act—set the stage for an era without any significant financial panics. Between 1943 and the mid-1970s, bank failures never exceeded single digits in a year.[248] The tax policies of the era likewise helped facilitate economic equality. In 1942, the top marginal tax rate was 88 percent and reached those above a taxable income of $200,000. From 1942 to 1963, the top marginal tax rate remained above 80 percent, hitting 91 percent from 1951 to 1963, and it applied to those above $400,000. Top rates remained at or above 70 percent until 1981.[249]

Nothing captured the economic model of the glorious postwar years better than the approach to wages and benefits. In 1948, Walter Reuther, the head of the United Automobile Workers (UAW), was engaged in fierce negotiations with General Motors for a thirty-five-cent raise for his workers. At first the best he could get was a cost-of-living adjustment. But over time GM's Charlie Wilson came around to a better offer. Wilson wanted labor peace and stability so GM could make long-term plans for growth. Despite the 1947 Taft-Hartley Act (which restricted labor's power to strike and boycott and even allowed states to nullify federal law allowing union workplaces), the UAW still had considerable power to disrupt the carmaker's future plans.[250] So Wilson declared that his generation of industrialists would be "the Jeffersonians to [his predecessor] Mr. Sloan's Federalists." Reaching out to labor, he offered a two-year contract with an eleven-cent wage increase—but in addition, quarterly cost-of-living adjustments and a 2 percent "annual improvement factor" wage increase, which was effectively a raise based on productivity improvements. Reuther agreed to the proposal.[251] Two years later, in May 1950, Reuther and Wilson agreed to a new five-year deal. There were improvements in the cost-of-living adjustments and the annual improvement factor, but GM would now also cover a $125-per-month pension and half the costs of a new health-care plan for its workers. The plan would mean a 20 percent increase in the standard of living of GM workers over five years, and it was immediately recognized as a bombshell. *BusinessWeek* called it a moment of "industrial statesmanship." *Fortune* referred to it as the "Treaty of Detroit."[252]

The Treaty of Detroit defined an era of American social and economic policy. On the one hand, it marked the end of an era whose aspiration was to structure corporations to create a "republic" or "democracy" within industry. As Daniel Bell noted at the time, the treaty "unmistakably accepts the existing distribution of income between wages and profits as 'normal' if not as 'fair.' "[253] On the other hand, the treaty established a social policy model by which private firms, rather than government, provided workers with the benefits of the welfare state. The treaty's provisions spread and eventually became standard throughout much of unionized industry, non-unionized industry (employers hoped to avoid unionization), and even for manufacturers' white-collar workers.[254] To be sure, women and African Americans were less likely to benefit from the treaty's employer-based benefits model because of the industries and firms they worked in.[255] But the Treaty of Detroit regime nonetheless established the basic framework for American social policy, led to a generation of broadly shared economic growth, and helped build the postwar middle class.

Constitutionally, debates over economic power became far less prominent during the postwar years due in part to the success of progressive economic policies. The New Deal constitutional consensus permitted broad democratic power over economic regulation.[256] Since that time, legal scholars have generally accepted that economic regulation is subject to a lower standard of judicial scrutiny.[257] The New Deal consensus seems to have been so strong that, as Professor Suzanna Sherry has persuasively shown, it never needed to be thoroughly defended.[258] The breadth of the postwar consensus is also visible when it comes to the commerce clause. Many commentators—perhaps even most—would likely have thought it unthinkable that Congress did not have the power to regulate health insurance under the commerce clause (one of the issues in *National Federation of Independent Business v. Sebelius,* the Obamacare case).[259] That debate was settled during the New Deal.[260] The fact that the Supreme Court's shift away from the New Deal constitutional paradigm is referred to as a "revolution" is evidence itself of the strength of the preexisting consensus.[261] During this period, economic debates increasingly shifted from the constitutional realm into the policy and regulatory realm. As President Kennedy said in a 1962 speech, economic issues were now "technical problems" and "administrative problems," requiring "very sophisticated judgments" that "do not lend themselves to the great sort of 'passionate movements' which have stirred this country so often in the past."[262]

But there were passionate movements, and they did involve economic issues. After all, when Dr. Martin Luther King Jr. delivered his famous "I Have a Dream" speech in 1963, it was at the March on Washington for *Jobs* and Freedom. And it was King who said that "the inseparable twin of racial injustice was economic injustice."[263] Kennedy was right, though, that the movements of the early 1960s were different from the labor strikes of the late 1870s or the mobilizations against corruption in the Progressive Era. The movements of the early 1960s were primarily in the tradition of inclusion: they were about expanding the political and economic community to include African Americans, other minorities, and women.

Since the end of Reconstruction, African Americans had been stripped of voting rights, political participation, and equal justice under the law through intimidation, bloody violence, and fraud. When *Brown v. Board of Education* required school desegregation in 1954, pro–Jim Crow southerners raised constitutional claims in their fight against equality. William F. Buckley Jr. declared, "The Fourteenth and Fifteenth Amendments to the Constitution are regarded by much of the South as inorganic accretions to the original document, grafted upon it by victors-at-war by force." James J. Kilpatrick, editor of *The Richmond News Leader,* resurrected John C. Calhoun's old theory of nullification. What he called "interposition" was the constitutional companion to "massive resistance," holding that it was the right of the southern states to block federal efforts at integration.[264]

African Americans had never been treated equally in the economic realm either. While income grew for everyone during the postwar boom years, African Americans consistently made about half as much as whites. In 1950, the median African American man had an income of $12,600. His white counterpart took home $23,000. By 1960, incomes had grown, but the gap remained: $15,800 compared with $30,000.[265] African American veterans had been eligible for GI Bill education benefits but found few schools that would admit them, and those that would were quickly oversubscribed.[266] Racially restrictive deeds, unscrupulous lending, redlining, and other policies kept African Americans from building wealth and economic security through homeownership.[267]

The civil rights revolution was therefore a great triumph, and not just for African Americans. Won only after a 534-hour filibuster in the Senate, Title VII of the Civil Rights Act of 1964 declared that discrimination based on "race, color, religion, sex, or national origin" was an unlawful employment practice and banned discrimination in facilities that serve the general public.[268] Soon followed the Voting Rights Act in 1965 and the Fair Housing Act in 1968. By prohibiting discrimination and protecting women and minorities from unequal treatment, the laws of the civil rights revolution substantially expanded America's political and economic community, promising everyone a place in America's middle class.

The inclusion of "sex" in the Civil Rights Act was crucial for expanding America's opportunities to women. After the Civil War, suffragettes like Elizabeth Cady Stanton and Susan B. Anthony petitioned Congress to enfranchise women in the new constitutional amendments. Women had long been thought of as members of the political community who were virtually represented by their husbands. Suffragettes challenged the argument that the family would be destroyed if women got the vote, arguing that there was "an order of nobility" when "one class of citizens" had the "right to make, interpret, and execute the law for another class wholly unrepresented in government." Universal manhood suffrage, Elizabeth Cady Stan-

ton said, made "all women slaves—the most odious form of aristocracy."[269] By the time of the Nineteenth Amendment, ratified in
1920, the women's movement was internally divided. In the wake of
the *Lochner* decision, progressives discovered that while they could
not get the Court to uphold labor wages and hours laws that were
generally applicable, the Court would uphold laws designed to help
women and children, who were seen as "weak" and in need of special protection. Progressive advocates and labor feminists pragmati-
cally used "protective legislation" to improve working conditions for
women. Others, however, like Alice Paul and the National Woman's
Party, opposed special protections and supported an equal rights
amendment to the Constitution. At times they even allied with the
National Association of Manufacturers and southern Democrats
who sought primarily to undermine social welfare programs.[270]

The post–World War II boom years saw a growth in women in
the workforce. The percentage of working mothers with children
between ages six and seventeen rose from 30.5 percent in 1950 to
41.5 percent in 1963.[271] Still, the New Deal's social and economic policy approach was one of "breadwinner liberalism," in which the goal
was a "family wage" earned by a single male breadwinner, who had
access to benefits (like a pension and unemployment).[272] The result,
as Simone de Beauvoir wrote in *The Second Sex,* was that women
were, like African Americans, "only partially integrated in a civilization that nevertheless considers them an inferior caste."[273] By the
1960s, the lawyer and activist Pauli Murray had coined the phrase
"Jane Crow" and gained a spot on President Kennedy's Commission on the Status of Women, where she argued that the Fourteenth
Amendment could be interpreted as applicable to women, thereby
forgoing the need for an equal rights amendment.[274] The commission did not go as far with its recommendations as many wanted, but
it did expose sex discrimination policies in American law and create
momentum toward the 1963 Equal Pay Act. It also spurred efforts
around the country, because many states established commissions of
their own; the influential, moderate leaders who constituted the state
commissions found discrimination in their laws.[275]

After the Civil Rights Act was passed, the civil rights movement
became a model for women, and equal opportunity became the

approach to combating sex discrimination.[276] The Equal Employment Opportunity Commission was immediately overwhelmed with complaints from women. Women across America received less generous life insurance, health insurance, and pension and retirement plans, not to mention that jobs were arbitrarily classified by sex and women were often not hired (or were fired) if they got married or pregnant.[277] Groups like the National Organization for Women's Legal Defense and Education Fund (modeled on the NAACP's litigation group) and the ACLU, with star attorney Ruth Bader Ginsburg, used the law in court to push for greater equality.[278]

The 1960s also saw the *growth* of the political community. In the mid-nineteenth century, Ralph Waldo Emerson praised "the energy of the Irish, Germans, Swedes, Poles, and Cossacks, and all the European tribes—and of the Africans, and of the Polynesians" who would make Americans a new people and America a "smelting pot" of cultures.[279] But many Americans did not share Emerson's sentiments, and even in the 1840s nativists organized against the growing numbers of Irish and German immigrants in America. By the economic crises of the 1870s, opinion turned against the Chinese, whom many saw as racially inferior, culturally different, and economically threatening. In 1882, for the first time in American history, Congress passed a law restricting immigration by race and nationality—the Chinese Exclusion Act.[280] As economic insecurity persisted, this "selective" approach to immigration grew more popular with nativists, who now opposed immigrants from southern and eastern Europe.[281] In the early 1920s, Congress passed restrictive laws massively reducing the number of immigrants allowed into the country, setting up quotas based on national origin, and closing America to "undesirable races."[282] In 1914, European immigration to the United States was over one million. By 1929, it had dropped to 158,000. The restrictive laws of the early 1920s virtually eliminated Asian immigration and severely reduced the numbers of southern and eastern Europeans. In 1914, more than 200,000 Italians came to the United States. After 1924, the yearly average was less than 15,000. In 1921, 95,000 Poles immigrated; the rest of the decade saw an average of 8,000.[283] The result was that America became less and less of a "nation of immigrants." The number of foreign born living in America dropped from

13.1 percent in 1920 to 6.9 percent in 1950, eventually reaching a low of about 5 percent in the 1960s.[284]

Of course, even during restrictive eras, there were exceptions. Some were for geopolitical reasons, including allowing some displaced Europeans to enter the country after World War II.[285] Others were economic. Growers in the Southwest, for example, argued through the 1920s and again during World War II that they needed more agricultural labor. With uncanny echoes of James Henry Hammond's mudsill theory, they said that they needed "a class of labor that will do this back-breaking work," in part so that whites wouldn't have to.[286] Although foreign contract labor had been abolished in 1885, as contrary to the system of "free labor" that emerged victorious during the Civil War, Congress responded in 1943 with the bracero program for Mexican contract laborers (often called guest workers).[287] In its agreement with Mexico, the United States promised that these workers "shall not suffer discriminatory acts of any kind."[288] Despite this guarantee, braceros were paid less and labored under worse working and living conditions.[289]

In 1965, Congress passed immigration legislation abolishing the quotas based on national origin that had existed since the 1920s.[290] As Vice President Hubert Humphrey said of the reforms, "We want to bring our immigration law into line with the spirit of the Civil Rights Act of 1964."[291] Reforms ended the bracero program, and immigrants entered the country from all over the world, particularly from developing countries in Latin America, Asia, and Africa.[292] With the model of the civil rights movement in mind, nonprofit groups like the Mexican American Legal Defense and Educational Fund and the National Council of La Raza emerged to protect and advance the interests of immigrants and new Americans.[293]

Many of the inclusionary efforts of civil rights reformers centered on the fact that the New Deal model that was responsible for the middle-class family of the 1950s had deliberately excluded minorities and women. White supremacist southern Democrats excluded agricultural labor and domestic services, sectors that were largely African American, from the National Labor Relations Act and from the Social Security Act (which also discriminated against women, because it was designed with a male breadwinner as its paradigm case). The Fair

Labor Standards Act, which included the federal minimum wage, did not apply to textiles, tobacco processing, and lumber, all heavily southern industries. Some New Deal programs were implemented through the states and localities—unemployment, Aid to Families with Dependent Children, housing—and local white officeholders could therefore redirect funds away from African Americans. And of course, New Deal labor policies could simply be ignored: employers would engage in illegal firings and intimidation of workers, with little risk of enforcement from their white brethren.[294] During the war, Roosevelt had established a Fair Employment Practices Committee to help end job discrimination in the defense industry. But when it came time to make the progressive agency permanent after the war, Congress killed it.[295]

Still, during the war civil rights and fundamental labor reform had often gone hand in hand. Attorney General Francis Biddle and the Justice Department envisioned the Thirteenth Amendment as guaranteeing free labor, which they believed required national markets, national regulation, and union organization. Their vision took aim not only at unjust individual employer-employee relationships but also at the broader structure of the economy, particularly in the South, where peonage (debt-bonded labor) and sharecropping still persisted.[296] But in the words of a classic essay, the "opportunities found" during World War II were ultimately "lost."[297] Employers put labor unions on the defensive after the war. Conservatives used fears of communism to attack economic reform. The institutionalization of collective bargaining as the dominant form of industrial relations made it harder to mobilize African Americans. And liberal institutions like unions and African American advocacy groups increasingly shifted toward a legal and administrative approach to winning citizenship rights.[298] Civil rights lawyers, in particular, made strategic litigation choices that ultimately led to the great victory in *Brown* but at the same time established desegregation and antidiscrimination as the paradigm for civil rights reform rather than a more economically focused approach.[299] As one legal historian puts it, "*Brown* thus constructed a partial and particular image of Jim Crow. . . . It divorced the seventy-five-year-old caste system from its economic roots, from its material inequities, from the farmworkers who complained about their immobility and the industrial workers who complained about their inability to make a living."[300] The result is that the core legislation in the civil rights revolution was fundamentally about including previously excluded groups in the political and economic system as it existed, not about reshaping the postwar economic structure as a whole.

The leaders of the civil rights movement understood, however, that economic opportunity was central to the challenges facing women and minorities. "What will [the Negro] gain by being permitted to move to an integrated neighborhood if he cannot afford to do so because he is unemployed?" Bayard Rustin asked at the 1964 Democratic National Convention.[301] When Lyndon Johnson spoke at Howard University in 1965, he cited statistics—unemployment, income, poverty, infant mortality—showing that America's rising prosperity had not fully reached African Americans. Equality as a "right and a theory," he said, was not enough.[302] So Johnson declared war on poverty and passed Medicare, Medicaid, Head Start, and the Elementary and Secondary Education Act. A. Philip Randolph proposed "A Freedom Budget for All Americans," which would spend $355 billion over ten years in hopes of achieving full employment and adequate incomes, wiping out slum ghettos and providing housing, ensuring modern medical care and educational opportunities, purifying the air and water, and updating transportation needs.[303] Martin Luther King Jr. spent his later years launching the Poor People's Campaign. The civil rights revolution had made so many Americans full and equal members of the political and economic community. The question now was whether they would have access to the booming economy. As one historian puts it, "The Great Society was built on the premise that the New Deal generation had solved the major structural problems and that the New Deal order would persist." Those who hadn't yet made it "simply needed help in doing so."[304]

THE CONSTITUTION AND THE WAR ON POVERTY

In the midst of a generation of rising prosperity, an expanding middle class, increasing equality, and fears of communism, it is not surprising that constitutional debate on economic issues shifted away from the fundamental structural questions that motivated reformers from the start of the industrial age. In the postwar era, the most compelling, innovative thinking was not about restraining the influence of the rich or restructuring the economy to improve the stake of the middle class. The most interesting economic thinking was about poverty—about how to help Americans whose boats had not been lifted by the rising tide of the glorious years. In politics, this effort was best captured by President Lyndon Johnson's War on Poverty. For constitutional thinkers and activists, the goal was to constitutionalize Roosevelt's economic bill of rights.

The origins of the effort to constitutionalize the rights of the poor are located in the 1941 case of *Edwards v. California*.[305] California passed a law making it a misdemeanor for any person to bring a poor person into the state. The Supreme Court struck down California's ban, because the state was trying to regulate interstate commerce, a power granted to the federal government in the Constitution. But the Court also suggested that the philosophy of the "Elizabethan poor laws," in which each locality must care for its own poor, was outdated. New Deal efforts from farm assistance to Social Security to works programs showed that America was now a national community.[306] Perhaps most instructive was Justice Robert Jackson's comments (the same Jackson who had been at the antitrust division before Thurman Arnold):

> Any measure which would divide our citizenry on the basis of property into one class free to move from state to state and another class that is poverty-bound to the place where it has suffered misfortune is not only at war with the habit and custom by which our country has expanded, but is also a shortsighted blow at the security of property itself. Property can have no more dangerous, even if unwitting, enemy than one who would make its possession a pretext for unequal or exclusive civil rights.[307]

The ethos of the middle-class constitution lived on in Jackson's statement. It would be opposed to America's "habit and custom" to divide our people into different classes "on the basis of property."

Indeed, property owners, Jackson implies, would face the danger of revolt if a class emerged without property but with civil rights.

Starting in the late 1950s, the Supreme Court decided a series of cases that ensured that the poor had equal legal rights to the wealthy. "Providing equal justice for poor and rich, weak and powerful alike is an age-old problem," the Court observed in *Griffin v. Illinois*.[308] Illinois charged a fee for getting the transcript from a trial, an important document for appealing a case. The Court held that under the Constitution's equal protection clause, poor people had to have access, for "[t]here can be no equal justice where the kind of trial a man gets depends on the amount of money he has."[309] In the celebrated 1963 case of *Gideon v. Wainwright,* the Court announced that criminal defendants had to be given access to defense counsel.[310] Legal counsel in appealing a criminal conviction came next.[311] The Court then struck down one-year residency requirements for receiving welfare benefits and nonemergency health care, and in 1970 declared in *Goldberg v. Kelly* that if the government wanted to deny welfare benefits, it had to provide due process.[312] The Court was not alone in its efforts. Scholars and commentators during this period pushed the Court to think about the rights of the poor and provided legal and philosophical justifications for these efforts.[313]

But with the election of Richard Nixon to the presidency and his new appointees on the Supreme Court, the possibility that the Constitution would provide minimal protections for the poor came to an end.[314] The turning point was the 1973 case *San Antonio Independent School District v. Rodriguez*.[315] Texas had a system of financing public schools that was based on geography, leading to widespread disparities in school funding based on locality. For every $1,000 that went to a wealthy school, poor schools only received $370.[316] The challengers thought that Texas's system violated the Constitution's guarantee of equal protection of the law. The poor did not have the same educational opportunities as the wealthy, because Texas had designed its system of school financing in a way that guaranteed inequality that benefited the wealthy. Justice Lewis Powell, writing for a 5–4 majority, upheld Texas's system, declaring that "[i]t is not the province of this Court to create substantive constitutional rights in the name of guaranteeing equal protection of the laws."[317] Education was not explicitly mentioned in the Constitution, Powell said, and therefore it is not protected explicitly or even implicitly under the equal protection clause. Education might be helpful for exercising free speech or the right to vote, but it was not the job of the Court to ensure that Americans had access to the prerequisites of constitutional rights.[318]

In dissent, Justice Thurgood Marshall criticized virtually every aspect of Powell's reasoning. As to Powell's claim that the Court should not recognize rights that are not explicitly mentioned in the Constitution, Marshall parried that the right to procreate, the right to vote in state elections, the right to have access to appeal a criminal conviction—rights everyone would support and the Court *had* in fact recognized as constitutionally protected—would fail Powell's test.[319] While the task of identifying constitutionally protected rights was difficult, Marshall said, it was not impossible. The test "in every case," he explained, "should be to determine the extent to which the constitutionally guaranteed rights are dependent on interests not mentioned in the Constitution."[320]

> As the nexus between the specific constitutional guarantee and the nonconstitutional interest draws closer, the nonconstitutional interest becomes more fundamental and the degree of judicial scrutiny applied when the interest is infringed on a discriminatory basis must be adjusted accordingly.[321]

In other words, there were certain prerequisites without which constitutionally protected rights were meaningless. The task for judges was to consider the alignment between the preconditions for constitutional rights and the rights that were outlined in the document. What Marshall understood is that the Constitution had built into it a set of assumptions about underlying social, political, and legal conditions. It did not mention every possible right in detail. The task for judges was to look for the links between the underlying conditions and the fulfillment of the Constitution's vision. Even though education was not mentioned explicitly in the text of the Constitution, the constitutional system relied upon it. Jefferson and many of the other founders would have recognized this style of argument;

indeed, they often made the argument that education was essential to preserving America's republican Constitution.

After *San Antonio*, however, the project of recognizing the constitutional rights of the poor largely came to an end.[322] In some ways, the rise and fall of the constitutional movement to protect the poor confirms the exceptional nature of the glorious postwar years. In previous eras, those who feared the disconnect between America's economic equality and its political structure had focused on restructuring the economy or the political system. They advocated for industrial democracy, regulation, antitrust, the direct election of senators, popular referenda, and campaign finance reforms. Now, in an age of relatively equitable growth, the focus shifted from how to make capitalism compatible with our republican Constitution to how to alleviate burdens for those who were left behind. And just as the goals changed, so too did the tactics. In previous eras, economic and political reformers were *hostile* to the courts. They routinely condemned judges, lawyers, and the Supreme Court as an improper barrier to achieving their Constitution-preserving goals that the people demanded. Now, bolstered by judicial decisions brought to bear in the battle against racism in the Jim Crow South, reformers saw the Court as an ally rather than a foe. But the exception was short-lived. The Court soon went back to its historic role of blocking efforts to preserve America's middle-class republic.

THE EPHEMERAL DEAL

Starting in the 1960s, the civil rights, women's, and LGBT movements achieved victories that increasingly ended discrimination and made the promise of America's middle-class republic open regardless of race, national origin, gender, sexuality, and identity. But while these movements were transformative, they were not primarily about reforming or reshaping the structure of industrial capitalism. These movements did not attempt to destroy the institutions of finance, as the Jacksonians did; or suggest that corporations become cooperatives, as the Knights of Labor did in the Gilded Age; or push for breaking up corporate juggernauts, as the Progressive trustbusters did. In the rising tide era of growth and prosperity, the problem with the economic regime was not that it failed to create a middle class or that the middle class was collapsing. The problem was that it had long blocked women and minorities from equal access and treatment.

A century before, some of the Reconstruction Republicans had an economic plan to guarantee that the freedmen of the South would enter the middle class that the Constitution demands. President Lyndon Johnson and some civil rights leaders recognized this need as well in the late 1960s. But would the expansion of the population included in America's middle-class community lead to economic reforms? Would it lead to solidarity between black and white working-class men and women? Or would it lead to fragmentation?

Within the Democratic Party, the critical event in this shift was the 1971 McGovern-Fraser Commission, which suggested revising the process of delegate selection and participation in advance of the 1972 Democratic National Convention. The reformed system expanded representation among women, minorities, and young people, establishing the "new politics" coalition that has characterized the Democratic Party since.[323] While the convention was the most diverse in the Democratic Party's history to that point, some labor leaders were furious, complaining that the Democratic Party had been hijacked by these new entrants and that the party was fundamentally changing (which it was).[324] Many working-class whites started to believe that inclusionary reforms meant a zero-sum game between their economic fortunes and those of minorities.[325] An Atlanta man thus complained that the problem since *Brown v. Board of Education* "was not race, but the have-nots taking what the haves had produced and achieved" to the point "of us middle class people" being "liquidated."[326] Resentment was on the rise and was identified even by 1969 in Pete Hamill's influential *New York* magazine article "The Revolt of the White Lower Middle Class."[327] Some Republicans capitalized on this shift, using racial polarization to gain political benefits. Decades later, in 2005, Republican National Committee chairman Ken Mehlman would declare that the party was "wrong" to have done so.[328]

Just as these changes were under way, the economy of the 1970s brought what one historian has called the "crisis of industrial society."[329] In 1971, the United States ran a trade deficit for the first time since 1893.[330] Two years later came the Arab oil embargo and an energy crisis, in addition to a recession in which the stock market lost half of its value.[331] That year was also the last year in which the median male worker's wages continued to increase; after that, wages flattened out.[332] By the 1970s, Japan, China, and former European colonies around the world were now industrializing and producing basic goods that were once limited to Western industry.[333] A stagnant economy combined with increasing inflation led to the portmanteau "stagflation" and at the same time transformed historically thrifty American savers into borrowers, spenders, and (eventually) debtors.[334] The industrial workforce also began to shift. Between 1967 and 1977, manufacturing dropped by a third in Boston, Philadelphia, Pittsburgh, and Chicago.[335] As a percentage of the workforce, union membership declined from 25 percent in 1970 to 16 percent in 1981.[336] Industry started moving to the non-union Sunbelt, made possible in part by the widespread adoption of air-conditioning.[337] Commentators at the time worried about what these massive shifts meant. Daniel Bell declared the "coming of post-industrial society,"[338] the name itself reflecting uncertainty. Michael Harrington called it the "twilight of capitalism" and saw in the future either a resurgent liberal state or the outright corporate domination of society.[339]

In corporate America, things were changing as well. In 1971, two months before he was appointed a justice on the Supreme Court, Lewis Powell (the same Powell whose opinion in *San Antonio* killed off the attempt to address poverty through constitutional law) wrote a memo to one of the leaders of the U.S. Chamber of Commerce. "[T]he American economic system is under broad attack," Powell wrote.

> [I]ndependent and uncoordinated activity by individual corporations . . . will not be sufficient. Strength lies in organization, in careful long-range planning and implementation, in consistency of action over an indefinite period of years, in the scale of financing available only through joint effort, and in the political power available only through united action and national organizations.[340]

Powell advised the Chamber of Commerce to take aggressive action to promote advantageous economic positions. He pushed it to cultivate political power and use it "aggressively and with determination."[341] He even suggested that corporate America start focusing on helping supportive academics and evaluating textbook content, to shape the information environment in which they would operate.

Powell's memo came in the midst of an era of significant economic reform. With the support of the middle-class consumer, Congress passed a flurry of reform-oriented legislation between 1969 and 1974: the National Environmental Policy Act, the Clean Air Act amendments, the Occupational Safety and Health Act, the Consumer Product Safety Act, the Federal Water Pollution Control Act, the Equal Employment Opportunity Act, and the Employee Retirement Income Security Act, among others. Each of these laws involved the victory of public interests over private profits. In the months and years after Powell's memo, corporations reacted by getting into the political game, creating trade associations, political action committees, and lobbying arms. The goal was not just to educate legislators on policy issues or play defense to protect their bottom line but also to define the playing field itself.[342] Indeed, some even hoped that the ideal CEO would have "one foot in the boardroom and the other in Washington."[343]

The portents appeared in 1978 in the legislative fights over full employment and labor reform. With the election of 1976, Democrats gained control of the White House and both houses of Congress, including a filibuster-proof Senate majority. Since the time of Franklin Roosevelt's second bill of rights, full employment had been one of the prize goals of the New Deal coalition. Roosevelt's attempt to guarantee every American a job was stripped from the Employment Act of 1946. By the 1970s, full employment was an opportunity to break free from the trade-off between economic access for women and minorities and the economic crisis that was limiting opportunity. Instead of workers' fighting over slices in the pie, full employment would expand the pie. The draft Humphrey-Hawkins Full Employment Act was a mix of New Deal economics and 1960s civil rights talk. It would guarantee a universal right to a job, establish policy planning to achieve a full-employment economy, and give individuals a right to sue in court for a job.[344] The 1978 labor law reform bill was, in contrast, a modest bill—one that had been watered down from the start to eliminate the most controversial goals. It was designed to pass easily.[345]

Both bills met with disastrous fates. Humphrey-Hawkins was gutted, stripped of the universal right of employment, access to the courts, and a policy-planning regime to achieve full employment.[346] At the time, as one historian has said, "joblessness tended to be regarded as either an individual or a racial problem rather than a structural one."[347] There was simply no appetite—or popular energy—for such a bold reform. The labor reform bill was an even bigger surprise. Organizations that Powell hoped would use political power "aggressively and with determination" sprang into action. Business Roundtable, the National Association of Manufacturers, the Chamber of Commerce, the National Right to Work Committee— all jumped into the fight. In the end, more than one hundred major corporations took part, including U.S. Steel, GM, AT&T, and Bank of America.[348] George Meany, the head of the AFL-CIO, called it "an all out attack on the American labor movement." It was "no longer a fight on the bill but an attack by every anti-union group in America to kill the labor movement." Writing in *The Wall Street Journal,* he asked America's business leaders about their opposition, "Why should law-abiding companies seek to continue a system that allows some employers to break the law with impunity? . . . Do you secretly seek a death sentence for the collective bargaining system you so often hail in public forums?"[349] The bill was defeated by one vote. Senator Orrin Hatch (one of the leaders of the opposition) said it was the "starting point for a new era of assertiveness by big business in Washington."[350]

With the failure of the labor bill in July 1978, UAW president Douglas Fraser resigned from the Labor-Management Group, a forum for collaboration in the Treaty of Detroit era. The bill, he said in his resignation letter, was "an extremely moderate, fair piece of legislation that only corporate outlaws would have had need to fear." Instead of supporting it, "[t]he leaders of industry, commerce and finance in the United States have broken and discarded the fragile, unwritten compact previously existing during a past period of growth and progress."[351] The fight was a wake-up call for labor leaders. A. H. Raskin, writing in *The New York Times,* said that this "crucial battle marked the end of a thirty-year entente cordiale."[352]

Looking back, it is clear that the glorious postwar years "rested on an ephemeral deal, not a permanent realignment of class power," writes historian Jefferson Cowie.[353] By the start of the 1980s, Americans were left "with a set of individual rights to non-discrimination amidst a more brutal economy—a multi-cultural neo-liberalism."[354]

PART III

THE CRISIS OF THE
MIDDLE-CLASS CONSTITUTION

How Economic Inequality Threatens the Republic

In his best-selling *Capital in the Twenty-First Century,* economist Thomas Piketty argues that the mid-twentieth century was economically exceptional. Prior to that time, economic inequality had been pronounced, with economic gains flowing mainly to the wealthiest in the United States and Europe. Two world wars and the Great Depression wiped out much of their wealth, ushering in an age of unprecedented economic equality, broad-based economic growth, and relative economic stability. Since the 1970s, economic wealth has once again become increasingly stratified. Unless public policy changes, Piketty predicts the twenty-first century will look more and more like the Gilded Age of the late nineteenth century.[1]

The 2008 financial crash brought the decades-long trend of widening inequality to the forefront of public attention. Since the 1970s, globalization, technology, and public policy choices have fundamentally reshaped American economic and political life. Working families have been increasingly squeezed by flat wages and rising expenses, while the wealthiest Americans did better and better—capturing a larger and larger share of America's growing economy. Long before the 2008 crash, the age of America's great middle class was receding.

For those on the losing end of the economy, both economic and political power seem out of balance. This isn't just felt among progressives. According to a 2014 Pew survey, 48 percent of steadfast *conservatives* believe the economic system unfairly favors the powerful, and 71 percent of steadfast conservatives believe too much power is concentrated in the hands of a few large companies.[2]

Everywhere people look there seems to be evidence that the system serves to perpetuate the privileges of the economically powerful. Bankers who engage in criminal activities don't get prosecuted. Hedge fund managers pay lower tax rates than their secretaries. And no matter who is in charge in Washington, it seems as if many of these policies never change.

These two phenomena—the collapse of the middle class and America's increasingly rigged political system—are connected. But the truly terrifying thing is that they reinforce each other. As wealth is concentrated in the hands of elites and corporations, they use their wealth and influence to rewrite laws and regulations in ways that help them amass even greater wealth and power. The result is a downward spiral, a vicious circle in which economic inequality and the capture of the political system reinforce each other. This dynamic makes it more and more likely with each passing day that modern America is losing its character as a republic.

THE CRISIS OF THE MIDDLE CLASS

Port Clinton is located along the southern shore of Lake Erie, in Ottawa County, Ohio. The county, writes Harvard social scientist Robert Putnam, is the bellwether county—the best at predicting election returns—in the bellwether state in America. It is also Putnam's hometown and the subject of his book *Our Kids: The American Dream in Crisis,* which traces the fate of Port Clinton and its residents from 1959 (when Putnam graduated from high school) to 2015. In the glorious postwar 1950s, Port Clinton was a classic American middle-class city, an industrial Lake Wobegon. But over the next half century, its fate was far from above average. Manufacturing in Ottawa County accounted for 55 percent of all jobs in 1965. But by 1995, the Standard Products factory, army base, and gypsum mines had closed. Manufacturing dropped to just 25 percent of jobs. Wages in the 1970s were slightly above the national average, but forty years later they were 25 percent below the national average. In 2012, the average worker in Ottawa County was paid 16 percent less than his grandparents were in the early 1970s. The population had grown steadily from World War II through 1970 but soon flatlined and then dropped by 17 percent. Businesses disappeared. Juvenile delinquency rates grew from average to three times the national average by 2010. Single-parent households doubled. The divorce rate quintupled. Unwed births doubled to almost 40 percent between 1990 and 2010. And in just fourteen years, from 1999 to 2013, child poverty in Port Clinton jumped from 10 percent to 40 percent.[3]

At the same time as Port Clinton's working class collapsed, the town saw the emergence of a new upper class. Wealthy midwesterners noticed Port Clinton's location on Lake Erie and started building gated communities and massive mansions, particularly in the Catawba area, just northeast of town. It is now possible, Putnam says, to walk "from wealthy estates on the shoreline to impoverished trailer parks inland" in only ten minutes. When Putnam was a kid, one of his wealthiest classmates, Frank, was embedded in the town's middle-class community. Although his parents owned a fishing business, shopping center, restaurant, and farm, and were members (and leaders) of the Port Clinton Yacht Club, Frank lived four blocks away from Don, a working-class kid whose father had an eighth-grade education and worked on the line at a manufacturing plant. Frank's neighbors included a truck driver, a cashier at A&P, a fire chief, and a gas station owner. Frank even worked summers at his family's restaurant. While the 1950s were hardly perfect for minorities, Putnam tells the story of Jesse, an African American classmate whose family fled Jim Crow Mississippi after his sister was killed. Jesse became president of the student council, MVP of the football team, and went to college—all before the civil rights revolution of the 1960s.[4] By 2010, the picture in Ottawa County was different. The median household income in Catawba was now twice as much as the median income in the neighborhood next door. In 2011, the Catawba area had a child poverty rate of 1 percent; the census tract across the road from Catawba had a child poverty rate of 51 percent.[5] The kids Putnam talks to now have nothing like the lives his classmates had. They are separated by geography, segregated educationally, and divided socially, including by stability of their families, incidence of drug use, and support they get from the community—all along lines of class. In the 1950s, Putnam writes, "affluent kids and poor kids lived near one another, went to school together, played and prayed together, and even dated one another. . . . Nowadays, by contrast, fewer and fewer of us, in Port Clinton and elsewhere, are exposed in our daily lives to people outside our own socioeconomic niche."[6]

Putnam's story of the collapse of the middle class and the fraying of his hometown's community isn't a memoir of one idiosyncratic spot in America. Putnam shows that the trends and challenges facing Port Clinton over the last half century are representative of those faced all around the country. In recent years, more and more analysts have documented the collapse of America's middle-class communities over the last thirty years. Conservative intellectual Charles Murray's *Coming Apart: The State of White America, 1960–2010* traces how American whites have become increasingly divided into an upper class and a lower class, segregated from each other and with different habits and behaviors. Instead of using the "real" Port Clinton, he traces the story of a fictional "Belmont" and "Fishtown," neighborhoods that track the changes in America from 1960 to 2010.[7] Liberal commentator George Packer's *The Unwinding* provides an "inner history of the new America" through vignettes from across the country.[8] Indeed, the list of books describing the collapse of the middle class and the rise of the upper and lower classes seems to be growing: Barbara Ehrenreich's *Bait and Switch: The (Futile) Pursuit of the American Dream,* Kathryn Edin and Luke Shaefer's *$2.00 a Day: Living on Almost Nothing in America,* Chrystia Freeland's *Plutocrats: The Rise of the New Global Super Rich and the Fall of Everyone Else.*[9] Together, these books and many others show the growing divide between the wealthy and the poor.

Looking back from the early twenty-first century, the post–World War II era—the era of the Great Compression in wages and the industrial system symbolized by the Treaty of Detroit—increasingly looks exceptional. For a generation, economic growth meant shared prosperity. But since the late 1970s and early 1980s, the Great Compression has turned into what Paul Krugman has called the "Great Divergence."[10] Today, economic growth increasingly benefits only the wealthiest Americans, the middle class is increasingly being hollowed out, and economic inequality threatens faith in the American dream.

From 1948 to 1978, wages and productivity marched upward together. But since then, growth has far outstripped wages. By 2013, productivity in America was up 243.1 percent since 1948. But wages had only risen 108.9 percent.[11] Where did all the benefits from growth go? Between 1979 and 2008, 100 percent of the growth in income went to the top 10 percent of Americans. During this period, the income for the bottom 90 percent actually declined.[12]

In the last generation, the wealthiest Americans have taken home a larger and larger share of America's income and wealth. In 1979, the top 10 percent of Americans captured 32 percent of American income, excluding capital gains; in 2014, they captured 47 percent of income.[13] That number is *higher* than the peak during the Roaring Twenties (46 percent).[14] Looking within the top 10 percent of Americans, it is the truly super-rich who have picked up most of these gains. In 1928, the top 1 percent of Americans took home almost 24 percent of the nation's income, including capital gains. By 1976, they were only drawing 8.86 percent of America's income. That number was back up to 21 percent by 2014.[15] The numbers are even more striking when considering the smallest slice of the super-rich. *Forbes* magazine calculates the four hundred wealthiest Americans each year. A report analyzing this list found that the Forbes 400 has as much wealth as the entire African American population and a third of the Latino population combined. The twenty wealthiest individuals in America alone are wealthier than the bottom half of the American population—152 million people.[16]

The collapse of the middle class in the meantime has been slow and gradual, with each decade since the 1970s seeing a smaller percentage of middle-class adults than the prior decade.[17] In 2015, for the first time in generations, the American middle class no longer comprised the majority of Americans. According to the Pew Research Center, in 1971, 80 million Americans were middle class. This amounted to 61 percent of Americans. Combined, the upper and lower classes were 51.6 million.[18] By 2015, America's population had grown. The middle class was now 120.8 million, but the upper and lower classes together are now more than 50 percent of the population—some 121.3 million Americans.[19]

Coupled with the shrinking middle class are their dwindling fortunes. According to Pew, middle-income households took home 62 percent of the nation's aggregate income in 1970. By 2015, they were taking home only 43 percent. In the same period, the upper class's share rose from 29 percent to 49 percent of income.[20] The data shows that the percentage of Americans in the upper class is increasing. The number of highest-income Americans more than doubled from 4 percent to 9 percent between 1971 and 2015.[21] This is partly desirable; some Americans are getting wealthier. But the data also shows that the number of lower-income people is rising—from 16 percent in 1971 to 20 percent in 2015.[22] In addition, there are demographic differences in who is doing better and who is doing worse. Married adults and those over sixty-five are more likely to be wealthy instead of poor, as are whites and Asians.[23]

Looking at specific metropolitan areas, the data confirms these trends. According to a Pew Research study of 229 metro areas—which covers 76 percent of the U.S. population—the share of adults living in middle-class households fell in 203 of them, and in 53 the decrease in the share of the middle class was more than 6 percent.[24] In some cases, the shrinking middle class meant a growing upper class. In Midland, Texas, for example, the share of adults in middle-income households dropped from 53 percent of the population to 43 percent, but the share in upper-income households skyrocketed from 18 percent to 37 percent. However, in other areas, the shrinking middle meant the growth of the poor. In Goldsboro, North Carolina, the share of adults in middle-income households fell from 60 percent to 48 percent, and the share in lower-income households jumped from 27 percent to 41 percent. Both the upper class and the lower class grew, shrinking the middle class, in 108 out of the 229 metro areas.[25] In 2014, there were only 10 metro areas in which more than 60 percent of adults lived in middle-class households, and in 222 out of 229 metro areas middle-income households lost ground financially. For example, 63 percent of adults in Sheboygan, Wisconsin, are middle class, but the median income for these adults fell by 17 percent between 1999 and 2014—from $80,000 to about $66,000.[26] Pew's analysis also shows that income inequality and the share of adults in middle-income households are directly correlated: a smaller middle class means greater inequality.[27]

What about the bargain struck with the Treaty of Detroit? In the 1930s and 1940s, union membership shot up, reaching more than

30 percent of the workforce and hovering above 25 percent through the mid-1970s. Unions and other workers benefited from the treaty's health, unemployment, and retirement benefits model. But since that time, union membership has plummeted to only about 11 percent of the workforce in 2012.[28] Why does this matter? A 2015 International Monetary Fund (IMF) study of twenty advanced economies found that lower unionization is linked to an increase in the share of income going to the top 10 percent. More interestingly, the study found that the decline of unionization contributes to about *half* of the increase in inequality from 1980 to 2010.[29] The IMF study explains that unions give workers bargaining power and influence over corporate decisions. With reduced worker power, corporate managers and shareholders can capture more of the wealth of the corporation. Indeed, CEO compensation has grown alongside this trend in reduced worker power. In 1979, the CEOs of America's most successful companies made on average 29.9 times as much as their workers. By 2013, they made 295.9 times as much as their workers.[30] The second reason unionization matters is that unions shape the labor market overall. Unions exert political influence, pushing political parties toward policies that help working people. Weaker unions mean that working people have less political influence. In addition, as Professors Bruce Western and Jake Rosenfeld have shown, unions help "institutionalize norms of equity," which means that union wage levels actually influence non-union wage levels.[31] Recall that in the Treaty of Detroit era, non-unionized companies adopted the treaty approach voluntarily. With the eclipse of the treaty system as the dominant norm, the model of generous benefits becomes less of a benchmark.

Economic inequality also threatens the ideal of economic mobility—the idea that people can do better than their parents. In what is now known as the "Great Gatsby Curve," economist Alan Krueger demonstrated the relationship between economic mobility and inequality. Looking across developed countries, Krueger plotted a measure of intergenerational mobility—the likelihood that people will inherit their parents' level of income—and the Gini coefficient, the standard measure of inequality. What he found was a clear correlation: as inequality rises, mobility declines.[32] Countries with the highest mobility had the lowest levels of inequality. What that means is that the idea that everyone has an equal shot of becoming wealthy is highly unlikely in an unequal society. It is more likely, over time, that children of the wealthy will remain wealthy, and those who are unlucky enough to be born to a working-class family won't be able to move up. Indeed, economists have shown the limited extent of upward mobility in America. An important recent study found that children born in the bottom 20 percent of the income distribution only have a 7.5 percent chance of making it into the top 20 percent.[33] If intergenerational equality of opportunity was perfect, it would be a 20 percent chance for these kids to make it to the top 20 percent. On some level, Americans viscerally understand this. A 2014 *Wall Street Journal*/NBC News poll found that fully 76 percent of Americans do not feel confident that their children will have a better life than they do.[34]

For those who are on the losing end of the economic bargain, the situation is dire. Fifty-one percent of all workers in the United States—more than half—make less than $30,000 a year.[35] Forty-seven percent of Americans say they are so strapped for cash that they could not cover a $400 emergency without borrowing money or selling something.[36] Sociologist Victor Tan Chen tells the story of a forty-seven-year-old Detroit factory worker he interviewed. The worker lost his $11-an-hour job when he crashed his forklift into a ladder by accident. Nothing was damaged and no one was hurt, but he was an at-will employee without a union and he was fired. His wife, who made $8 an hour at a cleaning company, left him. He couldn't find work, got stressed out, and ultimately started taking antidepressants.[37] Unfortunately, his story is far too common. When asked in surveys, people with a high-school education or less are more likely to say that they don't have anyone to discuss "important matters" with; their social support network has disappeared.[38] Economists have recently even documented that there has been an increase in the mortality rate of middle-aged white men and women that is largely a function of drug and alcohol poisoning, suicide, and chronic liver disease.[39]

Economic disparities are also growing by race. In 1963, median family wealth was $43,000 higher for whites than for African Americans. By 2013, it was $123,000 higher (and $120,000 higher than for Hispanics, for whom there isn't data from 1963).[40] Even in the few years since the financial crash, wealth inequality has grown along racial lines.[41] Important wealth-building measures, like homeowner-ship, remain widely disparate. In 1983, 68 percent of whites owned their own home, compared with 45 percent of African Americans and 41 percent of Hispanics. Little had changed by 2013: 69 percent of whites were homeowners, compared with 43 percent of African Americans and 45 percent of Hispanics.[42] In other areas, the racial inequality divide is also persistent: African Americans' unemploy-ment rate is higher than whites', and the gap has remained consistent since the 1970s. Black unemployment rates are higher than white rates at every level of education. The percentage of thirty-year-olds with a college degree has widened. And the pay gap has widened over time.[43]

With the shrinking middle class and rising levels of inequality, Americans are becoming more and more segregated by income and, as a result, less and less likely to interact with people who are dis-similar to themselves.[44] One study of metro areas, focused on areas larger than 500,000, showed that in 1970, 6.6 percent of families lived in affluent neighborhoods and 8.4 percent lived in poor neighbor-hoods. By 2012, these numbers had more than doubled: 15.7 per-cent lived in affluent neighborhoods, and 18.6 percent lived in poor neighborhoods. The increase in income segregation has come with a decline in the number of families living in middle-class neigh-borhoods. In 1970, 64.7 percent of families lived in middle-income neighborhoods. By 2012, it was only 40.5 percent.[45] But it isn't just geography. Scholars have recently shown that the upper-middle class and everyone else are increasingly drifting apart on a variety of met-rics: the upper-middle class and the wealthy reach higher education levels, get married (often to each other) at higher rates, stay mar-ried at higher rates, and have different cultural tastes and values.[46] The consequences of these changes are significant. Investments that the wealthy make in their communities will be less likely to bene-fit middle-class or poor families as well, and as social empathy for others drops, people are less likely to support public programs that benefit people unlike themselves.[47]

Americans don't want to live in a country with a collapsing middle class and such extreme inequality. In an important study, Michael Norton and Dan Ariely asked a representative sample of Americans about their views on the distribution of wealth. In one survey, they showed Americans three different possible distributions of wealth: The first divided Americans into five groups by wealth, and each group (for example, the top 20 percent, the bottom 20 percent) had the same amount of wealth. The second distribution mimicked the distribution of wealth in Sweden (but wasn't stated as such). The third was the actual distribution of wealth in America. Not only did Americans prefer complete equality and Swedish levels of equality to the American distribution of wealth, but both Republicans and Democrats preferred the Swedish levels to the American, with more than 90 percent support.[48] In a second survey, Norton and Ariely asked Americans what they thought the actual distribution of wealth was in America and what they think it should be. Respondents in their study estimated that the top 20 percent in America held 59 percent of the wealth, when in fact it was about 84 percent at the time of the study. Their preference, however, was for the top 20 percent to only have about 32 percent of the country's wealth.[49] In other words, Americans dramatically *under*estimate the amount of inequality in America—and want a country that is far more economically equal.

From the standpoint of a republican system of government, what is most important is that the data shows the collapse of the middle and an increasing divide between the wealthy and the poor— something that is incompatible with our middle-class constitution.

HOW ECONOMIC INEQUALITY THREATENS THE REPUBLIC

In his book *The Twilight of the Elites*, Chris Hayes identifies what he calls the "Iron Law of Meritocracy." A meritocratic system is based on two principles: the principle of difference recognizes that people have different abilities; the principle of mobility holds that we should reward performance and punish failure. The problem, Hayes argues, is that over time the two principles conflict. Rewarding merit leads to inequality in conditions, and inequality "subvert[s] the mechanisms of mobility." "Unequal outcomes make equal opportunity impossible. . . . Those who are able to climb up the ladder will find ways to pull it up after them, or to selectively lower it down to allow their friends, allies, and kin to scramble up. In other words: 'Whoever says meritocracy says oligarchy.'"[50]

Hayes's account of meritocracy gets to the heart of the tension between equality of opportunity, which politicians like to support, and equality of condition, which they often oppose. The hard truth, however, is that the two concepts are far more closely linked than people think. Imagine two people who are perfectly equal in every way. Even with equal opportunities, one of them will end up doing better than the other, due to natural differences, talent, hard work, and dumb luck. This means that our two people are now *unequal* in their condition. We might not have a problem with that. After all, they might have earned it or at least become successful by being lucky. But what happens when our two unequal people now try to start a business? Or lobby Congress? And what happens when it is time for their *children* to enter the world? Now the more successful, wealthier person has a leg up in the competitive marketplace or an advantage in getting access to elected officials. And the wealthier parent, of course, can send her kids to better kindergartens and test prep courses, pay for their educational trips, and support them in unpaid internships. The two children are now both unequal in the conditions they grow up with and unequal in their opportunities. Inequality does not absolve these kids of the need to work hard and take initiative; individual success depends on effort. But formally claiming there is equality of opportunity for these kids is a comforting story we tell ourselves to feel better. In the real world, it is simply wrong to say these kids have equal opportunities.[51]

What emerges from inequality is a new cultural norm. In a relatively economically equal society, no one will think they are "better" than anyone else, or even terribly different from anyone else. Each person has pretty close to the same opportunities, lives in similar conditions, and has reasonably similar life outcomes. Members of the middle class therefore are less likely to think they are inherently better than anyone else, and if they vote their material interests, they are likely to support policies that benefit the strong middle-class majority. Similarity also enhances trust, reciprocity, and understanding between people.[52] This is why Aristotle, Giannotti, Harrington, and Hume so lavishly praised the middle class.

But when economic inequality grows, one of two things can happen. Aristotle reminds us of the first, which we can think of as the inherent ethos of inequality. Because the rich are unequal with respect to their wealth, Aristotle says, they start thinking they are unequal in all respects (moral worth, intelligence, ability to govern). Hayes suggests the same thing happens to the winners in a meritocratic system. They believe that because they succeeded in a fair competitive system, they are inherently better than those who did not succeed. Over time, inequality leads to an erosion of trust as people become more dissimilar, interact less, and begin to see themselves as different from others in society.[53] In political terms, the elites soon begin to believe they are more capable of governing society. This kind of thinking is inherently at odds with republican government, which is rooted directly in the right of the people to govern themselves.

For some people, however, the ethos of inequality isn't just psychological and self-justifying but, more important, material and self-interested. It is often hard to tell the difference between the two ways inequality changes people. The old adage "What's good for General Motors is good for America" is perhaps the best example of people trying to justify their self-interest as the general interest. But as inequality increases, economic elites want to preserve and expand on their wealth. Because they are no longer part of the middle class, the policies that will preserve and expand their wealth now diverge from the policies that help the middle class. For example, the middle class might support raising taxes on the extremely wealthy in order to pay for high-quality public schools that are a gateway to opportunity for their children, but the wealthy will prefer lower tax rates for themselves and less spending on public education because they can afford private schooling.

The wealthy, in the words of Jeffrey Winters, a leading scholar of oligarchy, turn toward policies of *wealth defense*.[54] As fortunes become larger and larger, the wealthy now focus less on the financial well-being of the general public or middle-class families and more on protecting their wealth. They want to defend their property (what they already have), their income (what they can earn), and what they can pass on to their children in the form of inheritance in the future.[55] In medieval times, they engaged in what Winters calls *property defense* by quite literally building castles and fortifications to defend property. Today, in most developed countries, legal rights protecting property serve that function.[56] Likewise, income was once a function of a system of extraction from serfs with limited freedom; the threat to that income was universal freedom, and so feudal lords resisted democracy. In modern republics, the threat to income is taxation, so the wealthy engage in *income defense* by advocating for lower taxes.

With the spread of an ethos of inequality, economic elites increasingly aim to exercise power and influence. They seek out any and every opportunity to shape public policy. Some of their pathways to power are formal. Economic elites, for example, can run for office, seek out political appointments, donate money to campaigns, and engage in lobbying efforts in ways that are all 100 percent legal. Other pathways are informal and indirect. Campaign contributions are pernicious not only because of a reality or appearance of quid pro quo bribery; they are pernicious because they force elected officials to spend so much of their time with economic elites. Candidates for office hear the concerns of the elites more frequently and, as is natural, are informed and acculturated to the views of those elites. Lobbying operates in a similar way. Hearing a skewed set of views from lobbyists, dominated by business and wealthy interests, means that elected officials become accustomed to one side of an argument—and in some cases might never have heard the other side. More indirectly, the creation of an ecosystem of think tanks and media outlets that develop and spread ideological policies and narratives can further skew the views of policy makers. Over time and through this variety of pathways, the economically powerful gain undue influence over policy and shape the actions of those crafting it.

Power soon turns into entrenched privileges, which ultimately reshape the very structure of government and the economy. Economic elites try to adopt policies to insulate themselves from competition and to preserve and expand their wealth—even when it means special privileges. Franklin Roosevelt put it best in his Commonwealth Club address in 1932. "The same man who tells you that he does not want to see the government interfere in business," he said, "is the first to go to Washington and ask the government for a prohibitory tariff on his product." And when "things go bad enough," he will "go with equal speed to the United States government and ask for a loan." The problem, Roosevelt recognized, is that every "group has sought protection from the government for its own special interest, without realizing that the function of government must be to favor no small group at the expense of its duty to protect the rights of personal freedom and of private property of all its citizens."[57] Once economic elites and corporations start to see the role that government can play in helping them, it creates a downward spiral that doesn't just harm the political system but starts to harm the economy. Instead of making money through innovative technologies or marketing, companies look for economic gains through lobbying.[58] Some business schools now even teach courses in "non-market strategies," explaining how business can use legislatures, government agencies, and courts to advance their bottom line.[59]

Privilege doesn't stop at special-interest policies, like the government loans or tariffs Roosevelt mentioned. The truly significant shift happens when economic elites start to manipulate and deform the *structures* of government and of the economy. They attempt to reformulate economic laws like antitrust to reduce competition overall, making it harder to dislodge their privileged positions. And they attempt to alter government—and even the Constitution—making it harder to prevent any policy changes that would block their influence over politics or end the system of special privileges. Economic power through political manipulations then becomes self-sustaining.

As political structures are hobbled to prevent reform and economic policy is skewed to preserve and expand the wealth of those who already have it, economic inequality continues to grow. With greater inequality comes a stronger ethic of inequality, in which the wealthy see their interests as different from everyone else's. The result is a vicious cycle or, as one commentator has put it, the "doom loop of oligarchy."[60]

A cyclical dynamic would have been no surprise to Aristotle, Polybius, Machiavelli, and other political theorists throughout history. Monarchy, aristocracy, republics, tyranny, oligarchy, mobocracy—these were never permanent forms of government. Internal dynamics would lead to a cycle of regimes and intermittent revolution. The critical task of constitutional and political theory was figuring out how to stabilize, or ideally end, the cycle. The worry was that either the rich would oppress the poor or the poor would overthrow the rich. One answer was the class warfare constitution; another, the middle-class constitution.

As economic inequality turns into political inequality, the threat to the republic comes in two forms. First is that the rich will oppress the poor. In other words, the republic will no longer be a republic. A republic is a representative democracy; it involves the rule of the people.[61] But as public policy becomes more focused on wealth defense and eventually the entrenchment of privilege, the form of government changes; it becomes an oligarchy. Winters shows that there are four types of oligarchies in history, classified according to how much the oligarchs directly use force to coerce others and how institutionalized or personalized the oligarchy is. Warring oligarchies—think warlords—are highly coercive and highly personal. Ruling oligarchies, like mafia governance, are highly coercive but more institutionalized. Sultanistic oligarchies, like Indonesia during the rule of Suharto, are not directly coercive, but they are highly personal. Civil oligarchies are neither directly coercive nor personal.[62]

Winters argues that America has *already* become a civil oligarchy. The oligarchs never directly use force, but their property defense comes from the coercive power of the state. The oligarchs also do not usually rule in their personal capacity but instead exert influence through highly institutionalized political and bureaucratic processes.[63] But make no mistake, Winters says, this impersonal, noncoercive, and institutionalized system is not any less oligarchical. The key to oligarchy is that the political system is focused on defending the wealth of the oligarchs. In civil oligarchies, the oligarchs use their wealth to ensure that the government (as the guarantor of the legal rights and civil society) defends their position, even (or perhaps especially) when it means creating special privileges that benefit them and perpetuate their wealth and power at the expense of everyone else. What makes the civil oligarchy so pernicious is that it *appears* to have all the trappings of a rule-of-law-based constitutional republic.

No formal revolution takes place for the oligarchy to emerge. There is no constitutional moment in which there is a decision to change the form of government. Republics descend into oligarchy quietly, through the slow shifting of power from the people to the economic elites. As John Taylor of Caroline put it in 1814, when the "rich plunder the poor," it is always "slow and legal."[64]

The second possibility is that the poor will overthrow the rich. This need not happen through some kind of anarchical populist uprising. More likely, it happens through the emergence of a demagogue with authoritarian tendencies. In recent years, political scientists have documented that authoritarians are likely to emerge from a situation in which people increasingly feel deep anxiety over demographic, economic, and security threats. Political scientists have shown that some people hold latent authoritarian tendencies that are activated when they experience destabilizing social and economic change or significant physical threats.[65] Authoritarian tendencies have also led to political polarization and extreme views in America across a variety of issues including immigration and the use of military force.[66] Even *non*authoritarians can become sufficiently scared—usually by physical threats—that they will adopt authoritarian political beliefs.[67]

Throughout history, republican thinkers feared demagogues. They worried that these charismatic leaders would channel the disaffections and fears of the people to gain power and overthrow the regime.[68] As Alexander Hamilton said in *Federalist* No. 1, "[O]f those men who have overturned the liberties of republics, the greatest number have begun their career by paying an obsequious court to the people; commencing demagogues, and ending tyrants."[69]

This, then, is how economic inequality threatens the republic. Under a middle-class constitution, the republic thrives when there is relative economic equality. But if the middle class collapses and the gap between the rich and everyone else expands, economic inequality will soon lead to political inequality. Policies will shift from protecting broad-based economic growth to defending the wealth of the economic elites. Eventually, the political system itself will be deformed to stack the deck in favor of the economic elites. Either the republic will transform into an oligarchy, or the people will be seduced by an authoritarian demagogue.

PREFERENCES AND PARTICIPATION

In recent years, political scientists have turned to the question of how much influence those with economic power have over American politics and public policy.[70] This still-emerging but already-voluminous literature confirms what the famed political scientist E. E. Schattschneider once noted: in politics, "the heavenly chorus sings with a strong upper-class accent."[71] What the data shows is that there are stark differences between economic elites and everyone else in the population. The preferences of economic elites diverge from those of the rest of the population, and economic elites participate in politics and policy making to a far greater degree than the rest of the population. Perhaps more troubling is the disparity of influence between economic elites and everyone else. Some political scientists have called our system "democracy by coincidence"[72] because the majority only gets its way when, by coincidence, their preferences happen to align with the views of economic elites.[73] Even with data's inevitable limitations, a consistent pattern emerges across these studies: economic elites have disproportionate influence over American public policy.

Start with preferences. When political scientists have compared the preferences of the wealthiest Americans—the top 1 percent and 0.1 percent—with those of the general public, they find stark differences.[74] As people get wealthier, they become more opposed to regulation and more interested in cutting domestic social programs like Social Security, education, food stamps, and jobs programs.[75] The wealthy think deficits are one of the most important problems facing the country, compared with the general public, which is more worried about unemployment and education.[76] The wealthiest Americans tend to be far less supportive of increasing the earned income tax credit or making sure that the minimum wage can keep workers above the poverty line.[77] By significant majorities, the general public strongly supports spending whatever is necessary to have good public schools, and they want to make sure everyone who wants to attend college can do so; only a minority of the wealthiest Americans agree with these goals.[78] The general public is also far more supportive of efforts to regulate Wall Street, oil companies, and big corporations than are the wealthiest Americans.[79]

Divergences in policy preferences extend to the individuals and interest groups that participate in politics as well. According to a study of the economic backgrounds of elected officials, lawmakers who are from different economic backgrounds "tend to think, vote, and advocate differently on economic issues."[80] Similarly, political scientists have shown that views on economic issues diverge between those who are inactive, those who vote, those who volunteer on campaigns, and those who donate to campaigns.[81] With greater participation (which is linked to economic class), people become more hostile to economic and social policies that benefit the working class. The preferences of interest groups also diverge substantially from the views of the general public.[82] Studies conclude that interest group views are almost totally unrelated to the preferences of average citizens and that business interest groups actually have views that are the opposite of ordinary citizens".[83]

Still, the fact that economic elites and everyone else have different policy preferences might not matter much to political outcomes if the people who participate in politics are drawn from the general public. Maybe the people in government are ordinary, rather than drawn from the elites. Alas, no. Those with a higher socioeconomic status are more likely to vote, engage in political activities, and especially donate to political campaigns.[84] At the top 1 percent, levels of access and participation are particularly notable, with more than half of the people in this group contributing to campaigns and contacting government officials.[85] Wealth-based political inequality also holds when a variety of other factors are taken into account. For example, differences exist even when controlling for whether people participate in nonpolitical activities (for example, church), for age cohort, for generational and life cycle effects, and for race.[86] It turns out that the median voter is not the same as the "median campaign volunteer, the median campaign donor, or—because contributors give such different amounts—the person giving the median dollar."[87]

These disparities in participation also extend to interest groups. Under the classic political science approach to interest group politics, the kind we associate with James Madison's idea in *Federalist No. 10*, the barriers to entry into politics should be sufficiently low that the interest group environment is fluid.[88] Interests spring up easily, entering and exiting politics as relevant policy debates come to the fore. According to this theory, there are so many interests, and so many conflicting interests, that no one group wins every time. Early challengers to this rosy view of interest group theory suggested that the interest group ecosystem was biased in favor of businesses and the well-to-do.[89] They also pointed out that ordinary citizens would have a harder time getting organized to participate in politics because they hold a wide variety of views.[90]

Looking at tens of thousands of lobbying organizations in Washington, D.C., over a thirty-year period, Professors Kay Schlozman, Sidney Verba, and Henry Brady have demonstrated that Schattschneider was right: the interest group environment is, in their play on his classic phrase, an "unheavenly chorus," skewed toward business and other elite economic interests. More than half of organizations that are active in Washington represent business interests.[91] Only about one in eight organizations are voluntary associations made up of individuals.[92] Less than 1 percent of organizations are focused on the poor and social welfare.[93] When one looks deeper into the types of organizations, the tilt in the playing field becomes even clearer. Blue-collar workers make up 24 percent of the population but only 6.9 percent of membership organizations and 1.1 percent of all economic organizations that have a presence in Washington.[94] In contrast, executives (a category they separate from professionals and general white-collar workers) make up 9.6 percent of the population but are represented by 13.9 percent of membership organizations and a whopping 73.9 percent of all economic organizations.[95] Breaking up the categories by sector of the economy leads to similar results. In higher education, for example, 50 percent of research universities that award doctoral degrees are represented in Washington, compared with only 2 percent of two-year schools.[96] This is not due to two-year schools' having no stake in public policy: two-year schools rely heavily on the Federal Pell Grant Program, just as research universities rely on federal research dollars. Other studies have shown that even *within* groups that advocate for the disadvantaged, more emphasis is placed on supporting the subgroups that are better off rather than those that are worst off.[97]

Political scientists continue to debate whether political participation is a causal factor in shaping policy outcomes, but they share the view that the composition of those who participate is skewed.[98] As the leading study concludes, "[T]he evidence indicates unambiguously that neither active individuals nor active organizations represent all politically relevant segments of society equally."[99]

"DEMOCRACY BY COINCIDENCE"

Even with divergent preferences and differences in participation, it might be the case that economic elites do not exert disproportionate influence over policy outcomes. That is, representatives might nonetheless follow the will of the majority instead of the economic elites' preferred policies when there are disagreements. Political scientists have tested this possibility, and the results are not encouraging. In a well-known study of voting patterns in the Senate, Professor Larry Bartels found that senators were more responsive to affluent constituents than to constituents of modest means. Strikingly, he found that the views of constituents in the bottom third of the income distribution had almost no impact whatsoever on the senators' behavior.[100]

Another political scientist, Martin Gilens, has conducted the most comprehensive study of the relationship between wealth and political influence, based on an analysis of public policy over two decades. He finds that government policy across all policy areas reflects the policy preferences of the affluent and that the views of the poor and the middle class have no effect on outcomes.[101] Gilens assessed the preferences of people at the 10th, 50th, and 90th percentiles in the income distribution in comparison to policy outcomes in government. As the views of people in the 10th and 90th percentile diverge, the poor and the middle class have less and less influence over policy outcomes. When the gap in preferences between rich and poor increases from less than 5 percentage points to more than 10 percentage points, the poor lose any influence over policy they might have.[102] One might think this is just majoritarianism at work: the poor, after all, could be outvoted by the wealthy and the middle class. But the same effect operates for those at the 50th income percentile and at the 70th income percentile.[103] Gilens even tested coalitions in which the preferences of the poor and the middle class are aligned against those of the wealthy, and he still found that policy was unresponsive to the lower-income groups' combined power.[104] What that means is that when the poor and the middle class—when 70 percent of the people—disagree with the views of the richest 10 percent, their views have no effect on public policy outcomes. But the views of the richest 10 percent are still highly predictive of public policy outcomes. Gilens's findings operate across all areas of policy: foreign policy, economic and tax policy, religious/values issues, and social welfare policy, though the effects vary somewhat by area.[105] Interestingly, the data looks the same even when taking education into account. More educated people get their policy preferences instantiated into law more frequently than the less educated. But if you want political influence, it is much better to be rich than smart. Someone at the 90th percentile in income (very rich) and the 10th percentile in education (low education) has about the same influence as someone at the 90th percentile for both income and education (both rich and educated). But a person at the 90th percentile in education (very well educated) and only 10th percentile in income (poor) has about *half* as much policy influence as his counterpart who is both well educated and rich.[106]

Policy responsiveness to the general public also changes based on when presidential elections are looming, but elections do not fully counteract the influence of economic elites. During presidential election years, policies are more consistent with the views of all Americans than in years without a presidential election, but they are still the *most* responsive to the views of the affluent.[107] In midterm election years, however, this isn't the case.[108] In other words, policies adopted in nonelection years favor the elites the most. Policies adopted during midterm election years favor them a little less. And policies adopted during presidential election years favor economic elites the least. While this finding might be somewhat promising, because it suggests that elections can serve as a partial check on the influence of the wealthy, it turns out that policies adopted during presidential election years are also more likely to be cut over time than those adopted during years without a presidential election.[109] In other words, the policies most likely to align with the preferences of ordinary Americans are first on the chopping block when the people lose the influence that comes from an imminent presidential election.

Some of the most interesting political science research in recent years has explored how elected officials are shaped by their personal experiences. For example, scholars have found that male representatives' views on women's issues are partly influenced by whether they have daughters.[110] So what about economic class? In the most extensive study on the topic, Nicholas Carnes concludes that "[o]n the important economic issues of the day, members of Congress routinely vote with class."[111] Controlling for party, age, race, gender, religion, constituent demographics, ideology, donor base, and margins of victory, Carnes shows that economic class is a significant driver of policy views, making a bigger difference even than race, income differences in constituents, gender, and union membership among constituents.[112] Only partisan affiliation is a better predictor. Carnes finds that if Congress had truly been representative of the economic backgrounds of Americans, major economic legislation passed between 1999 and 2008 favoring the rich and big business would have failed, including the 2001 Bush tax cuts, laws limiting liability for business from the Y2K problem, and the Gulf of Mexico oil-drilling legislation.[113]

Carnes's data raises the possibility that partisanship, not economic class, drives all decisions. But political scientists have shown that economic inequality and political polarization are related. Economic inequality, scholars have demonstrated, leads to polarization because the wealthy devote themselves to a party that is focused on preserving their economic interests. Polarization leads to inequality because the wealthy use their political influence to block efforts to address inequality.[114] In their study of the top 1 percent, the political scientists Benjamin Page, Larry Bartels, and Jason Seawright find that wealth has a significant effect on preferences independent of party and that wealthy Democrats were "more conservative than Democrats in the general population."[115] When it comes to how responsive politicians are, political scientists have found that *both* parties are more responsive to the wealthy than to ordinary Americans, but Republicans are even more responsive to the wealthy than are Democrats.[116] A shift in the views of the wealthy can completely neutralize the effects of party affiliation.[117]

What about polarization and gridlock? Does a divided government—government split between Democrats and Republicans—do any better? Party polarization combined with gridlock from divided government turns out to be more responsive to the general public, but only at the cost of blocking a substantial amount of policy change. When there is gridlock, only policies that are uncontroversial can run the legislative gauntlet.[118] But the news isn't all good. When partisan gridlock combines with divergent preferences, the 90th income percentile *still* has the most influence over outcomes.[119]

What does all this data mean for how we should think about American politics? Traditionally, there have been four basic theories for how to view American politics, two focused on individuals and two on interest groups. Majoritarian electoral democracy focuses on the will of average citizens, suggesting that the majority rules in American politics. Economic elite domination suggests that people with high wealth (or, in some theories, high socioeconomic status) are the primary driver of American public policy. Majoritarian pluralism takes the optimistic view of interest group activity, suggesting that the "wants or needs of the average citizen tend to be reasonably well served by the outcomes of interest-group struggle" in part because there are many interest groups, they can enter and exit politics, and the winners of this interest group struggle are not always the same. Biased pluralism takes the pessimistic view of interest group politics, arguing that politics is dominated by business and elite economic interest groups.[120] In an important article, Gilens and Page tested these four approaches to see how well they explain policy outcomes across a twenty-year period. Unlike most previous work, which compares a single theory with policy outcomes, Gilens and Page use a new data set and test the theories against each other. Their conclusion: "[E]conomic elites and organized groups representing business interests have substantial independent impacts on U.S. government policy, while mass-based interest groups and average citizens have little or no independent influence."[121]

While many Americans think of majoritarian democracy or majoritarian pluralism as the archetypical image of American politics, the data suggests that economic elites—individuals and business interest groups—dominate. Elites' preferences diverge from those of the average American (and the majority of Americans). Elites participate at much greater rates in all aspects of politics. And elite preferences—not those of average Americans—are the primary driver of policy change. To be sure, this does not mean that the wealthy *always* get what they want. Given the barriers to making policy, there is a status quo bias in seeking policy change, and it is often the case that the wealthy and business interest groups may seek to preserve the status quo by blocking reform rather than to advance policy change.[122] But the fundamental reality of our political system is that it is best characterized no longer as majority rule but as rule by economic elites.

"[U]nder most circumstances," Martin Gilens concludes, "the preferences of the vast majority of Americans appear to have essentially no impact on which policies the government does or doesn't adopt."[123] Rather, "for Americans below the top of the income distribution, any association between preferences and policy outcomes is likely to reflect the extent to which their preferences coincide with those of the affluent."[124] In America, all that matters is the views of the economic elites. Ordinary Americans' views only matter when the elites happen to agree. This is democracy by coincidence.

THE BANALITY OF CAPTURE

In October 2015, *The New York Times* reported that 158 families contributed $176 million to the early phase of the 2016 presidential campaign. That was nearly half of all spending on the 2016 race at that time and almost as much as what was spent on the entirety of the 2000 presidential campaign.[125] The *Times* showed that these families, and the companies they own or control, tend to support candidates "who have pledged to pare regulations; cut taxes on income, capital gains and inheritances; and shrink entitlement programs."[126] Responding to the story, a writer on the liberal blog *Daily Kos* declared, "This is what the death of American democracy looks like. It's time to acknowledge that we no longer have a democracy, but a plutocracy: Government of the rich, by the rich, for the rich, brought to you by *Citizens United* and the Supreme Court."[127]

While there is "so damn much money" in campaigns and elections, to use Robert Kaiser's memorable phrase, there remains some debate on *how exactly* money matters in shaping public policy.[128] In a famous 2003 article, "Why Is There So Little Money in U.S. Politics?," Professors Stephen Ansolabehere, John de Figueiredo, and James Snyder argued that campaign contributions were unconnected to legislative voting.[129] Money, they said, doesn't buy votes. If it did, we should see a lot *more* money in American politics. Even if we accept this conclusion, there are still good reasons to think that money might influence politics in ways that are not so direct as quid pro quo bribery—a trade of campaign contributions for votes. Former congressman Hamilton Fish (R-NY) described the relationship between money and his votes as a "'thank you' for the position that I took, not as expecting that I would take a position in the future. . . . [It was] a reward, not a bribe."[130] Former congressman Tim Penny (D-MN) once observed that there is a subtle influence nonetheless: "There's no tit for tat in business, no check for a vote. But nonetheless, the influence is there. Candidates know where their money is coming from."[131] Former representative Eric Fingerhut (D-OH) took a similar position: "[P]eople consciously or subconsciously tailor their views to where they know what the sources of campaign funding can be."[132] Even if there isn't a direct money-for-votes connection, former members of Congress think that the role of money implicitly shapes behavior.

But it does more than just that. Members and candidates for Congress spend most of their time—30 to 70 percent according to some estimates—raising money.[133] Florida Republican David Jolly was elected to Congress in March 2014 in a special election. When he went to party headquarters, he was told that he had six months until the election and that he had to raise $2 million. "Your first responsibility is to make sure you hit $18,000 a day," Jolly remembered.[134] Rick Nolan, a Democrat from Minnesota, said that "both parties have told newly elected members of the Congress that they should spend 30 hours a week . . . dialing for dollars."[135] A Democratic Congressional Campaign Committee model schedule for members of Congress suggested that representatives spend four hours a day raising money in "call time" and only two hours a day on congressional business like committee work and floor votes.[136] Even if they are not interested in quid pro quo bribery, constant fund-raising can have a significant impact on the views of members of Congress and the work that they do (or don't do). First, as Harvard Law School professor and campaign finance reformer Lawrence Lessig has argued, devoting time to fund-raising means devoting less time to other things, like learning about and debating policy.[137] As evidence, Lessig looks at the decline of non–Appropriations Committee meetings from 1983 to 1997. During that period, the House of Representatives committee meetings dropped from 782 in 1983 to 287 in 1997. In the Senate, the number of committee meetings dropped from 429 to only 175 by 1997.[138] Congresspeople now routinely spend only a few days each week working in Washington and more and more time campaigning and raising money back home. Indeed, Jolly discovered upon his arrival in Congress that the House of Representatives' schedule was arranged to accommodate fund-raising.[139] This means less time to learn, less time to develop relationships with other members, and less time to debate.

Time spent raising money does something else too: it substantively shapes representatives' views on what issues are important. Lessig calls this "substantive distortion" and "agenda distortion."[140] It is important to see how this kind of distortion emerges in the fund-raising context. Candidates host fund-raisers—events, big or small, in which people pay to attend. Big donor events might require each person to "max out," contributing the maximum allowable amount to the candidate, and they can raise tens of thousands of dollars in a single night. The hosts of these events are particularly important, because they have the social network to bring together people who can contribute $1,000 or even $5,000 without blinking. For a candidate in a competitive race, fund-raising means spending considerable amounts of time at these events, mingling with big donors, answering their questions, hearing their concerns. Fund-raising also means calling up these donors and asking for money and in the process talking to them about the race and their views. Hosts and other big donors will even call up the candidate and offer their advice and opinions on different topics.

The consequence is that candidates hear quite a bit from wealthy people about what *they* think is important to America, what they think the problems are, what they think the solutions are. And the candidates need to answer questions and offer a vision that doesn't run totally counter to what their donors want. Just imagine how awkward it would be to enter a room of people who just gave $5,000 each to see you and then tell them you disagree with everything they believe—their priorities and their views. Not a good strategy for funding a campaign.

If most of the people you hear from most of the time are wealthy elites, it is only natural that you start thinking that their views are the same as what "people" think. Researchers have found this phenomenon in a variety of contexts. If a group is made up of people who take risks, after deliberation the group will be prone to risky behavior; in contrast, a risk-averse group will skew even further away from risk taking.[141] Liberals and conservatives become more polarized on issues like affirmative action, climate change, and marriage equality if they deliberate in groups with like-minded partisans.[142] Even federal judges suffer from herd mentality: studies show that three-judge panels are more likely to shift to extremes if all members were appointed by a president of the same political party.[143]

Why does this happen? There are a variety of theories. Psychologists have shown that social conformism might be part of it. People tend to conform to the views of the social group around them, even when they know better. In one of the most famous experiments in social psychology, Solomon Asch placed a research subject in a room with other subjects, who were secretly working with Asch. Everyone was shown a line and asked which of three additional lines was the same length. The subjects working with Asch all picked a line that was obviously not the same length. The research subject was then asked and agreed with the group with surprising frequency.[144] Other explanations are more about how individuals perceive group information. The concept of groupthink suggests that people are less likely to engage in critical thinking when they deliberate in a cohesive group.[145] Scholars have also argued that people in a group might think the opinions they get from people around them are unbiased and independent, when in fact they are getting a single perspective.[146]

Lobbying can shape opinion in a similar way. Lobbyists develop relationships with members of Congress and their staffs over time. By providing information (that of course supports the client's interests), they engage in what one technology lobbyist calls "thought leadership."[147] In essence, through repeated interactions, lobbyists can shape members' views and actions. An important recent study of lobbying in America shows when lobbying is most effective and how lobbying creates its own vicious cycle that reinforces the power and influence of lobbyists and their clients. First a company hires lobbyists. The lobbyists teach the company's leaders about political threats and opportunities, and they advocate for more lobbying (in part because more lobbying is good for their pocketbooks). Now better informed, company leaders see the benefits of lobbying, and they realize that ramping up their lobbying presence is a great return on investment.[148] One study finds that for every dollar spent on lobbying, a firm will receive between $6 and $20 in tax benefits.[149] So once the company starts lobbying, it will keep lobbying.

Now shift from the company-lobbyist relationship to the lobbyist-government relationship. With more and more companies lobbying, there are more interests represented for any given piece of legislation. Change becomes harder, and that also helps the lobbyists. To get different interest groups on board, legislation becomes longer and more complicated, with carve-outs for this group, special benefits for that group. As the legislation becomes more complicated, the debate becomes one over technical details rather than political values. Members of Congress and their staffs are less likely to have strongly held views, which means lobbyists' "thought leadership" exerts more influence. The other by-product of complexity is that lobbyists with technical information about the industry are also needed to help members of Congress and their staffs understand the impact of legislation. The need for lobbyists to explain legislation means more jobs for lobbyists, and that in turn means congressional staff have financially lucrative job prospects. With congressional staff departing for K Street lobbying shops, members of Congress don't have experienced staffs with well-developed expertise and institutional memory. The decline in congressional capacity once again means that members need to rely more on lobbyists.[150]

The rise in lobbying over the last generation—and the fact that lobbyists are stacked in favor of business interests—makes this dynamic extremely concerning. Between 1971 and 1979, the number of firms with registered lobbyists jumped from 175 to 650. The number of corporations with political action committees skyrocketed from 294 in 1976 to 1,204 in 1980.[151] In 1983, politically active organizations are estimated to have spent roughly $200 million on direct lobbying. By 2002, they were spending $1.82 billion. In 2012, politically active organizations spent $3.31 billion on direct lobbying. Adjusted for inflation, that is seven times more than they spent in 1983, and three-fourths of this spending was to benefit corporate America.[152] In fact, 56 percent of all disclosed spending on lobbying in 2012 came from just 3,587 corporations. If we add trade associations and business-wide associations, the number jumps to 78 percent of all lobbying money.[153] Between 1998 and 2010, corporations increased spending on lobbyists by 85 percent (to $2.09 billion), while trade associations increased spending by 53 percent (to $590 million).[154] Membership and public interest organizations can't keep up with their corporate counterparts in the amount spent or in the percentage increases. In that same period, public interest and membership groups increased spending by only 23 percent (to $41.3 million). Unions increased their lobbying by 32 percent (to $486 million) but then severely decreased lobbying expenditures to $45.6 million in 2012.[155] Public Citizen, a leading public interest group, has an annual budget of around $3 million, and it can spend about $9 million more through a nonprofit arm. In 2012, the Chamber of Commerce's budget was $207 million. The Chamber of Commerce's CEO alone makes more than $5 million in compensation—more than Public Citizen's annual budget.[156] More money means more lobbyists. In 2014, the financial, insurance, and real estate sectors of the economy employed 2,349 lobbyists. That's more than four lobbyists for every member of Congress.[157]

Within corporate lobbying, the participants are skewed toward the biggest corporations. More than 45.7 percent of all lobbying in 2007 was on behalf of only 127 companies. And the 297 companies that each spent more than $1 million on lobbying make up 62.6 percent of all lobbying expenditures.[158] On average, small firms have 1.16 lobbyists or firms representing them; the 297 companies that spend more than $1 million have 13.9 lobbyists or firms representing them.[159] When lobbyists engage in "thought leadership," it isn't fair and balanced. It is stacked to benefit a small number of the biggest companies.

Thought leadership goes beyond lobbying to shaping the wider information environment.[160] Outside the media, think tanks are some of the most important institutions that shape public policy. The first think tanks—nonprofit organizations dedicated to policy research and dissemination—emerged during the Progressive Era. The Russell Sage Foundation, New York's Bureau of Municipal Research, the Institute for Government Research, the Brookings Institution—all were created with the intent of "depoliticizing public decision making."[161] The funders behind these think tanks were the industrial titans of the age: John D. Rockefeller, Andrew Carnegie, E. H. Harriman, J. P. Morgan. But these business leaders largely believed in "reform through objective, scientific research."[162]

Starting in the 1970s, there was a burst of new think tanks. Between 1970 and 2000, the number of think tanks jumped from seventy to more than three hundred.[163] Corporate titans also funded the new generation of think tanks, but with important differences. More than half of the new think tanks are ideological, rejecting the earlier generation's mission of neutral, objective research.[164] More than two-thirds are focused on limiting government and promoting unregulated markets (which in many cases happen to support the corporate bottom line).[165] And far more than the older think tanks, the more recent vintage spends less on research and much more on shaping the information environment. In 2004, for example, the Brookings Institution (founded in 1916) spent 3 percent of its $39 million budget on communications. The conservative Heritage Foundation (founded in 1973) spent 20 percent of its $33 million budget on communications.[166] In recent years there has been growing concern that even the older, seemingly neutral think tanks are subject to corporate influence. They often partner with and receive funding from corporations, and some think tank scholars act as corporate consultants.[167]

The result is that elected officials (and their staffs) spend much of their time talking to and listening to economic elites in order to raise money. When they have a minute to stop fund-raising and actually consider the issues, they are bombarded with information from lobbyists. And in case they look beyond lobbyists, they are most likely to find research produced by the new generation of ideological think tanks that spend considerable resources on communications. If most of the people they talk to, most of the people they learn from, and most of the information they have access to is consistently skewed in favor of economic elites, it is not surprising that eventually they start to believe it. Scholars have a name for this phenomenon: intellectual capture.[168] It means that you naturally start thinking in a way that serves special interests.

The reality of our system is not that there is widespread quid pro quo bribery taking place. The reality of our system is far more pernicious. It is that some of our public officials may not even realize they've been captured. They think they are following the views of the people or engaging in technical debates on complex provisions of law. But in reality, they become unwitting accomplices, acculturated to an agenda that conflicts with the will of the people.

PERSONNEL IS POLICY

There was a saying in the Reagan administration: "Personnel is policy."[169] The basic idea was simple. Reagan officials wanted to make sure that their government appointees had the same philosophy and agenda as President Reagan. If they did, then it guaranteed that the president's policies would be pursued faithfully and aggressively, even without constant monitoring from top leadership. The idea is an old one in politics, but it is often ignored. Commentators frequently celebrate the idea of a "team of rivals," only to wonder in retrospect why the personnel chosen didn't have the same agenda and views as the president.[170]

The views of personnel in government matter, so when it comes to economic policy, what is so troubling is who fills the government. Start with elected officials. When Alexander Hamilton and Melancton Smith debated during the New York ratifying convention for the new U.S. Constitution, Smith worried that Congress would be composed of elites. Hamilton parried that it would not, because it would be drawn from the American people at large. So what do our elected officials look like today? Less than 2 percent of members of Congress had working-class jobs before entering public life, and only 20 percent were raised in working-class households.[171] The median net worth of members serving in Congress in 2013 was above $1 million.[172] That same year, the median net worth of an American household was $56,335.[173] The data looks better at the state and local level, but not by much. Only 3 percent of state legislators are blue-collar workers themselves, and only 9 percent of city council members.[174] After analyzing this data, political scientist Nicholas Carnes concludes that we have a "white-collar government."

And it isn't just elected officials. Government agencies are filled with political appointees. Political appointees come from a wide variety of backgrounds, but what is surprising is how many powerful officials are part of Washington's "revolving door." They go back and forth from regulatory agencies to the very industries that they are supposed to regulate. Senator Elizabeth Warren has done the most to expose the breadth and scope of the revolving door, particularly when it comes to Wall Street banks' influence over financial agencies. In December 2014, Warren observed that "three of the last four Treasury secretaries under Democratic presidents have had Citigroup affiliations before or after their Treasury service. The fourth was offered, but declined, Citigroup's CEO position."[175] The vice-chairman of the Federal Reserve worked at Citigroup as an executive, and "directors of the National Economic Council and Office of Management and Budget, our current U.S. trade representative, and senior officials at the Treasury Department also have had Citigroup ties." And this was just for a *single* Wall Street firm.

Of course, the economic status or employment status of a government official doesn't necessarily mean that the official will always, or even mostly, take positions that support his or her personal, industry, or class interests. Theodore and Franklin Roosevelt were famously considered "traitors to their class." But think about how hard it is for leaders to be traitors to their class. They would have to ignore calls and meetings from former colleagues. They would have to enforce the law against their former friends, colleagues, and employers, especially when they engage in questionable or illegal behavior. They would have to regulate or restructure their former industry, changing the business model they themselves used to make money. It gets even harder if they think about their future: if leaders suspect they might want to return to industry *after* government, it might influence the decisions they make when they are *in* government. All of these pressures are on top of the fact that the wealthy's preferences diverge from those of ordinary people and that intellectual capture can emerge from living in a skewed information environment.

STACKING THE DECK

The collapse of the middle class. Different preferences and participation levels between the rich and everyone else. The influence of money on policy choices. The consequence of these trends is that the public policy deck is increasingly stacked in favor of the wealthy and their interests. But it isn't just that policy benefits the wealthy; policy creates the conditions for the wealthy to keep their wealth and get even wealthier. The perverse consequence is that public policy can often reinforce economic inequality.

Consider a few features in the tax code. The top marginal tax rate, for an individual's federal income taxes, has dropped from a high of above 90 percent in the early 1960s to 70 percent in the 1970s to under 40 percent today.[176] This precipitous decline, as economist Emmanuel Saez has shown, coincides with a spike in the share of income going to the top 1 percent of Americans. Inequality jumped at precisely the same moment that marginal tax rates dropped.[177] The same downward trajectory applies to other tax rates as well. The tax rates on capital gains—on investments, which is how many wealthy Americans make their money—fell from a high of 39.9 percent in 1977 to 15 percent today.[178] Perhaps the most prominent example of the benefit from the low tax rate on capital gains was the 2012 Republican presidential nominee, Mitt Romney. For 2010, Romney paid an effective tax rate of only 13.9 percent, even though he earned $21.6 million that year.[179] There was nothing illegal about Romney's tax rate. But that is precisely the point: Romney paid less than many ordinary Americans, even though his income was much higher.

The ability to pass on wealth to the next generation was one of the founders' great fears. They were concerned about hereditary wealth, which at the time manifested itself through land inheritance policies. That is why Jefferson called the abolition of the entail one of his greatest accomplishments. A century later, Theodore Roosevelt echoed the founders' fears of inherited wealth, calling for a progressive tax on "large fortune[s]" to "preserve a measurable equality of opportunity" and ensure "at least an approximate equality in the conditions under which each man obtains the chance to show the stuff that is in him."[180] Where are tax rates today on estates? According to data from the Tax Policy Center, only about 3,800 estates in the entire country—which amounts to 0.14 percent or one in every seven hundred people who die—pay any estate tax at all.[181] In 1976, by comparison, 139,115 estates paid the tax (which was 7.65 percent of deaths).[182] In 2013, the top rate on estate taxes was 40 percent, but because of special exemptions the average estate pays only a 17 percent rate in taxes.[183]

Corporate taxes have followed a similar path with egregious carve-outs for powerful companies in some areas. Between 1960 and today, the tax rate on corporate income has been cut from 52 percent to 35 percent, and that is the *statutory* rate, before any special tax breaks or loopholes.[184] In some cases, reductions to the statutory rate might be desirable as a matter of public policy. For example, one can imagine a reasonable policy case for giving tax breaks to producers of the steam engine in the nineteenth century or renewable energy today. The goal of the tax break would be to foster investment in those technologies. But when wealthy interest groups gain political power, tax breaks can become more about protecting incumbents rather than accelerating innovation. For example, in 2013, the five biggest oil companies—BP, Chevron, ConocoPhillips, ExxonMobil, and Shell—made combined profits of $93 billion. With that much in profit, oil companies clearly don't need taxpayer subsidies to survive or develop new technologies and bring them to market. They could simply reinvest their profits.

But these big oil companies benefit from $2.4 billion per year in special tax breaks that are not available to other industries.[185] It is hard to understand why profitable, well-established industries should get special tax breaks, except for the fact that they've lobbied heavily to advance their financial interests.

The phenomenon isn't limited to tax policy. In 2003, Congress passed the Medicare Modernization Act, which added a prescription drug benefit to Medicare. With Medicare buying prescription drugs in huge numbers, one would think that the health insurance program could negotiate with the pharmaceutical companies to get a discount for buying in bulk. That's what other insurance companies would do. But Congress inserted a provision into the law that banned Medicare from negotiating drug prices. Republican congressman Walter Jones of North Carolina told *60 Minutes,* "The pharmaceutical lobbyists wrote the bill." His Democratic colleague John Dingell agreed, saying that the law "was written by their lobbyists."[186] And just a few months after the 2003 law was passed, the chairman of the House committee responsible for the bill quit his job in Congress to become the head lobbyist for the pharmaceutical industry, with a salary of $2 million per year.[187] How much could the federal government save if Medicare negotiated drug prices? There are a range of estimates: If Medicare gets the same deal that Medicaid and the Veterans Health Administration currently get, it would save $15 to $16 billion per year.[188] If it negotiates as well as Canada, then $230 billion over ten years. And if it negotiates like Denmark, $541 billion.[189] More than 80 percent of Americans support drug-price negotiations, and yet negotiations still haven't happened.[190] Why not? Another way of framing those numbers is that they represent reduced profits for the pharmaceutical companies, so the pharma companies lobby hard to prevent negotiations. In 2014, the pharmaceutical industry employed more than fourteen hundred lobbyists and spent more than $229 million lobbying.[191]

As another example, consider a recent regulatory proposal. Many Americans who save for retirement rely on investment advisers to give them advice on where to put their money, when to buy and sell, and how to shape their portfolio so they can save for their future. While most retirement advisers are honest and want to give good advice to their clients, there are some bad apples. In some cases, retirement advisers steer their customers toward financial investments with high fees and expenses, thereby boosting their own profits.[192] In other cases, they get perks—vacations, cars, or electronic devices—for selling certain products.[193] What is surprising is that investment advisers have no fiduciary duty—no legal obligation—to provide their customers with good investment advice. It is perfectly legal for them to push customers toward products that are *worse* for their customers but more profitable for the investment company or for the salesperson. This conflict of interest is estimated to cost Americans $17 billion each year.[194] Or to put it another way, the industry makes $17 billion extra from deliberately giving *bad* advice to consumers.

In early 2015, after years of proposals and ample opportunity for public comments, the Department of Labor proposed a regulation to address these conflicts of interest.[195] Retirement advisers would now have a duty to give their clients the best advice for the client's interests. In response to the proposed rule, the industry and its supporters immediately began to work hard to defeat it. Republican congresswoman Ann Wagner introduced legislation prohibiting the Department of Labor from issuing the regulation, commenting at a hearing that "[m]y broker-dealers and financial advisors are my friends."[196] Big interest groups like the Financial Services Roundtable lobbied for the bill, and the Chamber of Commerce issued a "key vote alert" on Wagner's legislation.[197] Industry even started pushing out its own studies on the financial effects of the rule, in hopes of combating the argument that the rule was beneficial. For example, the Investment Company Institute, which represents big finance companies, released a study saying that the rule would lead to net losses of $109 billion.[198]

In the summer of 2015, Jane Dokko, a fellow in economic studies at the Brookings Institution, warned that industry-supported research on the Labor Department's rule was questionable because the methods and conclusions were strikingly different from the "careful, independent research" that had taken place. "Research not funded by special interest groups," Dokko wrote, "concludes that when they are paid to recommend certain financial products over others, advisors tilt their recommendations so that they receive higher pay."[199] Dokko's comments—and her Brookings affiliation—took on greater meaning a few months later in September, when her colleague and longtime Brookings affiliate Robert Litan testified before the Senate on the Labor Department's rule. Litan contradicted Dokko and argued that the rule would be bad for consumers, and he supported his argument with a study he had conducted. His study, however, was commissioned by a consulting firm and funded by Capital Group, a mutual fund manager, which paid Litan $38,800 for his work.[200] When it became public that Litan's study might be compromised because of the conflict of interest, Litan resigned from Brookings, which noted he had not upheld rules to preserve the think tank's independence.[201]

Perhaps most interesting is what the opponents to the fiduciary rule said themselves about its impact. In the spring of 2016, members of Congress called out some of the largest insurance and financial companies for talking out of both sides of their mouths. When lobbying Congress, they predicted disaster for middle-class Americans if the fiduciary rule took effect. Leaders of some insurance companies said it would have a "potentially devastating impact" that would force Americans to pay more for financial products. But when talking to their investors, these same insurance companies assured them that the regulation would not be a "significant hurdle" and that they would still be able to make products "available on terms that work for everybody."[202] Their outcry over the impact of the rule appeared more like posturing than serious analysis.

Even if tough laws and regulations do get passed, there is another problem: enforcing the rules. Take the case of the "too big to prosecute" banks. These are financial institutions that have grown so powerful economically that they now evade law enforcement, even when they take part in illegal activities. In 2012, for example, the U.S. arm of the British bank HSBC admitted to allowing the laundering of $881 million for drug cartels in Mexico and Colombia. It also violated economic sanctions against Iran, Cuba, Sudan, Libya, and Burma by allowing $660 million in transactions with those countries.[203] What was the result? No one—not a single person—was prosecuted. Instead, HSBC paid a fine. The result is a two-tiered system of justice.[204] A kid who is caught with a small bag of marijuana gets thrown in jail. But white-collar bankers can launder $800 million in drug money and they don't go to jail. They don't even pay the fine; their company pays.

Why does this happen? At a Senate hearing in 2013, then–attorney general Eric Holder admitted that the banks were so large that they were above the law. "I am concerned that the size of some of these institutions becomes so large that it does become difficult for us to prosecute them," he said. "[I]f you do bring a criminal charge, it will have a negative impact on the national economy, perhaps even the world economy."[205] Holder later backtracked on his comments, but his point speaks directly to how economic power becomes political (or in this case legal) privilege.[206] Equal justice under law simply doesn't apply to the biggest banks.

THE CRISIS OF THE CONSTITUTION

When Lewis Powell wrote his 1971 memo to the U.S. Chamber of Commerce stating that the "American economic system is under broad attack" and that business needed to fight back, he argued that the courts were a "vast area of opportunity for the Chamber" because "the judiciary may be the most important instrument for social, economic and political change."[207] Over the next four decades, groups such as the Chamber of Commerce, Business Roundtable, the Heritage Foundation, the Cato Institute, and the Federalist Society advanced an economic vision for the Constitution that took aim at the New Deal consensus.[208] Conservatives and libertarians have increasingly criticized Supreme Court decisions enabling government regulation of commerce, and some have even sought to rehabilitate the *Lochner* era's vision of economic regulation.

As Steven Teles explains in *The Rise of the Conservative Legal Movement,* conservative activists undertook a concerted effort to fund and support public interest activists, academic education in law and economics, and social and professional networks such as the Federalist Society. Activists at the Pacific Legal Foundation, the oldest conservative public interest legal organization (founded in 1973), mobilized around property rights.[209] In the educational world, big donors like the Olin Foundation supported the growth of the "law and economics" movement, funding a new generation of scholars and in part seeking to counteract the influence of liberal legal schol-ars.[210] Indeed, in the case of George Mason Law School, they turned a less well-known law school into a national powerhouse by estab-lishing and supporting the school's Law and Economics Center—perhaps the preeminent home for libertarian legal thinkers.[211]

Most significant, however, was the Federalist Society.[212] Started in the early 1980s, the Federalist Society took no position on particular issues. Rather, it served as a home for conservative and libertarian law students on otherwise liberal law school campuses. By creating a safe space for conservative thought, building a social and profes-sional network of students, and eventually connecting those students to lawyers, judges, and senior government officials, the Federalist Society succeeded in constructing a conservative legal movement that was widespread enough to challenge the New Deal consensus.

Under the Rehnquist Court, New Deal precedents were increas-ingly overturned, challenged, or distinguished, as conservatives pushed to bring back the pre–New Deal vision of the Constitution, which came to be known as the "Constitution in Exile."[213] From 1937 to 1995, the Supreme Court never once found that Congress had exceeded its powers under the commerce clause. The Rehnquist Court, for the first time since the New Deal, restricted this federal regulatory power, striking down provisions of the Gun-Free School Zones Act and the Violence Against Women Act.[214] While both laws were on key topics in the culture wars, the underlying legal question was inextricably linked with economic power: whether the federal government would have expansive power to regulate under the com-merce clause.

But that wasn't all. In 1941, the Supreme Court had rejected the idea that the Tenth Amendment created a zone of activities for exclu-sive state control—a provision that had been used in the infamous 1918 case, *Hammer v. Dagenhart,* to strike down a federal law pro-hibiting child labor.[215] In two cases in the 1990s, the Rehnquist Court appeared to revive the Tenth Amendment, restricting congressional authority to deal with radioactive waste and ensure background checks before gun permits are granted.[216] The Tenth Amendment has since sparked a conservative movement called the "Tenthers," who argue that virtually everything the federal government does—

Medicare, Medicaid, Social Security, Veterans Administration health care, the GI Bill, transportation funding—is unconstitutional.[217] Legal scholar Erwin Chemerinsky summed up the developments as "The Rehnquist Revolution."[218] Two decades later, it is clear that these changes did not amount to a complete constitutional revolution, but the insurgents did succeed in breaking the great consensus and reintroducing economic debate into constitutional law.

Under the Roberts Court, economic debates have continued, with the Constitution as the battlefield. The most prominent and controversial case was *National Federation of Independent Business v. Sebelius*, the Obamacare case.[219] When the Supreme Court upheld the Affordable Care Act as an exercise of Congress's taxing power, the decision was widely seen as a victory for liberals and the Obama administration. But just as important was Chief Justice Roberts's discussion of the commerce clause. Usually, if the Supreme Court can uphold a law, it will not address alternate theories. Yet in the Obamacare case, the chief justice went out of his way to find that Congress did not have power to enact the Affordable Care Act under the commerce clause. Even as he was attacked by conservatives for upholding Obamacare, in the grand sweep of constitutional history, the chief justice managed to whittle away at the New Deal consensus on the commerce power, just as Chief Justice Rehnquist had in the mid-1990s.

While the debate over the commerce clause is long-standing in our history, some recent economic battles are not as obvious. In 2010, the Supreme Court decided *Free Enterprise Fund v. Public Company Accounting Oversight Board*.[220] At first glance, the case appears to be a decision about presidential power and the structure of government agencies. The issue was whether the structure of the Public Company Accounting Oversight Board (PCAOB) violated the separation of powers because the agency was located within the Securities and Exchange Commission. The broader context of the case, however, is illuminating. At the heart of the Sarbanes-Oxley Act of 2002 was the PCAOB, an agency that was designed to bring oversight to accounting firms that many believed had been too lax, leading to scandals at companies such as Enron, Tyco, WorldCom, and Global Crossing. PCAOB was created to audit the auditors. Because the law did not have a "severability clause," which protects the remainder of a bill from being struck down if one clause is found unconstitutional, the conservative group Free Enterprise Fund thought that by challenging the constitutionality of the PCAOB, it could kill the entire law. The Court declined to go as far as Free Enterprise Fund wanted: it ultimately struck down the specific provisions of the law relating to PCAOB's structure but did not overturn the legislation entirely. Still, the context of the case is striking: two years after the biggest financial crash since the Great Depression, Free Enterprise Fund was asking the Supreme Court to strike down a law passed to oversee accounting firms—firms whose practices led to corporate scandals so massive that even a pro-business Republican president supported legislation to oversee them. The group even managed a limited victory.

Movement conservatives and libertarians have also increasingly been developing and resurrecting arguments to challenge other core tenets of the New Deal constitution. Even the infamous *Lochner* decision is being reframed. Some scholars now argue that the case turned not on laissez-faire ideology but on "partial legislation," laws that further the interest of special-interest groups rather than the public good as a whole. Others argue that the case correctly focused on "fundamental rights" to economic liberty.[221] The *Lochner* revisionists have uncovered some new historical facts—including that the Supreme Court of the *Lochner* era was not as hostile to legislation as some have suggested—but their intellectual project has the odd feature of implying that elected officials cannot protect bakers who were being forced to work more than sixty hours a week.

It is striking that recent economic debates over the Constitution have been dominated by conservatives and libertarians who by and large seem less concerned with the concentration of economic power and the possibility that private actors can be oppressive. Couched in language of freedom and liberty, recent books like Randy Barnett's *Restoring the Lost Constitution,* David Bernstein's *Rehabilitating Lochner,* and Richard Epstein's *Classical Liberal Constitution* all press strong, sophisticated cases for overturning the theory underlying the New Deal constitution and replacing it with a new set of laissez-faire constitutional rules.[222] But the catch is that their new rules are likely to increase the economic and political power of wealthy individuals and corporations.

THE CORPORATE TAKEOVER OF THE FIRST AMENDMENT

While cases on the structure and powers of government are significant, the most radical constitutional change has been how the Supreme Court interprets the First Amendment. For virtually all of American history, the First Amendment was largely irrelevant when it came to corporate rights. Corporations were highly regulated, only able to undertake activities the public allowed in their charters, and subject to common-law regulations as well. In the *Lochner* era, as we have seen, the Supreme Court adopted a laissez-faire theory of the Constitution that restricted democratic power to regulate corporate malfeasance. By the mid-twentieth century, the First Amendment was virtually sacred for liberals, who saw it as protecting protesters, students, and freethinkers. Conservatives like Robert Bork saw the First Amendment as protecting only an extremely narrow category of speech. As he said in 1971, "Constitutional protection should be accorded only to speech that is explicitly political. There is no basis for judicial intervention to protect any other form of expression, be it scientific, literary or that variety of expression we call obscene or pornographic."[223]

How quickly things change. In 1976, the Supreme Court decided *Virginia Pharmacy,* a case striking down a state law that prevented pharmacists from advertising drug prices.[224] Virginia was concerned that advertising would reduce pharmacists' professionalism, but at the same time price information would surely be useful to customers. Striking down the law, the case was the first in which the Court recognized a right for businesses to speak for primarily business purposes (advertising prices) rather than for expressive purposes (making movies, publishing a newspaper). That same year, the Court declared in *Buckley v. Valeo* that money was speech for election purposes.[225] Two years later, the Court extended First Amendment rights to corporate political activity in campaigns and elections.[226]

Virginia Pharmacy marks a moment from which we can see a

palpable shift in how the First Amendment works. In an important article, Harvard Law School professor John Coates has shown that businesses were involved in 26 percent of First Amendment cases prior to *Virginia Pharmacy* but 34 percent afterward.[227] Business's "win" rate was only 20 percent before 1976; after *Virginia Pharmacy* it jumped to 55 percent.[228] The critical period was the mid-1970s to the mid-1980s, when the number of business-related First Amendment cases increased sharply from about 20 percent of the Court's docket to around 40 percent. That period, Coates shows, coincides precisely with the tenure of Justice Lewis Powell, the conservative judge who wanted to reshape the Constitution to support business interests.[229]

While liberals have long celebrated the First Amendment as a defender of the little guy, today it is as likely to serve as a weapon of the powerful—a way for corporations to block even highly sensible regulations. In fact, the trend has skewed so far in this direction that scholars now routinely refer to "First Amendment *Lochner*ism," harking back to the case from the first Gilded Age.[230]

The debate has advanced furthest in the law of campaign finance reform. For decades, reformers have tried across the country to place limitations on the ability of corporations and the wealthiest individuals to dominate elections. At virtually every turn, they have encountered a hostile Supreme Court wielding the First Amendment. In 2010, the Court in *Citizens United* considered the constitutionality of federal restrictions on corporate spending in campaigns.[231] Under federal law, corporations were prohibited from making "independent expenditures"—like advertisements—close to elections. Striking down the law, Justice Anthony Kennedy famously noted that corporate speech was no different from individual speech and held that Congress could not restrict corporations from shaping elections. A year later, in *Arizona Free Enterprise Club's Freedom PAC v. Bennett,* the Supreme Court struck down an Arizona law that provided matching funds to publicly financed candidates who were being swamped by privately funded candidates.[232] Arizona's legislature did not directly restrict anyone's speech, but the Court found that trying to level the playing field by *increasing* speech also violated the Constitution because privately funded candidates might feel pressure to spend less money on campaigns.

In 2014, in *McCutcheon v. FEC,* the Supreme Court struck down yet another campaign finance law, what lawyers call "aggregate contribution limits"—limits on the total amount of campaign contributions someone can make in a two-year cycle.[233] Shaun McCutcheon, the CEO of an electrical company and the treasurer of a conservative super PAC, wanted to donate more than the $123,200 total limit for political action committees and candidates. Under Supreme Court precedent, Congress was allowed to regulate campaign finance if it could justify the regulations based on a concern about "corruption" or "the appearance of corruption." Corruption was understood as more than just quid pro quo bribery, and the appearance of corruption extended to a broad democratic concern with "undue influence" in the legislative process. In *McCutcheon,* Chief Justice Roberts essentially eliminated the broader understanding of corruption: "[T]he Government's interest in preventing the appearance of corruption is . . . confined to the appearance of *quid pro quo* corruption."[234] If the only justification for campaign finance laws is outright bribery, or its appearance, it is hard to imagine what restrictions on big contributions remain. In all of these cases, the core question is simple: Can Congress regulate the corrupting influence of money in politics? In recent years, the Court has repeatedly said no, giving economically powerful interests outsized influence over the political system.

The First Amendment has also been at the forefront of the war on unions. By law, unions must represent the interests of all employees—even those who are not members of the union. This creates what economists call a "free rider" problem that could make unions unworkable: individuals have an incentive not to join the union (so they don't have to pay union dues), but they still get all the benefits of the union's efforts. To address the free rider problem, unions are allowed to charge fees to nonmembers to cover the costs of collective bargaining. This system was critical to the Treaty of Detroit model that sustained the boom of the post–World War II era. Union bargaining is what allowed labor to improve the financial well-being of its members (and, indirectly, of all other workers). In a 1977 case called *Abood v. Detroit Board of Education,* the Supreme

Court upheld this structure of labor relations.[235] Then, in 2012, in a case called *Knox v. Service Employees International Union, Local 1000*, Justice Samuel Alito called the free rider justification "an anomaly" and suggested that it violated the First Amendment rights of non-union members.[236]

In *Harris v. Quinn* (2014), Justice Alito took direct aim at *Abood* and all but overturned it.[237] The majority opinion attacked *Abood*'s reasoning and refused to extend *Abood* to the Illinois home health-care workers at issue in *Harris*. The case doesn't mean the end of unions, but *Abood* is on death row. To be sure, *Harris v. Quinn* covers a relatively complex matter of labor law, but as a matter of American economic history the dismantling of labor unions is significant. Unions have been partly responsible for reducing economic inequality and for many of the major workplace legislative victories of the last few generations. Weaker unions mean a weaker middle class— economically and politically.

Corporations have also aggressively used the First Amendment to strike down regulations related to privacy, health, safety, and competitive markets. Consider an important Supreme Court case, *Sorrell v. IMS Health* from 2011.[238] Pharmacies have a great deal of data about prescription drugs, in part because they have records of what drugs doctors prescribe. Pharmacies started selling this data to a company called IMS Health. IMS Health would use the data to create individualized profiles of doctors' prescription practices and then sell those profiles to drug companies, which could better target their sales (especially for the most expensive drugs). Concerned that selling medical records could infringe on privacy and that the use of this data would increase drug prices, Vermont, New Hampshire, and Maine banned the practice. By 2010, twenty-six other states were considering laws prohibiting the sale of this data.[239] IMS Health challenged the law, claiming that the ban on buying and selling data violated the company's free speech under the First Amendment. Even though the case had nothing to do with speech per se, the Supreme Court agreed and struck down the law. Justice Kennedy wrote that the law burdened speech because it limited the ability of pharmaceutical companies to market their drugs. "The State may not burden the speech of others in order to tilt public debate in a preferred direction. 'The commercial marketplace, like other spheres of our social and cultural life, provides a forum where ideas and information flourish.'"[240] As law professor Jedediah Purdy has said, "There is, of course, something otherworldly about describing as 'public debate' companies' targeted pitches to physicians."[241]

The corporate First Amendment is not just about speech; it also extends to religion.[242] Consider the 2014 case of *Burwell v. Hobby Lobby Stores*.[243] Although it principally concerned a federal law, the case involved religious freedom claims. Under the Affordable Care Act, employers have a choice between paying a tax and providing health care to their employees (this is the poorly named "employer mandate"; legally, of course, there is a choice to provide health care or pay a tax).[244] If employers choose to provide health care, their plans must cover a variety of preventive services, including birth control. Hobby Lobby claimed that its owners' freedom of religion is burdened by the mandate to cover birth control and that it should therefore be exempt from following the law. The conventional view, as Linda Greenhouse has argued, is that *Hobby Lobby* is simply the most recent battle in the ongoing culture wars.[245] But some commentators, like Jeffrey Rosen, have worried that the Court's ruling could "drive a stake into the heart of the regulatory state."[246] The Court's decision can be interpreted either way. Justice Alito's majority opinion goes to great pains to argue that this ruling cannot circumvent civil rights laws and other laws. But in dissent, Justice Ruth Bader Ginsburg disagreed, stating that the majority's decision opens the door to "commercial enterprises . . . opt[ing] out of any law (saving only tax laws) they judge incompatible with their sincerely held religious beliefs."[247] Justice Alito could not come up with a principled distinction that would stop a company from claiming that religious beliefs prevent them from serving African Americans or Jewish Americans, or refusing to follow health and safety regulations for customers and workers.

"[T]he corporate takeover of the First Amendment," Professor Coates argues, "represents a pure redistribution of power over law with no efficiency gain." Coates is no anti-corporation socialist; prior to becoming a law professor, he was a partner at the white-shoe New York law firm of Wachtell, Lipton, Rosen & Katz. But he concludes in his study that the new First Amendment takes power from "ordinary individuals with identities and interests as voters, owners, and employees" and gives it to "corporate bureaucrats." "This is as radical a break from Anglo-American business and legal traditions as one could find in U.S. history."[248]

THE CORPORATE CAPTURE OF THE FEDERAL COURTS

If personnel is policy, the identities, views, and backgrounds of judges are critical. But whether it is federal judges appointed for life or state and local judges subject to election, the courts are increasingly being tilted toward the interests of the most economically powerful in our society.

It is often noted that the New Deal justices were picked to decide economic cases but that civil rights issues defined their careers. It could be argued that the opposite is true now. Over the last few decades, the conventional wisdom is that presidents chose judicial nominees, in part, based on their views on hot-button civil rights and cultural issues—first school desegregation, then abortion. Consider, however, the most controversial conservative nominees in recent years. President George W. Bush nominated some fiercely libertarian judges, no one more vocal than Judge Janice Rogers Brown. Judge Brown once said the New Deal "inoculated the federal Constitution with a kind of underground collectivist mentality" and declared that "[i]n the heyday of liberal democracy, all roads lead to slavery."[249] Although she was strongly opposed by Democrats, she was still confirmed to the D.C. Circuit. Meanwhile, disputes over President Obama's appointment of liberal judges have turned back to civil rights and cultural issues. Goodwin Liu, a leading scholar of affirmative action and civil rights, for example, ultimately withdrew his nomination (he was later appointed to the California State Supreme Court). Liu's area of expertise—civil rights—was and remains hugely important, but with the collapse of the middle class over the last generation it should be as important to nominate individuals with populist views on economic issues, people who are ready to joust with Judge Brown.

Yet judicial nominations from both parties are consistently skewed in favor of economic elites. In a speech to the American Constitution Society in 2013, Senator Elizabeth Warren noted the "striking lack of professional diversity" on the federal bench. Citing a 2008 study, she noted that of 162 judges listed in the *Almanac of the Federal Judiciary,* 85 percent had worked in private practice, many for large corporate law firms. In contrast, only 3 percent—5 judges out of 162—had substantial experience working for nonprofit organizations, and only one judge out of 162 appeared to have substantial experience arguing consumer protection cases. Troubled by this data, Warren criticized the increasing "corporate capture of the federal courts."[250]

To be sure, not all lawyers who work for corporations have the same personal views as their clients, but the stunning lack of diversity is particularly concerning when considered in light of studies of corporate influence and success in the courts. Adam Chandler of *SCOTUSblog* has shown that the groups that are best at getting the Supreme Court to take their cases are "pro-business, anti-regulatory, and ideologically conservative," including the Chamber of Commerce, the Cato Institute, the National Federation of Independent Business, the pharmaceutical industry lobby, and the American Bankers Association.[251] And when they get to the Supreme Court, these interest groups increasingly find a receptive audience. According to the Constitutional Accountability Center, the Chamber of Commerce has improved from a losing record—43 percent—in the early 1980s to a 69 percent win rate with the Roberts Court.[252] Professor Lee Epstein, Professor William Landes, and Judge Richard Posner (a Reagan appointee to the federal court of appeals) have also shown that the five conservative judges on the Supreme Court prior to Justice Antonin Scalia's death in 2016 were in the top ten of the most pro-business justices in history and that Chief Justice Roberts and Justice Alito are numbers one and two.[253]

In many states, judges are elected, creating another set of opportunities for interest groups to skew the judicial system in their favor. According to the Brennan Center for Justice, during the 2011–12 cycle of state supreme court elections, political parties and interest groups spent $24.1 million on advertising supporting or attacking judges—more than twice the amount spent in the 2010 cycle and almost *ten times* more than they spent in 2001–02.[254] As the amount of money goes up in judicial elections, so too does the likelihood that campaign spending will influence judges' views, whether consciously or subconsciously. Scholars have shown that there is a strong relationship between campaign contributions and elected judges' rulings. When interest groups—business, insurance, medical, labor groups—contribute to judges' campaigns, those judges are more likely to decide in favor of the interest group.[255] In a study of every state supreme court case during a four-year period, researchers found that as the amount of campaign contributions from business interests increases, the probability that an elected judge will vote in favor of business litigants also increases.[256] Researchers have also shown that the increase in television advertising in judicial elections makes judges less likely to rule in favor of defendants in criminal appeals cases.[257] In other words, even when issues of fundamental rights are at issue, big money in judicial campaigns can influence whether someone gets a fair hearing in court. All of this data raises a troubling question: Can we really be confident that our judicial system is prioritizing the rule of law over economic power?

THE MEANING OF 2016

The election of Donald Trump over Hillary Clinton shocked the political world. A businessman who never served in government or in the military defeated the most qualified candidate quite possibly in the history of the country. Despite Clinton's substantial victory in the popular vote, the campaign season and election results leave little room for interpretation.

The defining feature of the 2016 election was the strength of anti-establishment candidates who channeled popular discontent with elites and with the current functioning of American politics. In the primaries, Senator Bernie Sanders received more than twelve million votes, Donald Trump received more than thirteen million votes, and Senator Ted Cruz won more than seven-and-a-half-million votes. Together, explicitly anti-establishment candidates took more than thirty million primary votes, out of around fifty-six million cast.[258] Trump ran his campaign as a populist, promising to "drain the swamp" in Washington of lobbyists and end the "rigged" system. Even Clinton, who was considered by many to be more of an establishment candidate, ran a campaign that tried to channel populist disaffection. In a video announcing her run for president, Clinton said "Americans have fought their way back from tough economic times, but the deck is still stacked in favor of those at the top."[259] On Election Day, a Reuters poll found that 72 percent of voters believed "the American economy is rigged to advantage the rich and powerful."[260]

The anti-establishment populist revolt didn't come out of nowhere. It had roots in Ross Perot's taking 19 percent of the vote in 1992 and in the election of Jesse Ventura in Minnesota in 1998. On the right it gained steam with the rise of the Tea Party after the financial crash. On the left it was visible in Howard Dean's insurgent campaign in 2004, and it became clear with Occupy Wall Street and Black Lives Matter. These were all different movements, taking place over decades. But they all expressed a growing dissatisfaction with the governing order.

Since the end of the 1970s, the central challenge for our republic has been how to ensure relative economic equality in a more inclusive country—how to guarantee the promise of a middle-class life to *everyone*, regardless of region, race, gender, or sexual orientation. A generation of policymakers has largely failed in this task, and the result has been not just economic inequality but social fragmentation. After thirty years of a collapsing middle class; after thirty years of changing social, demographic, and globalizing trends; after thirty years of an economy designed to stack the deck in favor of the big guys; after thirty years of a political and constitutional system increasingly rigged to work for economic elites—after all this, the people revolted. They revolted over economic change, social change, demographic change. They revolted because, in Walter Lippmann's terms, the country was at "drift" and the elites had done little to show "mastery" over the forces transforming the nation.

If there is anything that defines the populist revolt of 2016—both right and left—it is that the populists demand structural changes, not technocratic changes. They believe the system as a whole is rotten. Incremental reforms that keep the system intact while making tweaks around the edges will not satisfy them. The populists of the right want structural changes to immigration, social mores, and government authority. Some of them seek to turn back the clock to a time when America was predominantly blue-collar and white. The populists of the left want structural changes to break up the accumulation of economic power, to stop political corruption, and to fight structural racism. In some cases—trade and antitrust, for example—the populists on both sides overlap. In other cases—racial equality and inclusiveness—they are opposed. But in spite of their many differences, they do not ask for reform on the margins. They cry for revolution.

CHAPTER SIX

The Future of the Middle-Class Constitution

Looking back on the Gilded Age, the great-grandson of John Adams despaired. Like his famous ancestors, Henry Adams had "never in his life taken politics for a pursuit of economy."[1] But with the changes of the late nineteenth century, every instinct, lesson, and ideal the historian had inherited from his forebears seemed less and less relevant. He watched as "[a]ll one's friends, all one's best citizens, reformers, churches, colleges, educated classes" rejected the old model of politics and instead "joined the banks to force submission to capitalism."[2] But Adams refused to go along. As a young man, he had sat in Rome, contemplating the decline and fall of the Eternal City. Now, after the panic of 1893, he thought he had to make his last stand—against the banks, trusts, corporations, the gold standard, against all the forces that were bringing the decline and fall of the American republic. He "stood up for his eighteenth-century, his constitution of 1789, his George Washington."[3] But it was to no avail. He was an old man, and his views were now antiquated. "Modern politics," Adams lamented, "is, at bottom, a struggle not of men but of forces."[4]

Adams turned to developing a theory of history. At first he toyed with history as a pendulum, swinging back and forth, from unity to complexity. But in his era, history didn't seem so predictable; it was wholly new, accelerating faster and faster until the world would eventually go smash, crushed by the dynamic forces that industrial man had unleashed. Many think Adams was opposed to modernity outright. But what he really feared was the inability of society to control what it had created. The only glimmer of hope was that a "new kind of man" would emerge, one who understood both the values of the old regime and the realities of the new.[5]

Half a century after Adams, another historian, Arthur Schlesinger Sr., looked back at American history and saw cycles, rather than the acceleration of forces and an inevitable crash. The tides of American politics ebbed and flowed between periods of public purpose and private interest. With surprising regularity, he said, the "[e]mphasis on the welfare of property has given way to emphasis on human welfare," only to return back over time.[6] Schlesinger's son, the more famous historian of the two, later added to his father's theory. The cycles of American history were partly self-generating: the dynamics of each new phase emerged from the conditions and contradictions of the previous phase.[7]

Whether the story is one of the decline and fall requiring Adams's "new kind of man" or one of tides in American politics, as the Schlesingers posited, the urgent question today is how to break free of the increasingly vicious cycle that threatens our republican form of government. Our constitutional system assumes a relatively equal distribution of wealth in society—a big middle class, no extreme rich or poor. The founding generation rejected the class warfare constitutions of the ancient world because of the new nation's unique economic conditions. And throughout American history, there was a tradition of leaders who remained faithful to this constitutional prerequisite, fighting to uphold it and adapt it when economic conditions changed. Since World War II, we have largely forgotten this tradition. But with the collapse of the middle class in the last thirty years, we can no longer ignore the constitutional significance of economic inequality. Today, we live in an America in which the middle class is being hollowed out and political power is increasingly in the hands of the wealthiest individuals and corporations. As economic power and political power come into alignment, our system will become less and less amenable to reform. Adams will matter more than Schlesinger. Decline and fall will become more likely than the cycles of reform. So what can we do?

SHOULD WE REVIVE CLASS WARFARE CONSTITUTIONS?

In the grand sweep of the Western tradition, the conventional strategy for controlling the power of economic elites was to incorporate economic class directly into the constitutional structure through a system of countervailing powers.[8] If we were to revive the tradition of class warfare constitutions, our system would speak less of the "separation of powers" and more of the "separation of economic powers." While this form of design was common in the ancient world, it is not just extremely unlikely in our modern context but also undesirable.

Still, it is worth outlining what a modern class warfare constitution might look like, if only to show why it would be undesirable. We could imagine reviving class warfare constitutions along legislative and executive lines. The legislative approach involves dividing power between two branches of the legislature while restricting admission to each by wealth. The medieval notion of the "estates of the realm" offers one example of this strategy, dividing society into nobles and commons and entrenching each into the political process.[9] Another example is one of the Florentine republic's governing bodies, the *Signoria,* whose members were selected through "occupational-specification and randomization."[10] Of the six available seats on that body, two were reserved for representatives of each of the three major occupational guilds.[11]

Literally applying this approach to our American legislature is wildly unrealistic. Imagine reforms to the qualifications for entrance into the House and the Senate. Instead of simply focusing on age requirements, as our Constitution does in providing minimum ages for elected officials, constitutional reformers could focus on wealth requirements—for example, a cap on the wealth of eligible candidates for the House of Representatives or a requirement that one senator from each state not exceed a certain wealth level. A special body restricted *only* to the wealthy might not be necessary, because the wealthy have sufficient ability to protect their interests through elections and political advocacy generally.[12] As surprising as these proposals sound, variations on them were proposed during the Progressive Era.[13]

The legislative approach is not the only path for reviving class warfare constitutions. Republican Rome instituted countervailing powers into the structure of government through the creation of what we would consider an executive branch position: the tribune of the plebeians. Political theorists throughout history have drawn on the tribunate to inspire constitutional design, and at least one contemporary commentator has called for such a position. The University of Chicago political theorist John McCormick has recently argued for the creation of a modern American tribunate, composed of fifty-one citizens, chosen by lottery, for a one-year term. They would be compensated, get their jobs back when their service is complete, and be given other incentives (such as free college for their children). Tribunes would be chosen from the population at large, but the top 10 percent by household wealth would be excluded, as would elected officeholders. The tribunate would be empowered to veto one statute, executive order, and Supreme Court decision per yearly term, in addition to calling one national referendum in which campaign spending would be severely restricted. Three-fourths of the tribunate would have the power to institute impeachment proceedings against federal officials. Tribunes themselves would be disciplined by future tribunates having the authority to indict prior tribunes for misconduct. Finally, his modern tribunate's powers could not be weakened, only strengthened.[14]

There are good reasons why we should be opposed to—or at least skeptical of—proposals to bring back class warfare constitutions in a formal capacity. First, class warfare constitutions are antithetical to the American tradition and to American aspirations. The founding generation rejected class warfare constitutions in favor of a system of government defined by relative economic equality, opportunity, and mobility. And throughout our history, Americans have fought to preserve the middle-class republic that was established in the late eighteenth century. Even for those who were excluded from the promise of America—perhaps especially for those who were excluded—the aspiration was to achieve the American dream for everyone, not to abandon it by explicitly adopting a class-based hierarchy.

There are also some potentially undesirable practical consequences to returning to a constitutional system of class warfare. In particular, attempts to address economic power could have the opposite and unintended effect of entrenching economic class, in the process exacerbating class-based divisions and making class tensions worse. At the level of the individual, explicitly recognizing or designing policies based on economic class could undermine mobility between economic classes. Sociological and psychological theories suggest that perceptions about class status can influence an individual's ability to successfully undertake actions that are outside the class status. In 1948, Robert Merton famously identified the phenomenon of a "self-fulfilling prophecy," which he defined as a "false definition of the situation evoking a new behavior which makes the originally false conception come true."[15] If we apply this theory, people who identify as part of a lower economic class might perceive the system as hostile to economic mobility (the false definition) and therefore not act in ways that will enable them to move up economically (the new behavior), resulting in their remaining in a lower economic class. One prominent example of this phenomenon has been shown to operate in classrooms, in which teachers' expectations influence student performance.[16] Variations on this idea are also common in social psychology, in which studies on "behavioral confirmation" suggest that incorrect perceptions can trigger responses that confirm those perceptions.[17]

At a societal level, explicit class recognition might result in a society that is stuck with more pronounced class divisions and a greater potential for conflict between classes. Consider the dynamics of constitutional design for divided societies, in which designers often use power sharing and other strategies to mitigate conflict between ethnic, religious, language, or other groups. Some studies show that these design strategies can lead to further entrenching—and even radicalizing—the different groups, increasing the likelihood of the political or military conflict that they were meant to alleviate.[18] Explicit power-sharing arrangements risk greater instability rather than greater stability.

While turning our Constitution into a class warfare constitution is not desirable, there are elements consistent with the function of a tribunate that currently exist in some of our institutions. In light of well-known economic inequality in the criminal justice system, jury participation could be interpreted as serving a similar function to the Roman tribune's clemency power. Local juries are drawn from a non-elite, non-expert, non-economically powerful general public, so they can counterbalance a political process that is skewed toward elites. Some scholars have also advocated that juries should issue a verdict of not guilty, even when the defendant is guilty, if the jury believes that the underlying law is unjust. This more extreme measure is akin to a tribunate's clemency and veto powers.[19]

In an executive capacity, the position of "public advocate" or "ombudsman" that many states and cities have established focuses on investigating citizen complaints.[20] First adopted in the United States in the 1960s, ombudsmen serve investigatory, oversight, and advocacy functions, with a focus on protecting individuals from "the excesses of public and private bureaucracies."[21] American ombudsmen and public advocates are nowhere near as strong as the Roman tribunes were, but they are watchdogs with the public interest in mind. The American Bar Association has also recommended strengthening ombudsmen by granting them subpoena power and the ability to initiate litigation or administrative actions.[22] These and other less formalized checks on power might be useful, even if the strong form of a class warfare constitution is not.

SAFEGUARDING THE POLITICAL PROCESS

A second option is to try to sever the link between economic power and political power. Perhaps, in other words, we can have economic inequality in society but design a system in which money doesn't infect political decision making. Institutional design should therefore protect, or safeguard, the political process from the influence of economic elites. According to this approach, the problem is not that there are economic elites in society but simply that they have outsized influence over policy.

Traditionally, campaign finance reform efforts have followed this strategy. The logic is simple: Money corrupts the political process, and disparities in money corrupt the political process in a direction that favors the wealthy. Therefore, money must be restricted from politics.[23] This approach has "defined the modern era of campaign finance reform," and it is best exemplified by the newly defunct "undue influence" justification for campaign finance restrictions.[24] Until *Citizens United* and *McCutcheon v. FEC,* the Supreme Court generally recognized two versions of corruption: quid pro quo corruption and its appearance, and undue influence.[25] According to the undue influence theory, "the source of corruption was large expenditures capturing the marketplace of political ideas."[26] In the 1990 case of *Austin v. Michigan Chamber of Commerce,* the Supreme Court recognized the special corruption that comes with "immense aggregations of wealth that are accumulated with the help of the corporate form."[27] While the Court focused in that case on corporations, its recognition that wealth can distort political outcomes applies more broadly to wealth inequality. The Court's "antidistortion" rationale for campaign finance reform was targeted at curbing the undue influence of the wealthy in the political marketplace.

With the Supreme Court's decisions in *Citizens United* and *McCutcheon* foreclosing the "undue influence" route to campaign finance reform, a number of scholars and activists have turned instead to restrictions on lobbying.[28] This version of safeguarding politics operates further downstream in the political process from campaign finance restrictions. Instead of restricting influence in campaigns, these proposals restrict influence in lobbying Congress. Lobbying restrictions, such as anti-revolving-door laws, fund-raising restrictions, and restrictions on gifts, are all designed to make it harder for individuals or interest groups to purchase influence with lawmakers.[29]

We can also think of the professional civil service as a strategy for insulating policy making from economic influence. Although the common way of thinking about bureaucracies is rooted in technical expertise, the rise of the bureaucracy was intimately interconnected with the rise of economically powerful actors in society and seen at the time as a mechanism for combating their power.[30] Theodore Roosevelt and Herbert Croly's New Nationalism and James Landis's justifications for the regulatory state both indicate a desire to curb the influence of powerful economic interests. Viewed in this light, expertise is a strategy to prevent economically powerful actors from capturing public policy. A professional, expert-driven civil service should insulate policy making from economic influence. Because civil servants are chosen for their technical knowledge rather than by election, political preferences, or connections, they will be less likely to cower to influence.

The motivation underlying this strand of progressive and New Deal thought is instructive as a matter of design. It suggests that contemporary attention to protecting bureaucratic independence and preventing agency capture may be a promising way to rebalance government policy making away from economic elites.[31] At the congressional level, we could develop a more professional, expert-based civil service of congressional staffers. In the executive branch, we could expand the civil service, extend terms of office for higher officials, and restrict revolving-door employment between agencies and their regulated industries.[32] All of these reforms would strengthen the capacity of civil servants and comparatively weaken the power that special interests have.

As promising as it might seem, this approach to safeguarding politics is unlikely to solve the problem of economic power alone. Historically, the best examples of safeguarding tactics were never seen as exclusive or independent. We know that even under class warfare constitutions, such as the Roman republic, wealthy elites attempted to bribe the tribunes in order to influence their actions.[33] In ancient Athens, the practice of ostracism (a particularly extreme safeguarding tactic) was combined with lotteries, paid participation, and rotation in office to maintain democracy. The safeguarding strategy is better understood as a complement and supplement to other design structures.

The reason why safeguarding strategies are complements to and not substitutes for other strategies is that the ethos of inequality will push economic power to find a way to influence political power. Campaign finance scholars call this the "hydraulic" problem. Put simply, the hydraulic problem states that any regulatory effort to restrict the flow of money through one channel of campaign spending will inevitably result in money flowing through another channel.[34] Money is like water: it will follow whatever path is open to it.

The hydraulic problem applies not just to campaign finance efforts but to any effort to cabin the influence of money in politics. The most obvious example is regulatory capture. While the attempt to create a professional bureaucracy with expert civil servants was at least partly an effort to bypass economic influence over policy making, there is evidence that economic elites and industry interest groups have nonetheless succeeded in capturing regulatory agencies.[35] Some pathways for capture, like revolving-door personnel, are obvious, but others are less so.[36] Consider participation in an agency's regulatory process. There is an elaborate system that ensures notice and an opportunity for commenting on a federal agency's proposed regulations in advance of their taking effect. This system is designed to ensure transparency and create a level playing field for any group—public or private—that wants to participate in the regulatory process. But administrative law scholars have shown that private industry has been able to bypass this process. Industry groups often exert influence *before* a proposal is even announced for public comment.[37]

Other safeguarding strategies suffer from the hydraulic problem as well. The Jacksonians saw political parties as a solution to economic power. The Democratic Party of the 1830s was supposed to unite the country against the "money power" that had captured government. But scholars have shown that parties can also be captured by wealthy donors.[38] Even broader structural solutions suffer from the hydraulic problem. Imagine the traditional version of a class warfare constitution, in which the wealthy exert influence through one chamber of the legislature and the working classes through another chamber. What is to stop the wealthy from seeking to capture the working-class chamber through bribes, campaign advertising, lobbying, or less perceptible routes of influence, such as educational activities?

A second problem is what administrative law scholars have called "the paradox of process."[39] Put simply, if we adopt rules and regulations to increase public participation or prevent capture, the well-to-do and their associated interest groups will in practice be better suited to navigate those rules and regulations.[40] As a result, increasing procedural safeguards might have the perverse consequence of actually exacerbating capture rather than reducing it.

The paradox of process arises from the ability of an individual or group to overcome the barriers to participation. Wealthy individuals and interest groups can hire lawyers and lobbyists to navigate a complex political and regulatory process, thereby jumping over the hurdles to participation. Members of the public generally do not have such resources. As a result, there are disparities in participation and influence at every stage of the political process.[41] Moreover, when wealthy individuals and interest groups do participate, their input is often more technically sophisticated, again giving them greater influence. For example, scholars have shown not only that most public comments on proposed regulations come from business groups but also that when the general public comments on proposed regulations, their comments tend to be "form comments" rather than sophisticated analyses.[42] It is therefore not surprising that studies have found that agencies are more responsive to regulated industry groups than to the general public's comments on proposed regulations.[43] The expertise-driven nature of regulatory policy making serves as the barrier to entry for the general public but not for the wealthy and organized elites.

The paradox of process operates not just in lobbying Congress and regulatory agencies. Consider access to the Supreme Court. While the United States has developed a variety of interest groups and private law firms that take on constitutional law cases with an eye toward bringing them to the Supreme Court, as a starting point access to the high court requires considerable resources. Litigants have to make it through a trial court and potentially multiple appeals before they can petition the Supreme Court to take their case, even when constitutional issues are at stake. Or take campaign and election requirements. A well-financed candidate can more easily get on the ballot, identify arcane rules about filing deadlines, and comply with campaign finance reporting requirements because she can hire campaign professionals to navigate these procedures. These rules are designed to create a fair process, but they are complicated, and a less well-financed candidate will have a harder time complying with them.

The hydraulic problem and the paradox of process are serious challenges, but they are not fatal. While any particular reform might be imperfect, that does not mean that doing nothing is better. The right comparison is between a system in which certain channels of influence are restricted and a system in which no channels are restricted. Think about it this way: Laws criminalizing bribery are imperfect because they do not address campaign spending. But most people concerned about the influence of wealth on politics would still think a system with anti-bribery laws is superior to one without any laws. So even if particular reforms are imperfect, a package of reforms—a whole set of reforms—might significantly improve the political system.[44] Multiple, overlapping strategies might make it hard enough to influence politics that the hydraulic problem doesn't disappear but at least becomes much less significant.

The paradox of process is also not an insurmountable problem. In some areas, a leveling-up strategy—creating resources for those who do not have their own—can help increase the ability of ordinary people to navigate the process. In the judicial context, public defenders and pro bono lawyers are examples of the leveling-up approach; they allow people without means to access the courts. Some scholars have argued that we can use a leveling-up strategy to enable greater public access to the regulatory process and to ensure more balanced information in legislative lobbying.[45] A second option is to reduce the procedural hurdles in the first place. In the regulatory context, commentators have suggested that technology could make rulemaking more democratic: proposed regulations can be more easily accessed online and more people can therefore comment on drafts.[46] Some countries have gone so far as to simply bypass procedural hurdles altogether when they get in the way of access. In India, for example, the Supreme Court can exercise "epistolary jurisdiction"—the Court can take a case based on a letter from an ordinary individual.[47] While procedural safeguards are likely to restrict access and reinforce inequality, these effects can be mitigated at least in some cases.

REBUILDING THE MIDDLE CLASS

Reviving class warfare constitutions is undesirable. Safeguarding politics is only a partial answer. What's left? The third option is that we can try to rebuild the middle class in order to bring economic power and political power back into realignment. This solution reaches back to Harrington's philosophy and the economic prerequisites for the American Constitution. In order to work, our republic requires a relatively equal distribution of wealth. The distribution of wealth has become unequal, Harrington would observe, and so our politics has become unequal as well. If we want to preserve our republic, the only sustainable answer is to rebuild our middle class.

Some of the economic policy answers are well-known and have been long-sought goals for American political and economic reformers:

TAX POLICY: Throughout American history, those who have wanted to preserve the Republic have believed that the wealthiest Americans should pay more in taxes and have been concerned about intergenerational transfers of wealth.[48] Jefferson said that ending land-inheritance policies would block the rise of an American "Pseudoaristocracy." The first tariff was thought to shift the tax burden from ordinary people to wealthier coastal merchants. The progressives passed a constitutional amendment to implement an income tax. And yet today, top marginal tax rates are significantly lower than they were in the glorious postwar years; tax loopholes and preferences mean that wealthy individuals and corporations get special benefits, and the estate tax applies to fewer and fewer people. Tax reforms can close loopholes and entrench more progressive rates.

WAGES, BENEFITS, AND EXPENSES: Working families have basic needs, including housing, food, clothing, health care, child care, education, transportation, and retirement funds. To pay for these daily needs, they either need sufficient income or need to get these benefits from their employer, government, or other associations. Populists and progressives called for minimum wages and maximum hours laws during the industrial era, and the New Dealers and Great Society liberals of the mid-twentieth century instituted Social Security, Medicare, and other social programs. Increasing the minimum wage is one path. Today, the federal minimum wage is $7.25 an hour. If the minimum wage in 1968 had been indexed to rise with inflation, it would have been $10.52 in 2012. During that same time period, productivity also rose considerably. Had the minimum wage instead kept pace with productivity, in 2012 it would have been almost $22.[49] Whatever the right number is, higher wages can help struggling families. The other side of the ledger is expenses on necessities like health care, retirement, and education. In the Treaty of Detroit era, many of these basic needs—health care, retirement (through pensions)—were paid for by employers. But workers do not spend their entire careers with one employer, and in many cases workers are contractors, subcontractors, or independent freelancers.[50] Obamacare makes progress in trying to ensure that health care does not depend on employment. But in other areas, like retirement, the system is not designed to make savings easy for those who switch jobs or are independently employed. Reforms to decouple these benefits from employment and make them universal could also help reduce economic insecurity and help preserve the middle class.

EDUCATION: Education has been a ticket to the middle class for many Americans. Efforts to improve early childhood education and ensure high-quality K–12 education are therefore critical to guaranteeing opportunity for all Americans. But it is also essential that every American can access higher education—either skills training or college—without drowning in debt. In recent decades, however, the cost of education has skyrocketed. A college student today paying only in-state tuition and fees at a four-year public school will pay almost four times as much as her counterpart would have paid in 1971.[51] Total student loan debt in America is now above $1.2 trillion.[52] Ensuring affordable or even free access to college could help families and young people with a major expense that is not just beneficial for them and for society but is also a significant financial pressure.

But these specific reforms might not be enough. The economic assumptions of our Constitution were not just egalitarian but agrarian. The crisis of our middle-class constitution began with commercialization and industrialization. The economic structure of society changed significantly—the closing of the frontier, the move to cities, communications, industrial production, the rise of the corporation. Americans from the Knights of Labor to the populists to the progressives tried to reform the *structure* of the economic system. They knew that an economic system designed to concentrate wealth and power in the hands of the few was antithetical to the republic of the founders. Despite their different approaches, these reformers were still committed to capitalism and competition. Roosevelt and Croly saw big business as a reality but wanted to tame its influence, not eradicate corporations altogether. Brandeis and Wilson emphasized a marketplace of small competitors. Even the cooperative commonwealth of the Knights of Labor still involved private business. Industrial democracy was emphatically *not* the communist idea of socializing the means of production. What united these thinkers is that they set out to reform the structure of an economic system that resulted in fraud, special privileges, and concentrated economic and political power. They didn't want to keep the system as it was and just mitigate its negative effects after the fact through redistribution. They wanted significant structural changes to how the system worked in the first place.

Today, one of the central divides in American public policy is whether economic and political reforms should be structural or technocratic. Technocratic reforms keep the basic structure of the regulatory system intact and make incremental or modest changes to improve the worst aspects of the system. The technocratic approach trusts that bureaucrats can manage and monitor private firms, without taking a myopic view or becoming captured. While technocratic reforms benefit from being incremental and less politically controversial, they suffer from a few significant drawbacks. First, technocratic reforms take an overly optimistic view of regulators, policy makers, and the system itself. Should we really believe that expert regulators can keep up with the dynamic changes in the markets? Will they be truly independent? Second, technocratic reforms assume that the current way that an industry is designed to function is morally and socially desirable. Technocratic reforms tend to focus on market optimization and risk management; they do not engage with the broader question of whether certain practices are desirable in the first place. In contrast, structural reforms often tackle these questions. They seek to restructure economic encounters in a more fundamental way. As a result, these changes can often be simpler and less technical than technocratic reforms and can even be self-regulating because they change the behavior, culture, and actions of powerful economic actors.[53]

The easiest place to see the contrast between structural and technocratic thinking is in the financial sector. The philosophy underlying the Dodd-Frank financial reforms of 2010 was largely technocratic. The law didn't break up the "too big to fail" banks. Instead, the central approach was to keep the financial sector largely the same as it was before the crash. The law gave authority to financial regulators (indeed, many of the same regulators who were partly responsible for the crash) to make additional reforms and changes to (hopefully) improve the safety and soundness of the financial sector. Key reforms focused on collecting more and better data and giving financial regulators power to assess the risk that financial institutions pose to economic stability. In other words, the law didn't change the basic structure of the financial industry. This is a classic technocratic approach.[54]

Advocates for structural reforms emphasize instead that the financial sector has fundamental problems. Some of these reformers focus on the size of financial institutions, noting that they are too big to fail, too big to prosecute, too big for trial, too big to manage, and too big to jail.[55] Others focus on a modernized Glass-Steagall Act. The Glass-Steagall regime, originally passed in the wake of the Great Depression and repealed in 1999, separated depository banking from investment banking and insurance. Glass-Steagall's philosophy was that different functions within the financial system should be separated. In 1933, that meant depository and investment banking. Later reformers added insurance. Today, separating functions might involve even more fragmentation. Separation prevents cross subsidies between the risky, speculative parts of a financial institution and the essential activities that the government guarantees (such as insurance on consumer deposits). Division makes it less likely that taxpayers will be on the hook if an institution's bets go bad. Separation also could change the culture of financial institutions. It protects traditional banking from getting caught up in speculation. Even two former Citigroup CEOs, Sanford Weill (the architect of Glass-Steagall's repeal) and John Reed, have said that repealing Glass-Steagall was a mistake.[56]

Structural reform along the lines of Glass-Steagall also has political consequences. When an industry is consolidated into conglomerates, it is harder to play interest groups off each other and pass reform legislation. In contrast, when an industry is fragmented—for example, small versus large banks, retail versus financial services—"the influence of the competing groups can be cancelled out, leaving legislators and regulators space for more neutral policy analysis."[57] The critical insight is that government regulations *create* these interest group environments by allowing or disallowing industry to organize itself. The Glass-Steagall regime, for example, did not just separate different lines of business within the financial sector; it also broke up "the political power of the financial services industry."[58] When different parts of an industry are not always aligned, it becomes harder to capture members of Congress. Legislators might end up supporting one faction against another, and they could then pass legislation that might not have been viable otherwise.[59]

Today, critics of reinstating a modernized Glass-Steagall argue that it had little to do with the immediate causes of the financial crash in 2008. But they miss the bigger point. Today's financial reformers are trying to do more than just find Band-Aids to patch up the holes from the last economic crash. They are trying to build a healthier structure—both economic and political—than the one that currently exists.[60]

It should be no surprise that structural reforms were most prominent during the Gilded Age and the Progressive Era. Reformers in those periods confronted the many changes wrought by the Industrial Revolution and the rise of corporations, and they recognized that they had the power to shape the structure of the new industrial economy. Indeed, some of the most promising structural reforms today find inspiration in the reforms of the Gilded Age and the Progressive Era.

ANTITRUST: The historian Richard Hofstadter observed that Americans once had a robust antitrust movement without antitrust enforcement but by the mid-twentieth century had robust antitrust enforcement without an antitrust movement. Today, it would be more accurate to say that Americans have neither a robust antitrust movement nor robust antitrust enforcement.[61] Industry consolidation and concentration, leading either to oligopoly or monopoly, have a variety of downsides. They make it harder for entrepreneurs and small businesses to enter markets and compete. They mean higher prices for consumers. They mean greater pressure on businesses that depend on monopolists. And they concentrate power in just a handful of companies. Journalists and scholars are increasingly documenting the emergence of a new era of monopolistic capitalism in sectors ranging from telecommunications and technology to agriculture and consumer goods.[62] As a result, economists and commentators have argued for revitalizing antitrust law.[63] Today's antitrust reformers emphasize benefits ranging from greater competition to reduced political power—all from reshaping how sectors of industry are structured.

PUBLIC UTILITY AND COMMON CARRIER REGULATIONS: In the late nineteenth and early twentieth centuries, populists and progressives developed public utility and common carrier regulations as ways to address the emergence of powerful corporations. Public utility regulation can apply to goods and services that are part of the basic infrastructure of modern life, particularly where the market for those services is a monopoly. For example, electricity, water, and sewage provision are classic public utilities. Everyone needs them, and yet their delivery is hardly competitive because of the infrastructure to homes and businesses. Regulation is therefore appropriate. Similar to public utility regulation, common carrier rules traditionally apply when private companies serve basic functions in society and are therefore seen to have public duties, the most important of which is ensuring that members of the general public have equal access to their services.

Today, some reformers have advocated for resurrecting public utility and common carrier principles for the modern age. Modern reformers have argued that some technology companies' products should be considered like traditional public utilities because they are "platforms" that are effectively monopolies.[64] Common carrier regulations have also seen a renaissance. In February 2015, the Federal Communications Commission announced new regulations treating Internet service providers like Comcast as common carriers, in order to guarantee "net neutrality."[65]

LONG-TERMISM: Still others have focused on ending economic structures and incentives that lead to short-termism in corporate decision making. Opponents of short-termism argue that changes in tax and securities laws have created incentives for corporations and especially their CEOs to engage in behavior that maximizes short-term profits and short-term bumps in their stock prices, even at the expense of higher long-term profits and growth. A short-term focus skews corporate choices in ways that are bad not only for the corporation in the long run but also for workers and for society. The worry is that short-termism leads to lower levels of corporate investment in growth and innovation and that it contributes to societal inequality by boosting executive pay and shareholder payouts.[66] Advocates for long-termism argue for a variety of reforms that would therefore flip core incentives for how CEOs run corporations.[67]

INDUSTRIAL DEMOCRACY: The old idea of industrial democracy, or the cooperative commonwealth, is also making a comeback in different forms. The Knights of Labor, the populists, and the progressives all saw that the locus of economic power and decision making had shifted from the individual to the corporation. Translating the spirit of the independent yeoman farmer into the industrial age, they argued that wage workers and employees should have a role in making corporate decisions and in sharing in the profits of the corporation. Today, proposals loosely inspired by these ideas are making a comeback. Some have argued for creating or expanding profit-sharing and stock ownership plans for workers.[68] A proposal in California would tie corporate tax rates to the ratio of CEO-to-worker pay. Corporations who pay their workers well would benefit from lower tax rates, creating an incentive to spend more on wages and less on CEO compensation.[69] There have also been efforts to expand employee participation in decision making, often called co-determination. Kaiser Permanente, for example, created a labor-management partnership in 1997 that includes workers and their union representatives in a range of managerial decisions.[70] Co-determination is also prominent in Germany, where major corporations use "works councils" to empower workers to participate in workplace decision making.

THE NEW LABOR MOVEMENT: Since the New Deal, the traditional model for labor unions has focused on enterprise bargaining. Unions organize workers within a single firm and then represent those workers in collective bargaining with management. Over the last few decades, as union membership has declined, reformers have sought to make the traditional model of union organizing more effective. The proposed Employee Free Choice Act, for example, would accelerate the process of recognizing a union within a workplace. But the traditional model is increasingly under stress from contracting, independent workers, and other changes in the economy. As a result, reformers are also looking beyond the existing structure of labor-management relations, pushing the labor movement to focus less on enterprise bargaining and more on worker empowerment. In some cases, this means organizing workers to reform entire industrial sectors or geographies at once rather than targeting a single firm. In other cases, it means organizing workers and negotiating with both government and business to adopt society-wide policies rather than policies only within one firm or one sector. For example, raising the minimum wage helps all workers regardless of firm, sector, or union status. Industrial democracy ideas—like worker profit sharing and co-determination—are also part of this new movement. The core goal is to empower working people to have a role in setting policies and benefits, participating in decision making, and enforcing the rules.[71]

These categories of reform are all focused on the basic organization of corporations and the economy. By making changes at the structural level, they hope to achieve more fundamental—and far-reaching—change.

THE ECONOMIC ULYSSES

Even if we adopted structural economic and political reforms, there is another tricky problem. A society may be economically equal when its constitution is written, but it might not remain economically equal as changes in the economy occur over time. Even if we could therefore design a workable middle-class constitution for today, how can constitutional design ensure that democratic majorities will continue to rule *over time* given changes in the economic background conditions? Or to put it another way: We might be able to get our middle-class constitution back, but what if the vicious cycle emerges once again?

One answer comes from ancient Greece. Ulysses was the hero of Homer's *Odyssey*. At one point, his ship is about to pass the island of the Sirens. Any sailor who hears their song will be drawn to them, only to have his ship destroyed on the rocks beneath their lair. Ulysses orders his men to put beeswax in their ears so they will not be tempted by the Sirens' song. But he wants to hear the song, so he has his men tie him to the ship's mast and orders them not to free him until they have passed the Sirens' island. Ulysses feared that his future self—the one passing the Sirens—would be tempted. So he restrained himself *beforehand*.

The Ulysses story captures one function of our legal system, and particularly of our Constitution. Constitutions are a way for people to bind themselves to the mast—to a set of policies that in the future they might find hard to maintain.[72] This "precommitment" strategy allows the people to remain on their predetermined path, even if there are changes in the future.[73]

With precommitment theory as inspiration, we might consider

binding ourselves to policies that prevent the emergence of economic inequality, or at least elite economic domination of policy making. This is in fact precisely what Harrington advised when he outlined the theory of the equal commonwealth. At a time when wealth was held primarily in land, Harrington argued that the most important law for any society was its "agrarian" legislation—the laws governing the distribution, transmission, and redistribution of land. The Roman republic, Harrington thought, had failed because of "negligence" in maintaining and enforcing its agrarian laws. By the time of the Gracchi and their attempted economic reforms on behalf of the plebeians, it was too late. Rome was already too unequal. Eventually, the republic descended into civil war.

In our modern context, wealth isn't held solely in land, but there are many different kinds of policies that could precommit the country to preserving a large middle class and relative economic equality. A few examples will be helpful. At the most radical end of the spectrum, imagine a constitutional provision stating that if wealth inequality (however defined) reached a certain level, income, wealth, and estate tax rates would immediately take effect for those at the highest wealth echelons. This self-correcting provision would precommit the society to preventing widespread wealth disparities from turning into a hereditary economic elite. Importantly, the proposal accounts for the possibility that in the future, when there is significant wealth inequality, it might not be possible for popular majorities to institute such a policy through ordinary legislative means precisely because wealth inequality has led to economic elites having outsized influence in politics. Another possibility would be to structure such a proposal with respect only to political influence. Imagine a provision stating that if wealth inequality reaches a certain level, a variety of politically relevant laws would be triggered immediately, including more severe campaign finance restrictions and lobbying rules. Again, society would be precommitting itself to restricting the political power of economic elites as the risks of their disproportionate influence grow stronger. At a more mundane level, we can understand policies like indexing Social Security (or other economic benefits) to inflation as a version of the precommitment story. In the future, it might be harder to increase benefits for the poor or the working class. Tying benefits to inflation means they keep up with the times, without any action from the political system.

Of course, these economic variations on the Ulysses story have their benefits and drawbacks. On the positive side, precommitment gets around the possibility that rising economic inequality will create a political process failure that makes public policy reforms to advance populist or democratic influence unlikely. At the same time, it is not obvious whether the precommitted design strategies (taxes, campaign finance rules, or what have you) would be responsive to the pathways that economic elites are using to influence politics at the moment when the precommitment policies are triggered. Still, a precommitment strategy provides a possible path forward in addressing the problem of changing conditions.

FOXES GUARDING THE HENHOUSE

Perhaps the most significant roadblock to reform of any kind is the problem of foxes guarding the henhouse.[74] If economic elites run the government, why would they act against their interests? Should we really expect them to restructure the political system if it means they lose power? Should we really expect them to restructure the economic system if it means they would lose their wealth?

For example, in the constitutional context, people might look to the federal courts for a solution. But given that the political process is driven by economic elites, and that the president and the Senate choose federal judges, it is not clear why judges would interpret laws and statutes in favor of ordinary-income majorities rather than skew them in the direction of economic elites.[75] Indeed, this was one of the progressives' arguments for moving toward the direct election of senators. Direct election, they hoped, would make it less likely that the selection process for judges would be skewed toward corporate interests.[76] This basic problem applies to all of the branches of government.

Still, the foxes-guarding-the-henhouse problem is not necessarily fatal. Obviously, there have been constitutions that incorporate economic power into their design, laws that curb campaign spending, progressive taxes, industry regulation, and the like. How did these laws come about?

First, individuals in government may not always be captured by economic elites, or not all be captured to the same degree. Some people might be public-spirited or have personal life experiences that push them toward opposing elite preferences. Throughout our history, there have been leaders who understood that preserving the Republic required supporting the middle class and preventing the emergence of a plutocracy. Leaders from Thaddeus Stevens to Theodore Roosevelt to Louis Brandeis recognized the economic preconditions necessary for our republic. Finding and supporting such people is critical to having political leaders that will stand up for reforms to rebuild the middle class, even in the face of pressure from economic elites.

Second, social movements, mass mobilization, and populist energy can put pressure on political elites to force them to change the system. Throughout our history, the biggest political changes have required leadership, but they haven't been the result only of political insiders. Shays's Rebellion, the Jacksonian Democracy, abolitionists, suffragettes, populists, progressives, union organizers, civil rights reformers—all mobilized people throughout the country to put pressure on political elites. The path to change requires energy from the bottom up, not just the top down. Indeed, many of the boldest changes to American public policy have come from grassroots demands for action. Shays's Rebellion involved widespread, even violent, uprisings that forced elites to revise the charter of American government, creating the Constitution. The labor strikes of the Gilded Age raised the specter of class warfare and ultimately resulted in a flurry of progressive reforms to the political and economic system. The peaceful protests of the civil rights movement and the violent response from white supremacist elites led to the end of Jim Crow. In every case, pressure from the outside was crucial for reform.

Third, reform-oriented changes might be more likely during emergencies, when political leaders are willing to experiment with policies outside elite norms simply to address the immediate conditions.[77] Many significant economic reforms—the first corporate income tax in 1895 and the New Deal, for instance—came in the midst of economic emergencies. In addition, if the wealthy lose much of their wealth due to a war or an emergency, they may have less influence over policy. Thomas Piketty hints at this possibility in his study of inequality since the nineteenth century. He argues that the two world wars and the Great Depression wiped out much of the wealth of Western elites and that fact is what led to the mid-twentieth century's unprecedented levels of economic equality.[78] In America, that period also coincides with new government efforts in economic regulation and steeply progressive taxation, among other things. A similar argument can be made in the context of environmental disasters and reform legislation: after a crisis, interest groups that would block legislation in normal times often have less influence.[79] We might want to give special emphasis to reforms adopted in these times. During these extraordinary situations, economic elites have less influence, and the people themselves express their will.[80]

Finally, mass mobilization and legal fragmentation can together lead to *conservative* reforms. Worried about revolt or simply frustrated by popular ferment, economic elites might agree to reforms out of a fear that more radical changes might be adopted. Or they might want reforms simply to take an issue off the table. In the Progressive Era, for example, the corporate tax came about in part as a way to forestall income taxes.[81] Similarly, economic elites might want reform if the legal system is fragmented and complicated. Scholars have suggested that legal fragmentation was a factor in the shift from state to federal environmental law. Instead of a patchwork of rules (with the attendant complexity and costs), elites might prefer a simpler legal regime and be willing to accept reforms as part of that bargain.[82]

THE NEW OREGON SYSTEM

The fox-guarding-the-henhouse problem was the same one that faced populists and progressives who were trying to pass a constitutional amendment to have the people choose their senators. The way they solved this problem was with the "Oregon System." In Oregon, the people passed an initiative allowing the people to vote on their senatorial preference. They then forced state legislators to pledge to support whoever the people's choice was. This meant that the state legislatures now had to either ratify the people's selection when choosing a senator or break their promises and defy the popular will. Needless to say, state legislators followed the people's choice. As a result, senators knew that they owed their allegiance to the people, and because they were already bound, the state legislatures were not giving up much power by ratifying the Seventeenth Amendment. Political reformers need to revive and adapt the Oregon System for today. Activists should push people not to support any candidate for elected office—local, state, or federal—who does not pledge to reform the political system.

Campaign finance reform and voting reforms will be at the forefront of the New Oregon System. Between *Citizens United, Arizona Free Enterprise Club,* and *McCutcheon,* the Court has made clear that it will strike down any attempt to get big money out of politics unless it is tied narrowly to quid pro quo corruption. Indeed, in *Arizona Free Enterprise Club* the Court even rejected a leveling-up strategy—an attempt to get *more* spending into the system by matching funds for those who aren't wealthy—because increasing money would indirectly water down the influence of wealthy donors. Under the New Oregon System, voters should reject any candidate for any office who does not pledge support for a constitutional amendment to overturn the Court's campaign finance decisions or for Supreme Court justices who recognize the problems with the Court's campaign finance decisions.

In addition to campaign finance reform, we need a leveling up of influence in the lobbying context so the playing field isn't skewed toward those who can hire lobbyists. There are different ways to achieve this goal: create research consultants for legislators or establish a public defender approach for lobbying by public-interest organizations. Either way, the aim should be to give legislators more access to information from all sides. We could also adopt policies that will enable Congress to build up a more professional, expert staff. Higher salaries will certainly be part of it, but restrictions on lobbying and the revolving door would complement that effort.

We will also need to reform our system of voting. The ancient

Greeks and the progressives understood that popular involvement in politics would counteract the influence of the wealthy. That is why the Greeks paid a per diem for participation, and it is why the progressives wanted popular election of senators. In America today, however, participation at every level is skewed toward the wealthy. Leveling up campaign funding and lobbying resources will help. But we can make other changes too. Some of the barriers to voting are simple and practical. Shifting elections from Tuesdays, when most people have to work, to a weekend day, or expanding the number of days for elections—to include weekdays and weekends—would make it far easier for working people, people with children, and those who need help getting around to vote. Voter ID laws and felon disenfranchisement without the possibility for rehabilitation have the disproportionate effect of locking out the poor and minorities. Reforming these rules would make a difference.

All of these policies increase participation, but another option—bolder (and thus less likely)—would be to flip the default rule and start from the assumption that everyone should participate. Courts could look with even higher scrutiny at the constitutionality of laws that have the consequence of making it harder to vote. Or the United States could follow the Australian approach of compulsory voting with a protest option. Australians are required to submit a ballot, but they do not have to vote for any of the candidates. This kind of system expands participation among ordinary people but accommodates those who want to protest the election.[83] What is most interesting is at least one study suggests that compulsory voting leads to a decrease in economic inequality and increased income for the bottom quintiles of the population.[84]

THE POLITICS OF REFORM: THE NEW POPULISTS AND PROGRESSIVE CONSERVATIVES

Change of any kind, big or small, bold or incremental, requires a political context in which change is feasible and a political coalition that will take action. Two groups will be necessary for political change: the new populists and progressive conservatives.

There is a story about Franklin Roosevelt meeting with some

reformers who outlined an aggressive agenda for change. Roosevelt said he agreed with them and wanted to act. But he then told the reformers, "Now make me do it." The story is probably false, because no president enjoys getting pressured, but the point is instructive. The apocryphal Roosevelt understood that there has to be external pressure on political actors for them to be able to undertake reform.

The role of the new populists in this system is to bring that pressure to bear on political leaders. Whether on the right or on the left, economic populists can raise bold ideas and then mobilize supporters to pressure elected leaders to undertake reform. Their role is to establish a vision for change, even if unlikely or unachievable, that becomes a stake in the ground against which policy can be measured. On occasion, their bold visions might become reality. But their true purpose is to help the imagination, spark vigorous debate about fundamental issues, and shape the political context. Big ideas, coupled with popular mobilization, can succeed at putting reform on the agenda and at pressuring leaders to do *something*. The key lesson for anyone interested in preserving America's republic is that a robust populist movement is not an enemy of moderate reform but an ally. By bringing pressure from the flank, the new populists pressure elites in the center to change course.

A second group, the seemingly oxymoronic *progressive conservatives,* is just as important to restoring America's middle-class constitution. Throughout history, true conservatives have sought to preserve the status quo and maintain continuity with the best traditions of the past. Many conservatives today do not follow this tradition, instead seeking to impose an ideological vision on the country and the world. True conservatives like Edmund Burke and Theodore Roosevelt wanted to *conserve*. But they also recognized that conservation required reform. "If you do not give the people social reform, they will give you social revolution," said the British conservative Quintin Hogg.[85] The world is constantly changing. Without incremental reforms to adapt to those changes, society faces the possibility of more radical revolution. Conservatives of this mold were defined by their courage to embrace popular reform. In Britain, Lord Randolph Churchill, father of the future prime minister Winston Churchill, referred to this position as "Tory Democracy." In America,

Theodore Roosevelt was the country's leading progressive conservative. "Those who oppose all reform," he said, "will do well to remember that ruin in its worst form is inevitable if our national life brings us nothing better than swollen fortunes for the few and the triumph in both politics and business of a sordid and selfish materialism."[86]

Saving the Republic will require the Republican Party to reclaim its tradition of progressive conservatism, of conservatives who believe in reform in order to preserve the best of America's traditions and avoid more radical change. The challenge for Republicans is that they will need to find the courage to push back against their more ideological allies. The historian Arthur Schlesinger Jr. once observed that this has always been a challenge for American conservatives because their leaders are drawn from the wealthy. They "think . . . in terms of class and not of nation, in terms of profit and not of social obligation."[87] Progressive conservatives will have to revisit their position on policies that privilege the wealthy and instead focus on rebuilding the middle class. In recent years, some conservatives have begun to revive this tradition.[88] It is too early to tell whether these "reformicons" will emerge as a leading force in Republican politics over the next decades, but their efforts—or something like them—will be critical to restoring America's middle-class constitution.

THE WISDOM OF THE WISEST PATRIOTS

When James Madison looked forward from 1830, he recognized that one day "[t]he institutions and laws of the country" would have to "be adapted" to address the "proportion being without property." This task, he said, would require "the wisdom of the wisest patriots."

The wisest patriots of Madison's day understood Harrington's dictum that power follows property, and they knew that America could not be a republic without relative economic equality. "The great object of terror and suspicion to the people of the thirteen provinces was *power*," Henry Adams wrote in 1870. "Not merely power in the hands of a president or a prince . . . but power in the abstract, wherever it existed and under whatever name it was known."[89] These days, most commentators look back to the founding era and equate the fear of power with the fear of *government* power. But for much of American history, the fear of power extended beyond tyrannical government to the accumulation of private power and in particular economic power. Fear of economic power and the belief that America had an exceptional level of economic equality were central to the origins of our Constitution. And as time passed and the economic structure of the country shifted, the wisest patriots recognized that reforms would be needed to preserve our republican form of government.

Today, with economic inequality rising, the middle class collapsing, and power increasingly concentrated in the hands of economic elites, our middle-class constitution is once again at risk. The central question we must ask is one John Adams raised more than two hundred years ago: Is there "such a rage for Profit and Commerce" that we no longer have "public Virtue enough to support a Republic"?[90]

Acknowledgments

When I started working on this book, everyone at Vanderbilt Law School was enthusiastic. Dean Chris Guthrie, Kevin Stack, Jim Rossi, and the program on law and government provided critical support for the project at every stage. Rebecca Haw Allensworth, Margaret Blair, Ed Cheng, Paul Edelman, Tracey George, Sara Mayeux, Morgan Ricks, Dan Sharfstein, Chris Slobogin, and Ingrid Wuerth suffered through innumerable conversations and read and commented on portions of the text. The Vanderbilt Law Library staff—in particular Libby Byington, Catherine Deane, LaRentina Gray, Carolyn Hamilton, and Sara Saddler—were cheerful, attentive, and dedicated, even in the face of my unending requests at all hours of the day and night. Amanda Blain, Ariel Doblein, Kim Jackson, Katelyn Marshall, Greg Miraglia, Sarah Dotzel, Laura McKenzie, and Laura Dolbow fact-checked or proofed the entire book. And my assistants Emily Padget Applegate and then Quenna Stewart kept the machinery running.

Along the way, many friends and colleagues were helpful interlocutors or read and commented on drafts: Bruce Ackerman, Einer Elhauge, Dan Epps, Richard Fallon, Joey Fishkin, David Fontana, Willy Forbath, Barry Friedman, Jamie Galbraith, Heather Gerken, Sarah Igo, Jim Kloppenberg, Bob Kuttner, Melissa Lane, Larry Lessig, Daryl Levinson, Michael Lind, Jon Margolick, Tom McGinn, Jon Michaels, Martha Minow, Emily Nacol, Bill Novak, Dave Pozen, Claire Priest, Richard Primus, Richard Re, Cristina Rodriguez, Shalev Roisman, Laura Phillips Sawyer, Elizabeth Sepper, Damon

Silvers, and Nick Stephanopolous. A few brave souls went above and beyond, reading the entire manuscript and providing exhaustive and extraordinarily helpful comments and suggestions: Kate Andrias, Jeremy Kessler, Bruce Mann, Jed Purdy, Sabeel Rahman, Chris Serkin, Suzanna Sherry, Kevin Stack, and Danny Yagan.

The law schools at Columbia University, Harvard University, UCLA, the University of Minnesota, New York University, the University of Richmond, the University of Texas at Austin, William and Mary, and Yale gave me the opportunity to present portions of the book, and faculty and students provided helpful comments, as did the audience at the annual conference for the Society of U.S. Intellectual History in 2015. The editors at the *Cornell Law Review, Texas Law Review, Politico,* and University of Wisconsin Press significantly improved earlier articles, portions of which appear here in substantially revised form: "America's Post-Crash Constitution," *Politico Magazine,* Oct. 5, 2014; "*Drift and Mastery* in the Twenty-First Century," foreword to *Drift and Mastery,* by Walter Lippmann (University of Wisconsin Press, 2015); "The Puzzling Absence of Economic Power in Constitutional Theory," 101 *Cornell Law Review* 1445 (2016); "Economic Structure and Constitutional Structure: An Intellectual History," 94 *Texas Law Review* 1301 (2016).

My parents and sister were patient when I disappeared from their lives for weeks at a time, buried in books or writing fiercely. Years of working with Dan Geldon and Jon Donenberg were crucial to my thinking on so many political and economic issues. My friends Moira Weigel, Ben Tarnoff, Joe Green, and Lindsay Voigt went above and beyond in providing advice, support, and encouragement. And my intrepid agent Chris Parris-Lamb and terrific editor Keith Goldsmith helped shape the text and bring it into existence.

Although the themes in this book had been in my mind for many years, I would never have started writing the book—or written it in this way—had I not spent years working with Elizabeth Warren. For more than a decade, we discussed how the American middle class was getting squeezed, chipped at, and hammered, and the many ways in which the political system was rigged against working families. Those experiences, as a student, co-author, and adviser, have shaped much of my thinking over the years. When I left her office in 2013, this book grew naturally from my interest in the history of American political thought and my reflections on our time working together. I cannot thank her enough for our conversations, for her friendship, and for the opportunity to make a difference.

Notes

Introduction

1. For a discussion of these challenges, see "Who's in the Middle?," *Economist,* Feb. 12, 2009.
2. "Burgeoning Bourgeoisie," *Economist,* Feb. 12, 2009 (describing the middle class as having sufficient discretionary income). The point about guaranteeing the future as the rich can is implied from the definition.
3. *Federalist* No. 1, at 1 (Hamilton) (Clinton Rossiter ed., 1999).
4. Steve Fraser, *The Age of Acquiescence: The Life and Death of American Resistance to Organized Wealth and Power* 68–69 (2015) makes a version of this point.

Chapter One: From Athens to America: The Two Traditions

1. These paragraphs follow Gordon Wood's interpretation of Adams's political thought. See Gordon S. Wood, *The Creation of the American Republic* 567–92 (1969). The quotation to a friend is from Wood, *Creation,* at 581.
2. Wood, *Creation,* at 569.
3. John Adams, *Defence of the Constitutions of Government of the United States,* 5 *The Works of John Adams* 488 (Charles Francis Adams ed., 1851); John Adams, *Discourses on Davila,* 6 *The Works of John Adams* 257, 280 (Charles Francis Adams ed., 1851).
4. Adams, *Discourses on Davila,* at 246; Adams, *Defence,* in 6 *Works,* at 68 ("In every society where property exists, there will be a struggle between rich and poor.... They will either be made by numbers, to plunder the few who are rich, or by influence, to fleece the many who are poor. Both rich and poor, then, must be made independent").
5. Adams, *Defence,* in 4 *Works,* at 401; Wood, *Creation,* at 571.

6. Adams, *Defence,* in 4 *Works,* at 290, 414.

7. Adams to Thomas Jefferson, Oct. 9, 1787, in 12 *The Papers of Thomas Jefferson* 220–21 (Julian P. Boyd ed., 1955).

8. Adams, *Defence,* in 4 *Works,* at 290. For a discussion, see Luke Mayville, *John Adams and the Fear of American Oligarchy* (2016).

9. See Wood, *Creation,* at 582–83.

10. John Taylor, *An Inquiry into the Principles and Policy of the Government of the United States* 355–56 (1814).

11. Simon Hornblower, "Creation and Development of Democratic Institutions in Ancient Greece," in *Democracy* 1, 3 (John Dunn ed., 1992).

12. John Dunn, *Setting the People Free: The Story of Democracy* 32 (2005).

13. See Plutarch, 1 *Lives* 437 (Bernadotte Perrin trans., 1914).

14. Melissa Lane, *The Birth of Politics: Eight Greek and Roman Political Ideas and Why They Matter* 34 (2014).

15. Josiah Ober, *Mass and Elite in Democratic Athens: Rhetoric, Ideology, and the Power of the People* 61 (1989).

16. Id.

17. Plutarch, 1 *Lives,* at 447. On redistribution, see Dunn, *Setting the People Free,* at 32; Ober, *Mass and Elite,* at 198.

18. Thucydides, *History of the Peloponnesian War* 145 (Rex Warner trans., 1972).

19. Mogens Herman Hansen, *The Athenian Democracy in the Age of Demosthenes* 34 (1991); Hornblower, "Creation," at 7; Ober, *Mass and Elite,* at 70–71.

20. Hansen, *Athenian Democracy,* at 35–36.

21. Id. at 36; Ober, *Mass and Elite,* at 76. The officials were the archons, in 487 B.C.

22. Ober, *Mass and Elite,* at 78–81. Property requirements were reduced in 457 B.C.

23. Hansen, *Athenian Democracy,* at 40–42.

24. Dunn, *Setting the People Free,* at 35–36; Lane, *Birth of Politics,* at 103–4; Ober, *Mass and Elite,* at 54, 98.

25. Dunn, *Setting the People Free,* at 36.

26. Id. at 37; Ober, *Mass and Elite,* at 7–8. On the Athenian justice system and its relationship to democracy more broadly, see Adriaan Lanni, *Law and Justice in the Courts of Classical Athens* 175–80 (2006).

27. Dunn, *Setting the People Free,* at 37; Ober, *Mass and Elite,* at 7–8.

28. Hornblower, "Creation," at 9; Lane, *Birth of Politics,* at 118.

29. Ober, *Mass and Elite,* at 7.

30. Id. at 26–27.

31. All facts in the paragraph are from id. at 128–35. Ober has slightly

different estimates in *The Rise and Fall of Classical Greece* 92 (2015): of about 29,900 Athenians in the late fourth century, there were 400 elite citizen men, 24,500 middling, and 5,000 at subsistence levels. His pessimistic account is 400 elite citizen men, 19,500 middling men, and 10,000 at subsistence levels.

32. Ober, *Rise and Fall,* at 95–97.
33. Id. at 89–90.
34. Id. at 80.
35. Dunn, *Setting the People Free,* at 35–37; Ober, *Mass and Elite,* at 7–8, 54, 78–81, 98; Lane, *Birth of Politics,* at 103–4.
36. Plutarch, 7 *Lives* 19 (Bernadotte Perrin trans., 1919).
37. Id. at 21.
38. Lane, *Birth of Politics,* at 125; Ober, *Mass and Elite,* at 54–55, 109–10.
39. Bernard Manin, *The Principles of Representative Government* (1997).
40. Andrew Lintott, *The Constitution of the Roman Republic* 46 (2003).
41. Jon Elster, *Solomonic Judgments* 81–85 (1989); Manin, *Principles,* at 54–63; John P. McCormick, *Machiavellian Democracy* 108–9 (2011).
42. Manin, *Principles,* at 42, 63.
43. Id. at 79.
44. See, for example, Montesquieu, *The Spirit of the Laws* 2.2 (13) (Anne M. Cohler et al. trans., 1989) ("[V]oting by lot is in the nature of democracy, voting by choice is in the nature of aristocracy").
45. Manin, *Principles,* at 132–60 (making this argument thoroughly). See also John Ferejohn and Frances Rosenbluth, "Electoral Representation and the Aristocratic Thesis," in *Political Representation* (Ian Shapiro et al. eds., 2009).
46. Manin, *Principles,* at 83–85 (social contract and natural rights), 88–89 (Middle Ages); see also Monica Brito Vieira and David Runciman, *Representation* 25–26 (2008) (describing the radical changes stemming from Hobbes's theory of representation). For a contemporary discussion of lottery as a way to choose representatives, see Akhil Reed Amar, Note, "Choosing Representatives by Lottery Voting," 93 *Yale Law Journal* 1238 (1984).
47. See Polybius, *The Histories* 6.2 (371) (Brian McGing ed., Robin Waterfield trans., 2010).
48. Polybius, *Histories,* at vii–ix, xi–xiii, xiv, 6.2 (371), 6.3–6.5 (372–74), 6.11–6.18 (379–85); Fergus Millar, *The Roman Republic in Political Thought* 24 (2002); Lane, *Birth of Politics,* at 250–67. For an older analysis of Polybius's idea of the mixed constitution, see Kurt von Fritz, *The Theory of the Mixed Constitution in Antiquity: A Critical Analysis of Polybius' Political Ideas* (1954).

49. David E. Hahm, "The Mixed Constitution in Greek Thought," in *A Companion to Greek and Roman Political Thought* 178, 178–98 (Ryan K. Balot ed., 2009); Lane, *Birth of Politics*, at 69; Andrew Lintott, "Aristotle and the Mixed Constitution," in *Alternatives to Athens* 152, 156–57 (Roger Brock and Stephen Hodkinson eds., 2000).

50. Fred D. Miller Jr., *Nature, Justice, and Rights in Aristotle's Politics* 191, 252 (1995); see also Aristotle, *Politics* 4.1.1288b23–24 (92) (Stephen Everson ed., 1996).

51. Aristotle, *Politics*, at 3.7.1279a22–1279b5 (71).

52. Id. at 3.7.1279a25–33 (71).

53. Id. at 4.3 (94).

54. Josiah Ober, "Aristotle's Political Sociology: Class, Status, and Order in the *Politics*," in *Essays on the Foundations of Aristotelian Political Science* 112 (Carnes Lord and David K. O'Connor eds., 1991).

55. Aristotle, *Politics*, at 2.1.1260b40–41 (31), 3.4.1276b30 (65).

56. See Hahm, "Mixed Constitution," at 186. My focus here is on the "corrupt" versions rather than the "true" or perfect versions of government. As Aristotle says, "[T]he best is often unattainable, and therefore the true legislator and statesman ought to be acquainted, not only with what is best in the abstract, but also with that which is best relatively to circumstances." Aristotle, *Politics*, at 4.1.1288b25–29 (92).

57. Aristotle, *Politics*, at 3.7.1279b8–9 (71–72), 3.8.1279b16–20 (72).

58. Id. at 3.8.1279b40–1280a1–3 (72).

59. Id. at 4.4.1290b3–4 (95).

60. Id. at 5.1.1301a28–30 (120).

61. Id. at 3.10.1281a14–20 (75).

62. Id. at 5.1.1301a30–33 (120).

63. See id. at 3.10.1281a25–27 (75).

64. See id. at 5.3.1303b4–7 (125).

65. Id. at 4.8.1293b33 (103) (describing the "fusion of oligarchy and democracy"), 4.8.1294a23 (104) (describing "the admixture" of wealthy and poor).

66. Id. at 4.9.1294a35–1294b14 (104–5).

67. See Polybius, *Histories*, at 6.11–6.18 (379–85).

68. Id. at 6.18 (385).

69. Livy, *The Rise of Rome* 2.23 (93) (James T. Luce trans., 2008).

70. Id.

71. Id. at 2.24–27 (95–97).

72. Id. at 2.30–31 (101–2).

73. Id. at 2.32 (103–4). Livy points out that others say it was the Aventine Hill, but he doesn't believe this.

74. Id. at 2.33 (104–5). For scholarly discussions, see T. J. Cornell, *The Beginnings of Rome* 259–64 (1995); Christopher S. Mackay, *Ancient Rome* 35–37 (2004); Lintott, *Constitution,* at 32–33, 121–25; Lily Ross Taylor, "Forerunners of the Gracchi," 25 *Journal of Roman Studies* 19, 20 (1962). For a skeptical view of Livy's history of the tribunate's origins, structure, and relationship to other offices including the consulate, see Gary Forsythe, *A Critical History of Early Rome* 159, 162–65, 166, 170–75 (2005).

75. For example, it is unlikely the first secession was an uprising of infantry. Had it been, Cornell notes, "the conflict of the orders would not have lasted two days, let alone two centuries." Cornell, *Beginnings,* at 257. Similarly, the veteran's story isn't entirely accurate, because the tax supposedly imposed on him didn't exist at the time. Id. at 267. The central problem is that our historical sources from early Rome, and particularly from the fifth century B.C., are limited. In many cases, the stories come from later-republic historians who are drawing on events in their own time and reading them backward into earlier Roman history. For a discussion of the reliability of sources, see Forsythe, *Critical History,* at 59–77; see also Kurt A. Raaflaub, "The Conflict of the Orders in Archaic Rome: A Comprehensive and Comparative Approach," in *Social Struggles in Archaic Rome: New Perspectives on the Conflict of the Orders* 9–11, 24, 28–31 (Kurt A. Raaflaub ed., 2nd ed. 2005). Some historians, however, argue that the basic "structural" and factual evidence is accurate, though rhetorically embellished. Timothy J. Cornell, "The Value of the Literary Tradition Concerning Archaic Rome," in *Social Struggles in Archaic Rome,* at 48, 53. For this approach through Roman history, see generally Cornell, *Beginnings.* While I will make note of many of the historical challenges, my primary interest is less in the "true" history of what happened and more in the basic structures of the history, which is what thinkers throughout history received and what we can use to think about constitutional design. For a close study of the former, see Millar, *Roman Republic.*

76. The Roman historical tradition was primarily "interested in providing practical examples for the statesman and citizen," rather than explicating history with conservative accuracy, and later political theorists and statesmen who looked back at Roman history generally took the statements of Roman historians at face value. Jürgen von Ungern-Sternberg, "The Formation of the 'Annalistic Tradition': The Example of the Decemvirate," in *Social Struggles in Archaic Rome,* at 88; see also Forsythe, *Critical History,* at 66–67 ("Like many other ancients, [Livy] believed that the value of history lay in providing people with good

and bad models of conduct to be emulated and to be avoided respectively."). This is more a problem for historians than for political theorists.

77. The "struggle" or "conflict" of the orders is the subject of considerable debate. Some, including the later Roman historians, suggest that Romulus divided the people into patricians and plebeians. Forsythe, *Critical History,* at 157 (describing Livy's and Dionysius's accounts). In the late nineteenth and early twentieth centuries, historians focused on geography and race as possible grounds for the division. Some scholars today believe that the conflict in the fifth century was likely between poor plebeians and rich landowners, rather than "social orders," but that by the fourth century it had shifted to "orders" due to the passage of various laws. Cornell, *Beginnings,* at 244, 333. Others, agreeing that "orders" is a better interpretation for the later period, think the focus was on personal status, property, and social relations rather than class or social distinctions like rich and poor. Kurt A. Raaflaub, preface to *Social Struggles in Archaic Rome,* at xi. Still others believe the distinction was religious and legal. Richard E. Mitchell, "The Definition of Patres and Plebs: An End to the Struggle of the Orders," in *Social Struggles in Archaic Rome,* at 129. The classic work distinguishing between order, class, and status (and favoring status) is M. I. Finley, *The Ancient Economy* 45–50 (2nd ed. 1985). For a recent account that notes Finley's response to Marxist interpretation and brings economics back into the story, see Emanuel Mayer, *The Ancient Middle Classes: Urban Life and Aesthetics in the Roman Empire, 100 BCE–250 CE* 2 (2012). It is worth noting that even scholars who take a Marxist approach to interpreting the history and thus emphasize the economic aspects of the "struggle of the orders" recognize the distinction between economic class and juridical orders. G. E. M. de Ste. Croix, *The Class Struggle in the Ancient Greek World* 332–37 (1981). Indeed, even historians with different views on these questions believe economic issues and political power were relevant to the struggle of the orders. See, for example, P. A. Brunt, *Social Conflicts in the Roman Republic* 47 (1971) ("[T]he distinction [between patricians and plebeians] was one of birth, not wealth; the conflict of the orders is unintelligible unless there were rich plebeians, but no doubt property was originally concentrated more in the hands of the patricians ... the rich plebeians, who desired to gain a share in political power, from time to time made themselves the champions of their oppressed brethren"); Kurt A. Raaflaub, "From Protection and Defense to Offense and Participation: Stages in the Conflict of the Orders," in *Social Struggles in Archaic Rome* 189 (the

conflict is "only intelligible if there was at the outset no substantial nonpatrician, but otherwise comparable, rich and noble upper class"); Karl-J. Holkeskamp, *Reconstructing the Roman Republic* 31, 78 (Henry Heitmann-Gordon trans., 2010) (taking a status approach but noting that the "social structure of Rome was always characterized by a distinct, and indeed steep, stratification into classes, based on enormous differences in wealth, income, and status"). As a matter of history, the "struggle of the orders" story that we have inherited from the Roman republic's later historians suffers from a variety of problems: (1) it is suspicious that the subjects and factions of a political contest were identical for 150 years, even though the policy and political context changed; (2) the dichotomy is quite simplistic; (3) there are clearly anachronistic elements that have been imported into the early history by later Roman historians; (4) there is very little evidence from the fifth century. Forsythe, *Critical History,* at 158–59. Indeed, the conflict might have evolved over time. Raaflaub suggests the first stage was between aristocracy and non-aristocracy, between the powerful and wealthy and the middle/lower classes who were trying to address imbalances in economic, political, and social power. The second stage saw the emergence of a plebeian elite that was wealthy and socially not so different from patricians. In the third stage, this plebeian upper class challenges the patricians to gain access to office holding, at the same time addressing some issues facing lower-class plebs. Finally, economic issues are addressed more directly, and the plebs gain full political integration and the right to hold offices. Raaflaub, "From Protection and Defense," at 189–90. For a fascinating re-periodization of the entire history of the Roman republic, see Harriet I. Flower, *Roman Republics* (2010). Despite these challenges, the fact remains that the Roman historians of the later republic characterized their history in these terms and these histories were what passed down to later generations of political theorists and statesmen.

78. Mackay, *Ancient Rome,* at 33–35 (discussing economic goals, including debt, hunger, and land distribution); Cornell, *Beginnings,* at 267–68.
79. Cornell, *Beginnings,* at 268–70.
80. Id.
81. Id. at 270.
82. Id. at 328–29.
83. Id.
84. Mackay, *Ancient Rome,* at 33–35; Cornell, *Beginnings,* at 272.
85. Brunt, *Social Conflicts,* at 54.
86. Cornell, *Beginnings,* at 272–73; Livy, *Rise,* at 3.44–72.

87. Livy, *Rise,* at 3.44–72. See also Cornell, *Beginnings,* at 272–73. This is the traditional story, though it may be highly unreliable. See Forsythe, *Critical History,* at 202, 209–10, 222–23, 225–26, 230, 262–67; Cornell, *Beginnings,* 273–74; Mary Beard, *SPQR: A History of Ancient Rome* 149–51 (2015).

88. Cornell, *Beginnings,* at 277–78.

89. Lintott, *Constitution,* at 37; Kurt A. Raaflaub, "Between Myth and History: Rome's Rise from Village to Empire (the Eighth Century to 264)," in *A Companion to the Roman Republic* 140 (Nathan Rosenstein and Robert Morstein-Marx eds., 2006). Consul in 367 B.C.; dictator in 356 B.C.; praetor in 337 B.C. There's some debate about the date when the censorship opened. Raaflaub says 339 B.C.; Lintott says 351 B.C.

90. Lintott, *Constitution,* at 37 (this took place in 342 B.C.); Mackay, *Ancient Rome,* at 37–38.

91. Lintott, *Constitution,* at 37 (interest rates and debt repayment were reformed in 357 B.C. and 355 B.C.; debt bondage reforms were in 326 B.C.).

92. Cornell, *Beginnings,* at 277; Lintott, *Constitution,* at 38, 122; Brunt, *Social Conflicts,* at 57.

93. By tradition, the struggle of the orders ended in 287 B.C. Raaflaub, "From Protection and Defense," at 185; Raaflaub, "Conflict of the Orders," at 4. But some historians question that date as the appropriate periodization. Mitchell, "Definition of Patres and Plebs," at 129; Jürgen von Ungern-Sternberg, "The End of the Conflict of the Orders," in *Social Struggles in Archaic Rome.*

94. Cicero, *On the Republic* 1.26–27 (67–69) (Clinton W. Keys trans., 1928).

95. Id. at 1.29 (71).

96. Id. at 2.23 (151), 1.29 (71).

97. Id. at 2.1 (111–12), 2.25–26 (155–57).

98. Id. at 2.33 (169).

99. Cicero, *On the Laws,* at 3.9 (483).

100. Id. at 3.10–11 (485–87).

101. Id. at 3.11–12 (491).

102. Id. at 3.8 (480) (author's translation) (Clinton W. Keys trans., 1928).

103. Mackay, *Ancient Rome,* at 61–75; H. H. Scullard, *From the Gracchi to Nero: A History of Rome from 133 B.C. to A.D. 68* 3–4 (5th ed. 1959).

104. *Nobiles* were those whose ancestors had held the consulship. Mackay, *Ancient Rome,* at 38. The shift toward the *nobiles* is emphasized most prominently by Flower, who creates new periods for the Republic based in part on the rise of the *nobiles* and their role in the Republic.

See Flower, *Roman Republics,* at 24–28. For recent scholars emphasizing the role of plebeians and ordinary people, rather than the *nobiles* and their client-based networks, see Fergus Millar, *The Crowd in Rome in the Late Republic* (1998); Henrik Mouritsen, *Plebs and Politics in the Late Roman Republic* (2001). For an overview of the debate between the orthodox approach, which emphasized elite rule, and the scholarship suggesting an important popular role, see Holkeskamp, *Reconstructing the Roman Republic,* at 1–11.

105. Flower, *Roman Republics,* at 64; Scullard, *Gracchi to Nero,* at 12–13.

106. Mackay, *Ancient Rome,* at 96–97 (describing the spoils of war and contracts going to the equestrians); Flower, *Roman Republics,* at 64; Scullard, *Gracchi to Nero,* at 12–13.

107. Sallust, *The War with Jugurtha* 41 (225) (J. C. Rolfe trans., 1921).

108. Mackay, *Ancient Rome,* at 97–98; Scullard, *Gracchi to Nero,* at 19.

109. Scullard, *Gracchi to Nero,* at 21.

110. Mackay, *Ancient Rome,* at 98; Flower, *Roman Republics,* at 64; Brunt, *Social Conflicts,* at 17.

111. Mackay, *Ancient Rome,* at 98–99.

112. Id. at 99.

113. Sallust, *The War with Catiline* 10 (19) (J. C. Rolfe trans., 1921).

114. Brunt, *Social Conflicts,* at 17.

115. On the military link, see Mackay, *Ancient Rome,* at 107; Brunt, *Social Conflicts,* at 78. On the origins of his interest in helping the poor, see Beard, *SPQR,* at 221.

116. Mackay, *Ancient Rome,* at 107–8; Scullard, *Gracchi to Nero,* at 25–26; Beard, *SPQR,* at 222–23.

117. Sallust, *Jugurtha,* at 42 (225).

118. Mackay, *Ancient Rome,* at 108; Scullard, *Gracchi to Nero,* at 26.

119. Mackay, *Ancient Rome,* at 108; Lintott, *Constitution,* at 207; Scullard, *Gracchi to Nero,* at 27; Beard, *SPQR,* at 223.

120. Mackay, *Ancient Rome,* at 108; Scullard, *Gracchi to Nero,* at 27.

121. Mackay, *Ancient Rome,* at 108–9; Scullard, *Gracchi to Nero,* at 27; Beard, *SPQR,* at 223. When the king of Pergamum died and unexpectedly left his wealth to the Roman people, Tiberius threatened to bring to the assembly a bill to use the money for his land project. Although he got the funding, his attempt called into question the Senate's control of finances and foreign affairs alike and furthered resentment against him.

122. Lintott, *Constitution,* at 209; Scullard, *Gracchi to Nero,* at 27; Mackay, *Ancient Rome,* at 109.

123. Lintott, *Constitution*, at 209.

124. Brunt, *Social Conflicts*, at 78–81; Scullard, *Gracchi to Nero*, at 28; Beard, *SPQR*, at 224; Mackay, *Ancient Rome*, at 109.

125. Flower, *Roman Republics*, at 95; Scullard, *Gracchi to Nero*, at 29; Beard, *SPQR*, at 225.

126. Scullard, *Gracchi to Nero*, at 29; Beard, *SPQR*, at 224.

127. Brunt, *Social Conflicts*, at 84–86; Scullard, *Gracchi to Nero*, at 32–33.

128. Mackay, *Ancient Rome*, at 112; Brunt, *Social Conflicts*, at 84–86; Scullard, *Gracchi to Nero*, at 32–33.

129. Mackay, *Ancient Rome*, at 113; Brunt, *Social Conflicts*, at 87–89.

130. Mackay, *Ancient Rome*, at 114; Brunt, *Social Conflicts*, at 90; Scullard, *Gracchi to Nero*, at 36–37; Beard, *SPQR*, at 228–32.

131. Scullard, *Gracchi to Nero*, at 38.

132. Brunt, *Social Conflicts*, at 92.

133. Id.

134. Mackay, *Ancient Rome*, at 125–27; Scullard, *Gracchi to Nero*, at 70–71; Lintott, *Constitution*, at 210–11.

135. Mackay, *Ancient Rome*, at 128–29; Scullard, *Gracchi to Nero*, at 74–76.

136. Scullard, *Gracchi to Nero*, at 80–81.

137. Flower, *Roman Republics*, at 94–95, 121; Scullard, *Gracchi to Nero*, at 80–81.

138. Flower, *Roman Republics*, at 119–32 (describing Sulla's reforms to the Republic); Mackay, *Ancient Rome*, at 131; Beard, *SPQR*, at 245–47; Millar, *Crowd in Rome*, at 53–54; Scullard, *Gracchi to Nero*, at 82; Catherine Steel, *The End of the Roman Republic, 146 to 44 BC* 108–9 (2013); Eric J. Kondratieff, "Reading Rome's Evolving Civic Landscape in Context: Tribunes of the Plebs and the Praetor's Tribunal," 63 *Phoenix* 322, 323 (2009).

139. Kondratieff, "Reading Rome's Evolving Civic Landscape," at 334 (quoting Velleius).

140. Scullard, *Gracchi to Nero*, at 83; Beard, *SPQR*, at 245.

141. Kondratieff, "Reading Rome's Evolving Civic Landscape," at 334–35.

142. Lintott, *Constitution*, at 212; Scullard, *Gracchi to Nero*, at 94.

143. Millar, *Crowd in Rome*, at 73.

144. The classic work is J. G. A. Pocock, *The Machiavellian Moment: Florentine Political Thought and the Atlantic Republican Tradition* (2002). Other helpful studies include Philip Bobbitt, *The Garments of Court and Palace: Machiavelli and the World That He Made* (2013); Felix Gilbert, *Machiavelli and Guicciardini: Politics and History in Sixteenth Century Florence* (1965); Harvey C. Mansfield Jr., *Machiavelli's New Modes and Orders* (1979); Harvey C. Mansfield, *Machiavelli's Virtue*

(1996); Quentin Skinner, *Machiavelli* (1981). The best account of his populism is McCormick, *Machiavellian Democracy,* which my account draws upon heavily.

145. McCormick, *Machiavellian Democracy,* at 108–9.

146. Id. at 108.

147. James B. Atkinson and David Sices, introduction to *The Sweetness of Power* xiv–xv (James B. Atkinson and David Sices trans., 2002).

148. McCormick, *Machiavellian Democracy,* at 3–4.

149. Id.

150. Atkinson and Sices, *Sweetness of Power,* at xiv–xv.

151. Niccolò Machiavelli, *Discourses on the First Ten Books of Titus Livy* 1.2 (28), in *Sweetness of Power.*

152. Id. at 1.2 (28–29).

153. For further discussion, see Pocock, *Machiavellian Moment* 189–90.

154. Machiavelli, *Discourses,* at 1.2 (30).

155. Id. at 1.5 (36–37).

156. Id. at 1.6 (40–41).

157. Id. at 1.6 (42).

158. Id. at 1.2 (30).

159. Id. See Millar, *Roman Republic,* at 74, for a discussion.

160. Machiavelli, *Discourses,* at 1.4 (34–35).

161. Id.

162. Id.

163. Id. at 1.37 (105–6).

164. Id.

165. Id. at 1.37 (107).

166. McCormick, *Machiavellian Democracy,* at 4–5, makes this point.

167. Machiavelli, *Discourses,* at 1.5 (37).

168. Id. at 1.55 (141).

169. Id. at 1.2 (30), 1.3 (33).

170. Id. at 1.2 (30), 1.4 (35).

171. Id. at 1.3 (34).

172. Id. at 1.58 (148).

173. McCormick, *Machiavellian Democracy,* at 103.

174. Id. at 103–6.

175. Pocock, *Machiavellian Moment,* at 273–74, 296.

176. Id. at 296–97.

177. Id. at 308.

178. Id. at 308–9.

179. Id. at 309. Contemporary constitutional theorists have offered devastating criticisms of separation and balance of powers theories, but sur-

prisingly, Giannotti's argument is not among their central objections. See Eric A. Posner, "Balance-of-Powers Arguments and the Structural Constitution" (University of Chicago Institute for Law and Economics, Working Paper No. 622, 2012); M. Elizabeth Magill, "Beyond Powers and Branches in Separation of Powers Law," 150 *University of Pennsylvania Law Review* 603 (2001); M. Elizabeth Magill, "The Real Separation in Separation of Powers Law," 86 *Virginia Law Review* 1127 (2000).

180. Pocock, *Machiavellian Moment,* at 309–10.

181. Id. at 278, 287.

182. Id. at 297–98.

183. Id. at 302.

184. Id. at 297–98.

185. Id. at 298, 300.

186. Id. at 300.

187. There are traces of the idea in the writings of Nicole Oresme, a distinguished fourteenth-century French scientist, economist, mathematician, and bishop. Oresme seems to have understood mixed government's blend of democracy and oligarchy as implying that "the people of middle estate who are neither very rich or very poor hold the rule." James A. Blythe, *Ideal Government and the Mixed Constitution in the Middle Ages* 203, 228 (1992).

188. Pocock, *Machiavellian Moment,* at 295.

189. Aristotle, *Politics,* at 4.3.1289b30–32 (94), 4.11.1295b1–2 (107) ("Now in all states there are three elements: one class is very rich, another very poor, and a third in a mean").

190. Id. at 4.11.1295b5–28 (107); 3.4.1277a25–27 (66); Miller, *Nature,* at 264–66.

191. Aristotle, *Politics,* at 4.11.1295b29–33 (107–8), 4.11.1295b5–20 (107).

192. Id. at 4.11.1295b29–33 (107–8), 4.11.1295b5–20 (107).

193. Id. at 4.11.1296a1–5 (108).

194. Id. at 4.11.1296a13–18 (108).

195. Id. at 4.11.1295b21–23 (107).

196. Id. at 4.11.1296a7 (108).

197. Id. at 4.11.1295b.24–26 (107); Jill Frank, *A Democracy of Distinction* 177 (2005).

198. Political commentators have long held this view. Today, it is perhaps most prominent in explanations for Scandinavia's successful social democracy: a small homogeneous population creates a unified political community that is willing to invest—often great sums—in supporting each other. Scandinavia's greatest threat, according to this theory, is

losing its homogeneity. In the history of political thought, this idea undergirded the conventional wisdom that republican governments had to be small. The celebrated French philosopher Montesquieu argued in the eighteenth century that republican governments needed homogeneity and virtue to succeed and that this was only possible in a small republic. Montesquieu, *Spirit of the Laws,* at 8.16 (124). For a helpful analysis of the small republic thesis, see Jacob T. Levy, "Beyond Publius: Montesquieu, Liberal Republicanism, and the Small-Republic Thesis," 27 *History of Political Thought* 50 (2006). Large states inevitably had greater inequality and a variety of interests among citizens, making it harder for there to be a common good. Worse yet, even if there is a truly common good in a large state, it would be harder to identify. Montesquieu, *Spirit of the Laws,* at 8.16. In *Federalist* No. 10, James Madison famously argued that republics could exist in a large society because clashing factions would cancel each other out, allowing leaders with the common good in mind to emerge. *Federalist* No. 10 (Madison); for a discussion, see "Book Note: The Relevance and Irrelevance of the Founders," 120 *Harvard Law Review* 619 (2006). Aristotle had a different view. He actually suggested that *large* states were "less liable to faction than small ones" because "the middle class is large; whereas in the small states it is easy to divide all the citizens into two classes who are either rich or poor and leave nothing in the middle." Aristotle, *Politics,* at 4.11.1296a9–12 (108). Aristotle's point about size suffers from the same problem that afflicted Montesquieu and Madison. Size isn't the decisive variable. The decisive variable is the unity of the population in a political community. While Aristotle mistakenly linked unity to size, his more important insight was recognizing that a society with a large middle class will be relatively unified economically and therefore less likely to have strife along class lines.

199. Miller, *Nature,* at 266, 268.

200. Id. at 268 develops the game theory idea. Aristotle, *Politics,* at 4.11.1295b34–39 (108). For a discussion of the arbiter, see Aristotle, *Politics,* at 4.12.1296b35–1297a6 (110).

201. Aristotle, *Politics,* at 4.11.1295b34–39 (108), 4.11.1295b24–26 (107).

202. Id. at 4.11.1296a22–38 (108).

203. H. F. Russell Smith, *Harrington and His Oceana: A Study of a 17th Century Utopia and Its Influence in America* 3 (1914); John Aubrey, 1 *Brief Lives* 288 (Andrew Clark ed., 1898).

204. J. G. A. Pocock, introduction to James Harrington, *Commonwealth of Oceana; and, A System of Politics* viii (J. G. A. Pocock ed., 1992).

205. Id.; Aubrey, *Brief Lives,* at 288.

206. Aubrey, *Brief Lives*, at 288.

207. Id. at 288–89.

208. Pocock, *Machiavellian Moment*, at 383–84.

209. Harrington, *Commonwealth of Oceana*, at 10.

210. Pocock, *Machiavellian Moment*, at 386–87.

211. Harrington, *Commonwealth of Oceana*, at 11.

212. Id. at 11–12.

213. J. G. A. Pocock, *The Ancient Constitution and the Feudal Law* 128 (1987).

214. On Harrington as an English Machiavelli, see Pocock, *Machiavellian Moment*, at 385. On his agreement and disagreement with Machiavelli, see Eric Nelson, *The Greek Tradition in Republican Thought* 110, 112 (2004). My interpretation of Harrington aligns with Nelson's economic reading.

215. Harrington, *Commonwealth of Oceana*, at 33.

216. Id. at 155.

217. Nelson, *Greek Tradition*, at 112.

218. Harrington, *Commonwealth of Oceana*, at 20.

219. Id. at 33.

220. Pocock, *Machiavellian Moment*, at 387–88.

221. Harrington, *Commonwealth of Oceana*, at 33.

222. Id. at 13.

223. Id. at 37.

224. Id. at 44.

225. Id. at 37.

226. Id. at 43.

227. Id. at 54–56; Pocock, *Ancient Constitution*, at 139.

228. Id. at 55; Pocock, *Ancient Constitution*, at 139.

229. For discussion, see Pocock, introduction, at xix; Pocock, *Machiavellian Moment*, at 387–89; Smith, *Harrington and His Oceana*, at 29–30.

230. Smith, *Harrington and His Oceana*, at 30.

231. Pocock, *Machiavellian Moment*, at 385, 387; Smith, *Harrington and His Oceana*, at 30.

232. Harrington, *Commonwealth of Oceana*, at 60.

233. John Trenchard and Thomas Gordon, *Cato's Letters* 3.84 (Ronald Hamoway ed., 1995).

234. Nelson, *Greek Tradition*, at 141; Trenchard and Gordon, *Cato's Letters*, at 3.85; see also Pocock, *Machiavellian Moment*, at 474.

235. Nelson, *Greek Tradition*, at 141; Trenchard and Gordon, *Cato's Letters*, at 3.85.

236. David Hume, "Of the First Principles of Government," in *Selected Essays* 24, 25 (Stephen Copley and Andrew Edgar eds., 1993).

237. Id. at 27.

238. Hume, "Of the Middle Station of Life," in *Selected Essays,* at 5, 5.

239. Id. at 6.

240. Id. at 6–7.

241. Montesquieu, *Spirit of the Laws,* at 5.5 (45). For a discussion of Montesquieu along these lines, see Nelson, *Greek Tradition,* at 155–95.

242. Id. at 27 (523).

243. Id. at 5.5 (45).

244. Id. at 5.5 (46–47).

245. For scholars who have recognized the importance of Aristotle to Harrington, see Nelson, *Greek Tradition,* at 197; J. R. Pole, *Political Representation in England and the Origins of the American Republic* 8 (1966); Smith, *Harrington and His Oceana,* at 20. See also C. B. Macpherson, *The Political Theory of Possessive Individualism,* 162–63 (1962) (taking an economic approach to Harrington). For the more conventional view that Machiavelli is the key to Harrington, see Pocock, *Ancient Constitution,* at 129; Pocock, *Machiavellian Moment,* at 385. Pocock's revival of Harrington and placement of Harrington at the center of the post-Machiavellian story does extend, importantly, to America. See Pocock, *Machiavellian Moment,* at 506–52. Of particular note is his treatment of Noah Webster's views. Id. at 534–35. Nelson's study is the best recent treatment of Harrington's egalitarianism, and he also traces the tradition into early America.

Chapter Two: America's Middle-Class Constitution

1. "The Constitution: Prof. Beard's Startling Theory as to Influences Affecting Origin of the Famous Document," *New York Times,* Nov. 23, 1913, at 17.

2. "'Classes' in the Constitution," *Sun,* Aug. 17, 1913, at sec. 6, p. 6.

3. Forrest McDonald, *We the People: The Economic Interpretation of the Constitution* (1958); Robert E. Brown, *Charles Beard and the Constitution* (1956). For recent criticism from a "neo-Beardian," see Woody Holton, "The Readers' Reports Are In," 2 *American Political Thought* 264 (2013).

4. By "Beardian," I mean a focus on material, and especially economic, interests. For a discussion separating Beard from the broader Beardian argument, see Mark A. Graber, "Beard and Uber-Beard," 29 *Constitutional Commentary* 293 (2014).

5. Classics that fit in this tradition include J. Allen Smith, *The Spirit of American Government* (1907); Vernon Parrington, *Main Currents in American Thought* (1927); Merrill Jensen, *Articles of Confederation: An*

Interpretation of the Social-Constitutional History of the American Rev-olution, 1774–1781 (1940); Merrill Jensen, *The New Nation: A History of the United States During the Confederation, 1781–1789* (1950). Of course, there is a robust tradition that has opposed this line of think-ing, arguing instead that the Constitution was the culmination of the Revolutionary project and there can be no revolution without a new founding. See Hannah Arendt, *On Revolution* (1963) (arguing that rev-olutions require a new founding); Bruce Ackerman, *We the People,* vol. 1, *Foundations* (1991) (emphasizing the founding moment). See also Bernard Bailyn, "The Central Themes of the American Revolution: An Interpretation," in *Essays on the American Revolution* 3, 22 (Stephen G. Kurtz and James H. Hutzon eds., 1973) (noting that the Constitution "was neither a repudiation of '76, nor an instrument devised to protect aristocracies threatened in the states, nor the mark of a slaveholders' plot. It is a second-generation expression of the original ideological impulses of the Revolution applied to the everyday, practical problems of the 1780s").

6. Robert A. McGuire, *To Form a More Perfect Union: A New Economic Interpretation of the United States Constitution* (2003); Terry Bouton, *Taming Democracy: "The People," the Founders, and the Troubled Ending of the American Revolution* (2007); Woody Holton, *Unruly Americans and the Origins of the Constitution* (2007); Bartholomew Sparrow and Shannon Bow O'Brien, "Pulling Punches: Charles Beard, the Proper-tyless, and the Founding of the United States," 29 *Constitutional Com-mentary* 409, 410 (2014) ("The argument here is . . . not that Beard overplays his hand, but that he understates his case"). A different kind of Beardian argument, focusing on politics rather than economics, is Michael J. Klarman, *The Framers' Coup: The Making of the United States Constitution* (2016).

7. For a recent discussion of the dichotomy between ideas and interests in the context of Beard's history, see Jonathan Gienapp, "Using Beard to Overcome Beardianism: Charles Beard's Forgotten Historicism and the Ideas-Interests Dichotomy," 29 *Constitutional Commentary* 367 (2014). See also Morton J. Horwitz, "Republicanism and Liberalism in American Constitutional Thought," 29 *William and Mary Law Review* 57, 66 (1987) ("Bailyn's work is also directed primarily against Beard-ianism in American history. To the extent that Beard is a stand-in for Marx, Bailyn, like Pocock, focused his analysis on the reductionist base-superstructure methodology of orthodox European Marxism").

8. The classic texts are Bernard Bailyn, *The Ideological Origins of the American Revolution* (1967); Gordon S. Wood, *The Creation of the*

American Republic, 1776–1787 (1969); J. G. A. Pocock, *The Machiavellian Moment: Florentine Political Thought and the Atlantic Republican Tradition* (rev'd ed., 2002) (1975); Robert E. Shalhope, "Toward a Republican Synthesis: The Emergence of an Understanding of Republicanism in American Historiography," 29 *William and Mary Quarterly* 49 (1972). Legal scholars took up the republican mantle in the 1980s. See, for example, Cass R. Sunstein, "Interest Groups in American Public Law," 38 *Stanford Law Review* 29 (1985); Frank Michelman, "Law's Republic," 97 *Yale Law Journal* 1493 (1988); Cass R. Sunstein, "Beyond the Republican Revival," 97 *Yale Law Journal* 1593 (1988).

9. The classic statement is Louis Hartz, *The Liberal Tradition in America* (1955). See also Joyce Appleby, *Liberalism and Republicanism in the Historical Imagination* (1992); Jennifer Nedelsky, *Private Property and the Limits of American Constitutionalism* (1990); John Patrick Diggins, *The Lost Soul of American Politics* (1986).

10. By that, I don't mean the distinction between liberalism and republicanism. After decades of battle along those lines, a new generation of historians has largely reached a détente, agreeing that the founding era cannot be defined by a single philosophical tradition. See, for example, Jeffrey C. Isaac, "Republicanism vs. Liberalism? A Reconsideration," 9 *History of Political Thought* 349 (1988); James T. Kloppenberg, "The Virtues of Liberalism: Christianity, Republicanism, and Ethics in Early American Political Discourse," 74 *Journal of American History* 9 (1987); Michael Zuckert, *The National Rights Republic* 209 (1996) (describing the change as moving from "either/or" to "both/and"); Lance Banning, "Jeffersonian Ideology Revisited: Liberal and Classical Ideas in the New American Republic," 42 *William and Mary Quarterly* 11 (1987); Forrest McDonald, *Novus Ordo Seclorum: The Intellectual Origins of the Constitution* (1985). For a helpful overview, see Alan Gibson, "Ancients, Moderns, and Americans: The Republicanism-Liberalism Debate Revisited," 21 *History of Political Thought* 261 (2000).

11. Notably, there have been historians and political theorists who have recognized the importance of economic democracy. See, for example, Douglass Adair, *The Intellectual Origins of Jeffersonian Democracy* (2000); J. Franklin Jameson, *The American Revolution Considered as a Social Movement* 27–28 (1925) ("political democracy came to the United States as a result of economic democracy, that this nation came to be marked by political institutions of a democratic type because it had, still earlier, come to be characterized in its economic life by democratic arrangements and practices"); Robert E. Brown, "Economic Democracy Before the Constitution," 7 *American Quarterly*

257 (1955); Jackson Turner Main, *The Social Structure of Revolutionary America* 42 (1942) ("The outstanding feature of northern society was not its small wealthy class but the very large proportion of substantial middle-class property owners"); Arendt, *On Revolution*, at 68 ("The reason for success and failure [of the American Revolution] was that the predicament of poverty was absent from the American scene but present everywhere else in the world"). Notably, while the central takeaway from Wood's *Creation of the American Republic* was republicanism and the importance of social and ideological rather than economic factors, Wood also presents considerable evidence of egalitarian economic conditions. Some scholars have noticed this. See Horwitz, "Republicanism and Liberalism," at 66. This egalitarian tradition has recently been revived and explored thoroughly in excellent books: Eric Nelson, *Greek Tradition in Republican Thought* (2004); John P. McCormick, *Machiavellian Democracy* (2011). Legal scholars make this claim less frequently. For an example, see Akhil Reed Amar, "Republicanism and Minimal Entitlements: Of Safety Valves and the Safety Net," 11 *George Mason Law Review* 47 (1988) ("it is very difficult for a democracy to operate properly if it lacks a middle class").

12. William Manning, *The Key of Liberty* 157 (Michael Merrill and Sean Wilentz eds., 1993) (1799).

13. Gordon S. Wood, *The Radicalism of the American Revolution* 112 (1991). In comparison, the Earl of Derby's estates in England produced an annual income of more than £40,000. Id.

14. Id.

15. Id. at 113.

16. Id. at 122.

17. Peter H. Lindert and Jeffrey G. Williamson, *Unequal Gains: American Growth and Inequality Since 1700* 38 and table 2-4 (2016); Peter H. Lindert and Jeffrey G. Williamson, "American Incomes Before and After the Revolution," 73 *Journal of Economic History* 755–56 and table 7 (2013).

18. Anthony B. Atkinson and Salvatore Morelli, "Economic Inequality in USA," Chartbook of Economic Inequality, http://www.chartbookofeconomicinequality.com/inequality-by-country/usa/.

19. Id.

20. Lindert and Williamson, *Unequal Gains*, at 38 and table 2-4.

21. Atkinson and Morelli, "Economic Inequality in USA"; Anthony B. Atkinson and Salvatore Morelli, "Measures of Economic Inequality," Chartbook of Economic Inequality, http://www.chartbookofeco

nomicinequality.com/economic-inequality/measures-of-economic
-inequality/.

22. Atkinson and Morelli, "Economic Inequality in USA"; Atkinson and
Morelli, "Measures of Economic Inequality."

23. Atkinson and Morelli, "Economic Inequality in USA."

24. Lindert and Williamson, *Unequal Gains,* at 38 and table 2-4.

25. Id.

26. See Wood, *Radicalism,* at 21–22.

27. George Mason, draft of the Virginia Declaration of Rights, May 1776,
http://www.gunstonhall.org/georgemason/human_rights/vdr_first
_draft.html; http://www.loc.gov/exhibits/treasures/tr00.html#obj6.

28. David Ramsay, "An Oration on the Advantages of American Independence, Spoken Before a Public Assembly of the Inhabitants of
Charleston, in South Carolina, on July 4th, 1778," in *Republication of
the Principles and Acts of the Revolution in America* 375 (Hezekiah Niles
ed., 1876).

29. Drew R. McCoy, *The Elusive Republic: Political Economy in Jeffersonian
America* 20, 62–63, 121 (1980). This aligned with the four-stage theory
of political economy—hunting, pastorage, agriculture, and commerce.
America was in the agricultural stage, and many hoped it would stay
there. Id. at 19.

30. Benjamin Franklin, "Observations Concerning the Increase of Mankind, Peopling of Countries, &c." (1751), in 4 *The Papers of Benjamin
Franklin* 225 (Leonard W. Labaree ed., 1961).

31. Wood, *Creation,* at 72.

32. Main, *Social Structure,* at 163, 164–65 ("What made it even more
admired was the ease and rapidity with which the poor man could
become economically independent, and the remarkable opportunity for the man of modest property to become rich. Thus economic
abundance together with high mobility combined to minimize those
conflicts which might have grown out of the class structure and the
concentration of wealth").

33. Wood, *Radicalism,* at 197.

34. Wood, *Creation,* at 86–87.

35. Wood, *Radicalism,* at 287.

36. Charles Rappleye, *Robert Morris: Financier of the American Revolution*
(2010); Robert McCloskey, introduction to 1 *The Works of James Wilson* 44 (Robert McCloskey ed., 1967).

37. See, for example, Woody Holton, *Forced Founders* (1999); Carol Berkin,
Revolutionary Mothers: Women in the Struggle for Independence (2005);

Peter Silver, *Our Savage Neighbors: How Indian War Transformed Early America* (2008); Alfred F. Young, Gary B. Nash, and Ray Raphael, eds., *Revolutionary Founders: Rebels, Radicals, and Reformers in the Making of the Nation* (2011); Alan Taylor, *The Internal Enemy: Slavery and War in Virginia, 1772–1832* (2013).

38. Gary B. Nash, *The Unknown American Revolution* 63 (2005).

39. Id. at 289.

40. Id. at 288–89; Judith Apter Klinghoffer and Lois Elkins, "'The Petticoat Electors': Women's Suffrage in New Jersey, 1776–1807," 12 *Journal of the Early Republic* 159 (1992).

41. Bouton, *Taming Democracy*, at 53.

42. Wood, *Radicalism*, at 186.

43. Lindert and Williamson, *Unequal Gains*, at 39 and table 2-5.

44. Brazil was .527 in 2012; Haiti was .608 in 2012; South Africa was .634 in 2011. See World Bank GINI Index, http://data.worldbank.org/indi cator/SI.POV.GINI/countries?order=wbapi_data_value_2012%20 wbapi_data_value&sort=asc&display=default.

45. Lindert and Williamson, *Unequal Gains*, at 39 and table 2-5.

46. Id. at 38–39 and tables 2-4 and 2-5.

47. Id. at 37.

48. Wood, *Radicalism*, at 123.

49. Samuel Peters, *General History of Connecticut* 220–21 (1877) (1781). Peters also notes that "estates pass from generation to generation by gavelkind," which was a rule that divided lands among sons, as opposed to primogeniture. "A general mediocrity of station being thus constitutionally promoted, it is no wonder that the rich man is despised, and the poor man's blessing is his poverty." For discussion of these themes, see Wood, *Radicalism*, at 123.

50. For a full discussion of the founders' extensive knowledge of the classics from ancient Greece and Rome, see Carl J. Richard, *The Founders and the Classics* (1994); see also Fergus Millar, *Roman Republic in Political Thought* 120–34 (2002); Andrew Lintott, *The Constitution of the Roman Republic* 251–56 (1999). For a contemporary discussion of the distinction between possessing property and the distribution of property, see Frank I. Michelman, "Possession vs. Distribution in the Constitutional Idea of Property," 72 *Iowa Law Review* 1319 (1987). Modern property theorists have also recognized the importance of the distribution of property to the structure of government. See, e.g., Joseph W. Singer, "Property as the Law of Democracy," 63 *Duke Law Journal* 1287 (2014); Joseph W. Singer, "Original Acquisition of Property: From Conquest and Possession to Democracy and Equal

Opportunity," 86 *Indiana Law Journal* 763 (2011). Joseph W. Singer, "Democratic Estates: Property Law in a Free and Democratic Society," 94 *Cornell Law Review* 1009 (2009).

51. Adams to James Sullivan, May 26, 1776, in 9 *The Works of John Adams* 376–77 (Charles Francis Adams ed., 1854).

52. An anonymous Charleston writer in 1783 held that "[n]atural law imparts an equality of property" and that "America has not yet departed far from the rule of right." Citing *Cato's Letters* and echoing Harrington, the nameless writer noted that "men in moderate circumstances, are most virtuous. An equality of estate, will give an equality of power; and equality of power is a natural commonwealth." Nelson, *Greek Tradition,* at 211. Federal Farmer agreed, "If there are advantages in the equal division in our lands . . . we ought to establish governments calculated to give duration to them." Federal Farmer V, Oct. 13, 1787, in Herbert Storing, 2 *The Complete Anti-Federalist* 251 (1981). The Massachusetts arch-Federalist Fisher Ames, in 1796, asked, "Can liberty, such as we understand and enjoy, exist in societies where the few only have property . . . ?" Clement Fatovic, *America's Founding and the Struggle over Economic Inequality* 13 (2015). The First Kentucky Convention, in the winter of 1784–85, also recognized the point: "That to grant any Person a larger quantity of Land than he designs Bona Fide to seat himself or his Family on, is a greevance, Because it is subversive of the fundamental Principles of a free republican Government to allow any individual, or Company or Body of Men to possess such large tracts of Country in their own right as may at a future Day give them undue influence." Jackson Turner Main, *The Antifederalists: Critics of the Constitution, 1781–1788* 1 (1961).

53. Nelson, *Greek Tradition,* at 210.

54. Id. at 221; Centinel I, Oct. 5, 1787, in Storing, *Complete Anti-Federalist,* at 136, 139.

55. Noah Webster, *An Examination into the Leading Principles of the Federal Constitution,* in *Pamphlets on the Constitution of the United States* 25, 57 (Paul Leicester Ford ed., 1968) (1787).

56. Id. at 59.

57. Id.

58. Id. at 57.

59. Id. at 57–58.

60. Id. at 59.

61. Id. at 60.

62. Noah Webster, "Remarks on the Manners, Government, and Debt of the United States," in *A Collection of Essays and Fugitiv Writings* 88

(1790, reprinted 1977). The quotation is revised to modernize the spelling.

63. Giles Hickory [Noah Webster] III, Feb. 1788, in *The Debate on the Constitution: Part II* 311 (Bernard Bailyn ed., 1993).

64. They didn't usually refer to the "middle class" per se. Instead they used a variety of terms: "neither rich nor poor," "middling class," "honest sober men, who mind their business," "middling," "the middling Kind," "middle sort," "middling Rank." For these and other class division terms from the era, see Main, *Social Structure,* at 230–33. Benjamin Franklin, for example, referred to the "happy Mediocrity" of people in America, compared with the "few rich and haughty Landlords, the multitude of poor, abject and rack'd Tenants, and the half-paid and half starv'd ragged Labourers" in Europe and concluded that "no Nation that is known to us enjoys a greater Share of human Felicity" than America. Fatovic, *America's Founding,* at 16.

65. Wood, *Creation,* at 231.

66. Nelson, *Greek Tradition,* at 213.

67. Wood, *Creation,* at 230.

68. Nelson, *Greek Tradition,* at 219. He noted that primogeniture laws were "gone or going, out of use" and that land could not be entailed, and so believed "the period must be distant, very far distant, when there can be such a monopoly of landed estates, as to throw the suffrages or even influence of electors into few hands . . . where is the risk of an *aristocracy* dangerous to liberty?" Arthur Browne, an Anglican clergyman, held that Americans were "without nobility, or orders of gentry." Wood, *Radicalism,* at 20.

69. James T. Kloppenberg, *Toward Democracy: The Struggle for Self-Rule in European and American Thought* 364 (2016).

70. The author was John Stevens in his *Observations on Government.* See Wood, *Creation,* at 583.

71. Or take Virginia. In *The Virginia Gazette* in 1776, "Hampden" wrote in support of revolution, linking America's equality with the possibility of republican government. Because of America's different system of "tenure of landed property, and the absence of *hereditary distinctions of rank,*" a monarchy or aristocracy was impossible. "Who among us," Hampden asked, "has pretensions to the *throne?*" Holton, *Forced Founders,* at 192. Future President James Monroe echoed the sentiment, observing in 1788, "the government of Rome acknowledged distinct orders of people, in which indeed the aristocracy prevailed, and can of course furnish no example for us." James Monroe, "Some

Observations on the Constitution," May 25, 1788, in 9 *The Documentary History of the Ratification of the Constitution* 855 (John P. Kaminski and Gaspare J. Saladino eds., 1990) (hereinafter cited as *DHRC*).

72. Wood, *Creation*, at 100. Another, Robert Goodloe Harper, said, "Fortunately for America, there are few *sans-culottes* among her inhabitants, very few indeed. Except some small portions of rabble in a few towns, the character is unknown among us; and hence our safety. Our people are all, or very nearly all, proprietors of land, spread over a vast extent of country, where they live in ease and freedom; strangers alike to oppression and want." Fatovic, *America's Founding*, at 15.

73. Speech of Charles Pinckney on Monday, June 25, 1787, in Max Farrand, 1 *Records of the Federal Convention of 1787* 398–402 (1911).

74. Civis [David Ramsay], "To the Citizens of South Carolina," *Columbian Herald* (Charleston, S.C.), Feb. 4, 1788, in 16 *DHRC* 26.

75. Wood, *Creation*, at 99. Another English radical, Richard Price, commented that America was made up of "only a body of yeomanry supported by agriculture, and all independent, and nearly upon a level." Id.

76. Nelson, *Greek Tradition*, at 230–31.

77. Wood, *Radicalism*, at 347. Wood concludes that "in America, in the North at least, already it seemed as if the so-called middle class was all there was." See also Gordon S. Wood, *Empire of Liberty* 28–30 (2009).

78. Wood, *Radicalism*, at 347–48.

79. Jefferson to John Adams, Oct. 28, 1813, in *The Founders' Constitution* (Philip B. Kurland and Ralph Lerner eds., 1986).

80. Noah Webster, "On the Education of Youth in America," in *Collection of Essays and Fugitiv Writings*, at 24. The quotation is revised to modernize the spelling.

81. James Madison, "Parties," *National Gazette*, Jan. 23, 1792, in *James Madison: Writings* 504 (Jack N. Rakove ed., 1999).

82. Adams to John Jebb, Aug. 21, 1785, in 11 *Works*, at 533.

83. Madison, "Parties," at 504.

84. See also Stanley N. Katz, "Republicanism and the Law of Inheritance in the American Revolutionary Era," 76 *Michigan Law Review* 1 (1977); Holly Brewer, "Entailing Aristocracy in Colonial Virginia: Ancient Feudal Restraints and Revolutionary Reform," 54 *William and Mary Quarterly* 307 (1997).

85. Thomas Jefferson, *Autobiography* 77, in 1 *The Works of Thomas Jefferson* (Paul Leicester Ford ed., 1904) (noting that these bills, along with education and freedom of religion, formed "a system by which

every fibre would be eradicated of antient or future aristocracy; and a foundation laid for a government truly republican"). Nelson, *Greek Tradition,* at 201–2.

86. Jefferson to Adams, Oct. 28, 1813, in *The Adams-Jefferson Letters* 389 (Lester J. Cappon ed., 1959).

87. Jefferson to James Madison, Oct. 28, 1785, in 8 *The Papers of Thomas Jefferson* 681–82 (Julian P. Boyd ed., 1953).

88. James Kent, 4 *Commentaries on American Law* 20 (1826).

89. Nelson, *Greek Tradition,* at 232.

90. St. George Tucker, 3 *Blackstone's Commentaries* 119n14 (1803). Of course, the history of these provisions is tied up in the political and economic context of the time. One scholar has argued that the entail's primary function was to protect family wealth from creditors and that abolition of the entail was partly related to the desire to promote fluid land markets in the context of a slave-based economy in the South. Claire Priest, "The End of Entail: Information, Institutions, and Slavery in the American Revolutionary Period," 33 *Law and History Review* 277 (2015).

91. Madison, "Parties," at 504.

92. Kloppenberg, *Toward Democracy,* at 307 (2016).

93. Jefferson to James Madison, Oct. 28, 1785, in 8 *Papers of Thomas Jefferson,* at 681–82. The Maryland Declaration of Rights declared that "the levying [of] taxes by the poll is grievous and oppressive, and ought to be abolished; that paupers ought not to be assessed for the support of the government; but every other person in the State ought to contribute his proportion of public taxes, for the support of government, according to his actual worth, in real or personal property, within the State." Even the elite Gouverneur Morris held, "It is confessed on all hands that taxes should be raised from individuals in proportion to their wealth." Fatovic, *America's Founding,* at 30. Thomas Tudor Tucker, an Anti-Federalist in South Carolina, said the "true principle of taxation is, that every man contribute to the public burthens in proportion to the value of his property." April 16, 1789, 1st Cong., 1st Sess., 1 *Debates and Proceedings of the Congress of the United States* 165–66 (Joseph Gales ed., 1834); Fatovic, *America's Founding,* at 140.

94. Nelson, *Greek Tradition,* at 212; Anonymous, "Rudiments of Law and Government Deduced from the Law of Nature," Charleston 1783, in 1 *American Political Writings During the Founding Era, 1760–1805* 579 (Charles S. Hyneman and Donald S. Lutz eds., 1983).

95. Jefferson to James Madison, Oct. 28, 1785, in 8 *Papers of Thomas Jefferson,* at 681–82.

96. Wood, *Radicalism,* at 179; Fatovic, *America's Founding,* at 211.

97. See Robert S. Hill, "Federalism, Republicanism, and the Northwest Ordinance," 18 *Publius* 41 (Autumn 1988); Matthew J. Festa, "Property and Republicanism in the Northwest Ordinance," 45 *Arizona State Law Journal* 409 (2013). The classic overview is Peter S. Onuf, *Statehood and Union: A History of the Northwest Ordinance* (1987).

98. Of course, Pocock in his classic study, *The Machiavellian Moment,* recognizes both aspects of Harrington. But the conventional "republican" emphasis is on virtue, not wealth. See Nelson, *Greek Tradition,* at 87–126. It is also worth pointing out that this tradition is not Marxist. The goal is not economic equality and abundance not for its own sake, but for the sake of preserving republican freedom. See Arendt, *On Revolution,* at 62–64 (discussing Marx's view that the goal of revolution became "[n]ot freedom but abundance").

99. Of course there were big differences as well. Locke, to be sure, saw politics and society as divided in a way that the ancients did not and that the egalitarian foundations of republicanism necessarily reject. For a nice discussion, with application to the American context, see Adair, *Intellectual Origins,* at 96–104.

100. Leonard L. Richards, *Shays's Rebellion* 8–9 (2002). Other helpful histories of Shays's Rebellion include David P. Szatmary, *Shays' Rebellion* (1980), and Robert A. Gross, ed., *In Debt to Shays* (1993). For an account of the Regulators' concerns with the court system, and of the court system at the time generally, see Claire Priest, "Colonial Courts and Secured Credit: Early American Commercial Litigation and Shays' Rebellion," 108 *Yale Law Journal* 2413 (1999).

101. Richards, *Shays's Rebellion,* at 9.

102. Id. at 10–11.

103. Id. at 12.

104. Id. at 11–12.

105. Id. at 53. For a rich discussion of debt during the founding period, see generally Bruce Mann, *Republic of Debtors* (2002). Mann also notes that the creditor/debtor split was not always sharp; often a single person could be both a creditor and a debtor. Id. at 188.

106. Richards, *Shays's Rebellion,* at 14.

107. Id. at 16–18.

108. Id. at 23–25, 29.

109. Id. at 34.

110. Holton, *Unruly Americans,* at 146.

111. Szatmary, *Shays' Rebellion,* at 124–26.

112. Holton, *Unruly Americans,* at 145.

113. Szatmary, *Shays' Rebellion*, at 126.
114. Hartz, *Liberal Tradition*, at 5.
115. For an overview of the histories on the American Revolution as a social movement, see Jack P. Greene, "The Social Origins of the American Revolution: An Evaluation and an Interpretation," 88 *Political Science Quarterly* 1, 2–4 (1973). See also Jensen, *New Nation*, at 21.
116. The modern, updated version is expressed well in Bouton, *Taming Democracy*, at 4–5. See also Fatovic, *America's Founding*, at 58 (The framers "sought to limit the ability of popular majorities to enact paper money laws and other policies that would threaten private property, damage the credit of the United States, drive away capital investment, and ultimately hamper economic development").
117. Arendt, *On Revolution*, at 68, 126, 142. There are some differences within this final camp. Arendt focuses more on public freedom. Ackerman emphasizes the mobilization and participation of the people. Ackerman, *Foundations*, at 206 (distinguishing his approach from that of Beard and Arendt). Gordon Wood notes the importance of virtuous leadership. Wood, *Creation*, at 65–70, 508. There are other explanations as well, including a generational explanation, see Stanley Elkins and Eric McKitrick, "The Founding Fathers: Young Men of the Revolution," 76 *Political Science Quarterly* 181 (1961), and a state-building explanation, see Max M. Edling, *A Revolution in Favor of Government* (2003).
118. To put it differently, Arendt agrees that America's lack of poverty was critical to its Revolutionary experience focusing on public freedom, rather than on "the social question" (of poverty). Arendt, *On Revolution*, at 68. But she ignores the possibility that the founding also had an economic component to it. My position aligns with a variety of historians who have emphasized the economic breakdown of the 1780s. See Holton, *Unruly Americans*, at 26–28 (although Holton reaches a different ultimate conclusion); Roger H. Brown, *Redeeming the Republic* (1993). It also echoes an earlier tradition in American history of emphasizing America's economic democracy. See Adair, *Ideological Origins;* Jameson, *Social Movement.* In the literature on republicanism, the best exponent is Drew McCoy. See McCoy, *Elusive Republic.*
119. Holton, *Unruly Americans*, at 26–28; Brown, *Redeeming the Republic*, at 36; Allan Kulikoff, "'Such Things Ought Not to Be': The American Revolution and the First National Great Depression," in *The World of the American Revolution and Republic: Land, Labor, and the Conflict for a Continent* 134, 144 (Andrew Shankman ed., 2014).
120. Nash, *Unknown American Revolution*, at 308–9.

121. Id. at 310.
122. Id. at 313.
123. Id. at 311–12.
124. Id. at 318–19.
125. Lindert and Williamson, *Unequal Gains,* at 93.
126. Bouton, *Taming Democracy,* at 92. Note that orders can be issued multiple times on the same property.
127. Id. at 91; Lindert and Williamson, *Unequal Gains,* at 85–86; Kulikoff, "'Such Things Ought Not to Be.'"
128. Pauline Maier, *Ratification* 11 (2010); Holton, *Unruly Americans,* at 67–69; Brown, *Redeeming the Republic,* at 12.
129. Brown, *Redeeming the Republic,* at 12, 26.
130. Id. at 12.
131. Holton, *Unruly Americans,* at 134–36.
132. Id. at 137, 140–43.
133. Id. at 136; Brown, *Redeeming the Republic,* at 22–24; Ferguson, *Power of the Purse,* at 152–53.
134. Brown, *Redeeming the Republic,* at 22–24; Ferguson, *Power of the Purse,* at 239–40.
135. There were six requisitions between 1781 and 1787, bringing in $5,071,237 to the Treasury. Each requisition, however, brought in less and less money. By the spring of 1787, "the states had paid two-thirds of the requisitions of October 1781 and April 1784, but only 35 percent of the September 1782 requisition, 20 percent of the 1785 requisition, and 2 percent of the August 1786 requisition. . . . In the six months before March 31, 1787, the Treasury received no more than $663 to meet current expenses." Edling, *A Revolution in Favor of Government,* at 155. See also Brown, *Redeeming the Republic,* at 25–26; Ferguson, *Power of the Purse,* at 220–25.
136. Holton, *Unruly Americans,* at 136; Brown, *Redeeming the Republic,* at 11–13.
137. Holton, *Unruly Americans,* at 65–66.
138. Brown, *Redeeming the Republic,* at 36–37.
139. Id. at 33.
140. Holton, *Unruly Americans,* at 128.
141. Brown, *Redeeming the Republic,* at 12.
142. Id. at 37–38.
143. Holton, *Unruly Americans,* at 29–30.
144. Id. at 65–66.
145. Farrand, 2 *Records,* at 307.
146. Holton, *Unruly Americans,* at 55, 58–61.

147. Not every state faced this backlash. Some states, like Connecticut, New York, North Carolina, and Georgia, already had relief-oriented majorities. See Edling, *Revolution in Favor,* at 156.

148. Holton, *Unruly Americans,* at 76. There seem to be some discrepancies on the exact percent of House members ousted. Brown claims it was 71 percent in the spring 1787 elections. Brown, *Redeeming the Republic,* at 119–20.

149. Holton, *Unruly Americans,* at 76.

150. Id. at 77, 81. For a state-by-state account, see Brown, *Redeeming the Republic,* at 53–140.

151. Holton, *Unruly Americans,* at 81–82.

152. Id. at 101–3.

153. Id. at 101–4.

154. Id. at 85–87. For a fascinating discussion of Adams, see Woody Holton, "Abigail Adams: Bond Speculator," 64 *William and Mary Quarterly* 821 (2007).

155. Holton, *Unruly Americans,* at 96–98.

156. Id. at 8–12, 23–25, 64, 275; Brown, *Redeeming the Republic,* at 3.

157. The sentiment was widespread. Other examples include Justice William Whiting of Berkshire County, Massachusetts, who linked interest rates to aristocracy, asking, "what more ready method can be devised to enrich and aggrandize a number of individuals at the expence of the community at large and thereby put it in their power to introduce that odious state of Aristocracy, to the utter subversion of our present republican constitution, than by permitting them to draw from the people near fifty p[er] Cent interest" on war bonds? Holton, *Unruly Americans,* at 108–9. Abraham Clark of New Jersey wrote in 1786 that the "inequality of property which is detrimental to a republican government" would turn America into an English-style land of "lords and tenants." Nash, *Unknown American Revolution,* at 447.

158. Main, *Social Structure,* at 237.

159. Holton, *Unruly Americans,* at 109.

160. Brown, *Redeeming the Republic,* at xi, 176–77. Madison "feared that a bankrupt Congress would disband and that the Union would devolve into regional republics. He also worried that the perceived instability of the state governments would turn the propertied classes against republican government and toward monarchy."

161. Id. at 176–77.

162. Remarks of James Madison, June 26, 1787; Alexander Hamilton, June 26, 1787, in Farrand, 1 *Records,* at 423–24.

163. See also Holton, *Unruly Americans,* at 211 (arguing that the biggest

compromises were between the framers and the absent, but influential, American people).

164. See, for example, Michael W. McConnell, "Contract Rights and Property Rights: A Case Study in the Relationship Between Individual Liberties and Constitutional Structure," 76 *California Law Review* 267 (1988). See also G. Edward White, "The Political Economy of the Original Constitution," 35 *Harvard Journal of Law & Public Policy* 61, 71 (2012) (noting the fear that private property was insecure from state legislatures' redistributive tendencies, but not mentioning the import-export clause).

165. See, for example, Boris I. Bittker and Brannon P. Denning, "The Import-Export Clause," 68 *Mississippi Law Journal* 521 (1998). See also Erik M. Jensen, "The Export Clause," 6 *Florida Tax Review* 1 (2003).

166. For a discussion, see Thomas W. Merrill, "Public Contracts, Private Contracts, and the Transformation of Constitutional Order," 37 *Case Western Reserve Law Review* 597 (1987); Richard A. Epstein, "Toward a Revitalization of the Contract Clause," 51 *University of Chicago Law Review* 703 (1984); Douglas W. Kmiec and John O. McGinnis, "The Contract Clause: A Return to the Original Understanding," 14 *Hastings Constitutional Law Quarterly* 525 (1987).

167. The tariff had another benefit: It had a built-in check on its abuse. If the tariff was set too high, smuggling would increase, leading to a reduction in revenues. See Edling, *Revolution in Favor,* at 185. Robin Einhorn has recently argued that the impost/tariff provisions were a way to generate federal revenue without having to calculate taxes, given the challenges of southern slavery. See Robin L. Einhorn, *American Taxation, American Slavery* 113, 147–49 (2006). As with many parts of the Constitution, slavery loomed in the background, but that does not mean the economic explanation is also not an essential one.

168. Fatovic, *America's Founding,* at 137; Fergus M. Bordewich, *The First Congress* 38–39 (2016) (discussing the first four bills Madison introduced—on the tariff, tonnage fees on ships discriminating based on origin, tariff collection at ports, and federal control of lighthouses, beacons, and buoys).

169. An Act for Laying a Duty on Goods, Wares, and Merchandises Imported into the United States, 1 Stat. 24, July 4, 1789. The first piece of legislation, signed into law on June 1, 1789, governed the oath that government officials would take. For a discussion of the tariff bill, see also Douglas A. Irwin, "Revenue or Reciprocity? Founding Feuds over Early U.S. Trade Policy," in *Founding Choices: American Economic Policy in the 1790s* 98–100 (Douglas A. Irwin and Richard Sylla eds.,

2011); Fatovic, *America's Founding,* at 137; Bordewich, *First Congress,* at 38–39; Einhorn, *American Taxation,* at 149–54.

170. Holton, *Unruly Americans,* at 267.

171. Edling, *Revolution in Favor,* at 211–12.

172. Id. at 212.

173. Alexander Hamilton, "New York Ratifying Convention. Notes for a Second Speech of July 17," 5 *The Papers of Alexander Hamilton* 173 (Harold Syrett ed., 1962). In his list of the vices of the Confederation, James Madison's first entry was the failure of the States to produce the needed revenue under the requisition system. James Madison, "Vices of the Political System of the United States," 9 *Papers of James Madison* 348 (William T. Hutchinson et al. eds., 1975).

174. Klarman, *The Framers' Coup,* at 27* (2016).

175. Holton, *Unruly Americans,* at 232–33.

176. Id. at 241.

177. One of the Middle-Interest, *Massachusetts Centinel,* Dec. 5, 1787, in 4 *DHRC,* at 387.

178. Id. at 388. This view was understood in other states as well. See, for example, A Native of Virginia, "Observations on the Proposed Plan of Federal Government," April 2, 1788, in 9 *DHRC* 663 (expecting that "impost duties will in all likelihood answer all the purposes of government," making direct taxation unnecessary).

179. A Farmer, "To the Farmers of Connecticut," *New Haven Gazette,* Oct. 18, 1787, in 3 *DHRC,* at 392–93.

180. Id. at 393.

181. Cincinnatus V, "To James Wilson, Esquire," *New York Journal,* Nov. 29, 1787, and Cato VI, *New York Journal,* Dec. 13, 1787, in 19 *DHRC,* at 325, 417.

182. Judge Dana, Massachusetts Convention Debate, Afternoon, Jan. 18, 1788, Rufus King, Massachusetts Convention Debate, Afternoon, Jan. 21, 1788, in 6 *DHRC,* at 1250, 1286–87; Robert Livingston, New York Convention Debate, Morning, June 19, 1788, in 22 *DHRC,* at 1684.

183. Holton, *Unruly Americans,* at 242.

184. Georgia and Pennsylvania were quick to ratify as well—Georgia largely because of conflict with the Creek Indians. In Pennsylvania, ratification was hurried and contentious. Brown, *Redeeming the Republic,* at 211–13. See also Main, *Antifederalists,* at 72–102 (noting states that would benefit from the impost, and the few limited states that would not, and their internal divides).

185. Brown, *Redeeming the Republic,* at 211–13; Holton, *Unruly Americans,* at 241. People at the time recognized this. Patrick Henry, for example,

argued to the Virginia ratifying convention that Connecticut and New Jersey supported the Constitution because they were non-importation states that benefitted from the impost provisions. Patrick Henry, "Debates in the Virginia Convention," June 9, 1788, in 9 *DHRC* 1057.

186. Maier, *Ratification,* at 345–48.
187. Id. at 347.
188. 22 *DHRC,* at 1750.
189. Id.
190. Id. at 1750–51.
191. Id. at 1751.
192. Id. at 1750.
193. Id. at 1751.
194. Id.
195. Id. at 1752.
196. Id. at 1751–52.
197. Id. at 1753.
198. Id. at 1771.
199. Id. at 1768.
200. Id.
201. Id. at 1771–72.
202. Id. at 1772.
203. Id.
204. Id. at 1796.
205. Wood, *Creation,* at 524.
206. *Federalist* No. 57, at 318 (Madison) (Clinton Rossiter ed., 1999). In *Federalist* No. 39, Madison makes a similar comment: "It is essential to [a republican] government that it be derived from the great body of the society, not from an inconsiderable proportion or a favored class of it; otherwise a handful of tyrannical nobles, exercising their oppressions by a delegation of their powers, might aspire to the rant of republicans and claim for their government the honorable title of republic." *Federalist* No. 39, at 209 (Madison).
207. *Federalist* No. 57, at 319 (Madison).
208. Id.
209. Id. at 320–21.
210. Bernard Manin, *The Principles of Representative Government* 112 (1997).
211. Federal Farmer VII, Dec. 31, 1787, in Storing, 2 *Complete Anti-Federalist,* at 267.
212. This may be because the Anti-Federalists did not develop their arguments sufficiently well and because the Federalists knew elections

would have aristocratic effects. Manin, *Principles,* at 114, 116. It is worth noting that John Adams worried deeply about informal distinctions in society. See, e.g., Adams, *Defence,* in 5 *Works,* at 488.

213. Nash, *Unknown American Revolution,* at 296–97.

214. Id. at 298–99; Pole, *Political Representation,* at 182–204; see also Wood, *Creation,* at 217–18.

215. Remarks of John Dickinson, June 7, 1787, in Farrand, 1 *Records,* at 150, 158.

216. Remarks of Charles Cotesworth Pinckney, June 26, 1787, in Farrand, 1 *Records,* at 426.

217. On suffrage, see Remarks of Gouverneur Morris, Thomas Fitzsimmons, and John Dickinson, Aug. 7, 1787, in Farrand, 2 *Records,* at 201–2. On fiscal legislation, see Remarks of James Wilson, Aug. 13, 1787, in Farrand, 2 *Records,* at 274–75. The power was one that even the British House of Lords did not have. Holton, *Unruly Americans,* at 194. Elbridge Gerry responded that "the acceptance of the plan [the Constitution] will inevitably fail, if the Senate not be restrained from originating Money bills." Remarks of Elbridge Gerry, Aug. 13, 1787, in Farrand, 2 *Records,* at 275. See also Holton, *Unruly Americans,* at 194–96.

218. Klarman, *The Framers' Coup,* at 180–81.

219. For a discussion of downstream ratification constraints, see Jon Elster, "Forces and Mechanisms in the Constitution-Making Process," 45 *Duke Law Journal* 364, 373 (1995).

220. For example, Edmund Randolph, in considering the power to initiate money bills, worried about the aggregation of a variety of provisions: "When the people behold in the Senate, the countenance of an aristocracy; and in the president, the form at least of a little monarch, will not their alarms be sufficiently raised without taking from their immediate representatives" the power to initiate appropriation bills? Remarks of Edmund Randolph, Aug. 13, 1787, in Farrand, 2 *Records,* at 278–79. Holton, *Unruly Americans,* at 194.

221. Remarks of James Wilson, June 7, 1787, in Farrand, 1 *Records,* at 153. I have modernized the abbreviation of "government."

222. Remarks of Elbridge Gerry, June 12, 1787, in Farrand, 1 *Records,* at 215. Holton, *Unruly Americans,* at 191.

223. Remarks of Oliver Ellsworth, Aug. 7, 1787, in Farrand, 2 *Records,* at 201.

224. M. J. C. Vile, *Constitutionalism and the Separation of Powers* 7, 14, 37 (2nd ed. 1998); Wood, *Creation,* at 584, 606–7.

225. Storing, 1 *Complete Anti-Federalist,* at 233.

226. Arendt, *On Revolution,* at 226.

227. Nedelsky, *Private Property,* at 67, 80.

228. Remarks of James Wilson, June 7, 1787, in Farrand, 1 *Records,* at 153.

229. Indeed, historians have shown that after the Revolution the state legislatures were composed of fewer elites and more men from modest backgrounds. See Jackson Turner Main, "Government by the People: The American Revolution and the Democratization of the Legislatures," 23 *William and Mary Quarterly* 391 (1966).

230. Arendt, *On Revolution,* at 226; see also Wood, *Creation,* at 553–62.

231. Remarks of James Madison, June 26, 1787, in Farrand, 1 *Records,* at 421. I have modified the text of Madison's notes to expand the abbreviated "agst." to "against."

232. Wilson, 1 *Works,* at 291, 414–17, 419.

233. Wilson, 2 *Works,* at 772.

234. Skeptics who seem to have preferred class warfare constitutional structures also interpreted the Constitution in these terms. Alexander Hamilton wondered at the Constitutional Convention how checks would work if "[a] democratic assembly is to be checked by a democratic senate, and both these by a democratic chief magistrate." Farrand, 1 *Records,* at 310. Hamilton seems to have believed that checks had to be based on class—and that the Senate did not accomplish this task. See also Daryl J. Levinson, "Foreword—Looking for Power in Public Law," 130 *Harvard Law Review* 1, 95 (2016).

235. Robert J. Dinkin, *Voting in Revolutionary America* 27 (1982).

236. Id. at 31–40. In some states, like Connecticut, Delaware, and Rhode Island, there were no changes. Id. at 35–36.

237. Id. at 31–33.

238. Id. at 36–39.

239. On New York and other lower-suffrage states, see id. at 38–39. For the transition, see Chilton Williamson, *American Suffrage: From Property to Democracy, 1760–1860* (1960). For updated accounts of the transition that are critical of Williamson's Whiggish history, see Robert J. Steinfeld, "Property and Suffrage in the Early American Republic," 41 *Stanford Law Review* 335 (1989); Jacob Katz Cogan, "The Look Within: Property, Capacity, and Suffrage in Nineteenth-Century America," 107 *Yale Law Journal* 473 (1997) (arguing that people in the eighteenth century looked to external factors like property to determine political participation but in the nineteenth century shifted to internal factors like innate capacity, inheritable traits, and intelligence).

240. Gordon S. Wood, *Revolutionary Characters* 16 (2006).

241. J. G. A. Pocock, *Virtue, Commerce, and History* 103 (1985) ("The citi-

zen possessed property in order to be autonomous and autonomy was necessary for him to develop virtue or goodness as an actor within the political, social and natural realm or order. He did not possess it in order to engage in trade, exchange or profit; indeed, these activities were hardly compatible with the activity of citizenship"); see also William Michael Treanor, "The Original Understanding of the Takings Clause and the Political Process," 95 *Columbia Law Review* 782, 819–25 (1995). Cf. Arendt, *On Revolution,* at 180 ("In the eighteenth century . . . property and freedom still coincided; who said property, said freedom, and to recover or defend one's property rights was the same as to fight for freedom"); Michelman, "Possession vs. Distribution," at 1329 (discussing this theory).

242. McCoy, *Elusive Republic,* at 68.

243. Treanor, "Original Understanding," at 822.

244. Nedelsky, *Private Property,* at 82; Robert Coram, a Revolutionary War veteran and newspaper editor, commented in 1791, "If they are dependent, they can neither manage their private concerns properly, retain their own dignity, or vote impartially for their country; they can be but tools at best." Fatovic, *America's Founding,* at 8. In England, Blackstone offered the same argument: "The true reason of requiring any qualification, with regard to property, in voters, is to exclude such persons as are in so mean a situation that they are esteemed to have no will of their own. If these persons had votes, they would be tempted to dispose of them under some undue influence or other. This would give a great, an artful, or a wealthy man, a larger share in elections than is consistent with general liberty." William Blackstone, 1 *Commentaries on the Laws of England* 165–66 (1765). Radical English Whigs like Joseph Priestley agreed. "[T]hose who are extremely dependent should not be allowed to have votes," Priestley said, "because this might . . . be only throwing more votes into the hands of those persons on whom they depend." Steinfeld, "Property and Suffrage," at 341.

245. Nedelsky, *Private Property,* at 82; Remarks of Gouverneur Morris, Aug. 7, 1787, in Farrand, 2 *Records,* at 202. I have expanded the abbreviation of "against." Morris also noted that the restriction would not be unpopular because "9/10 of the people" could meet the requirements.

246. See also Arendt, *On Revolution,* at 180 ("To the eighteenth century, as to the seventeenth before it and the nineteenth after it, the function of laws was not primarily to guarantee liberties but to protect property; it was property, and not the law as such, that guaranteed freedom"). For a discussion of how these views evolved from the eigh-

teenth into the nineteenth century, see generally Steinfeld, "Property and Suffrage."

247. Mary S. Bilder, *Madison's Hand* 15–16 (2015).

248. Id.

249. Montesquieu, *Spirit of the Laws*, at 8.16 (124); see also Jacob T. Levy, "Beyond Publius: Montesquieu, Liberal Republicanism, and the Small-Republic Thesis," 27 *History of Political Thought* 50 (2006).

250. *Federalist* No. 51, at 293 (Madison); *Federalist* No. 10, at 48 (Madison).

251. *Federalist* No. 10, at 47 (Madison).

252. *Federalist* No. 10; "Book Note: The Relevance and Irrelevance of the Founders."

253. *Federalist* No. 51, at 293 (Madison).

254. James Madison, Remarks on Mr. Jefferson's Draught of a Constitution, in *The Mind of the Founder* 34, 36–37 (Marvin Meyers ed., 1981).

255. Remarks of Alexander Hamilton, June 26, 1787, in Farrand, 1 *Records,* at 424; Notes of Alexander Hamilton, June 6, 1787, in Farrand, 1 *Records,* at 146–47; Adair, *Intellectual Origins,* at 154.

256. Adair, *Intellectual Origins,* at 155; Notes of Alexander Hamilton, June 6, 1787, in Farrand, 1 *Records,* at 146–47.

257. Adair, *Intellectual Origins,* at 155; McCoy, *Elusive Republic,* at 13–15. My reading of *Federalist* No. 10 in this section draws upon Adair's insightful reading and brilliant storytelling.

258. Alexis de Tocqueville, *Democracy in America* 578 (Harvey C. Mansfield and Delba Winthrop trans., 2000).

259. Jennifer Nedelsky takes a slightly different view. She argues that Madison recognized some element of the threat from the rich. Nedelsky, *Private Property,* at 18. But she says that fundamentally "the Madisonian approach neglected the relationship between economic and political power and the problems it would pose in the new republic." Nedelsky, *Private Property,* at 141. I agree that the Madisonian approach neglected the problem of the link between economic and political power, but because it presumed (albeit perhaps naively) that economic power would not be imbalanced.

260. Stephen Miller, *Special Interest Groups in American Politics* 48 (1983) (discussing the influence of *Federalist* No. 10 on David Truman, a leading political scientist associated with 1950s interest group theory).

261. Hartz, *Liberal Tradition,* at 86.

262. Eric Foner, *The Story of American Freedom* 33 (1998).

263. Id. at 35 (noting that some southern slaveowners voluntarily emancipated their slaves and that every northern state from New Hampshire

to Pennsylvania "took steps toward emancipation"); Klarman, *Framers' Coup,* at 260–61.

264. Annette Gordon-Reed and Peter S. Onuf, *"Most Blessed of the Patriarchs": Thomas Jefferson and the Empire of the Imagination* 282 (2016).

265. Speech of Charles Pinckney, Monday, June 25, 1787, in Farrand, 1 *Records,* at 397–402.

266. Speech of James Madison, Tuesday, June 26, 1787, in Farrand, 1 *Records,* at 422–23; Adair, *Intellectual Origins,* at 156–57.

267. McCoy, *Elusive Republic,* at 19–20 (describing the four stages of economic development: hunting, pasturage, agriculture, and commerce).

268. Scholars have wondered why the American Constitution does not have socioeconomic rights or guarantees built into it. Sunstein, for example, suggests four reasons: chronological (constitutions in the eighteenth century simply did not have such provisions), cultural (the absence of socialism in America), institutional (the United States not being as friendly to active judicial review as other countries), and realist (such rights were almost recognized in the 1970s). Cass R. Sunstein, "Why Does the American Constitution Lack Social and Economic Guarantees?," in *American Exceptionalism* (Michael Ignatieff ed., 2005). The background conditions argument presented here is somewhat distinct from the first two of these arguments. It holds that people at the time did think about the economic preconditions for republican government, but simply did not place guarantees into the Constitution. Instead they relied on economic conditions and legislative practices. That said, they were fiercely engaged in thinking about the question of social change and its relationship to legal change. See Phillip A. Hamburger, "The Constitution's Accommodation of Social Change," 88 *Michigan Law Review* 239 (1989).

269. Adair, *Intellectual Origins,* at 160. Others agreed with Madison that America's fate was deferred considerably. William Grayson commented at the Virginia ratifying convention, "I apprehend that among us, as the people in the lower country, find themselves straightened they will remove to the frontiers, which for a considerable period will prevent the lower country from being very populous, or having recourse to manufactures. . . ." William Grayson, June 12, 1788, in 10 *DHRC* 1189.

270. James Madison, "Property and Suffrage: Second Thoughts on the Constitutional Convention," in *Mind of the Founder,* at 396–97; Adair, *Intellectual Origins,* at 160–61.

271. James Madison, "Partnership of Power: The Virginia Convention of

1829–1830," in *Mind of the Founder,* at 406–8; Adair, *Intellectual Origins,* at 161.

Chapter Three: The Emergence of the Plutocracy

1. *New York Times,* Sept. 23, 1932, at 10.
2. James A. Haggerty, *New York Times,* Sept. 24, 1932, at 1.
3. Franklin D. Roosevelt, Campaign Address on Progressive Government at the Commonwealth Club of San Francisco, Sept. 23, 1932, in 1 *The Public Papers and Addresses of Franklin D. Roosevelt* (Samuel I. Roseman ed., 1938).
4. Daniel Webster, *A Discourse Delivered at Plymouth,* Dec. 22, 1820 (3rd ed. 1825).
5. Id. at 52.
6. Id. at 58.
7. Id. at 52.
8. Id. at 58–59.
9. Id. at 52.
10. Id. at 53–54.
11. Id. at 54.
12. Id. at 52–53.
13. Id. at 58–59.
14. Id. at 59.
15. Joseph Story, 1 *Commentaries on the Constitution of the United States* 166–67, para. 180 (1833).
16. Alexis de Tocqueville, *Democracy in America* xvii (Harvey C. Mansfield and Delba Winthrop trans., 2000).
17. Id. at 3.
18. Id. at 3, 40 (the latter quotation describes early Connecticut).
19. Id. at 292.
20. Id. at 52.
21. Id. at 223.
22. Id. at 200.
23. Id. at 549.
24. Id. at 607.
25. Id. at 4–5.
26. Id. at 485.
27. Id. at 47–49, 268–69, 294–95.
28. Id. at 530.
29. Id. at 531.
30. Id.

31. Id. at 532.

32. T. H. Breen, *The Marketplace of Revolution: How Consumer Politics Shaped American Independence* (2004).

33. Charles Sellers, *The Market Revolution: Jacksonian America, 1815–1846* 22 (1991).

34. Id. at 23.

35. Lance Banning, *The Jeffersonian Persuasion* 197, 199 (1978).

36. Bray Hammond, *Banks and Politics in America from the Revolution to the Civil War* 235–36 (1957). Clay made a similar argument. See id. at 237.

37. *McCulloch v. Maryland,* 17 U.S. (4 Wheat.) 316 (1819).

38. Sellers, *Market Revolution.* See also Howard B. Rock, *Artisans of the New Republic: The Tradesmen of New York City in the Age of Jefferson* (1979).

39. Sellers, *Market Revolution,* at 288.

40. Sven Beckert, *Empire of Cotton: A Global History* 180 (2014).

41. Kevin Phillips, *Wealth and Democracy* 23 (2002).

42. For a discussion of these thinkers, see Martin J. Burke, *The Conundrum of Class: Public Discourse on the Social Order in America* 76–107 (1995); Sean Wilentz, *Chants Democratic: New York City and the Rise of the American Working Class, 1788–1850* 164–67, 182–88 (1984).

43. Sellers, *Market Revolution,* at 339.

44. Some scholars suggest that the "crisis of the artisans" was not as significant as it might seem. See Stuart M. Blumin, *The Emergence of the Middle Class: Social Experience in the American City, 1760–1900* 74 (1989). But economic historians have argued that the incomes of artisans were declining, even though their numbers remained robust. Peter H. Lindert and Jeffrey G. Williamson, *Unequal Gains: American Growth and Inequality Since 1700* 132–34 (2016).

45. Sellers, *Market Revolution,* at 339. For a discussion of the workingmen's movement in Philadelphia, see Ronald Schultz, *The Republic of Labor: Philadelphia Artisans and the Politics of Class, 1720–1830* 211–34 (1993).

46. H. W. Brands, *The Money Men: Capitalism, Democracy, and the Hundred Years' War over the American Dollar* 79 (2006).

47. Hammond, *Banks and Politics,* at 409.

48. Id. at 410 (quoting the president of the Bank of the State of South Carolina).

49. John Bell, 8 Reg. Deb. 3348, 3357, June 8, 1832 (statement of Representative Bell).

50. Brands, *Money Men,* at 78.

51. Andrew Jackson, Veto Message Regarding the Bank of the United States, July 10, 1832, available at http://avalon.law.yale.edu/19th_century/ajveto01.asp.

52. Isaac Kramnick, *Bolingbroke and His Circle: The Politics of Nostalgia in the Age of Walpole* 111–27 (1968).

53. Bolingbroke, *Political Writings* 37 (David Armitage ed., 1997) (noting that the country party must be "formed on principles of common interest" and is opposed to "the prejudices and interests of particular sets of men").

54. Martin Van Buren, *The Origin and Course of Political Parties in the United States* 162 (1867). For an argument that Van Buren's party was an antiparty, see Gerald Leonard, *The Invention of Party Politics* 43 (2002). For classics on the party system and tradition of parties in America, see Richard Hofstadter, *The Idea of a Party System* (1970); Nancy Rosenblum, *On the Side of Angels: An Appreciation of Parties and Partisanship* (2010). For a discussion of the party system in the early republic, see Bruce Ackerman, *The Failure of the Founding Fathers* (2005).

55. Frederick Grimke, *Considerations upon the Nature and Tendency of Free Institutions* 105, 94 (1848).

56. For a discussion tying the Jacksonian party organization to the war over the Bank of the United States and fears of "court" corruption, see Major L. Wilson, "The 'Country' Versus the 'Court': A Republican Consensus and Party Debate in the Bank War," 15 *Journal of the Early Republic* 619 (1995).

57. Van Buren, *Political Parties*, at 376.

58. Rosenblum, *On the Side of Angels*, at 54–55.

59. Arthur M. Schlesinger Jr., *The Age of Jackson* 307–21 (1946).

60. The national bank was only the most prominent case of such a special charter. Thus, Thomas Hart Benton condemned the bank "on account of the exclusive privileges, and anti-republican monopoly, which it gives to its stockholders." The monopolistic bank was "too great and powerful to be tolerated in a Government of free and equal laws" and would "aggravate the inequality of fortunes; to make the rich richer, and the poor poorer; to multiply nabobs and paupers." Id. at 81.

61. Id. at 315; see generally William Leggett, *Democratick Editorials* (Lawrence H. White ed., 1984).

62. Theodore Sedgwick Jr., "What Is a Monopoly?," in *Social Theories of Jacksonian Democracy* 222 (Joseph L. Blau ed., 1954).

63. The Locofocos were not the same as the Working Men's Parties. On the Locofocos, see generally Daniel Walker Howe, *What Hath God Wrought: The Transformation of America, 1815–1848* 546 (2007); Sean

Wilentz, *The Rise of American Democracy* 421–22 (2005); Wilentz, *Chants Democratic*, at 235.

64. Schlesinger, *Age of Jackson,* at 197.

65. Id. at 313.

66. Id. at 316.

67. Robert V. Remini, *Andrew Jackson and the Bank War* 176 (1967). On bubbles, see Brands, *Money Men,* at 93.

68. Schlesinger, *Age of Jackson,* at 337.

69. Beckert, *Empire of Cotton,* at 119.

70. Id. at 120–21.

71. Id. at 106.

72. Edward E. Baptist, *The Half Has Never Been Told: Slavery and the Making of American Capitalism* 317 (2014).

73. My reading of Calhoun, and the other pro-slavery thinkers, draws upon and is heavily influenced by Michael O'Brien, 2 *Conjectures of Order: Intellectual Life and the American South* (2004), and Louis Hartz, *The Liberal Tradition in America* 145–202 (1955). At the same time, these scholars were also not the first to point out the links between Calhoun and the Roman tribunate. See, for example, Mitchell Franklin, "Roman Origin and the American Justification of the Tribunitial or Veto Power in the Charter of the United Nations," 22 *Tulane Law Review* 24 (1947); Mitchell Franklin, "Problems Relating to the Influence of the Roman Idea of the Veto Power in the History of Law," 22 *Tulane Law Review* 443 (1948).

74. John C. Calhoun, "The Fort Hill Address," in *Union and Liberty: The Political Philosophy of John C. Calhoun* 373 (Ross M. Lence ed., 1992).

75. John C. Calhoun, "A Disquisition on Government," in *Union and Liberty,* at 15–16.

76. John C. Calhoun, *A Discourse on the Constitution and Government of the United States,* in *Union and Liberty,* at 266.

77. Calhoun, "Disquisition," at 22.

78. Id. at 28–29; Calhoun, "Fort Hill," at 371.

79. Calhoun, "Disquisition," at 28–29; Calhoun, *Discourse,* at 190–91; Calhoun, "Fort Hill," at 371.

80. Calhoun, "Fort Hill," at 373–74, 366.

81. John C. Calhoun, "Speech on the Revenue Collection [Force] Bill," in *Union and Liberty,* at 456–58 (hereafter cited as Calhoun, "Force Bill"); Calhoun, "Disquisition," at 68–70; Calhoun, *Discourse,* at 191.

82. Calhoun, "Disquisition," at 70.

83. Calhoun, "Fort Hill," at 374–75.

84. Calhoun, "Force Bill," at 402.

85. Calhoun, "Fort Hill," at 388–89.

86. Calhoun, *Discourse,* at 260. O'Brien makes a version of this point in 2 *Conjectures of Order,* at 860.

87. Id. at 272.

88. Id. at 261–62.

89. Id. at 273–74.

90. John C. Calhoun, "Speech on the Reception of Abolition Petitions," in *Union and Liberty,* at 472–73.

91. Id. at 473.

92. Calhoun, *Discourse,* at 274.

93. Id. at 274–75.

94. Calhoun, "Disquisition," at 71.

95. Calhoun, "Fort Hill," at 397; Calhoun, *Discourse,* at 277.

96. Calhoun, "Disquisition," at 38, 36.

97. O'Brien, 2 *Conjectures of Order,* at 823, 941–42. For another helpful discussion, see Drew Gilpin Faust, "The Proslavery Argument in History," in *The Ideology of Slavery* (Drew Gilpin Faust ed., 1981).

98. O'Brien, *Conjectures of Order,* at 803.

99. Id. at 946–50.

100. Id. at 962–63.

101. Id. at 967–71.

102. George Fitzhugh, *Cannibals All! or, Slaves Without Masters* 353 (1857); O'Brien, *Conjectures of Order,* at 974–75.

103. C. Vann Woodward, "George Fitzhugh: *Sui Generis,*" in George Fitzhugh, *Cannibals All! or Slaves Without Masters* xxxiv (1960).

104. Fitzhugh, *Cannibals All!,* at 318.

105. Id. at 308.

106. Id. at 335.

107. Id. at 313–14.

108. John C. Calhoun, Speech on the Reception of Abolition Petitions, February 1837, in *Speeches of John C. Calhoun* 225 (1843). This argument is best summarized in Richard Hofstadter, *The American Political Tradition and the Men Who Made It* 81–89 (1948).

109. Fitzhugh, *Cannibals All!,* at 295; Faust, "Proslavery Argument," at 18.

110. O'Brien, *Conjectures of Order,* at 976.

111. Hartz, *Liberal Tradition,* at 150.

112. Drew Gilpin Faust, *James Henry Hammond and the Old South* 7–10, 241–43, 314–17 (1982). Hammond also weathered a personal and political scandal when it became public that he had sexually molested his four nieces. Hammond confessed in his diary that they had done "every thing short of direct sexual intercourse."

113. James Henry Hammond, "Speech on the Admission of Kansas, Under the Lecompton Constitution, Delivered in the United States Senate, March 4, 1858," in *Selections from the Letters and Speeches of the Hon. James H. Hammond* 318–19 (1866).

114. Matt Karp, "Arsenal of Empire: Southern Slaveholders and the U.S. Military in the 1850s," *Common-Place: The Interactive Journal of Early American Life* 12, no. 4 (July 2012); Matt Karp, "Slavery and American Sea Power: The Navalist Impulse in the Antebellum South," 77 *Journal of Southern History* 283 (2011); see also Walter Johnson, *River of Dark Dreams: Slavery and Empire in the Cotton Kingdom* 366–94 (2013).

115. Johnson, *River of Dark Dreams,* at 390–420.

116. For a discussion, see Eric Foner, *Free Soil, Free Labor, Free Men: The Ideology of the Republican Party Before the Civil War* (1970).

117. Wilentz, *Rise of American Democracy,* at 725.

118. Abraham Lincoln, "Address to Wisconsin State Agricultural Society, September 30, 1859," in *Speeches and Writings, 1859–1865* 97–98 (1989). On the harmony of interests between labor and capital more generally, see Martin J. Burke, *The Conundrum of Class: Public Discourse on the Social Order in America* 108–32 (1995) (discussing the economic thinking of Henry Carey, Frances Wayland, and others).

119. Eric Foner, *Reconstruction: America's Unfinished Revolution, 1863–1877* 67–69 (2002).

120. For an overview of this group of Republicans before, during, and after the Civil War, see Hans L. Trefousse, *The Radical Republicans* (1969). On a more theoretical level, see Akhil Reed Amar, "Forty Acres and a Mule: A Republican Theory of Minimal Entitlements," 13 *Harvard Journal of Law & Public Policy* 37, 38–39 (1990) (noting that there are two ways to fulfill the economic preconditions of republicanism: excluding some, or providing for all).

121. Foner, *Reconstruction,* at 67–69.

122. Id.

123. Id. at 236.

124. Thaddeus Stevens, "Reconstruction," Sept. 6, 1865, in 2 *The Selected Papers of Thaddeus Stevens* 18–19 (Beverly Wilson Palmer and Holly Byers Ochoa eds., 1998). For a recent and brief overview of Stevens, see A. J. Langguth, *After Lincoln: How the North Won the Civil War and Lost the Peace* 123–41 (2014).

125. Stevens, "Reconstruction," at 23.

126. Foner, *Reconstruction,* at 236.

127. Id. at 104.

128. Id. at 105.

129. Id.

130. Id. at 160–61.

131. Douglas R. Egerton, *The Wars of Reconstruction* 28, 97 (2014).

132. Id. at 99.

133. Claude F. Oubre, *Forty Acres and a Mule* 18–19 (1978). Sherman later said that he did not mean the settlement to be permanent, but after it was announced, the freedmen expected to keep the land. Foner, *Reconstruction*, at 70–71.

134. Oubre, *Forty Acres*, at 72–73.

135. Id. at 73.

136. Id. at 21; Mark A. Graber, "The Second Freedmen's Bureau Bill's Constitution," 94 *Texas Law Review* 1361, 1368 (2016).

137. Oubre, *Forty Acres*, at 84–89; Foner, *Reconstruction*, at 245–51.

138. Foner, *Reconstruction*, at 246. Michael L. Lanza, "'One of the Most Appreciated Labors of the Bureau': The Freedmen's Bureau and the Southern Homestead Act," in *The Freedmen's Bureau and Reconstruction* (Paul A. Cimbala and Randall M. Miller eds., 1999).

139. The exception was *Luther v. Borden*, 48 U.S. 1 (1849), in which the Court dodged the issue. See Jack M. Balkin, *Living Originalism* 240–44 (2011); Jack M. Balkin, "Republicanism and the Constitution of Opportunity," 94 *Texas Law Review* 1427, 1429 (2016).

140. Foner, *Reconstruction*, at 232.

141. Graber, "Second Freedmen's Bureau Bill," at 1373.

142. Id. at 1374.

143. Id. at 1373–74.

144. Id. at 1384 (emphasis added).

145. Id. at 1374.

146. Garrett Epps, *Democracy Reborn: The Fourteenth Amendment and the Fight for Equal Rights in Post–Civil War America* 136–37 (2006).

147. James Gray Pope, "The Thirteenth Amendment Versus the Commerce Clause: Labor and the Shaping of American Constitutional Law, 1921–1957," 102 *Columbia Law Review* 1, 18 (2002) ("Unlike the Fourteenth Amendment, which applied only to state action, the Thirteenth made no distinction between governmental and private conduct, and thus could support legislation banning employers as well as government from interfering with labor rights"). Some scholars, however, note that the Fourteenth Amendment's citizenship clause does not have a state action requirement, and that it too constitutes an expansive grant of power to Congress. Jack M. Balkin, "The Reconstruction Power," 85 *New York University Law Review* 1801 (2010).

148. The Civil Rights Cases, 109 U.S. 3, 23 (1883) ("Under the Thirteenth

Amendment, the legislation . . . may be direct and primary, operating upon the acts of individuals, whether sanctioned by State legislation or not; under the Fourteenth . . . it must necessarily be . . . corrective in its character, addressed to counteract and afford relief against state regulations or proceedings."); id. at 35–36 (Harlan, J., dissenting) ("[U]nder the Thirteenth Amendment, Congress has to do with slavery and its incidents; and that legislation . . . may be direct and primary, operating upon the acts of individuals, whether sanctioned by State legislation or not").

149. Jack M. Balkin and Sanford Levinson, "The Dangerous Thirteenth Amendment," 112 *Columbia Law Review* 1459, 1489 (2012).

150. Id. at 1489.

151. Lea S. VanderVelde, "The Labor Vision of the Thirteenth Amendment," 138 *University of Pennsylvania Law Review* 437, 440 (1989).

152. Id. at 490–91.

153. Balkin and Levinson, "Dangerous Thirteenth Amendment." See also Akhil Reed Amar and Daniel Widawsky, "Child Abuse as Slavery: A Thirteenth Amendment Response to *DeShaney*," 105 *Harvard Law Review* 1359 (1992).

154. Foner, *Reconstruction*, at 15.

155. Id. at 16.

156. *The Slaughterhouse Cases*, 83 U.S. (16 Wall.) 36 (1873). On *Slaughterhouse* as undermining the Fourteenth Amendment, see Barry Friedman, *The Will of the People: How Public Opinion Has Influenced the Supreme Court and Shaped the Meaning of the Constitution* 141–45 (2009).

157. Foner, *Reconstruction*, at 309.

158. For an overview of some of the central arguments for the failure of Reconstruction, see Egerton, *Wars of Reconstruction*, at 13–21. See also Nicholas Lemann, *Redemption* (2006).

159. Foner, *Reconstruction*, at 161–63; Egerton, *Wars of Reconstruction*, at 103–4.

160. Foner, *Reconstruction*, at 169–70.

161. Oubre, *Forty Acres*, at 186–87.

162. Foner, *Reconstruction*, at 374–75.

163. Id. at 199.

164. Egerton, *Wars of Reconstruction*, at 284–320; Lemann, *Redemption*. For a discussion of the post–Civil War era as an occupation and insurgency, see Gregory P. Downs, *After Appomattox* (2015).

165. On outrage, see Foner, *Reconstruction*, at 225, 232.

166. Id. at 585; Nicolas Barreyre, "The Politics of Economic Crises: The

Panic of 1873, the End of Reconstruction, and the Realignment of American Politics," 10 *Journal of the Gilded Age and Progressive Era* 403, 420 (2011).

167. Foner, *Reconstruction,* at 596–97.

168. Id. at 562. The most compelling account of the heights and failures of Reconstruction remains W. E. B. Du Bois, *Black Reconstruction in America* (2007) (1934). For overviews of post–Civil War transition into "redemption" including discussions of labor, politics, and race, see David Montgomery, *Citizen Worker: The Experience of Workers in the United States with Democracy and the Free Market During the Nineteenth Century* (1993); Heather Cox Richardson, *The Death of Reconstruction* (2001).

169. Claudia Goldin and Lawrence F. Katz, *The Race Between Education and Technology* (2008).

170. Macaulay to Randall, May 23, 1857, *New York Times,* March 24, 1860, http://www.nytimes.com/1860/03/24/news/macaulay-democracy -curious-letter-lord-macaulay-american-institutions-prospects.html.

171. Jack Beatty, *Age of Betrayal: The Triumph of Money in America, 1865–1900* 88–89 (2007).

172. Id. at 50.

173. Id. at 89.

174. Id.

175. Sean Dennis Cashman, *America in the Gilded Age* 10–11 (3rd ed. 1993).

176. Robert J. Gordon, *The Rise and Fall of American Growth* 98 (2016).

177. Foner, *Free Soil, Free Labor, Free Men,* at 17. For a discussion of how post–Civil War Americans grappled with debates over slavery and wage labor, see Amy Dru Stanley, *From Bondage to Contract: Wage Labor, Marriage, and the Market in the Age of Slave Emancipation* (1998).

178. Beatty, *Age of Betrayal,* at 303.

179. James L. Huston, "A Political Response to Industrialism: The Republican Embrace of Protectionist Labor Doctrines," 70 *Journal of American History* 35, 36 (1983).

180. Id. at 36. For accounts of the early labor reformers, see Wilentz, *Chants Democratic;* Burke, *Conundrum of Class;* Mark A. Lause, *Young America: Land, Labor, and the Republican Community* (2005). For Huston's broader account of labor, egalitarianism, and republican thought in the nineteenth century, see James L. Huston, *Securing the Fruits of Labor: The American Concept of Wealth Distribution, 1765–1900* (1998).

181. Huston, "Political Response," at 35.

182. Id. at 35, 37, 44.

183. James L. Huston, "Virtue Besieged: Virtue, Equality, and the General

Welfare in the Tariff Debates of the 1820s," 14 *Journal of the Early Republic* 523, 528–29 (1994).

184. Huston, "Political Response," at 43.

185. Id. at 44 n21.

186. Id. at 54. For a study of Republican economic policies during the period, see Heather Cox Richardson, *The Greatest Nation of the Earth* (1997).

187. Huston, "Political Response," at 55–56.

188. Id. at 56.

189. "Pingree Speaks at Night," *Indianapolis Journal*, Sept. 15, 1899, at 1, http://chroniclingamerica.loc.gov/lccn/sn82015679/1899-09-15/ed-1 /seq-1.pdf; Melvin G. Holli, *Reform in Detroit: Hazen S. Pingree and Urban Politics* (1969); Eli R. Sutton, "Hazen S. Pingree," 5 *Michigan Law Journal* 113, 113–17 (1896); V. V. McNitt, "Idol of the People," 63 *Michigan Alumnus Quarterly Review* 152, 152–58 (1956–57); *Cyclopedia of Michigan: Historical and Biographical* 144–46 (1900).

190. "Pingree Speaks at Night," at 1.

191. Hazen S. Pingree, "The Effect of Trusts on Our National Life and Citizenship," in *Chicago Conference on Trusts* 263–67 (1900).

192. For example, Orestes A. Brownson, the New England preacher and intellectual, explained America's almost unique situation in his 1866 book, *The American Republic:* "Whether [property] shall be made a basis of political power or not is a question of political prudence, to be determined by the supreme political authority." "In the Middle Ages" and "under feudalism," it was the "almost exclusive basis" of political power, and it remained so in most countries around the world. "France and the United States are the principal exceptions in Christendom," he said. "The American system . . . is not founded on antagonism of classes, estates, or interests." Orestes A. Brownson, *The American Republic* 136, 253–54 (1866).

193. For a monumental account of the many changes in this era, see Gordon, *Rise and Fall of American Growth.* For other accounts of this period, see Herbert Hovenkamp, *Enterprise and American Law, 1836– 1937* (1991); Richard Franklin Bensel, *The Political Economy of American Industrialization, 1877–1900* (2000).

194. Michael Lind, *Land of Promise: An Economic History of the United States* 152–53 (2012).

195. Cashman, *America in the Gilded Age,* at 23.

196. Lind, *Land of Promise,* at 153–55.

197. Id. at 153.

198. Id. at 163.

199. Id. at 220–21.

200. Id. at 161.

201. Henry Demarest Lloyd, *Wealth Against Commonwealth* 1 (1894).

202. Id. at 519, 6.

203. *United States v. E. C. Knight Co.,* 156 U.S. 1 (1895); Beatty, *Age of Betrayal,* at 203.

204. See, for example, *Knight,* 156 U.S. at 12.

205. Id. at 44–45 (Harlan, J., dissenting).

206. Beatty, *Age of Betrayal,* at 203. For an excellent account of the early years of antitrust law, before and after the Sherman Act, see Martin J. Sklar, *The Corporate Reconstruction of American Capitalism, 1890–1916* 86–179 (1988).

207. Naomi R. Lamoreaux, *The Great Merger Movement in American Business, 1895–1904* 2, 5 (1985).

208. Lind, *Land of Promise,* at 217.

209. Lamoreaux, *Great Merger Movement,* at 2.

210. Alan Trachtenberg, *The Incorporation of America: Culture and Society in the Gilded Age* 4 (1982).

211. H. W. Brands, *American Colossus: The Triumph of Capitalism, 1865–1900* 108–18 (2010).

212. James Green, *Death in the Haymarket: A Story of Chicago, the First Labor Movement, and the Bombing That Divided Gilded Age America* (2006).

213. Lind, *Land of Promise,* at 171.

214. Steve Fraser, *The Age of Acquiescence: The Life and Death of American Resistance to Organized Wealth and Power* 62 (2015).

215. Cashman, *America in the Gilded Age,* at 128–32 (describing reduction in wages and other factors leading to the strike).

216. Fraser, *Age of Acquiescence,* at 136.

217. *In re Debs,* 158 U.S. 564 (1895).

218. Cashman, *America in the Gilded Age,* at 132.

219. David Kinley, "Trusts," in *Political Economy, Political Science, and Sociology* 30 (1899).

220. M. W. Howard, *The American Plutocracy* 25 (1895).

221. Id. at preface.

222. Id. at 126–27.

223. Id. at 13–14.

224. Id. at 121.

225. Henry George, *Progress and Poverty* (4th ed. 1886) (1879).

226. George E. McNeill, "The Problem of Today," in *The Labor Movement* 456 (George E. McNeill ed., 1887).

227. Id. at 459.
228. Id. at 462.
229. Id.
230. For accounts of the Knights of Labor, see Leon Fink, *Workingmen's Democracy: The Knights of Labor and American Politics* (1983); Kim Voss, *The Making of American Exceptionalism: The Knights of Labor and Class Formation in the Nineteenth Century* (1993); Alex Gourevitch, *From Slavery to the Cooperative Commonwealth: Labor and Republican Liberty in the Nineteenth Century* (2015).
231. Fink, *Workingmen's Democracy*, at xii–xiii.
232. Gourevitch, *Cooperative Commonwealth*, at 99. Some estimate that in 1886 the Knights organized 8 to 12 percent of the industrial labor force, including with local assemblies in every state. Voss, *American Exceptionalism*, at 2.
233. Fink, *Workingmen's Democracy*, at 13.
234. Id.
235. Gourevitch, *Cooperative Commonwealth*, at 17; Voss, *American Exceptionalism*, at 84 ("Cooperatives were seen as a way to 'republicanize' industry; that is, as a way to reorganize work so that all workers— skilled and unskilled alike—would have an equal voice in deciding what to produce and how to produce it").
236. Laurence Gronlund, *The Co-operative Commonwealth: An Exposition of Modern Socialism* (1884). Frank Giddings thus said in 1886, "Co-operation differs from socialism. . . . It does not ask the State to take possession of all capital, and manage all industry, and order all men in their industrial life as it orders regiments of soldiers." F. H. Giddings, "Cooperation," in McNeill, *Labor Movement*, at 531.
237. Gourevitch, *Cooperative Commonwealth*, at 126 (emphasis added).
238. Knights of Labor, Preamble to the Constitutions of the General Assembly, in Record of the Proceedings of the General Assembly Held at Reading, Pennsylvania, January 1–4, 1878, https://archive.org/stream /RecordOfProceedingsOfTheGeneralAssemblyOfTheKnightsOf Labor/Knightslaborb#page/n15/mode/2up.
239. Gourevitch, *Cooperative Commonwealth*, at 148–49; see also Voss, *American Exceptionalism*, at 84–89.
240. Gourevitch, *Cooperative Commonwealth*, at 151.
241. Id.
242. Id. at 17, 149.
243. Id. at 158; Fink, *Workingmen's Democracy*, at 10–11.
244. Fink, *Workingmen's Democracy*, at 10.
245. McNeill, *Labor Movement*, at 466.

246. Voss, *American Exceptionalism,* at 81. They did not, however, allow Chinese immigrants into their ranks.

247. Gourevitch, *Cooperative Commonwealth,* at 2.

248. Knights of Labor, Preamble.

249. Charles Postel, *The Populist Vision* 12–13 (2007).

250. For an overview of the literature on the populists, see id. at 6–10. The classic works include John D. Hicks, *The Populist Revolt* (1931); Richard Hofstadter, *The Age of Reform* (1955); Lawrence Goodwyn, *The Populist Moment* (1978); Robert C. McMath Jr., *American Populism* (1993). For an account of the populists as heirs to the republican tradition, see Thomas Goebel, "The Political Economy of American Populism from Jackson to the New Deal," 11 *Studies in American Political Development* 109 (1997).

251. Postel, *Populist Vision,* at 38. John F. Willits, of the Jefferson County Kansas Farmers' Alliance, said, similarly, "We are today . . . in the midst of a mighty social revolution and the watchword—organization and practical cooperation—is the shibboleth of every successful business enterprise that marks the progress of this enlightened age. The word, co-operation, means more to us than any other word in the English language." Id. at 115–16.

252. Id. at 117.

253. Id. at 116.

254. Elizabeth Sanders, *Roots of Reform: Farmers, Workers, and the American State, 1877–1917* (1999).

255. Postel, *Populist Vision,* at 163, 139.

256. Id. at 164.

257. Id. at 143, 18.

258. Id. at 153; Fraser, *Age of Acquiescence,* at 97.

259. Populist Party Platform of 1892, in *A Populist Reader: Selections from the Works of American Populist Leaders* 90 (George Brown Tindall ed., 1966).

260. Postel, *Populist Vision,* at 159.

261. Jas. H. "Cyclone" Davis, *A Political Revelation* 9 (1894).

262. Id. at 111.

263. Id. at 13, 69–101.

264. C. Vann Woodward, *Tom Watson: Agrarian Rebel* 220 (1963) (1938).

265. Id. at 221.

266. Id. at 238–40.

267. Id. at 372.

268. Id. at 370–71, 432.

269. *Lochner v. New York,* 198 U.S. 45 (1905).

270. *Lochner,* 198 U.S. at 75 (Holmes, J., dissenting).

271. Cass R. Sunstein, *The Partial Constitution* 45–51 (1993).

272. Howard Gillman, *The Constitution Besieged: The Rise and Demise of Lochner Era Police Powers Jurisprudence* (1993).

273. David E. Bernstein, "*Lochner* Era Revisionism, Revised: *Lochner* and the Origins of Fundamental Rights Constitutionalism," 92 *Georgetown Law Journal* 1 (2003). For additional discussions of the many interpretations and problems with *Lochner,* see Jack M. Balkin, *Constitutional Redemption: Political Faith in an Unjust World* 174–225 (2011); Friedman, *The Will of the People,* at 167–77; David Strauss, "Why Was Lochner Wrong," 70 *University of Chicago Law Review* 373 (2003).

274. William E. Forbath, "The Ambiguities of Free Labor: Labor and the Law in the Gilded Age," 1985 *Wisconsin Law Review* 767 (1985).

275. Gourevitch, *Cooperative Commonwealth,* at 47; Stanley, *Bondage to Contract,* at 4.

276. William Graham Sumner, *What Social Classes Owe to Each Other* 26 (1883).

277. *In re Jacobs,* 98 N.Y. 98, 103–4, 106, 114–15 (1885); see also Forbath, "Ambiguities," at 795.

278. Forbath, "Ambiguities," at 796.

279. *Godcharles v. Wigeman,* 6 A. 354 (1886). For a discussion, see Laura Phillips Sawyer, "Contested Meanings of Freedom: Workingmen's Wages, the Company Store System, and the *Godcharles v. Wigeman* Decision," 12 *Journal of the Gilded Age and Progressive Era* 285 (2013); Forbath, "Ambiguities," at 796–97.

280. *Godcharles,* 6 A. at 356.

281. See Roscoe Pound, "Liberty of Contract," 18 *Yale Law Journal* 454 (1909).

282. McNeill, *Labor Movement,* at 456.

283. William E. Forbath, *Law and the Shaping of the American Labor Movement* 147 (1991).

284. Id. at 147.

285. See, for example, James Gray Pope, "Labor's Constitution of Freedom," 106 *Yale Law Journal* 941, 942, 958–59, 962–63 (1997).

286. Michael P. Malone, *The Battle for Butte: Mining and Politics on the Northern Frontier, 1864–1906* 80–83 (1981).

287. Id. at 86.

288. Id. at 88–91, 99–100; Jeff Wiltse, "The Origins of Montana's Corrupt Practices Act: A More Complete History," 73 *Montana Law Review* 299, 302–3 (2012).

289. Malone, *Battle for Butte,* at 111, 113, 115, 117.

290. Id. at 113.

291. Id.

292. Id. at 120.

293. Larry Howell, "Once upon a Time in the West: Citizens United, Caperton, and the War of the Copper Kings," 73 *Montana Law Review* 25, 35 (2012); Mark Twain, "Senator Clark of Montana," in *Mark Twain in Eruption* 72 (Bernard DeVoto ed., 1940).

294. Howell, "Once upon a Time in the West," at 33.

295. Malone, *Battle for Butte,* at 126–27.

296. *Western Tradition Partnership v. Attorney Gen.,* 363 Mont. 220, 230–31, at para. 24 (2011); Howell, "Once upon a Time in the West," at 40.

297. *Western Tradition Partnership,* 363 Mont., at 231, at para. 24; Howell, "Once upon a Time in the West," at 40.

298. Wiltse, "Origins," at 310–11.

299. Id. at 312.

300. Id.

301. Wiltse, "Origins," at 308–9.

302. Id. at 324, 333.

303. *American Tradition Partnership v. Bullock,* 132 S. Ct. 2490 (2012).

304. William D. P. Bliss, ed., "Plutocracy," in *Encyclopedia of Social Reforms* 1013 (1897).

305. John C. Reed, *The New Plutocracy* viii, ix (1903).

306. Frank Parsons, *The City for the People* 12 (1901).

307. R. F. Pettigrew, *Triumphant Plutocracy* 118 (1922).

308. Henry George Jr., *The Menace of Privilege* 1, 4 (1905).

309. Id. at vii.

310. Id. at 380.

311. Id. at 235–323.

312. Reed, *New Plutocracy,* at 120.

313. Pettigrew, *Triumphant Plutocracy,* at 197.

314. Bliss, "Plutocracy," at 1013.

315. James Bryce, 2 *The American Commonwealth* 460, 466 (1889).

316. Id. at 479.

317. Id. at 600.

318. Id. at 712, 479.

319. Beatty, *Age of Betrayal,* at xv.

320. Id. at xv. Mary Lease put it in similar terms: "It is no longer a government of the people, for the people, by the people, but a government of Wall Street, for Wall Street, and by Wall Street." Id. at 318.

Chapter Four: The Search for Solutions

1. Arthur M. Schlesinger Jr., "Walter Lippmann: The Intellectual v. Politics," in *Walter Lippmann and His Times* 197 (Marquis Childs and James Reston eds., 1959).

2. Background information in this and the subsequent paragraphs draws extensively from Ganesh Sitaraman, "*Drift and Mastery* in the Twenty-First Century," in Walter Lippmann, *Drift and Mastery* (2015).

3. Lippmann, *Drift and Mastery,* at 84.

4. Daniel T. Rodgers, "In Search of Progressivism," 10 *Reviews in American History* (Dec. 1982), at 113, 115.

5. Id. at 114.

6. Robert H. Wiebe, *The Search for Order, 1877–1920* 6 (1967).

7. Rodgers, "In Search of Progressivism," at 123.

8. Michael McGerr, *A Fierce Discontent* (2003).

9. Richard Hofstadter, *The Age of Reform,* at 5 (1995).

10. Lippmann, *Drift and Mastery,* at 38.

11. Id. at 93.

12. Id. at 16.

13. Id. at 138.

14. Id. at 148.

15. Id. at 147.

16. Id. at 16.

17. Theodore Roosevelt, "Two Noteworthy Books on Democracy," *Outlook,* Nov. 18, 1914, at 650–51.

18. Akhil Reed Amar, *America's Constitution* 405 (2005).

19. See, for example, Ajay K. Mehrotra, *Making the Modern American Fiscal State* 3–5, 38, 42–43, 50 (2013).

20. Id. at 91–93.

21. Id. at 27, 266.

22. Id. at 122–26.

23. Reuven S. Avi-Yonah, "Corporations, Society, and the State: A Defense of the Corporate Tax," 90 *Virginia Law Review* 1193, 1214–15 (2004); Steven A. Bank, "Entity Theory as Myth in the Origins of the Corporate Income Tax," 43 *William & Mary Law Review* 447, 452 (2001).

24. U.S. Const., art. I, sec. 2 and sec. 8. For a discussion of the direct tax clause from the founding through *Pollock* and the Sixteenth Amendment, see Bruce Ackerman, "Taxation and the Constitution," 99 *Columbia Law Review* 1 (1999).

25. Mehrotra, *Fiscal State,* at 130–31. The opinions were *Hylton v. United States,* 3 U.S. 171 (1796), and *Springer v. United States,* 102 U.S. 586 (1881).

26. *Pollock v. Farmers' Loan & Trust Co.*, 157 U.S. 429, 607 (Field, J., concurring).

27. Id. at 650–51 (White, J., dissenting).

28. Mehrotra, *Fiscal State,* at 143.

29. Avi-Yonah, "Corporations, Society, and the State," at 1219.

30. Id. at 1223.

31. Marjorie E. Kornhauser, "Corporate Regulation and the Origins of the Corporate Income Tax," 66 *Indiana Law Journal* 53, 53–54 (1990); see also Melvin I. Urofsky, "Proposed Federal Incorporation in the Progressive Era," 26 *American Journal of Legal History* 160 (1982).

32. Steven R. Weisman, *The Great Tax Wars* 224 (2002).

33. Representative Champ Clark of Missouri, July 12, 1909, Cong. Rec. 4392.

34. Mehrotra, *Fiscal State,* at 278.

35. Id. at 7.

36. Jay S. Bybee, "Ulysses at the Mast: Democracy, Federalism, and the Sirens' Song of the Seventeenth Amendment," 91 *Northwestern University Law Review* 500, 538–39n251 (1997) (statement of Representative Bushnell). There were other justifications as well. For a discussion, see Vikram David Amar, "Indirect Effects of Direct Election: A Structural Examination of the Seventeenth Amendment," 49 *Vanderbilt Law Review* 1347, 1353 (1996). The best encapsulation, however, is from the era itself. See George H. Haynes, *The Election of Senators* 36–50 (1906) (discussing deadlocks in the state legislatures regarding senatorial elections), 59–65 (vacancies in the Senate), 65–68 (interference with state business), 153–58 (popular interest in democracy). Another persuasive argument is that the rise of truly national parties encouraged direct election as a way to separate national policy debates, which were coming to dominate legislative elections, from state-level policy debates. See David Schleicher, "The Seventeenth Amendment and Federalism in an Age of National Political Parties," 65 *Hastings Law Journal* 1043 (2014).

37. Haynes, *Election of Senators,* at 53–56.

38. Jesse Hardesty, *The Mother of Trusts* 177–78 (1899).

39. Edgar Lee Masters, "The Federal Courts," *Watson's Magazine,* July 1906, at 381.

40. Haynes, *Election of Senators,* at 172.

41. Id. at 173.

42. Id. at 177n22.

43. Id. at 173.

44. Masters, "Federal Courts," at 381.

45. Hardesty, *Mother of Trusts,* at 177.

46. Walter Clark, "The Election of Federal Judges by the People," 67 *Albany Law Journal* 235, 236 (1905). See also Chief Justice Walter Clark, of North Carolina, "Some Defects in the Constitution of the United States" (an address to the Law Department of the University of Pennsylvania, April 27, 1906), printed July 31, 1911, in Senate Documents, 62nd Cong., 1st sess., vol. 30, doc. no. 87.

47. Clark, "Election of Federal Judges," at 236.

48. Id.

49. Id.

50. Albert M. Kales, *Unpopular Government in the United States* 211–12 (1914).

51. Haynes, *Election of Senators,* at 173.

52. Hardesty, *Mother of Trusts,* at 178.

53. Charles Erskine Scott Wood, "Impressions," 19 *Pacific Monthly* 479, 481 (April 1908); Hardesty, *Mother of Trusts,* at 178. Some modern commentators disagree. Bybee, "Ulysses at the Mast," at 541; Todd J. Zywicki, "Senators and Special Interests," 73 *Oregon Law Review* 1007 (1994).

54. See, for example, Bybee, "Ulysses at the Mast," at 540 ("William Jennings Bryan argued that 'great corporations . . . are able to compass the election for their tools and their agents through the instrumentality of Legislatures, as they could not if Senators were elected directly by the people'"); Masters, "Federal Courts," at 376 ("[A] plutocracy . . . cannot exist where the people retain control of the Government").

55. George H. Haynes, "The Changing Senate," 705 *North American Review* 222, 222 (1914).

56. William B. Murphy, "The National Progressive Republican League and the Elusive Quest for Progressive Unity," 8 *Journal of the Gilded Age and Progressive Era* 515, 522 (2009).

57. Adam Winkler, "'Other People's Money': Corporations, Agency Costs, and Campaign Finance Law," 92 *Georgetown Law Journal* 871, 882–83 (2004).

58. Robert H. Sitkoff, "Politics and the Business Corporation," 26 *Regulation* 30, 35 (Winter 2003–4); see also Winkler, "'Other People's Money,'" at 884.

59. Winkler, "'Other People's Money,'" at 883.

60. Id. at 884.

61. Id. at 883.

62. Robert E. Mutch, *Buying the Vote: A History of Campaign Finance Reform* 46 (2014).

63. Winkler, "'Other People's Money,'" at 885.

64. Mutch, *Buying the Vote,* at 46.
65. Id. at 38.
66. Winkler, "'Other People's Money,'" at 892.
67. Mutch, *Buying the Vote,* at 39.
68. Id. at 51.
69. Id. at 47.
70. Id. at 41.
71. Winkler, "'Other People's Money,'" at 879.
72. Sitkoff, "Politics and the Business Corporation"; Robert H. Sitkoff, "Corporate Political Speech, Political Extortion, and the Competition for Corporate Charters," 69 *University of Chicago Law Review* 1103, 1132 (2002).
73. Mutch, *Buying the Vote,* at 6–7.
74. Id. at 62.
75. Anthony Corrado, "Money and Politics: A History of Federal Campaign Finance Law," in *Campaign Finance Reform: A Sourcebook* 28 (Anthony Corrado et al. eds., 1997).
76. Id. at 28–29.
77. Mutch, *Buying the Vote,* at 75.
78. This isn't to say that constitutional scholars completely ignore the Progressive Era. See, for example, *America's Constitution,* at 403–30; Reva B. Siegel, "She the People: The Nineteenth Amendment, Sex Equality, Federalism, and the Family," 115 *Harvard Law Review* 947 (2002). Rather, the era is not usually considered one of the inflection points in constitutional history.
79. The leading account is Bruce Ackerman, *We the People,* vol. 1, *Foundations* (1991); Bruce Ackerman, *We the People,* vol. 2, *Transformations* (1998); Bruce Ackerman, *We the People,* vol. 3, *The Civil Rights Revolution* (2014).
80. Hofstadter, *Age of Reform,* at 252.
81. The literature on the Progressive Era is voluminous. Classics include id.; Wiebe, *Search for Order;* McGerr, *Fierce Discontent;* Charles Forcey, *The Crossroads of Liberalism* (1961); Gabriel Kolko, *The Triumph of Conservatism: A Reinterpretation of American History, 1900–1916* (1963); Eldon J. Eisenach, *The Lost Promise of Progressivism* (1994); Rodgers, "In Search of Progressivism." The standard works on the intellectual history of the period, with a focus on the transatlantic connections between the thinkers, are James T. Kloppenberg, *Uncertain Victory: Social Democracy and Progressivism in European and American Political Thought, 1870–1920* (1986); Daniel T. Rodgers, *Atlantic Crossings: Social Politics in a Progressive Age* (1998); Marc Stears, *Progres-*

sives, Pluralists, and the Problems of the State: Ideologies of Reform in the United States and Britain, 1909–1926 (2002).

82. Michael J. Sandel, *Democracy's Discontent* 217 (1996).

83. Theodore Roosevelt, Eighth Annual Message, Dec. 8, 1908, in *State Papers as Governor and President, 1899–1909* 495–96 (Hermann Hagedorn ed., 1925).

84. Martin J. Sklar, *The Corporate Reconstruction of American Capitalism, 1890–1916* 184–86 (1988).

85. Id. at 187, 192.

86. Id. at 191.

87. Id. at 189, 198.

88. Roosevelt, Annual Message, in *State Papers*, at 491.

89. Sklar, *Corporate Reconstruction*, at 201–3.

90. Herbert Croly, *The Promise of American Life* 22 (1965) (1909).

91. Id. at 23.

92. Herbert Croly, *Progressive Democracy* 46–47 (1998) (1914).

93. Id. at 51.

94. Id. at 57, 86, 88.

95. Id. at 95.

96. Id. at 97.

97. Id. at 98.

98. Id. at 103.

99. For an overview of Brandeis's life, see Melvin I. Urofsky, *Louis D. Brandeis: A Life* (2009).

100. Louis D. Brandeis, "True Americanism," in *Brandeis on Democracy* 29 (Philippa Strum ed., 1995).

101. Louis D. Brandeis, "The Living Law," in *Brandeis on Democracy*, at 61–62.

102. Philippa Strum, *Brandeis: Beyond Progressivism* 159 (1993) ("First we had the struggle for independence, and the second great struggle in our history was to keep the nation whole and abolish slavery. The present struggle in which we are engaged is for social and industrial justice"); see also Louis D. Brandeis, "Big Business and Industrial Liberty," in *Brandeis on Democracy*, at 127 ("[I]t is this social unrest of our people in this struggle with which none in our history save the Revolution and the Civil War can be compared").

103. Sandel, *Democracy's Discontent*, at 212.

104. Louis D. Brandeis, Testimony before the Commission on Industrial Relations, Jan. 23, 1915, in *Brandeis on Democracy*, at 97–98.

105. Brandeis, "True Americanism," at 28, 27.

106. Strum, *Brandeis*, at 158.

107. Id. at 36.

108. Sandel, *Democracy's Discontent*, at 212–13.

109. Strum, *Brandeis*, at 36. For discussions of industrial democracy, see Nelson Lichtenstein and Howell John Harris, eds., *Industrial Democracy in America* (1993); Joseph A. McCartin, *Labor's Great War: The Struggle for Industrial Democracy and the Origins of Modern American Labor Relations, 1912–1921* (1997); Milton Derber, *The American Idea of Industrial Democracy, 1865–1965* (1970).

110. Strum, *Brandeis*, at 38.

111. Brandeis, Testimony, at 99.

112. Id. at 101; Strum, *Brandeis*, at 38–39.

113. Louis D. Brandeis, Interview, in *Brandeis on Democracy*, at 96.

114. Sandel, *Democracy's Discontent*, at 212.

115. Strum, *Brandeis*, at 36, 83.

116. Id. at 84.

117. Sklar, *Corporate Reconstruction*, at 385–91.

118. Strum, *Brandeis*, at 87.

119. Herbert Hovenkamp, "Antitrust and Innovation: Where We Are and Where We Should Be Going," 77 *Antitrust Law Journal* 749, 749 (2011) ("The primary purpose of antitrust law is to promote competition"); Frank H. Easterbrook, "The Limits of Antitrust," 63 *Texas Law Review* 1, 1 (1984) ("The goal of antitrust is to perfect the operation of competitive markets").

120. Thomas B. Nachbar, "The Antitrust Constitution," 99 *Iowa Law Review* 57, 61 (2013).

121. Hovenkamp, "Antitrust and Innovation," at 750.

122. *Standard Oil Co. v. United States*, 221 U.S. 1, 50 (1911).

123. Sandel, *Democracy's Discontent*, at 211–12.

124. *Liggett v. Lee*, 288 U.S. 517, 565 (1933) (Brandeis, J., dissenting). For a helpful discussion of the anti-chain-store movement in the context of progressive constitutional theory, see Richard C. Schragger, "The Anti–Chain Store Movement, Localist Ideology, and the Remnants of the Progressive Constitution, 1920–1940," 90 *Iowa Law Review* 1011 (2005).

125. *Liggett*, 288 U.S. at 565 (Brandeis, J., dissenting).

126. Id. at 579 (Brandeis, J., dissenting).

127. *U.S. v. Columbia Steel Co.*, 334 U.S. 495, 536 (1948) (Douglas, J., dissenting).

128. Id.

129. Sandel, *Democracy's Discontent*, at 240–41.

130. Robert H. Bork, *The Antitrust Paradox* 51, 7 (1978).

131. Forcey, *Crossroads of Liberalism,* at 53, 59–60.
132. Walter E. Weyl, *The New Democracy* 8 (1912).
133. Id.
134. Id. at 20–21.
135. Id. at 76–77, 78.
136. Id. at 84, 95.
137. Id. at 117, 109.
138. Id. at 137, 120–22, 118.
139. Id. at 169–70.
140. Id. at 179.
141. Id. at 181.
142. Id. at 191.
143. Id.
144. Id. at 194.
145. Id. at 241, 244, 248.
146. Id. at 250.
147. Id. at 298, 303, 312, 316, 318.
148. Id. at 334, 145.
149. Id. at 297.
150. Id. at 163–64.
151. Sandel, *Democracy's Discontent,* at 226.
152. William J. Novak, *A New Democracy: Law and the Creation of the Modern American State* Ch. 5, at 7 (forthcoming 2017).
153. Id. at 2, 42.
154. Id. at 12–13, 15–16.
155. Id. at 17–20.
156. Id. at 35–36. The comment is Felix Frankfurter's.
157. Id. at 44.
158. Id. at 7.
159. For an account of this tradition, focusing primarily on the 1920s, see Ellis W. Hawley, *The Great War and the Search for a Modern Order* (2nd ed. 1992).
160. Arthur Jerome Eddy, *The New Competition* 24–25 (1912).
161. David M. Kennedy, *Over Here: The First World War and American Society* 93–143 (1980).
162. McGerr, *Fierce Discontent,* at 284. For a study of the War Industries Board, see Robert D. Cuff, *The War Industries Board* (1973).
163. McGerr, *Fierce Discontent,* at 285.
164. Id. at 285–86.
165. Arthur Krock, "Campaign Issue Defined," *New York Times,* June 28, 1936, at A1. The speech is available at 5 *Public Papers,* at 230–36.

166. For a helpful overview of the early years of Roosevelt's presidency, see Jonathan Alter, *The Defining Moment: FDR's Hundred Days and the Triumph of Hope* (2006).

167. Franklin Delano Roosevelt, Campaign Address at Madison Square Garden, Oct. 31, 1936, in 5 *Public Papers*, at 566, 568.

168. Alan Brinkley, *The End of Reform: New Deal Liberalism in Recession and War* 5 (1995).

169. William E. Leuchtenburg, "The New Deal and the Analogue of War," in *Change and Continuity in Twentieth-Century America* 117–19 (John Braeman, Robert H. Bremner, and Everett Walters eds., 1964).

170. David M. Kennedy, *Freedom from Fear* 151–52 (1999).

171. Franklin Delano Roosevelt, Address at Oglethorpe University, Atlanta, May 22, 1932, in 1 *Public Papers*, at 639, 646.

172. *Nebbia v. New York*, 291 U.S. 502 (1934); *Home Building & Loan Association v. Blaisdell*, 290 U.S. 398 (1934); *Norman v. Baltimore & Ohio Railroad Co.*, 294 U.S. 240 (1935).

173. William E. Leuchtenburg, *The Supreme Court Reborn* 87–88 (1995).

174. *Panama Refining Co. v. Ryan*, 293 U.S. 388 (1935); *Railroad Retirement Board v. Alton Railroad Co.*, 295 U.S. 330 (1935).

175. *A. L. A. Schechter Poultry v. United States*, 295 U.S. 495 (1935); *Louisville Joint Stock Land Bank v. Radford*, 295 U.S. 555 (1935).

176. Leuchtenburg, *Supreme Court Reborn*, at 90.

177. *United States v. Butler*, 297 U.S. 1, 67 (1936).

178. *Carter v. Carter Coal Co.*, 298 U.S. 238 (1936); *Ashton v. Cameron County Water Improvement District No. 1*, 298 U.S. 513 (1936); *Morehead v. New York ex rel. Tipaldo*, 298 U.S. 587 (1936).

179. *Tipaldo*, 298 U.S. at 636 (Stone, J., dissenting). On these cases, see Barry Friedman, *The Will of the People: How Public Opinion Has Influenced the Supreme Court and Shaped the Meaning of the Constitution* 203–5 (2009).

180. Leuchtenburg, *Supreme Court Reborn*, at 102.

181. *West Coast Hotel v. Parrish*, 300 U.S. 379, 391, 399 (1937).

182. *Wright v. Vinton Branch of Mountain Trust Bank of Roanoke, Va.*, 300 U.S. 440 (1937). For context on White Monday, see Friedman, *Will of the People*, at 226.

183. *National Labor Relations Board v. Jones & Laughlin Steel Corp.*, 301 U.S. 1 (1937).

184. *Steward Machine Co. v. Davis*, 301 U.S. 548 (1937); *Helvering v. Davis*, 301 U.S. 619 (1937).

185. See Friedman, *Will of the People*, at 225–26. Scholars have argued that Roberts's votes can be reconciled and that court-packing was not likely

to succeed and thus probably did not push Roberts to change his mind. But the public interpreted the Court's action as backing down. Id. at 227–34.

186. Harold Ickes, "Lawless Big Business Must Be Controlled to Save Democracy," Jan. 8, 1938, http://www.progressive.org/wx041409.html. The speech was delivered via NBC radio on Dec. 30, 1937. See Brinkley, *End of Reform,* at 56–57.

187. Brinkley, *End of Reform,* at 70–76.

188. Id. at 249–50.

189. Id. at 269; see also Reuel E. Schiller, "Reining in the Administrative State: World War II and the Decline of Expert Administration," in *Total War and the Law* 195–96 (Daniel R. Ernst and Victor Jew eds., 2002) (arguing that the shift toward Keynesianism contributed to a shift from autonomous agency action to greater judicial policing of agencies).

190. Ira Katznelson, *Fear Itself: The New Deal and the Origins of Our Time* (2013). For an argument that the southern cage was not as inevitable as Katznelson suggests, see Jeremy K. Kessler, "The Last Lost Cause," *Jacobin,* April 2013.

191. James T. Patterson, *Congressional Conservatism and the New Deal* 97–99, 109–10 (1967).

192. For discussion of the purge generally, see id. at 250–87; on southern senators, see id. at 278–79.

193. George B. Shepherd, "Fierce Compromise: The Administrative Procedure Act Emerges from New Deal Politics," 90 *Northwestern University Law Review* 1557, 1643 (1996).

194. Landon R. Y. Storrs, *The Second Red Scare and the Unmaking of the New Deal Left* 51–85 (2013).

195. Id. at 209–21.

196. Arthur Schlesinger Jr., *The Vital Center* (1949).

197. Storrs, *Second Red Scare,* at 2.

198. Ellen Schrecker, *Many Are the Crimes: McCarthyism in America* 368–86 (1998); Storrs, *Second Red Scare,* at 205, 227–35.

199. William M. Leiserson, "Constitutional Government in American Industries," 12 *American Economic Review* 56 (1922).

200. Nelson Lichtenstein, *State of the Union: A Century of American Labor* 36 (2002).

201. Indeed, there is a strong argument that it was the Wagner Act that first ended feudal labor relations in America because prior relations between employers and employees remained within common-law courts, which enforced an effectively feudal set of laws around master-

servant relations. See Karen Orren, *Belated Feudalism* (1991). One scholar argues that the Wagner Act was not intended to instantiate an adversarial model of labor-management relations but rather to lead to a cooperative organizational system. Mark Barenberg, "The Political Economy of the Wagner Act: Power, Symbol, and Workplace Cooperation," 106 *Harvard Law Review* 1379 (1993).

202. Nelson Lichtenstein, *Walter Reuther: The Most Dangerous Man in Detroit* 162–71 (1995); Nelson Lichtenstein, *Labor's War at Home: The CIO in World War II* 83–88 (2nd ed. 2003) (1982); Brinkley, *End of Reform*, at 206–9; Kennedy, *Freedom from Fear*, at 477.

203. Brinkley, *End of Reform*, at 209–11; Lichtenstein, *Labor's War at Home*, at 79–81.

204. Katznelson, *Fear Itself*, at 344; James T. Sparrow, *Warfare State: World War II Americans and the Age of Big Government* 6–7 (2011).

205. Brinkley, *End of Reform*, at 174.

206. Alan Brinkley, "The New Deal and the Idea of the State," in *The Rise and Fall of the New Deal Order* 103 (Steve Fraser and Gary Gerstle eds., 1989).

207. Brinkley, *End of Reform*, at 172.

208. Lichtenstein, *Labor's War at Home*, at 228–30.

209. Lichtenstein, *State of the Union*, at 117–18.

210. Id. at 148–49.

211. Shepherd, "Fierce Compromise," at 1561. The Supreme Court wasn't totally out of the picture, of course. For a suggestion that the Hughes Court participated in the administrative assault on the New Deal, see Jeremy K. Kessler, "The Struggle for Administrative Legitimacy," 129 *Harvard Law Review* 718, 749–50 (2016) (reviewing *Tocqueville's Nightmare*, by Dan Ernst) (discussing the *Morgan II* case of April 1938).

212. Shepherd, "Fierce Compromise," at 1590–92.

213. Id. at 1610.

214. Id. at 1617–18.

215. James M. Landis, *The Administrative Process* 7 (1938). For an account of Landis's life and work, see Justin O'Brien, *The Triumph, Tragedy, and Lost Legacy of James M. Landis* (2014).

216. Landis, *Administrative Process*, at 46, 120.

217. Id. at 36.

218. Id. at 36, 8.

219. Gerald E. Frug, "The Ideology of Bureaucracy in American Law," 97 *Harvard Law Review* 1276, 1318–34 (1984).

220. For a classic discussion of expertise in the administrative state, see generally id. at 1318–34.

221. Schiller, "Reining in the Administrative State," at 190–95.

222. Mariano-Florentino Cuellar, "Administrative War," 82 *George Washington Law Review* 1343 (2014).

223. Brinkley, *End of Reform,* at 60.

224. Id. at 114.

225. Id. at 111–12.

226. Katznelson, *Fear Itself,* at 233.

227. Id. at 44.

228. Benjamin L. Alpers, *Dictators, Democracy, and American Public Culture* 15 (2003).

229. Id. at 35. The NRA's head, Hugh Johnson, was partly responsible for this association, as he promoted corporatist ideas and was rumored to be a fan of Mussolini (though many others at the time were as well). James Q. Whitman, "Of Corporatism, Fascism and the First New Deal," 39 *American Journal of Comparative Law* 747 (1991).

230. Richard Polenberg, *Reorganizing Roosevelt's Government: The Controversy over Executive Reorganization, 1936–1939* 60 (1966).

231. Id. at 62.

232. Id. at 20; see also Barry Dean Karl, *Executive Reorganization and Reform in the New Deal* (1963).

233. Polenberg, *Reorganizing Roosevelt's Government,* at 55, 146–59; Patterson, *Congressional Conservatism,* at 222–25.

234. For further discussion, see generally Katznelson, *Fear Itself* (describing the democracy versus dictatorship choice in the 1930s and 1940s); Schiller, "Reining in the Administrative State," at 188–90 (linking the decline of administrative power to fears of totalitarianism, among other factors). The fear of totalitarianism continued in the postwar era. See Richard Primus, "A Brooding Omnipresence: Totalitarianism in Postwar Constitutional Thought," 106 *Yale Law Journal* 423 (1996); David Ciepley, *Liberalism in the Shadow of Totalitarianism* (2006).

235. Franklin Delano Roosevelt, Message to the Congress on the State of the Union, Jan. 11, 1944, in 13 *Public Papers,* at 32.

236. Claudia Goldin and Robert A. Margo, "The Great Compression: The Wage Structure in the United States at Mid-Century," 107 *Quarterly Journal of Economics* 1 (1992).

237. Economic Policy Institute, The Top Charts of 2014, at chart 2, Dec. 18, 2014, http://www.epi.org/publication/the-top-10-charts-of-2014/. U.S. Census Bureau, Historical Income Tables, table P-2: Race and Hispanic Origin by Median Income and Sex, http://www.census.gov /hhes/www/income/data/historical/people/; St. Louis Federal Reserve

Bank, Real Gross Domestic Product, FRED Economic Data, https:// research.stlouisfed.org/fred2/series/GDPC1.

238. Economic Policy Institute, Top Charts, at chart 2.

239. U.S. Census Bureau, Historical Census of Housing Tables, https:// www.census.gov/hhes/www/housing/census/historic/owner.html.

240. See tables A1 and A3, col. P90–100, http://elsa.berkeley.edu/~saez /TabFig2012prel.xls, updating Thomas Piketty and Emmanuel Saez, "Income Inequality in the United States, 1913–1998," 118 *Quarterly Journal of Economics* 1 (2003). The data covers income, excluding capital gains.

241. Emmanuel Saez and Gabriel Zucman, "Wealth Inequality in the United States Since 1913: Evidence from Capitalized Income Tax Data," at fig. 1, Oct. 2015, http://eml.berkeley.edu/~saez/SaezZucman2016QJE.pdf.

242. Carmen DeNavas-Walt, Bernadette D. Proctor, and Jessica C. Smith, Current Population Reports P60-238, *Income, Poverty, and Health Insurance Coverage in the United States: 2009* 56, U.S. Census Bureau (2010), http://www.census.gov/prod/2010pubs/p60-238.pdf.

243. Lizabeth Cohen, *A Consumers' Republic: The Politics of Mass Consumption in Postwar America* 141–42 (2003).

244. Staff of Subcommittee on Education and Health, Joint Economic Committee, 100th Cong., "A Cost-Benefit Analysis of Government Investment in Post-secondary Education Under the World War II GI Bill" 10 (Comm. Print 1988), reprinted in *The Future of Head Start: Hearing Before the Subcommittee on Education and Health, Joint Economic Committee,* 101st Cong. 92–113 (1990).

245. Stephen E. Ambrose, *Eisenhower: Soldier and President* 387 (1990).

246. "America's Interstate Highways: America's Splurge," *Economist,* Feb. 14, 2008.

247. This list is pared down, merging some of the overlap in lists from Charles Calomiris and Gary Gorton, "The Origins of Banking Panics: Models, Facts, and Bank Regulation," in *Financial Markets and Financial Crises* 109 (R. Glenn Hubbard ed., 1991); and Andrew J. Jalil, "A New History of Banking Panics in the United States, 1825–1929: Construction and Implications," 7 *American Economic Journal: Macroeconomics* 295 (2015).

248. FDIC, Failures and Assistance Transactions by Number of Institutions in U.S. and Other Areas, 1934–2016, https://www5.fdic.gov/hsob /HSOBSummaryRpt.asp?BegYear=2016&EndYear=1934&State =1&Header=0.

249. Internal Revenue Service, Table 23. U.S. Individual Income Tax: Personal Exemptions and Lowest and Highest Bracket Tax Rates, and Tax

Base for Regular Tax, Tax Years 1913–2015, https://www.irs.gov/uac
/soi-tax-stats-historical-table-23.

250. For a discussion of Taft-Hartley, see Christopher L. Tomlins, *The State and the Unions* 282–317 (1985).

251. Lichtenstein, *Most Dangerous Man,* at 277–79.

252. Id. at 280.

253. Id.

254. Id. at 280, 286–87.

255. Id. at 297.

256. See, for example, Ackerman, *Transformations,* at 279–311 (discussing the constitutional significance of the New Deal); Laura Kalman, *The Strange Career of Legal Liberalism* 13–59 (1996) (describing academic views toward judicial review in the generation after the New Deal); Gary Lawson, "The Rise and Rise of the Administrative State," 107 *Harvard Law Review* 1231, 1231 (1994) (arguing that the post–New Deal administrative state is unconstitutional and that its features have been "taken as unchallengeable postulates by virtually all players in the legal and political worlds, including the Reagan and Bush Administrations").

257. The classic case is *United States v. Carolene Products Co.,* 304 U.S. 144 (1938).

258. Suzanna Sherry, "Property Is the New Privacy: The Coming Constitutional Revolution," 128 *Harvard Law Review* 1452 (2015).

259. See, for example, Jamal Greene, "What the New Deal Settled," 15 *University of Pennsylvania Journal of Constitutional Law* 265, 266 (2012) (the commerce clause challenge "bordered on frivolous"); Jeffrey Rosen, "Economic Freedoms and the Constitution," 25 *Harvard Journal of Law and Public Policy* 13, 22 (2012) (arguing that overturning the Affordable Care Act would mean a "return to a pre–New Deal understanding of the Commerce Clause").

260. And yet five justices disagreed. *National Federation of Independent Business v. Sebelius,* 132 S. Ct. 2566 (2012).

261. See, for example, Erwin Chemerinsky, "Keynote Address: Rehnquist Court's Federalism Revolution," 41 *Willamette Law Review* 827 (2005); Erwin Chemerinsky, "The Rehnquist Revolution," 2 *Pierce Law Review* 1 (2004).

262. John F. Kennedy, Remarks to Members of the White House Conference on National Economic Issues, May 21, 1962, http://www.presidency.ucsb.edu/ws/?pid=867041.

263. Martin Luther King Jr., *Stride Toward Freedom: The Montgomery Story* 77 (2010) (1958).

264. Nancy MacLean, *Freedom Is Not Enough: The Opening of the American Workplace* 45–46, 48 (2006); Joseph J. Thorndike, "'The Sometimes Sordid Level of Race and Segregation': James J. Kilpatrick and the Virginia Campaign Against *Brown*," in *The Moderates' Dilemma: Massive Resistance to School Desegregation in Virginia* 51, 58 (Matthew D. Lassiter and Andrew B. Lewis eds., 1998). For a classic overview of the road to and through *Brown*, see Michael J. Klarman, *From Jim Crow to Civil Rights* (2004).

265. U.S. Census Bureau, Historical Income Tables: People, table P-2: Race and Hispanic Origin of People by Median Income and Sex, https://www.census.gov/hhes/www/income/data/historical/people/.

266. Cohen, *Consumers' Republic*, at 169–70.

267. Thomas J. Sugrue, *The Origins of the Urban Crisis: Race and Inequality in Postwar Detroit* 181–285 (2nd ed. 2005) (describing housing segregation in Detroit); Robert O. Self, *American Babylon: Race and the Struggle for Postwar Oakland* 11 (2003) ("Much of the modern civil rights movement, and its emphasis on economic rights, in the United States was dedicated to a critique of and confrontation with the two-tiered welfare state instantiated in the New Deal—especially its segregationist housing policies, its lack of fair employment and full employment provisions, its exclusion of hundreds of thousands of black workers from the protections of labor laws, and its deeply biased forms of social insurance, what is now called 'welfare'"); Richard R. W. Brooks and Carol M. Rose, *Saving the Neighborhood: Racially Restrictive Covenants, Law, and Social Norms* (2013); Cohen, *Consumers' Republic*, at 170–71; Ta-Nehisi Coates, "The Case for Reparations," *Atlantic*, June 2014.

268. Charles Whalen and Barbara Whalen, *The Longest Debate: A Legislative History of the 1964 Civil Rights Act* 200–201 (1985); see generally Ackerman, *Civil Rights Revolution*.

269. Siegel, "She the People," at 969, 978, 981, 989. For an additional discussion of objections to suffrage, see Reva B. Siegel, "Collective Memory and the Nineteenth Amendment: Reasoning About 'the Woman Question' in the Discourse of Sex Discrimination," in *History, Memory, and the Law* 149 (Austin Sarat and Thomas R. Kearnes eds., 1999).

270. Alice Kessler-Harris, *In Pursuit of Equity: Women, Men, and the Quest for Economic Citizenship in 20th-Century America* 30–33, 40–44 (2001); Alice Kessler-Harris, *Out to Work: A History of Wage-Earning Women in the United States* 185–86 (2003); MacLean, *Freedom Is Not Enough*, at 117–18; Dennis A. Deslippe, *"Rights, Not Roses": Unions and the Rise of Working-Class Feminism, 1945–80* 5 (2000); Dorothy

Sue Cobble, *The Other Women's Movement: Workplace Justice and Social Rights in Modern America* (2004); Linda K. Kerber, *No Constitutional Right to Be Ladies: Women and the Obligations of Citizenship* 183 (1998).

271. Deslippe, *"Rights, Not Roses,"* at 14, 20.

272. Kessler-Harris, *Pursuit*, at 4; Robert O. Self, *All in the Family: The Realignment of American Democracy Since the 1960s* 4 (2012).

273. Simone de Beauvoir, *The Second Sex* 311 (Constance Borde and Sheila Malovany-Chevallier trans., 2010) (1949).

274. MacLean, *Freedom Is Not Enough*, at 120; Kerber, *No Constitutional Right*, at 188–89; Kessler-Harris, *Pursuit*, at 229; Self, *All in the Family*, at 24.

275. Kerber, *No Constitutional Right*, at 192–93; Kessler-Harris, *Pursuit*, at 232–33.

276. Kessler-Harris, *Pursuit*, at 241.

277. Id. at 246–47.

278. MacLean, *Freedom Is Not Enough*, at 133–35; Kerber, *No Constitutional Right*, at 199.

279. Lucy E. Salyer, *Laws Harsh as Tigers: Chinese Immigrants and the Shaping of Modern Immigration Law* 3 (1995).

280. For an important treatment of pre–Exclusion Law immigration history, which argues that there were restrictions before 1875, albeit through different avenues, see Gerald L. Neuman, "The Lost Century of American Immigration Law (1776–1875)," 93 *Columbia Law Review* 1833 (1993).

281. Salyer, *Laws Harsh as Tigers*, at 1–35.

282. The restriction began earlier, and indeed immigration has risen and fallen throughout American history. For a discussion of the 1924 law and its racial and nationalistic origins, see Mae M. Ngai, *Impossible Subjects: Illegal Aliens and the Making of Modern America* 21–55 (2004). For general histories of American immigration policy, see Aristide Zolberg, *A Nation by Design: Immigration Policy in the Fashioning of America* (2006); Daniel J. Tichenor, *Dividing Lines: The Politics of Immigration Control in America* (2002).

283. Zolberg, *Nation by Design*, at 243.

284. Id. at 295.

285. See, for example, id. at 303–8; Tichenor, *Dividing Lines*, at 181–88.

286. Tichenor, *Dividing Lines*, at 174.

287. Ngai, *Impossible Subjects*, at 137–38.

288. Tichenor, *Dividing Lines*, at 173–74; Zolberg, *Nation by Design*, at 254–

58, 308–11; Ngai, *Impossible Subjects,* at 139–40, 127–66; MacLean, *Freedom Is Not Enough,* at 20.

289. Tichenor, *Dividing Lines,* at 174; Ngai, *Impossible Subjects,* at 139, 143–45.

290. Zolberg, *Nation by Design,* at 333. For a discussion of the lead-up to reform from the 1940s onward, and of the reforms themselves, see Ngai, *Impossible Subjects,* at 227–64.

291. Tichenor, *Dividing Lines,* at 215.

292. Zolberg, *Nation by Design,* at 340; Ngai, *Impossible Subjects,* at 261.

293. Zolberg, *Nation by Design,* at 340, 342; Tichenor, *Dividing Lines,* 230–35.

294. Lichtenstein, *State of the Union,* at 111–12; see also Katznelson, *Fear Itself;* Ira Katznelson, *When Affirmative Action Was White* (2005); Kari Frederickson, *The Dixiecrat Revolt and the End of the Solid South, 1932– 1968* 11–27 (2001); Patterson, *Congressional Conservatism,* at 40–76; V. O. Key, *Southern Politics in State and Nation* (1949). The FLSA also exempted certain white-collar workers. For a discussion of the relationship between FLSA and the middle classes, see Deborah C. Malamud, "Engineering the Middle Classes: Class Line-Drawing in New Deal Hours Legislation," 96 *Michigan Law Review* 2212 (1998). On the construction of the middle class in the New Deal era, see also Deborah C. Malamud, "Who They Are—Or Were: Middle Class Welfare in the Early New Deal," 151 *University of Pennsylvania Law Review* 2019 (2003).

295. MacLean, *Freedom Is Not Enough,* at 30; William E. Forbath, "Caste, Class, and Equal Citizenship," 98 *Michigan Law Review* 1, 82–83 (1999); Lichtenstein, *State of the Union,* at 111.

296. Risa L. Goluboff, *The Lost Promise of Civil Rights* 158–59 (2007); MacLean, *Freedom Is Not Enough,* at 7, 13.

297. Robert Korstad and Nelson Lichtenstein, "Opportunities Found and Lost: Labor, Radicals, and the Early Civil Rights Movement," 75 *Journal of American History* 786 (1988). Though perhaps not in California, where the situation was somewhat different. See Mark Brilliant, *The Color of America Has Changed: How Racial Diversity Shaped Civil Rights Reform in California, 1941–1978* (2010).

298. Korstad and Lichtenstein, "Opportunities Found and Lost," at 800–1; Karen M. Tani, *States of Dependency: Welfare, Rights, and American Governance, 1935–1972* (2016) (describing public administration and the legalization of American poor relief); Sophia Z. Lee, *The Workplace Constitution from the New Deal to the New Right* (2014) (describing

administrative efforts at civil rights); Paul Frymer, *Black and Blue: African Americans, the Labor Movement, and the Decline of the Democratic Party* (2008) (discussing the conflict between the court-based civil rights regime and the agency-based labor regime).

299. Goluboff, *Lost Promise,* at 13–15, 218, 243, 245–47. See also Jacquelyn Dowd Hall, "The Long Civil Rights Movement and the Political Uses of the Past," 91 *Journal of American History* 1250 (2005) (the NAACP "abandoned both economic issues and the battle against segregation in the North and devoted its considerable resources to clear-cut cases of de jure segregation in the South." This weakened the "link between race and class"); William H. Chafe, "Race in America: The Ultimate Test of Liberalism," in *The Achievement of American Liberalism: The New Deal and Its Legacies* 166 (William H. Chafe ed., 2002) ("The focus on economic and systemic change as a solution to racial inequality faded into oblivion [due to Cold War fears of communism], and more and more of the energies of civil rights groups went into legal challenges, within the constitutional structure, to patterns of segregation").

300. Goluboff, *Lost Promise,* at 251.

301. Forbath, "Caste, Class, and Equal Citizenship," at 86. For a discussion of King, Randolph, Rustin, and Ella Baker's views, see Tomiko Brown-Nagin, "The Civil Rights Canon: Above and Below," 123 *Yale Law Journal* 2698 (2014).

302. Lyndon B. Johnson, Commencement Address at Howard University, June 4, 1965.

303. A. Philip Randolph Institute, *A "Freedom Budget" for All Americans* 2–3, 9 (1966); Dona Cooper Hamilton and Charles V. Hamilton, *The Dual Agenda: Race and Social Welfare Policies of Civil Rights Organizations* 147–53 (1997).

304. Jefferson Cowie, *The Great Exception* 171, 170 (2015).

305. *Edwards v. California,* 314 U.S. 160 (1941).

306. Id. at 167, 174–75.

307. Id. at 185 (Jackson, J., concurring).

308. *Griffin v. Illinois,* 351 U.S. 12, 16 (1956).

309. Id. at 19.

310. *Gideon v. Wainwright,* 372 U.S. 335 (1963).

311. *Douglas v. California,* 372 U.S. 353 (1963).

312. *Shapiro v. Thompson,* 394 U.S. 618 (1969); *Memorial Hospital v. Maricopa County,* 415 U.S. 250 (1974); *Goldberg v. Kelly,* 397 U.S. 254 (1970).

313. The classic statements are Frank I. Michelman, "Foreword: On Protect-

ing the Poor Through the Fourteenth Amendment," 83 *Harvard Law Review* 7 (1969); Frank I. Michelman, "In Pursuit of Constitutional Welfare Rights: One View of Rawls' Theory of Justice," 121 *University of Pennsylvania Law Review* 962 (1973); Frank I. Michelman, "Welfare Rights in a Constitutional Democracy," 1979 *Washington University Law Quarterly* 659; Charles A. Reich, "The New Property," 73 *Yale Law Journal* 733 (1964). For later contributions, see Peter B. Edelman, "The Next Century of Our Constitution: Rethinking Our Duty to the Poor," 39 *Hastings Law Journal* 1 (1987); Goodwin Liu, "Rethinking Constitutional Welfare Rights," 61 *Stanford Law Review* 203 (2008). For an intellectual history of the evolution of constitutional welfare rights, see William E. Forbath, "Constitutional Welfare Rights: A History, Critique, and Reconstruction," 69 *Fordham Law Review* 1821 (2001). For a response, see Frank I. Michelman, "Democracy-Based Resistance to a Constitutional Right of Social Citizenship: A Comment on Forbath," 69 *Fordham Law Review* 1893 (2001).

314. Early cases are *Dandridge v. Williams,* 397 U.S. 471 (1970), and *Lindsey v. Normet,* 405 U.S. 56 (1972).

315. *San Antonio Independent School District v. Rodriguez,* 411 U.S. 1 (1973).

316. Cass R. Sunstein, *The Second Bill of Rights* 165–66 (2004).

317. *San Antonio,* 411 U.S. at 33.

318. Id. at 35–36.

319. Id. at 100 (Marshall, J., dissenting).

320. Id. at 102 (Marshall, J., dissenting).

321. Id. at 102–3 (Marshall, J., dissenting).

322. There were a few exceptions. See, for example, *Plyler v. Doe,* 457 U.S. 202 (1982); *Papasan v. Allain,* 478 U.S. 265 (1986).

323. Andrew Hartman, *A War for the Soul of America* 34 (2015); Self, *All in the Family,* at 261; Jefferson Cowie, *Stayin' Alive: The 1970s and the Last Days of the Working Class* 105 (2010); Judith Stein, *Pivotal Decade: How the United States Traded Factories for Finance in the Seventies* 52–57 (2010).

324. Hartman, *War for the Soul,* at 34; Cowie, *Stayin' Alive,* at 87–90.

325. MacLean, *Freedom Is Not Enough,* at 243.

326. Id. at 233.

327. Self, *All in the Family,* at 41. See Pete Hamill, "The Revolt of the White Lower Middle Class," *New York,* April 14, 1969.

328. Ian Haney Lopez, *Dog Whistle Politics: How Coded Racial Appeals Have Reinvented Racism and Wrecked the Middle Class* 1 (2014); Mike Allen, "RNC Chief to Say It Was 'Wrong' to Exploit Racial Conflict for Votes," *Washington Post,* July 14, 2005.

329. Charles Maier, "'Malaise': The Crisis of Capitalism in the 1970s," in *The Shock of the Global* 45 (Niall Ferguson et al. eds., 2010).

330. Daniel J. Sargent, "The United States and Globalization in the 1970s," in *Shock of the Global,* at 56.

331. Thomas Borstelmann, *The 1970s* 54 (2002).

332. In 1973, the median male worker earned $53,294 in 2014 dollars, a number that had been steadily increasing since 1960. From 1974 to 2014, the number has not again reached $53,000. Carmen DeNavas-Walt and Bernadette D. Proctor, Current Population Reports, P60-252, *Income and Poverty in the United States,* U.S. Census Bureau, table A-4: Number and Real Median Earnings of Total Workers and Full-Time, Year Round Workers by Sex and Female to Male Earnings Ratio: 1960 to 2014 (2015).

333. Maier, "Malaise," at 45.

334. Bruce J. Schulman, *The Seventies* 135–36 (2001). For more on debt, see, for example, Jacob S. Hacker, *The Great Risk Shift: The New Economic Insecurity and the Decline of the American Dream* (rev. ed. 2008); Elizabeth Warren and Amelia Warren Tyagi, *The Two-Income Trap* (2003).

335. Borstelmann, *1970s,* at 134.

336. Id.

337. Id. at 123–24; see also Jefferson Cowie, *Capital Moves* (1999).

338. Daniel Bell, *The Coming of Post-Industrial Society* (1973).

339. Michael Harrington, *The Twilight of Capitalism* (1976).

340. Powell to Eugene B. Snydor Jr., Confidential Memorandum: Attack on American Free Enterprise System 1, 11, Aug. 23, 1971, http://law2.wlu.edu/deptimages/Powell%20Archives/PowellMemorandumTypescript.pdf.

341. Id. at 26.

342. Lee Drutman, *The Business of America Is Lobbying* 55–59 (2015); Alyssa Katz, *The Influence Machine: The U.S. Chamber of Commerce and the Corporate Capture of American Life* 37–51 (2015); David Vogel, *Fluctuating Fortunes: The Political Power of Business in America* 37–113, 194 (1989); Cowie, *Stayin' Alive,* at 229–31. The list of reform legislation is from Cowie.

343. Cowie, *Stayin' Alive,* at 232.

344. Stein, *Pivotal Decade,* 190–91; Cowie, *Stayin' Alive,* at 267–69.

345. Stein, *Pivotal Decade,* at 182, 186; Cowie, *Stayin' Alive,* at 292.

346. Cowie, *Stayin' Alive,* at 286; Stein, *Pivotal Decade,* at 190–92.

347. Cowie, *Stayin' Alive,* at 286.

348. Stein, *Pivotal Decade,* at 182, 187–89; Cowie, *Stayin' Alive,* at 231, 293.

349. Cowie, *Stayin' Alive,* at 293.

350. Id. at 294, 231; Stein, *Pivotal Decade,* at 187.

351. Cowie, *Stayin' Alive,* at 296; Stein, *Pivotal Decade,* at 189–90. For an interesting discussion of the letter, see also Victor G. Devinatz, "Doug Fraser's 1978 Resignation Letter from the Labor-Management Group and the Limits of Trade Union Liberalism," 45 *Labor History* 323 (2004).

352. Cowie, *Stayin' Alive,* at 298.

353. Id.

354. Id. at 240.

Chapter Five: How Economic Inequality Threatens the Republic

1. Thomas Piketty, *Capital in the Twenty-First Century* (2013).

2. Pew Research Center, "Beyond Red vs. Blue: The Political Typology" 41, June 26, 2014.

3. Robert Putnam, *Our Kids: The American Dream in Crisis* 2, 20–21 (2015).

4. Id. at 3–5, 12–13, 22.

5. Id. at 3–5, 22.

6. Id. at 37.

7. Charles Murray, *Coming Apart: The State of White America, 1960–2010* (2012).

8. George Packer, *The Unwinding* (2013).

9. Barbara Ehrenreich, *Bait and Switch: The (Futile) Pursuit of the American Dream* (2005); Kathryn Edin and Luke Shaefer, *$2.00 a Day: Living on Almost Nothing in America* (2015); Chrystia Freeland, *Plutocrats: The Rise of the New Global Super-rich and the Fall of Everyone Else* (2012).

10. Paul Krugman, *The Conscience of a Liberal* 124 (2007).

11. Economic Policy Institute (EPI), "The Top 10 Charts of 2014," Dec. 18, 2014, Chart 2.

12. Economic Policy Institute, "The State of Working America," http://www.stateofworkingamerica.org/who-gains/#/?start=1979&end=2008. Restricting the data only to times when there was economic expansion (that is, excluding recessions), Pavlina Tcherneva has shown that most income growth went to the bottom 90 percent from 1949 to 1979. But since 1980, most income growth during expansions has gone to the top 10 percent, and in the most recent expansion, since 2009, the bottom 90 percent has actually seen their incomes decline. See Matthew Yglesias, "The Most Important Chart About the American Economy You'll See This Year," *Vox,* Sept. 25, 2014.

13. Data from Emmanuel Saez, table A1, col. P90–100, http://eml.berkeley.edu/~saez/TabFig2014prel.xls.

14. Id.
15. Data from Emmanuel Saez, table A3, col. P99–100 and col. P99.99–100, http://eml.berkeley.edu/~saez/TabFig2014prel.xls; for the number of families in 2012, see Emmanuel Saez, "Striking It Richer: The Evolution of Top Incomes in the United States," 10, Sept. 3, 2013, http://eml .berkeley.edu/~saez/saez-UStopincomes-2012.pdf.
16. Chuck Collins and Josh Hoxie, *Billionaire Bonanza: The Forbes 400 and the Rest of Us,* Institute for Policy Studies, Dec. 1, 2015.
17. Pew Research Center, "The American Middle Class Is Losing Ground," 7, Dec. 2015.
18. Id. at 4–5. Pew defined the middle class as those with an income of between two-thirds and double the median household income, adjusted for the size of household.
19. Id. at 4, 12, 25.
20. Id. at 4, 39.
21. Id. at 4–5.
22. Id.
23. Id. at 19–22.
24. Pew Research Center, "America's Shrinking Middle Class: A Close Look at Changes Within Metropolitan Areas," 5, May 11, 2016. Pew uses "middle income," defined as households between two-thirds and double the median household income, adjusted for the size of household, and occasionally uses "middle class" interchangeably. I use "middle class" for stylistic consistency.
25. Id. at 6.
26. Id. at 16–17, 22.
27. Id. at 34–36.
28. Larry Mishel, Elise Gould, and Josh Bivens, "Wage Stagnation in Nine Charts," fig. 9, Economic Policy Institute, Jan. 6, 2015.
29. Florence Jaumotte and Carolina Osorio Buitron, "Inequality and Labor Market Institutions," 25, IMF Staff Discussion Note, July 2015.
30. EPI, "Top 10 Charts," at chart 5.
31. Bruce Western and Jake Rosenfeld, "Unions, Norms, and the Rise in U.S. Wage Inequality," 76 *American Sociological Review* 513 (2011). See also Jake Rosenfeld, *What Unions No Longer Do* 74–79 (2014).
32. Alan B. Krueger, "The Rise and Consequences of Inequality in the United States," Jan. 12, 2012.
33. Raj Chetty et al., "Where Is the Land of Opportunity? The Geography of Intergenerational Mobility in the United States," 129 *Quarterly Journal of Economics* 1553, 1577–78 (2014).

34. Patrick O'Connor, "Poll Finds Widespread Economic Anxiety," *Wall Street Journal,* Aug. 5, 2014.

35. Social Security Administration, "Wage Statistics for 2014," May 13, 2016.

36. Neal Gabler, "The Secret Shame of Middle-Class Americans," *Atlantic,* May 2016.

37. Victor Tan Chen, "All Hollowed Out: The Lonely Poverty of America's White Working Class," *Atlantic,* Jan. 16, 2016.

38. Id.

39. Anne Case and Angus Deaton, "Rising Morbidity and Mortality in Midlife Among White Non-Hispanic Americans in the 21st Century," 112 *Proceedings of the National Academy of Sciences* 15078 (2015).

40. Urban Institute, Chart 3: Racial and Ethnic Wealth Disparities Are Also Growing, Nine Charts About Wealth Inequality in America.

41. Pew Research Center, "Wealth Inequality Has Widened Along Racial, Ethnic Lines Since End of Great Recession," Dec. 12, 2014.

42. Urban Institute, Chart 6: African Americans and Hispanics Lag Behind on Major Wealth-Building Measures, like Homeownership, Nine Charts About Wealth Inequality in America.

43. The data is helpfully collected at Neil Irwin, Claire Cain Miller, and Margot Sanger-Katz, "America's Racial Divide, Charted," *The Upshot* (blog), *New York Times,* Aug. 19, 2014.

44. For a discussion along a variety of lines, including cultural and political, see Bill Bishop, *The Big Sort: Why the Clustering of Like-Minded America Is Tearing Us Apart* (2008).

45. Sean F. Reardon and Kendra Bischoff, "The Continuing Increase in Income Segregation, 2007–2012," 7 and table 1, March 6, 2016. See also Sean F. Reardon and Kendra Bischoff, "Income Inequality and Income Segregation," 116 *American Journal of Sociology* 1092 (2011).

46. The literature emphasizes different features and causal mechanisms and comes from different political perspectives, but it is consistent on the trend of divergence along these lines. See, for example, Murray, *Coming Apart;* Putnam, *Our Kids;* Andrew Cherlin, *Labor's Love Lost: The Rise and Fall of the Working-Class Family in America* (2014); Bishop, *Big Sort;* Chen, "All Hollowed Out"; Richard V. Reeves, "The Dangerous Separation of the American Upper Middle Class," Brookings, Sept. 3, 2015; Reihan Salam, "The Upper Middle Class Is Ruining America," Slate.com, Jan. 30, 2015.

47. Reardon and Bischoff, "Continuing Increase in Income Segregation," at 14.

48. Michael I. Norton and Dan Ariely, "Building a Better America—One Wealth Quintile at a Time," 6 *Perspectives on Psychological Science* 9, 10 (2011). Americans have consistently wanted a more egalitarian society. See Leslie McCall, *The Undeserving Rich: American Beliefs About Inequality, Opportunity, and Redistribution* 186–212 (2013) (describing Americans' preference for a more egalitarian distribution of wealth from the 1980s onward); Benjamin I. Page and Lawrence R. Jacobs, "No Class War: Economic Inequality and the American Public," in *The Unsustainable American State* (Lawrence Jacobs and Desmond King eds., 2009) (noting that Americans dislike economic inequality and support progressive taxation to alleviate it).

49. Norton and Ariely, "Building a Better America," at 10–11.

50. Christopher Hayes, *Twilight of the Elites: America After Meritocracy* 56–57 (2012).

51. On the importance of equality beyond equality of opportunity, including a focus on the intergenerational issues and the distribution and structure of prizes for efforts, see Anthony B. Atkinson, *Inequality: What Can Be Done?* 11 (2015). For a sharp critique of equal opportunity, see Dylan Matthews, "The Case Against Equality of Opportunity," *Vox*, Sept. 21, 2015. For a philosophical argument that inequality is not the central issue, see Harry G. Frankfurt, *On Inequality* 7 (2015) (arguing that the core issue should be sufficiency rather than inequality). For a creative way to advance access to opportunities, see Joseph Fishkin, *Bottlenecks: A New Theory of Equal Opportunity* (2014).

52. David Madland, *Hollowed Out: Why the Economy Doesn't Work Without a Strong Middle Class* 37–41 (2015).

53. Id.

54. Jeffrey A. Winters, *Oligarchy* 6 (2011).

55. Id. at 6–7.

56. Id. at 23–24.

57. Franklin Delano Roosevelt, Campaign Address on Progressive Government at the Commonwealth Club of San Francisco, Sept. 23, 1932, in 1 *The Public Papers and Addresses of Franklin D. Roosevelt* (Samuel I. Roseman ed., 1938).

58. Michael Lind, "Private Sector Parasites," *Salon*, March 21, 2013. For a general discussion of how policy changes concentrate wealth and power, see Jacob S. Hacker and Paul Pierson, *Winner-Take-All Politics* (2010).

59. John C. Coates IV, "Corporate Speech & the First Amendment: History, Data, and Implications," 30 *Constitutional Commentary* 223, 270 and n161 (2015) (describing, for example, MGMT-450 Strategic Management in Non-market Environments, Kellogg School of Management, a

course which covers the strategic use of "legislatures, regulatory bodies, or courts").

60. Ezra Klein, "The Doom Loop of Oligarchy," *Vox*, April 11, 2014.

61. Indeed, even the founding generation thought republics were representative democracies. See *Federalist* No. 10 (James Madison) (Clinton Rossiter ed., 1999) ("A republic, by which I mean a government in which the scheme of representation takes place"); *Federalist* No. 14 (James Madison) ("[I]n a democracy, the people meet and exercise the government in person; in a republic, they assemble and administer it by their representatives and agents").

62. Winters, *Oligarchy*, at 34.

63. Id. at 208.

64. John Taylor, *Inquiry into the Principles and Policy of the Government of the United States* 259 (1814).

65. Karen Stenner, *The Authoritarian Dynamic* (2005).

66. Marc Hetherington and Jonathan Weiler, *Authoritarianism and Polarization in American Politics* (2009).

67. Marc Hetherington and Elizabeth Suhay, "Authoritarianism, Threat, and Americans' Support for the War on Terror," 55 *American Journal of Political Science* 546 (2011).

68. See generally Michael Signer, *Demagogue: The Fight to Save Democracy from Its Worst Enemies* (2009).

69. *Federalist* No. 1, at 3 (Hamilton).

70. Larry Bartels, "Rich People Rule!," *Monkey Cage* (blog), *Washington Post*, April 8, 2014 (noting that this turn in political science is relatively recent). The catalyst, or at least a focal point, for this newfound attention was Larry Jacobs and Theda Skocpol's 2003 to 2005 American Political Science Association Task Force on Inequality and American Democracy. See *Inequality and American Democracy* ix (Lawrence R. Jacobs and Theda Skocpol eds., 2007). But some scholars had been toiling on this issue for many years prior. See, for example, G. William Domhoff, *Who Rules America?* (7th ed. 2013); Thomas Ferguson, *Golden Rule* (1995).

71. E. E. Schattschneider, *The Semisovereign People* 34–35 (1975).

72. Martin Gilens and Benjamin I. Page, "Testing Theories of American Politics: Elites, Interest Groups, and Average Citizens," 12 *Perspectives on Politics* 564, 573 (2014).

73. A few brief methodological notes: First, the political science studies in this area sometimes use different metrics for identifying economic elites. Because a number of important studies use the top 10 percent income bracket as their metric, I will use that as an unstated default

throughout this section when referring to the "wealthy" or "economic elites." See, for example, Martin Gilens, *Affluence and Influence: Economic Inequality and Political Power in America* (2014); Martin Gilens, "Policy Consequences of Representational Inequality," in *Who Gets Represented?* (Peter K. Enns and Christopher Wlezien eds., 2011); Martin Gilens, "Preference Gaps and Inequality in Representation," 42 *PS: Political Science & Politics* 335 (April 2009); Martin Gilens, "Inequality and Democratic Responsiveness," 69 *Public Opinion Quarterly* 778 (2005). See also Benjamin I. Page and Lawrence R. Jacobs, *Class War?* 14 (2009) (describing public opinion and concluding that "[m]ajorities of Americans of all economic and political stripes actually agree that economic inequality has widened, that this is worrisome, and that the government should respond"); Andrew Gelman, *Red State, Blue State, Rich State, Poor State* (2010) (explaining how economic class, state wealth, and ideology are related); Jeffrey A. Winters and Benjamin I. Page, "Oligarchy in the United States?," 7 *Perspectives on Politics* 731 (2009) (suggesting that the United States might be better considered an oligarchy). When a study uses a different metric to define "wealthy" or "economic elites," I will specify the study's metric. Second, although the studies cited here are from leading political scientists, widely recognized as some of the most distinguished in their field, some might have questions about their methodologies and arguments. As with all interdisciplinary scholarship, I cannot explain or defend every methodological choice without repeating a decade's worth of books and articles. But the collection of studies all pointing in the same direction suggests that at the very least the patterns are real. For more on critics of this research and responses, see note 121.

74. Benjamin I. Page, Larry M. Bartels, and Jason Seawright, "Democracy and the Policy Preferences of Wealthy Americans," 11 *Perspectives on Politics* 51 (March 2013). The rest of the citations in this paragraph are all based on comparisons with the top 1 percent and 0.1 percent in income.

75. Id. at 64–65.

76. Id. at 55.

77. Id. at 57.

78. Id.

79. Id. at 61.

80. Nicholas Carnes, *White-Collar Government* 3, 17–21 (2013). In order to determine a legislator's class, Carnes focused on occupational background rather than on income, education, wealth, or other factors. He divided occupation prior to elected office into ten categories and also

grouped occupations into broader blue-collar and white-collar categories. Id. at 17–21.

81. Kay Lehman Schlozman, Sidney Verba, and Henry E. Brady, *The
Unheavenly Chorus* 126–33 (2012).

82. Frank R. Baumgartner et al., *Lobbying and Policy Change* 16 (2009).

83. Gilens and Page, "Testing Theories," at 570–71, 574. Indeed, preferences of individual economic elites and business groups are even misaligned: the former often want less government action, whereas the
latter sometimes seek support from the government for their industry.
Id. at 571.

84. Schlozman, Verba, and Brady, *Unheavenly Chorus,* at 122–26, 152–59.
Schlozman, Verba, and Brady use socioeconomic status, for which they
created their own measure, giving equal weight to family income and
education level. Id. at 123n9. They explicitly note the similarities of
their findings with other measures, particularly those that consider the
relationship between income and voting. Id. at 156n16.

85. Page, Bartels, and Seawright, "Democracy," at 54.

86. Schlozman, Verba, and Brady, *Unheavenly Chorus,* at 165–66, 199, 224,
228, 579. These authors rely on socioeconomic status.

87. Id. at 233.

88. I follow Schlozman, Verba, and Brady, *Unheavenly Chorus,* at 267–
77, in presenting the classic approach with broad strokes. For precise
statements of the theory, see Arthur F. Bentley, *The Process of Government* (1908); David B. Truman, *The Government Process* (1951); Robert Dahl, *A Preface to Democratic Theory* (1956).

89. Schattschneider, *Semisovereign People,* at 35.

90. Mancur Olson Jr., *The Logic of Collective Action* (1965).

91. Schlozman, Verba, and Brady, *Unheavenly Chorus,* at 322.

92. Id. at 319.

93. Id. at 331.

94. Id. at 329. Schlozman, Verba, and Brady use census data to categorize
occupations within the broader population. Id. at 328.

95. Id. at 329.

96. Id. at 371.

97. Dara Strolovitch, *Affirmative Advocacy: Race, Class, and Gender in
Interest Group Politics* (2007).

98. Compare Larry Bartels, *Unequal Democracy* 275 (2008) ("Income-
related disparities in turnout simply do not seem large enough to
provide a plausible explanation for the income-related disparities in
responsiveness documented here"), with Schlozman, Verba, and Brady,
Unheavenly Chorus, at 118 ("[A]ctivity by both citizens and organized

interests makes a difference for public policy, and, if anything, public officials are disproportionately responsive to the affluent and well-educated members of their constituencies").

99. Schlozman, Verba, and Brady, *Unheavenly Chorus,* at 118.
100. Bartels, *Unequal Democracy,* at 253–54. Bartels used National Election Studies data and, to correct for underrepresentation that is common in telephone surveys, post-stratified the sample. See id. at 254n9 for details.
101. Gilens, *Affluence and Influence;* Gilens, "Policy Consequences," at 247.
102. Gilens, *Affluence and Influence,* at 79; Gilens, "Policy Consequences," at 250–52.
103. Gilens, *Affluence and Influence,* at 79; Gilens, "Policy Consequences," at 252–53.
104. Gilens, *Affluence and Influence,* at 83–84.
105. Scholars have researched foreign policy issues in detail and found similar effects. See Benjamin I. Page, *The Foreign Policy Disconnect: What Americans Want from Our Leaders but Don't Get,* with Marshall M. Bouton (2006); Lawrence R. Jacobs and Benjamin I. Page, "Who Influences U.S. Foreign Policy?," 99 *American Political Science Review* 107 (2005); Benjamin I. Page and Jason Barabas, "Foreign Policy Gaps Between Citizens and Leaders," 44 *International Studies Quarterly* 339 (2000). On the other areas, see Gilens, *Affluence and Influence,* at 98–112; Gilens, "Policy Consequences," at 256–73.
106. Gilens, *Affluence and Influence,* at 94.
107. Id. at 163.
108. Id. at 171–72.
109. Id. at 173 and n24, describing findings based on data from Christopher R. Berry, Barry C. Burden, and William G. Howell, "After Enactment: The Lives and Deaths of Federal Programs," 54 *American Journal of Political Science* 1 (2010).
110. Ebonya L. Washington, "Female Socialization: How Daughters Affect Their Legislator Fathers' Voting on Women's Issues," 98 *American Economic Review* 311 (2008). The same effect has been found with smokers and pro-tobacco voting records. Barry C. Burden, *The Personal Roots of Representation* (2007).
111. Carnes, *White-Collar Government,* at 27.
112. Id. at 36–38.
113. Id. at 113–20.
114. Nolan McCarty, Keith T. Poole, and Howard Rosenthal, *Polarized America* 2 (2006).
115. Page, Bartels, and Seawright, "Democracy," at 66.

116. Gilens, *Affluence and Influence,* at 181; Bartels, *Unequal Democracy,* at 268–69.

117. Bartels, *Unequal Democracy,* at 264.

118. Gilens, *Affluence and Influence,* at 194, 211.

119. Id. at 212–13.

120. Gilens and Page, "Testing Theories," at 564–68.

121. Id. at 565, 568. Gilens and Page have recently been criticized by other political scientists. See Peter K. Enns, "Relative Policy Support and Coincidental Representation," 13 *Perspectives on Politics* 1053 (2015); Peter K. Enns, "Reconsidering the Middle: A Reply to Martin Gilens," 13 *Perspectives on Politics* 1072 (2015); Omar S. Bashir, "Testing Inferences About American Politics: A Review of the 'Oligarchy' Result," *Research & Politics* 1 (Oct.–Dec. 2015). While the political scientists make some good points, particularly around the extent to which majorities might win, many of their criticisms are covered by Gilens and Page's own work (for example, there is frequent overlap of preferences between the affluent and others, and there is a status quo bias that means there is a difference between accomplishing and blocking policies). For a response to the critics, see Martin Gilens, "The Insufficiency of 'Democracy by Coincidence': A Response to Peter K. Enns," 13 *Perspectives on Politics* 1065 (2015).

122. Gilens, *Affluence and Influence,* at 73–74; Baumgartner et al., *Lobbying and Political Change,* at 7; Gilens, *Affluence and Influence,* at 133.

123. Gilens, *Affluence and Influence,* at 1.

124. Id. at 83.

125. For the 2000 data, see Brennan Center, "2000 Presidential Race First in Modern History Where Political Parties Spend More on TV Ads Than Candidates," Dec. 12, 2004. Inflation-adjusted, the 2000 number is around $196 million.

126. Nicholas Confessore, Sarah Cohen, and Karen Yourish, "The Families Funding the 2016 Presidential Election," *New York Times,* Oct. 10, 2015. For the full list, see Eric Lichtblau and Nicholas Confessore, "From Fracking to Finance, a Torrent of Campaign Cash," *New York Times,* Oct. 10, 2015.

127. Stephen Wolf, "Just 158 Families Account for Nearly Half of All Presidential Campaign Donations," *Daily Kos,* Oct. 12, 2015. Wolf makes the comparison to 2000.

128. Robert Kaiser, *So Damn Much Money* (2009).

129. Stephen Ansolabehere, John de Figueiredo, and James Snyder Jr., "Why Is There So Little Money in U.S. Politics," 17 *Journal of Economic Perspectives* 105 (2003).

130. Lawrence Lessig, *Republic, Lost* 134 (2011).

131. Id. at 133.

132. Id. at 149.

133. Id. at 138.

134. Norah O'Donnell, "Are Members of Congress Becoming Telemarketers?," *60 Minutes*, April 24, 2016.

135. Id.

136. Ryan Grim and Sabrina Siddiqui, "Call Time for Congress Shows How Fundraising Dominates Bleak Work Life," *Huffington Post*, Jan. 8, 2013.

137. Lessig, *Republic, Lost*, at 138–39.

138. Id. at 139.

139. O'Donnell, "Are Members of Congress Becoming Telemarketers?"

140. Lessig, *Republic, Lost*, at 142, 151.

141. Edward L. Glaeser and Cass R. Sunstein, "Extremism and Social Learning," 1 *Journal of Legal Analysis*, 263, 268 (2009).

142. David Schkade, Cass R. Sunstein, and Reid Hastie, "What Happened on Deliberation Day?," 95 *California Law Review* 915, 921–22 (2007).

143. Cass R. Sunstein et al., *Are Judges Political? An Empirical Analysis of the Federal Judiciary* 14–15, 76–77 (2006).

144. See Solomon E. Asch, "Studies of Independence and Conformity: I. A Minority of One Against a Unanimous Majority," 70 *Psychological Monographs: General and Applied* 1 (1956); Solomon E. Asch, "Opinions and Social Pressure," 193 *Scientific American* 31 (1955).

145. Irving L. Janis, "Groupthink," *Psychology Today* 43, 44 (Nov. 1971); see generally Irving L. Janis, *Groupthink* (1982).

146. Glaeser and Sunstein, "Extremism and Social Learning."

147. Lee Drutman, *The Business of America Is Lobbying* 37 (2015).

148. Id. at 7–8.

149. Brian Kelleher Richter, Krislert Samphantharak, and Jeffrey F. Timmons, "Lobbying and Taxes," 53 *American Journal of Political Science* 893 (2009).

150. Drutman, *Lobbying*, at 24.

151. Id. at 58; David Vogel, *Fluctuating Fortunes: The Political Power of Business in America* 197 (1989).

152. Id. at 8.

153. Id. at 8–9.

154. Id. at 12.

155. Id.

156. Alyssa Katz, *The Influence Machine* 14 (2015).

157. OpenSecrets.org, "Finance, Insurance & Real Estate," Sector Profile,

2014, Center for Responsive Politics, http://www.opensecrets.org/lobby/indus.php?id=F&year=2014.

158. Drutman, *Lobbying*, at 85.

159. Id. at 91.

160. For a theory of how information shapes government, see Bryan D. Jones and Frank R. Baumgartner, *The Politics of Attention* (2005).

161. Andrew Rich, *Think Tanks, Public Policy, and the Politics of Expertise* 34–36, 38 (2004).

162. Id. at 35–37.

163. Andrew Rich, "War of Ideas," *Stanford Social Innovation Review* 20 (Spring 2005).

164. Id. at 20.

165. Id.

166. Id. at 25.

167. Eric Lipton and Brooke Williams, "How Think Tanks Amplify Corporate America's Influence," *The New York Times*, August 7, 2016; Eric Lipton, Nicholas Confessore, and Brooke Williams, "Think Tank Scholar or Corporate Consultant? It Depends on the Day," *The New York Times*, August 8, 2016.

168. Legal scholars call this epistemic or cognitive capture. See David Freeman Engstrom, "Corralling Capture," 36 *Harvard Journal of Law and Public Policy* 31, 32 (2013); James Kwak, "Cultural Capture and the Financial Crisis," in *Preventing Regulatory Capture* 71 (Daniel Carpenter and David A. Moss eds., 2013); Cass R. Sunstein, "The Office of Information and Regulatory Affairs: Myths and Realities," 126 *Harvard Law Review* 1838, 1860–61 (2013).

169. Lawrence B. Lindsey, *What a President Should Know*, with Marc Sumerlin, 21 (2008); Steven F. Hayward, *The Age of Reagan: The Conservative Counterrevolution, 1980–1989* 37 (2009).

170. Doris Kearns Goodwin, *Team of Rivals: The Political Genius of Abraham Lincoln* (2005). For a discussion of its failure, see Lawrence J. Korb, "Obama's 'Team of Rivals' Debacle," *National Interest*, Jan. 15, 2015.

171. Carnes, *White-Collar Government*, at 5.

172. Russ Choma, "Millionaires' Club: For First Time, Most Lawmakers Are Worth $1 Million-Plus," *OpenSecrets*, Jan. 9, 2014.

173. Fabian T. Pfeffer, Sheldon Danziger, and Robert F. Schoeni, "Wealth Levels, Wealth Inequality, and the Great Recession," Russell Sage Foundation, June 2014; see also Anna Bernasek, "The Typical Household, Now Worth a Third Less," *New York Times*, July 26, 2014.

174. Carnes, *White-Collar Government*, at 5.

175. Elizabeth Warren, Speech at the Managing the Economy Conference,

Dec. 9, 2014, https://www.bostonglobe.com/news/nation/2014/12/09/text-warren-speech-treasury-nominee/Atp2CqJDCraBLVR0x0goxL/story.html. See Jia Lynn Yang, "Jack Lew Had Major Role at Citigroup When It Nearly Imploded," *Washington Post,* Jan. 10, 2013; Craig Torres and Dakin Campbell, "Summers Suspends Citigroup Ties While Considered for Fed," *Bloomberg,* Sept. 14, 2013; Jonathan Stempel and Dan Wilchins, "Robert Rubin Quits Citigroup Amid Criticism," Reuters, Jan. 9, 2009.

176. Data from Emmanuel Saez, p. 1, http://eml.berkeley.edu/~saez/course/Labortaxes/taxableincome/taxableincome_attach.pdf.

177. Data from Emmanuel Saez, p. 7, table A, http://eml.berkeley.edu/~saez/course/Labortaxes/taxableincome/taxableincome_attach.pdf.

178. Data from Emmanuel Saez, p. 4, table A1, http://eml.berkeley.edu/~saez/course/Labortaxes/taxableincome/taxableincome_attach.pdf.

179. Richard Rubin and Jesse Drucker, "Romney's 13.9% Tax Rate Spotlights Wealthy Investors' Breaks," *Bloomberg,* Jan. 24, 2012.

180. Theodore Roosevelt, Seventh Annual Message, Dec. 3, 1907, in *State Papers as Governor and President, 1899–1909* 430 (Hermann Hagedorn ed., 1925).

181. Seth Hanlon and Sarah Ayres Steinberg, "Loopholes in the Estate Tax Show Why Revenue Must Be on the Table," Center for American Progress, Jan. 24, 2013.

182. Tax Policy Center, Taxable Estate Tax Returns as a Percentage of Adult Deaths, Selected Years of Death, 1934–2011, Nov. 30, 2011, http://www.taxpolicycenter.org/taxfacts/displayafact.cfm?Docid=52.

183. Hanlon and Steinberg, "Loopholes in the Estate Tax."

184. Data from Emmanuel Saez, p. 4, table A1, http://eml.berkeley.edu/~saez/course/Labortaxes/taxableincome/taxableincome_attach.pdf.

185. Daniel J. Weiss and Miranda Peterson, "With Only $93 Billion in Profits, the Big Five Oil Companies Demand to Keep Tax Breaks," Center for American Progress, Feb. 10, 2014.

186. Madland, *Hollowed Out,* at 97.

187. Paul Blumenthal, "The Legacy of Billy Tauzin: The White House–PhRMA Deal," Sunlight Foundation, Feb. 12, 2010, https://sunlightfoundation.com/blog/2010/02/12/the-legacy-of-billy-tauzin-the-white-house-phrma-deal/; Olga Price, "Medicare Drug Planners Now Lobbyists, with Billions at Stake," ProPublica, Oct. 20, 2009, https://www.propublica.org/article/medicare-drug-planners-now-lobbyists-with-billions-at-stake-1020.

188. Marc-André Gagnon and Sidney Wolfe, "Mirror, Mirror on the Wall: Medicare Part D Pays Needlessly High Brand-Name Drug Prices Com-

pared with Other OECD Countries and with U.S. Government Programs," Policy Brief, at 4, Carleton University and Public Citizen, July 23, 2015.

189. Dean Baker, "Reducing Waste with an Efficient Medicare Prescription Drug Benefit," Policy Brief, at 4, Center for Economic and Policy Research, Jan. 2013.

190. Bianca DiJulio, Jamie Firth, and Mollyann Brodie, "Kaiser Health Tracking Poll: August 2015," Aug. 20, 2015.

191. OpenSecrets.org, Industry Profile: Summary, 2014, Pharmaceuticals /Health Products, Center for Responsive Politics, http://www.open secrets.org/lobby/indusclient.php?id=H04&year=2014.

192. Sendhil Mullianathan, Markus Noeth, and Antoinette Schoar, "The Market for Financial Advice: An Audit Study" (NBER Working Paper No. 17929, March 2012); Susan E. K. Christoffersen, Richard Evans, and David K. Musto, "What Do Consumers' Fund Flows Maximize? Evidence from Their Brokers' Incentives," 68 *Journal of Finance* 201 (2013).

193. Stan Haithcock, "You Just Gave Your Annuity Agent a Great Vacation," *MarketWatch*, Aug. 12, 2014; Office of Senator Elizabeth Warren, "Villas, Castles, and Vacations: How Perks and Giveaways Create Conflicts of Interest in the Annuity Industry," Oct. 2015.

194. Council of Economic Advisers, "The Effects of Conflicted Investment Advice on Retirement Savings," White House, Feb. 2015, https://www .whitehouse.gov/sites/default/files/docs/cea_coi_report_final.pdf.

195. Department of Labor, "Fact Sheet: Department of Labor Proposes Rule to Address Conflicts of Interest in Retirement Advice, Saving Middle-Class Families Billions of Dollars Every Year."

196. Her bill would have required the SEC to act first. Press Release, "Rep. Wagner Statement on Labor Fiduciary Rule," April 14, 2015, https://wagner.house.gov/media-center/press-releases/rep-wagner -statement-on-labor-fiduciary-rule; Ashlea Ebeling, "DOL Fiduciary Rule Opponents Seek Delay, Perez Snubbed at House Hearings," *Forbes*, Sept. 14, 2015.

197. Press Release, "FSR Voices Support for Rep. Wagner's Retail Investor Protection Act to Pause Harmful DoL Rule," Financial Services Roundtable, Sept. 29, 2015; Chamber of Commerce, "Key Vote Alert!—H.R. 1090, the 'Retail Investor Protection Act,' and H.R. 1317," Oct. 27, 2015.

198. Statement of Sean Collins, Senior Director, Industry and Financial Analysis, Investment Company Institute, Department of Labor Hearing: Proposed Fiduciary Rules—Regulatory Impact Analysis, Aug. 11, 2015, https://www.ici.org/fiduciary_rule/resources/15_dol_fiduciary _ria_collins_oral.

199. Jane Dokko, "Caveat Emptor: Watch Where Research on the Fiduciary Rule Comes From," Brookings, July 29, 2015.

200. Daniel Strauss, "Warren Criticism Leads to Brookings Economist's Exit," *Politico,* Sept. 29, 2015.

201. Id.; Tom Hamburger, "How Elizabeth Warren Picked a Fight with Brookings—and Won," *Washington Post,* Sept. 29, 2015; Strobe Talbott, letter, "Warren Had Nothing to Do with Litan's Exit," *Wall Street Journal,* Oct. 8, 2015.

202. The quotations are from various insurance companies. See Representative Elijah Cummings and Senator Elizabeth Warren to Labor Secretary Thomas Perez and OMB Director Shaun Donovan, at 1, 4, Feb. 11, 2015, http://www.warren.senate.gov/files/documents/2016-2-11 _Letter_to_DOL_and_OMB.pdf.

203. Department of Justice, Press Release, "HSBC Holdings Plc. and HSBC Bank USA N.A. Admit to Money-Laundering and Sanctions Violations, Forfeit $1.256 Billion in Deferred Prosecution Agreement," Dec. 11, 2012.

204. Glenn Greenwald, "HSBC, Too Big to Jail, Is the New Poster Child for US Two-Tiered Justice System," *Guardian,* Dec. 12, 2012.

205. Mark Gongloff, "Eric Holder Admits Some Banks Are Just Too Big to Prosecute," *Huffington Post,* March 6, 2013.

206. Jason M. Breslow, "Eric Holder Backtracks Remarks on 'Too Big to Jail,'" *Frontline,* PBS, May 16, 2013.

207. Louis F. Powell Jr. to Eugene B. Snydor Jr., Confidential Memorandum: Attack on American Free Enterprise System 26–27, Aug. 23, 1971, http://law2.wlu.edu/deptimages/Powell%20Archives/PowellMemo randumTypescript.pdf.

208. For accounts of the rise of the conservative intellectual and legal movements, see Steven M. Teles, *The Rise of the Conservative Legal Movement: The Battle for Control of the Law* (2008); Amanda Hollis-Brusky, *Ideas with Consequences: The Federalist Society and the Conservative Counterrevolution* (2015); Michael Avery and Danielle McLaughlin, *The Federalist Society: How Conservatives Took the Law Back from Liberals* (2013); Jane Mayer, *Dark Money: The Hidden History of the Billionaires Behind the Rise of the Radical Right* (2016).

209. Teles, *Conservative Legal Movement,* at 61.

210. Id. at 182–207.

211. Id. at 207–16.

212. Id. at 135–80; Hollis-Brusky, *Ideas with Consequences;* Avery and McLaughlin, *Federalist Society.*

213. Jeffrey Rosen, "The Unregulated Offensive," *New York Times Magazine,* April 17, 2005.

214. *United States v. Lopez,* 514 U.S. 549 (1995); *United States v. Morrison,* 529 U.S. 598 (2000).

215. *Hammer v. Dagenhart,* 247 U.S. 251 (1918).

216. *New York v. United States,* 505 U.S. 144 (1992); *Printz v. United States,* 521 U.S. 898 (1997).

217. Rick Montes, "What Is a Tenther?," Tenth Amendment Center, May 6, 2010. For a discussion, see Ian Millhiser, "Rally 'Round the 'True Constitution,'" *American Prospect,* Aug. 25, 2009; Ian Millhiser, "What if the Tea Party Wins? They Have a Plan for the Constitution, and It Isn't Pretty," Center for American Progress, Sept. 2011.

218. Erwin Chemerinsky, "The Rehnquist Revolution," 2 *Pierce Law Review* 1 (2004).

219. *National Federation of Independent Business v. Sebelius,* 132 S. Ct. 2566 (2012).

220. *Free Enterprise Fund v. Public Company Accounting Oversight Board,* 561 U.S. 477 (2010).

221. The revisionist account is Howard Gillman, *The Constitution Besieged: The Rise and Demise of Lochner Era Police Powers Jurisprudence* (1995), though it is not necessarily libertarian. The leading libertarian account is David E. Bernstein, *Rehabilitating Lochner: Defending Individual Rights Against Progressive Reform* (2011).

222. Randy Barnett, *Restoring the Lost Constitution: The Presumption of Liberty* (2003); Richard A. Epstein, *The Classical Liberal Constitution: The Uncertain Quest for Limited Government* (2014).

223. Tim Wu, "The Right to Evade Regulation: How Corporations Hijacked the First Amendment," *New Republic,* June 2, 2013.

224. *Virginia State Board of Pharmacy v. Virginia Citizens Consumer Council,* 425 U.S. 748 (1976).

225. *Buckley v. Valeo,* 424 U.S. 1 (1976).

226. *First National Bank of Boston v. Bellotti,* 435 U.S. 765 (1978).

227. Coates, "Corporate Speech & the First Amendment," at 250.

228. Id. at 251.

229. Id. This isn't to say there were not First Amendment cases prior to the 1970s that supported business interests. See Jeremy Kessler, "The Early Years of First Amendment Lochnerism," *Columbia Law Review* (2016), http://papers.ssrn.com/sol3/papers.cfm?abstract_id=2758145.

230. For discussions of this trend, see Wu, "Right to Evade"; Jedediah Purdy, "The Roberts Court v. America," *Democracy: A Journal of Ideas* (Win-

ter 2012); Jedediah Purdy, "Neoliberal Constitutionalism: Lochnerism for a New Economy," 77 *Law and Contemporary Problems* 195, 195 (2014); Coates, "Corporate Speech & the First Amendment"; Amanda Shanor, "The New Lochner," 2016 *Wisconsin Law Review* 133 (2016); Howard M. Wasserman, "Bartnicki as Lochner: Some Thoughts on First Amendment Lochnerism," 33 *Northern Kentucky Law Review* 421, 458 (2006); Stuart Minor Benjamin, "Proactive Legislation and the First Amendment," 99 *Michigan Law Review* 281, 286 (2000); Cass R. Sunstein, "Lochner's Legacy," 87 *Columbia Law Review* 873, 883–84 (1987) (describing the Supreme Court's First Amendment restriction on campaign finance regulation as "a direct heir to Lochner" in its creation of "a kind of First Amendment 'taking'" doctrine); J. M. Balkin, "Some Realism About Pluralism: Legal Realist Approaches to the First Amendment," 1990 *Duke Law Journal* 375, 384 ("Business interests and other conservative groups are finding that arguments for property rights and the social status quo can more and more easily be rephrased in the language of the first amendment").

231. *Citizens United v. Federal Election Commission,* 558 U.S. 310 (2010).
232. *Arizona Free Enterprise Club's Freedom PAC v. Bennett,* 131 S. Ct. 2806 (2011).
233. *McCutcheon v. FEC,* 134 S. Ct. 1434 (2014).
234. Id. at 1451.
235. *Abood v. Detroit Board of Education,* 97 S. Ct. 1782 (1977).
236. *Knox v. Service Employees International Union, Local 1000,* 132 S. Ct. 2277, 2290 (2012).
237. *Harris v. Quinn,* 134 S. Ct. 2618 (2014).
238. *Sorrell v. IMS Health,* 131 S. Ct. 2653 (2011).
239. Wu, "Right to Evade."
240. *Sorrell,* 131 S. Ct. at 2671.
241. Purdy, "Roberts Court v. America."
242. Elizabeth Sepper, "Free Exercise Lochnerism," 115 *Columbia Law Review* 1453 (2015).
243. *Burwell v. Hobby Lobby Stores, Inc.,* 134 S. Ct. 2751 (2014).
244. Marty Lederman, "*Hobby Lobby* Part III—There Is No 'Employer Mandate,'" *Balkinization,* Dec. 16, 2013 (updated Dec. 19, 2013).
245. Linda Greenhouse, "Doesn't Eat, Doesn't Pray, and Doesn't Love," *New York Times,* Nov. 27, 2013.
246. Jeffrey Rosen, "These Two Cases Could Be Corporate America's Biggest Gift Since Citizens United," *New Republic,* Nov. 26, 2013.
247. *Hobby Lobby,* 134 S. Ct. at 2787.
248. Coates, "Corporate Speech & the First Amendment," at 265.

249. David G. Savage, "Nominee Is Critical of Big Government," *Los Angeles Times,* Nov. 6, 2003.

250. Elizabeth Warren, "The Corporate Capture of the Federal Courts," Speech to the American Constitution Society, June 13, 2013), http://www.warren.senate.gov/files/documents/ACSSpeech_ElizabethWarren.pdf.

251. Adam Chandler, "Cert.-Stage Amicus 'All Stars': Where Are They Now?," *SCOTUSblog,* April 4, 2013.

252. Doug Kendall and Tom Donnelly, "Not So Risky Business: The Chamber of Commerce's Quiet Success Before the Roberts Court—an Early Report for 2012–2013," Constitutional Accountability Center, May 1, 2013.

253. Lee Epstein, William M. Landes, and Richard A. Posner, "How Business Fares in the Supreme Court," 97 *Minnesota Law Review* 1431, 1449–51 (2013).

254. Alicia Bannon and Lianna Reagan, "New Politics of Judicial Elections, 2011–12," Brennan Center for Justice, Oct. 23, 2013. For the 2001–2 data, see Joanna Shepherd and Michael S. Kang, "Skewed Justice: Citizens United, Television Advertising, and State Supreme Court Justices' Decisions in Criminal Cases," fig. 2b, http://skewedjustice.org/.

255. Joanna M. Shepherd, "Money, Politics, and Impartial Justice," 58 *Duke Law Journal* 623, 670–72, and tables 7–8 (2009).

256. Michael S. Kang and Joanna M. Shepherd, "The Partisan Price of Justice: An Empirical Analysis of Campaign Contributions and Judicial Decisions," 86 *New York University Law Review* 69 (2011).

257. Shepherd and Kang, "Skewed Justice."

258. Vote totals exclude caucuses. Real Clear Politics, 2016 Democratic Popular Vote, http://www.realclearpolitics.com/epolls/2016/president/democratic_vote_count.html; Real Clear Politics, 2016 Republican Popular Vote, http://www.realclearpolitics.com/epolls/2016/president/republican_vote_count.html.

259. Hillary Clinton's 2016 Presidential Announcement, April 12, 2015, https://www.youtube.com/watch?v=N708P-A45D0

260. Chris Kahn, "U.S. Voters Want Leader to End Advantage of Rich and Powerful: Reuters/Ipsos Poll," Reuters.com, Nov. 8, 2016.

Chapter Six: The Future of the Middle-Class Constitution

1. Henry Adams, *The Education of Henry Adams* 1026 (1983) (1918).

2. Id. at 1035.

3. Id. at 1034.

4. Id. at 1105.

5. Id. at 1176.

6. Arthur M. Schlesinger, *Paths to the Present* 81 (1949).

7. Arthur M. Schlesinger Jr., *The Cycles of American Politics* 27 (1986).

8. I take countervailing power from John Kenneth Galbraith, *American Capitalism* 111 (1952). Galbraith argued that "the group that seeks countervailing power is, initially, a numerous and disadvantaged group which seeks organization because it faces, in its market, a much smaller and much more advantaged group," and he illustrated the concept with the rise of labor unions, vis-à-vis managers. Id. at 136, 114–15.

9. M. J. C. Vile, *Constitutionalism and the Separation of Powers* 7, 37 (2nd ed. 2012); James Harrington, *The Commonwealth of Oceana and a System of Politics* (J. G. A. Pocock ed., 1992).

10. John McCormick, *Machiavellian Democracy* 101 (2011).

11. Id. The structure still weighted power to the smaller set of major guilds (or wealthier and higher-status individuals), but it ensured participation from members of the minor guilds.

12. See generally Bernard Manin, *The Principles of Representative Government* 132–60 (1997) (discussing the aristocratic nature of elections).

13. See, for example, Albert M. Kales, *Unpopular Government in the United States* 211–12 (1914) (arguing for a more populist legislative system but with "a second legislative chamber in which the representatives of property interests shall sit").

14. Id. at 183–85.

15. Robert K. Merton, "The Self-Fulfilling Prophecy," 8 *Antioch Review* 193, 195 (Summer 1948) (emphasis omitted).

16. The classic is Robert Rosenthal and Lenore Jacobson, *Pygmalion in the Classroom* (1968).

17. Mark Snyder and William B. Swann Jr., "Behavioral Confirmation in Social Interaction: From Social Perception to Social Reality," 14 *Journal of Experimental Social Psychology* 148 (1978); Mark Chen and John A. Baugh, "Nonconscious Behavioral Confirmation Processes: The Self-Fulfilling Consequences of Automatic Stereotype Activation," 33 *Journal of Experimental Social Psychology* 541 (1997); Mark Snyder and Olivier Klein, "Construing and Constructing Others: On the Reality and the Generality of the Behavioral Confirmation Scenario," 6 *Interaction Studies* 53 (2005).

18. Kirsti Samuels, "Post-conflict Peace-Building and Constitution-Making," 6 *Chicago Journal of International Law* 663, 675 (2006); Kirsti Samuels and Vanessa Hawkins Wyeth, "State-Building and Constitutional Design After Conflict," International Peace Academy (2006); see

also Allison McCulloch, *Power-Sharing and Political Stability in Deeply Divided Societies* 79 (2014).

19. On jury participation serving a democratic function, the classic remains Tocqueville, *Democracy in America*. The classic article on jury nullification is Paul Butler, "Racially Based Jury Nullification: Black Power in the Criminal Justice System," 105 *Yale Law Journal* 677 (1995). Of course, juries are not necessarily representative of the population writ large, so a countervailing power justification for jury participation or nullification would probably need to be coupled with reforms of jury selection and peremptory challenge procedures.

20. For examples of states that have ombudsmen, see Public Counsel (Ombudsman's Office), Nebraska, http://nebraskalegislature.gov /divisions/ombud.php; Arizona Ombudsman: Citizen's Aide, http:// www.azleg.gov/ombudsman/; State of Hawaii, Office of Ombudsman, http://ombudsman.hawaii.gov; State of Iowa, Office of Ombudsman, https://www.legis.iowa.gov/Ombudsman/; Office of Ombudsman, Alaska, http://ombud.alaska.gov; Public Advocate of New York, http:// pubadvocate.nyc.gov.

21. See Mark Green and Laurel W. Eisner, "The Public Advocate for New York City: An Analysis of the Country's Only Elected Ombudsman," 42 *New York Law School Law Review* 1093, 1104–5 (1998). The 1809 Swedish Constitution first established a position of ombudsman, and debates from the time suggest that the Roman tribunate might have been an inspiration for the post. Stig Jägerskiöld, "The Swedish Ombudsman," 109 *University of Pennsylvania Law Review* 1077, 1080, 1079, and n.8 (1961). It seems that the more proximate inspiration was the role of attorney general. Id. at 1079. Among other things, the Swedish ombudsman serves as a prosecutor, with the formal power to try impeachment cases against the highest state officials (though not initiate them) and to initiate proceedings against lower judges. The ombudsman even has the power to prosecute members of a court, if she finds the court at fault in dismissing her actions (though this has never happened). Id. at 1087. For an early American treatment, see Kenneth Culp Davis, "Ombudsmen in America: Officers to Criticize Administrative Action," 109 *University of Pennsylvania Law Review* 1057 (1961). The quotation is from ABA, "Standards for the Establishment and Operation of Ombuds Offices," Feb. 2004.

22. ABA, "Standards," at 6–7, 12.

23. Samuel Issacharoff, "On Political Corruption," 124 *Harvard Law Review* 118, 118 (2010); Heather K. Gerken and Alex Tausanovitch, "A

Public Finance Model for Lobbying: Lobbying Campaign Finance, and the Privatization of Democracy," 13 *Election Law Journal* 75, 87 (2014).

24. Issacharoff, "Political Corruption," at 118. This model can be justified on a variety of theories. On markets, see David Cole, "First Amendment Antitrust: The End of Laissez-Faire in Campaign Finance," 9 *Yale Law & Policy Review* 236, 237 (1991). On responsiveness to citizens, see Heather Gerken, "Keynote Address: Lobbying as the New Campaign Finance," 27 *Georgia State University Law Review* 1155, 1156 (2011). On transaction costs, see Michael S. Kang, "The End of Campaign Finance Law," 98 *Virginia Law Review* 1, 56–57 (2012).

25. *Citizens United v. FEC*, 558 U.S. 310 (2010); *McCutcheon v. FEC*, 134 S. Ct. 1434 (2014). See *First National Bank of Boston v. Bellotti*, 435 U.S. 765, 790–92 (1978); *Buckley v. Valeo*, 424 U.S. 1, 26–28 (1976); see also *McConnell v. FEC*, 540 U.S. 93, 121 (2003) (distinguishing "real" and "apparent" quid pro quo corruption); *FEC v. Wisconsin Right to Life, Inc.*, 551 U.S. 449 (2007) (plurality opinion); *McConnell*, 540 U.S. at 143–45 (discussing the importance of prohibiting the appearance of "undue influence"). For a general discussion, see Issacharoff, "Political Corruption," at 121–22.

26. Issacharoff, "Political Corruption," at 122.

27. *Austin v. Michigan Chamber of Commerce*, 494 U.S. 652, 660 (1990); see also *Bellotti*, 435 U.S. at 809 (White, J., dissenting) (arguing that states have an interest in preventing institutions from "using . . . wealth to acquire an unfair advantage in the political process").

28. Richard L. Hasen, "Lobbying, Rent-Seeking, and the Constitution," 64 *Stanford Law Review* 191 (2012); Gerken, "Lobbying as the New Campaign Finance"; Zephyr Teachout, "The Forgotten Law of Lobbying," 13 *Election Law Journal* 4 (2014); Richard Briffault, "Lobbying and Campaign Finance: Separate and Together," 19 *Stanford Law & Policy Review* 105, 108 (2008) ("Lobbying and campaign finance, however, also raise common concerns about unequal wealth and improper influence over the political process"). Id. at 119 ("Prevention of improper influence over government decision-making is a primary concern for both campaign finance and lobbying regulation"); Richard Briffault, "The Anxiety of Influence: The Evolving Regulation of Lobbying," 13 *Election Law Journal* 160 (2014).

29. Hasen, "Lobbying, Rent-Seeking," at 198.

30. On the conventional view, see Gerald E. Frug, "The Ideology of Bureaucracy in American Law," 97 *Harvard Law Review* 1276, 1318–34 (1984); Richard B. Stewart, "The Reformation of American Administrative Law," 88 *Harvard Law Review* 1669, 1678 (1975); Cass R.

Sunstein, "Constitutionalism After the New Deal," 101 *Harvard Law Review* 421, 441–42 (1987); Elena Kagan, "Presidential Administration," 114 *Harvard Law Review* 2245, 2352–58 (2001).

31. For recent work on agency independence, see Adrian Vermeule, "Conventions of Agency Independence," 113 *Columbia Law Review* 1163 (2013); Lisa Schultz Bressman and Robert B. Thompson, "The Future of Agency Independence," 63 *Vanderbilt Law Review* 599 (2010); Kirti Datla and Richard L. Revesz, "Deconstructing Independent Agencies (and Executive Agencies)," 98 *Cornell Law Review* 769 (2013); Rachel E. Barkow, "Insulating Agencies: Avoiding Capture Through Institutional Design," 89 *Texas Law Review* 15 (2010); Daniel Carpenter and David A. Moss, eds., *Preventing Regulatory Capture* (2013).

32. For an argument in favor of civil service reform that would lead to greater professionalization of the bureaucracy, see Francis Fukuyama, "Why We Need a New Pendleton Act," *American Interest,* Nov. 3, 2013. On terms of office, see Daryl J. Levinson and Richard H. Pildes, "Separation of Parties, Not Powers," 119 *Harvard Law Review* 2311, 2378 (2006). See Arthur E. Wilmarth Jr., "Turning a Blind Eye: Why Washington Keeps Giving In to Wall Street," 91 *University of Cincinnati Law Review* 1283, 1407–17 (2013), for a discussion of the revolving door in the financial regulation context.

33. Andrew Lintott, "Electoral Bribery in the Roman Republic," 80 *Journal of Roman Studies* 1 (1990).

34. Samuel Issacharoff and Pamela S. Karlan, "The Hydraulics of Campaign Finance Reform," 77 *Texas Law Review* 1705, 1708 (1999) ("[P]olitical money, like water, has to go somewhere"). Deregulation, of course, allows money to flow back through the blocked channels. See also Kang, "End of Campaign Finance," at 40–52.

35. The literature is voluminous. For the classic theory, see George J. Stigler, "The Theory of Economic Regulation," 2 *Bell Journal of Economics and Management Science* 3 (Spring 1971). For a recent collection on the scope of the problem and how to prevent it, see Carpenter and Moss, *Preventing Regulatory Capture.*

36. For examples in the financial regulation context, see Wilmarth, "Turning a Blind Eye," at 1407–17.

37. Kimberly D. Krawiec, "Agency Lobbying and Financial Reform: A Volcker Rule Case Study," 32 *Banking & Financial Services Policy Report* 15 (Aug. 2013) (finding that 93 percent of pre-proposal meetings in the Volcker Rule context were with financial institutions, law firms, and financial industry groups and that only 4.2 percent were with public interest groups). See also Donald Elliott, "Re-inventing Rulemak-

ing," 41 *Duke Law Journal* 1490, 1492 (1992) ("Notice-and-comment rulemaking is to public participation what Japanese Kabuki theatre is to human passions—a highly stylized process for displaying something which in real life takes place in other venues").

38. Michael S. Kang, "Party-Based Corruption and *McCutcheon v. FEC*," 108 *Northwestern Law Review Online* 240 (2014).

39. Kevin M. Stack, "The Paradox of Process in Administrative Rulemaking," at 1 (forthcoming).

40. Id. at 1–2.

41. See Kay Lehman Schlozman, Sidney Verba, and Henry E. Brady, *The Unheavenly Chorus* (2012).

42. Jason Webb Yackee and Susan Webb Yackee, "A Bias Toward Business? Assessing Interest Group Influence on the U.S. Bureaucracy," 68 *Journal of Politics* 128, 133 (2006) (finding 57 percent of public comments from four agencies came from businesses); Krawiec, "Agency Lobbying and Financial Reform," at 16–17 (noting that 93 percent of comments on the "Volcker Rule" were from private individuals, but that more than half used the same form letter and 91 percent used a variation of that form letter).

43. Wendy Wagner, Katherine Barnes, and Lisa Peters, "Rulemaking in the Shade: An Empirical Study of EPA's Air Toxic Emissions Standards," 63 *Administrative Law Review* 99, 128 (2011).

44. Adrian Vermeule, "The Supreme Court 2008 Term—Foreword: System Effects and the Constitution," 123 *Harvard Law Review* 4, 18 (2009).

45. Stack, "Paradox of Process"; Gerken and Tausanovitch, "Lobbying."

46. Committee on the Status and Future of Federal E-rulemaking, American Bar Association, *Achieving the Potential* 3 (2008). Still, many have suggested reasons to be skeptical. Cynthia R. Farina et al., "Rulemaking 2.0," 65 *University of Miami Law Review* 395, 402 (2011); Cary Coglianese, "Citizen Participation in Rulemaking: Past, Present, and Future," 55 *Duke Law Journal* 943, 945 (2006).

47. Carl Baar, "Social Action in India: The Operation and Limits of the World's Most Active Judiciary," 19 *Policy Studies Journal* 140, 142 (1990).

48. For contemporary accounts of the importance of inheritance taxation, see Anne Alstott, "Equal Opportunity and Inheritance Taxation," 121 *Harvard Law Review* 469 (2007); Michael J. Graetz and Ian Shapiro, *Death by a Thousand Cuts: The Fight over Taxing Inherited Wealth* (2005).

49. John Schmitt, "The Minimum Wage Is Too Damn Low," Center for Economic and Policy Research, March 2012.

50. David Weil, *The Fissured Workplace* (2014).
51. College Board, "Tuition and Fees and Room and Board over Time," table 2, http://trends.collegeboard.org/college-pricing/figures-tables /tuition-and-fees-and-room-and-board-over-time-1.
52. Rohit Chopra, "Student Debt Swells, Federal Loans Now Top a Trillion," Consumer Financial Protection Bureau, July 17, 2013; Nicholas Rayfield, "National Student Loan Debt Reaches a Bonkers $1.2 Trillion," *USA Today,* April 8, 2015.
53. Ganesh Sitaraman, "Unbundling 'Too Big to Fail,'" Center for American Progress, July 2014. The most extensive discussion is in K. Sabeel Rahman, *Democracy Against Domination* chap. 6 (2016).
54. For a full discussion of Dodd-Frank as a technocratic piece of legislation, see K. Sabeel Rahman, "Envisioning the Regulatory State: Technocracy, Democracy, and Institutional Experimentation in the 2010 Financial Reform and Oil Spill Statutes," 48 *Harvard Journal on Legislation* 555, 562–67 (2011); see also Rahman, *Democracy Against Domination.*
55. Sitaraman, "Unbundling 'Too Big to Fail.'"
56. Heather Long, "Former Citigroup CEO: Big Banks Don't Work," CNN Money, Nov. 12, 2015; Donal Griffin and Christine Harper, "Former Citigroup CEO Weill Says Banks Should Be Broken Up," *Bloomberg,* July 25, 2012.
57. Adam J. Levitin, "The Politics of Financial Regulation and the Regulation of Financial Politics: A Review Essay," 127 *Harvard Law Review* 1991, 2059 (2014).
58. Id. at 2061.
59. Id. at 2062.
60. Sitaraman, "Unbundling 'Too Big to Fail.'"
61. For discussions of enforcement and the need for more competition in American markets, see Daniel A. Crane, "Has the Obama Justice Department Reinvigorated Antitrust Enforcement?," 65 *Stanford Law Review Online* 13 (2012); Lina Khan, "How to Reboot the FTC," *Politico,* April 13, 2016; Lina Khan, "The Next President Should Break Up Some Big Companies," *Washington Post,* Oct. 28, 2015; "Too Much of a Good Thing," *Economist,* March 26, 2016.
62. Susan Crawford, *Captive Audience: The Telecom Industry and Monopoly Power in the New Gilded Age* (2013); Barry C. Lynn, *Cornered: The New Monopoly Capitalism and the Economics of Destruction* (2010); Robert B. Reich, *Saving Capitalism* 29–47 (2015); Tim Wu, *The Master Switch: The Rise and Fall of Information Empires* (2010); Luigi Zingales, *A Capitalism for the People* 157 (2012); Franklin Foer, "Amazon Must

Be Stopped," *New Republic,* Oct. 9, 2014; Lina Khan, "What Everyone's Getting Wrong About Amazon," *Quartz,* Oct. 17, 2014.

63. See, for example, Reich, *Saving Capitalism,* at 29–47; Zingales, *A Capitalism for the People,* at 157; David Dayen, "Bring Back Antitrust," *American Prospect* (Fall 2015); David Dayen, "The Most Important 2016 Issue You Don't Know Anything About," *New Republic,* March 11, 2016.

64. K. Sabeel Rahman, "Curbing the New Corporate Power," *Boston Review,* May 2015. Others have discussed public utility regulation as appropriate for the health-care industry. See Nicholas Bagley, "Medicine as a Public Calling," 114 *Michigan Law Review* 57 (2015).

65. For a summary, see Federal Communications Commission, Press Release, "FCC Adopts Strong, Sustainable Rules to Protect the Open Internet," Feb. 26, 2015.

66. Joseph E. Stiglitz, *Rewriting the Rules of the American Economy* 33–36 (2015); Roger L. Martin, "Yes, Short-Termism Really Is a Problem," *Harvard Business Review,* Oct. 9, 2015 (reviewing studies and arguments for and against short-termism); William Lazonick, "Profits Without Prosperity," *Harvard Business Review* (Sept. 2014) (describing the increase and effects of stock buybacks); Laurence D. Fink, letter to S&P 500 chief executives, reprinted at http://www.businessinsider .com/blackrock-ceo-larry-fink-letter-to-sp-500-ceos-2016-2.

67. Mike Konczal, Amanda Page-Hoongrajok, and J. W. Mason, "Ending Short-Termism: An Investment Agenda for Growth," Roosevelt Institute, Nov. 6, 2015.

68. Joseph Blasi, Richard B. Freeman, and Douglas L. Kruse, *The Citizen's Share: Putting Ownership Back into Democracy* (2013). See also Danny Vinik, "How to Fight Inequality with Stocks," *Politico,* Jan. 26, 2016 (describing research on employee stock ownership plans and data suggesting that they reduce inequality).

69. The proposal is described in Reich, *Saving Capitalism,* at 196–97.

70. Thomas A. Kochan et al., *Healing Together: The Labor Management Partnership at Kaiser Permanente* (2009).

71. For a discussion, see Cynthia Estlund, *Regoverning the Workplace: From Self-Regulation to Co-Regulation* (2010); Kate Andrias, "The New Labor Law," *Yale Law Journal* (forthcoming 2016); David Rolf, "Toward a 21st-Century Labor Movement," *American Prospect,* April 18, 2016; Mark Barenberg, "Widening the Scope of Worker Organizing," Roosevelt Institute, Oct. 7, 2015. For a suggestion that union rules should be revised to enable greater political action, see Benjamin I.

Sachs, "The Unbundled Union: Politics Without Collective Bargaining," 123 *Yale Law Journal* 148 (2013).

72. The classic treatment of the theory is Jon Elster, *Ulysses Unbound* (2000).

73. Scholars have, of course, identified situations in which the theory is more or less persuasive. Jon Elster, "Don't Burn Your Bridge Before You Come to It: Some Ambiguities and Complexities of Precommitment," 81 *Texas Law Review* 1751, 1761 (2003) (some constitutional provisions emerge from a political haggle, not rational choices about the future); Jeremy Waldron, *Law and Disagreement* 266–75 (1999) (some provisions involve contestable moral questions that might change or manifest differently over time and with new information and norms); Adam M. Samaha, "Dead Hand Arguments and Constitutional Interpretation," 108 *Columbia Law Review* 606, 655–60 (2008) (discussing the problem of dead hand preferences dominating the current time). There is also the tricky problem of why any intertemporal commitment holds. For a discussion of this challenging issue, see Daryl J. Levinson, "Parchment and Politics: The Positive Puzzle of Constitutional Commitment," 124 *Harvard Law Review* 657 (2011).

74. Eric A. Posner and Adrian Vermeule, "Inside or Outside the System?," 80 *University of Chicago Law Review* 1743, 1744 (2013).

75. Id. at 1752–53.

76. It is possible that this problem affects courts less than the other branches. See Thomas W. Merrill, "Does Public Choice Theory Justify Judicial Activism After All?," 21 *Harvard Journal of Law & Public Policy* 219, 224–25 (1997) (arguing that the barriers to entry and costs of litigation are less significant than in other areas).

77. See, for example, Franklin D. Roosevelt, Address at Oglethorpe University, May 22, 1932 ("[T]he country demands bold, persistent experimentation").

78. Piketty, *Capital*.

79. See Richard J. Lazarus, "A Different Kind of 'Republican Moment' in Environmental Law," 87 *Minnesota Law Review* 999, 999n3, 1000, and n8 (2003); Daniel A. Farber, "Politics and Procedure in Environmental Law," 8 *Journal of Law, Economics, and Organization* 59, 66–67 (1992) (describing the 1970s "republican moment" in environmental law and noting the exceptional nature of the moment to overcome normal barriers to policy making).

80. See Ackerman, *Transformations*.

81. See Reuven S. Avi-Yonah, "Corporations, Society, and the State: A

Defense of the Corporate Tax," 90 *Virginia Law Review* 1193, 1216–17 (2004).

82. Richard L. Revesz, "Federalism and Environmental Regulation: A Public Choice Analysis," 115 *Harvard Law Review* 553, 573 (2001); E. Donald Elliott, Bruce A. Ackerman, and John C. Millian, "Toward a Theory of Statutory Evolution: The Federalization of Environmental Law," 1 *Journal of Law, Economics, and Organization* 313, 330–31 (1985).

83. Australian Electoral Commission, "Electoral Backgrounder: Compulsory Voting," http://www.aec.gov.au/About_AEC/Publications/backgrounders/compulsory-voting.htm; Australian Electoral Commission, "Informal Voting," http://www.aec.gov.au/voting/informal_voting/.

84. Alberto Chong and Mauricio Olivera, "Does Compulsory Voting Help Equalize Incomes?," 20 *Economics and Politics* 391 (2008). See also Anthony Fowler, "Electoral and Policy Consequences of Voter Turnout: Evidence from Compulsory Voting in Australia," 8 *Quarterly Journal of Political Science* 159 (2013).

85. Richard Carr, *One Nation Britain: History, the Progressive Tradition, and Practical Ideas for Today's Politicians* 27 (2014).

86. Theodore Roosevelt, *The New Nationalism* 29 (1910).

87. Schlesinger, *Vital Center*, at 13.

88. See, for example, Sam Tanenhaus, "Can the G.O.P. Be a Party of Ideas?," *New York Times Magazine*, July 2, 2014. For accounts of these ideas by the participants, see, for example, Reihan Salam and Ross Douthat, *Grand New Party* (2008); Yuval Levin, *The Fractured Republic: Renewing America's Social Contract in the Age of Individualism* (2016).

89. Henry Adams, "The Session," in *The Great Secession Winter of 1860–61, and Other Essays* 193 (George E. Hochfield ed., 1958).

90. Adams to Mercy Otis Warren, Jan. 8, 1776, 3 *Papers of John Adams* 398 (Robert J. Taylor et al. eds., 1979).

Index

A NOTE ABOUT THE AUTHOR

GANESH SITARAMAN is an associate professor of law at Vanderbilt Law School and a senior fellow at the Center for American Progress. From 2011 to 2013, he served as policy director to Elizabeth Warren during her successful Senate campaign and then as her senior counsel in the U.S. Senate. Professor Sitaraman has been a research fellow at the Counterinsurgency Training Center–Afghanistan in Kabul, the inaugural public law fellow and a lecturer at Harvard Law School, and a law clerk to Judge Stephen F. Williams on the U.S. Court of Appeals for the D.C. Circuit. Professor Sitaraman is the author of *The Counterinsurgent's Constitution: Law in the Age of Small Wars,* which won the 2013 Palmer Civil Liberties Prize. He lives in Nashville.

A NOTE ON THE TYPE

This book was set in Minion, a typeface produced by the Adobe Corporation specifically for the Macintosh personal computer and released in 1990. Designed by Robert Slimbach, Minion combines the classic characteristics of old-style faces with the full complement of weights required for modern typesetting.

Composed by North Market Street Graphics,
Lancaster, Pennsylvania

Printed and bound by Berryville Graphics,
Berryville, Virginia

Designed by Betty Lew